Contemporary Rhetoric

A Conceptual Background with Readings

Contemporary Rhetoric

A Conceptual Background with Readings

W. Ross Winterowd
University of Southern California

 HARCOURT BRACE JOVANOVICH, INC.

New York / Chicago / San Francisco / Atlanta

ISBN: 0-15-513715-8

Library of Congress Catalog Card number: 74-33006

Printed in the United States of America

COPYRIGHTS AND ACKNOWLEDGMENTS

For permission to use the selections reprinted in this book, the author is grateful to the following publishers and copyright holders:

NOAM CHOMSKY   For an excerpt from *Form and Meaning in Natural Language* by Noam Chomsky, pp. 66–67. Reprinted by permission of the author.

CITY LIGHTS BOOKS   For excerpts from "This Form of Life Needs Sex" and "The Change: Kyoto-Tokyo Express" from *Planet News* by Allen Ginsberg. Copyright © 1968 by Allen Ginsberg. Reprinted by permission of City Lights Books.

J. M. DENT & SONS, LTD   For excerpts from "Author's Prologue," "The hand that signed the paper," and "A Winter's Tale" from *Collected Poems* by Dylan Thomas. Reprinted by permission of J. M. Dent & Sons, Ltd. and the Trustees for the Copyrights of the late Dylan Thomas.

DOUBLEDAY & COMPANY, INC   For an excerpt from "The Longing," copyright © 1962 by Beatrice Roethke as Administratrix to the Estate of Theodore Roethke, and from "The Meadow Mouse," copyright © 1963 by Beatrice Roethke as Administratrix to the Estate of Theodore Roethke, from *The Collected Poems of Theodore Roethke* by Theodore Roethke. Reprinted by permission of Doubleday & Company, Inc.

EDICOM N. V.   For "The Problem of Style," pp. 40–73 from *A Quantitative Approach to the Style of Jonathan Swift* by Louis Tonko Milic. Published originally by Mouton & Co. (The Hague), 1967. Reprinted by permission of Edicom N. V.

ENGLISH IN EDUCATION   For an excerpt from *Growth Through English* by John Dixon. Reprinted by permission of *English in Education*.

FABER AND FABER, LTD   For excerpts from "East Coker" and "The Love Song of J. Alfred Prufrock" from *Collected Poems 1909–1962* by T. S. Eliot. Reprinted by permission of Faber and Faber, Ltd.

HARCOURT BRACE JOVANOVICH, INC   For excerpts from "East Coker" and "The Love Song of J. Alfred Prufrock" from *Collected Poems 1909–1962* by T. S. Eliot. Reprinted by permission of Harcourt Brace Jovanovich, Inc.

HARPER & ROW, PUBLISHERS, INC   For "A Generative Rhetoric of the Sentence." Originally appeared in *College Composition and Communication* (October 1963). And for "A Generative Rhetoric of the Paragraph." Originally appeared in *College Composition and Communication* (October 1965). Both reprinted from *Notes Toward a New Rhetoric* by Francis Christensen. Copyright © 1967 by Francis Christensen. By permission of Harper & Row, Publishers, Inc.

HARVARD EDUCATIONAL REVIEW   For "Toward a Modern Theory of Rhetoric: A Tagmemic Contribution" by Richard E. Young and Alton L.

Becker, *Harvard Educational Review* 35 (Fall 1965), 450–68. Copyright ©
1965 by The President and Fellows of Harvard College.

HARVARD UNIVERSITY PRESS   For "The Snow that never drifts—"
(#1133) and an excerpt from "They called me to the Window, for" (#628).
Reprinted by permission of the publishers and the Trustees of Amherst College from Thomas H. Johnson, Editor. *The Poems of Emily Dickinson*, Cambridge, Mass.: The Belknap Press of Harvard University Press, Copyright
1951, 1955, by The President and Fellows of Harvard College.

HERMES PUBLICATIONS   For "The Nature of Form" from *Counter-statement*
by Kenneth Burke. Reprinted by permission of Hermes Publications, Los
Altos, California 94022.

DAVID HIGHAM ASSOCIATES, LTD   For an excerpt from "The Don Juan
Triptych" from *Selected Poems* by John Heath-Stubbs. Published by Oxford
University Press, 1965. Reprinted by permission of David Higham Associates,
Ltd.

HOLT, RINEHART AND WINSTON, PUBLISHERS   For an excerpt from
Child, Language and Education by Courtney B. Cazden. For excerpts from
"Loveliest of trees, the cherry now" from "A Shropshire Lad"—Authorized
Edition—from *The Collected Poems of A. E. Housman*. Copyright 1939,
1940, © 1965 by Holt, Rinehart and Winston, Publishers. Copyright ©
1967, 1968 by Robert E. Symons. And for excerpts from "I Will Sing You
One-O" and "They Were Welcome to Their Belief" from *The Poetry of
Robert Frost* edited by Edward Connery Lathem. Copyright 1923, © 1969
by Holt, Rinehart and Winston, Publishers. Copyright 1936, 1951 by Robert
Frost. Copyright © 1964 by Lesley Frost Ballantine. All reprinted by permission of Holt, Rinehart and Winston, Publishers.

HOUGHTON MIFFLIN COMPANY   For an excerpt from "The Ballad of the
Lonely Masturbator" from *Love Poems* by Anne Sexton. Copyright © 1967,
1968, 1969 by Anne Sexton. Reprinted by permission of the publisher,
Houghton Mifflin Company.

ALFRED A. KNOPF, INC   For an excerpt from "The Motive for Metaphor"
by Wallace Stevens. Copyright 1947 by Wallace Stevens. Reprinted from
The Collected Poems of Wallace Stevens by permission of Alfred A. Knopf,
Inc.

LITTLE, BROWN AND COMPANY   For "The largest Fire ever known"
(#1114), Copyright 1929, © 1957 by Mary L. Hampson, and an excerpt
from "After great pain a formal feeling comes—" (#341), Copyright 1914,
1942 by Martha Dickinson Bianchi. Both from *The Complete Poems of
Emily Dickinson*, edited by Thomas H. Johnson. Reprinted by permission of
Little, Brown and Company.

MACMILLAN PUBLISHING COMPANY, INC   For an excerpt from "To a
Friend Whose Work Has Come to Nothing" from *Collected Poems* by William Butler Yeats (Copyright 1916 by Macmillan Publishing Company, Inc.,
renewed 1944 by Bertha Georgie Yeats). Reprinted by permission of the
publisher, Macmillan Publishing Company, Inc.

McGRAW-HILL BOOK COMPANY   For "The Printed Word," pp. 170–78
from *Understanding Media: The Extensions of Man* by Marshall McLuhan.
Copyright © 1964 by Marshall McLuhan. Used with permission of
McGraw-Hill Book Company.

NATIONAL COUNCIL OF TEACHERS OF ENGLISH   For "Response to
Janice Lauer, 'Counterstatement'" by Ann E. Berthoff from *College Composition and Communication* (December 1972). Copyright © 1972 by the
National Council of Teachers of English. For "The Problem of Problem

Solving" by Ann E. Berthoff from *College Composition and Communication* (October 1971). Copyright © 1971 by the National Council of Teachers of English. For "The Rhetorical Stance" by Wayne C. Booth from *College Composition and Communication* (October 1963). Copyright © 1963 by the National Council of Teachers of English. For Chapter One, pp. 7–28, "The Composing Process: Review of the Literature," from *The Composing Processes of Twelfth Graders* by Janet Emig. Copyright © 1971 by the National Council of Teachers of English. For "Form, Authority, and the Critical Essay" by Keith Fort from *College English* (March 1971). Copyright © 1971 by the National Council of Teachers of English. For "Some Tentative Strictures on Generative Rhetoric" by Sabina Thorne Johnson from *College English* (November 1969). Copyright © 1969 by the National Council of Teachers of English. For "Discovery Through Questioning: A Plan for Teaching Rhetorical Invention" by Richard Larson from *College English* (November 1968). Copyright © 1968 by the National Council of Teachers of English. For "Heuristics and Composition" by Janice Lauer from *College Composition and Communication* (December 1970). Copyright © 1970 by the National Council of Teachers of English. For "Response to Ann E. Berthoff, 'The Problem of Problem Solving' " by Janice Lauer from *College Composition and Communication* (May 1972). Copyright © 1972 by the National Council of Teachers of English. For "Assumptions and Hypotheses," pp. 15–30 from *Transformational Sentence-Combining* by John C. Mellon. Copyright © 1969 by the National Council of Teachers of English. For "Literature as Sentences" by Richard Ohmann from *College English* (January 1966). Copyright © 1966 by the National Council of Teachers of English. For "Four Forms of Metaphor" by Laurence Perrine from *College English* (November 1971). Copyright © 1971 by the National Council of Teachers of English. For a revised version of " 'Topics' and Levels in the Composing Process" by W. Ross Winterowd from *College English* (February 1973), 101–09. For a revised version of "Dispositio: The Concept of Form in Discourse" by W. Ross Winterowd from *College Composition and Communication* (February 1971). And for "The Grammar of Coherence" by W. Ross Winterowd from *College English* (May 1970). All reprinted by permission of the publisher and the author.

NEW DIRECTIONS PUBLISHING CORPORATION   For excerpts from "Author's Prologue," "The hand that signed the paper," and "A Winter's Tale" from *The Poems of Dylan Thomas*. Copyright 1939, 1946 by New Directions Publishing Corporation, copyright 1952 by Dylan Thomas. Reprinted by permission of New Directions Publishing Corporation.

PHILOSOPHY AND RHETORIC   For "Beyond Style" by W. Ross Winterowd. Originally appeared in *Philosophy and Rhetoric* 5 (Spring 1972), 88–110. Reprinted by permission of *Philosophy and Rhetoric*.

PRENTICE-HALL, INC   For "Report of the Committee on the Nature of Rhetorical Invention" by Robert L. Scott et al. in *The Prospect of Rhetoric*, Lloyd F. Bitzer and Edwin Black, Eds., © 1971. Reprinted by permission of Prentice-Hall, Inc., Englewood Cliffs, New Jersey.

RANDOM HOUSE, INC   For an excerpt from "Let Them Alone." Copyright © 1963 by Garth Jeffers and Donnan Jeffers. Reprinted from *Selected Poems* by Robinson Jeffers. And for excerpts from *Troilus and Cressida* by Geoffrey Chaucer, Englished anew by George Philip Krapp. Copyright 1932 and renewed 1960 by Elizabeth Krapp. Both reprinted by permission of Random House, Inc.

THE SOCIETY OF AUTHORS   For excerpts from "Loveliest of trees, the cherry now" from *Collected Poems* by A. E. Housman. Reprinted by permission of The Society of Authors as the literary representative of the Estate of A. E. Housman, and by permission of Jonathan Cape Ltd., publishers of A. E. Housman's *Collected Poems.*

SPEECH COMMUNICATION ASSOCIATION   For *"Topoi* and the Problem of Invention" by Karl R. Wallace from *QJS* 58 (December 1972), 387–95. Reprinted by permission of Mrs. Karl R. Wallace and the Speech Communication Association.

STYLE   For "The Application of Transformational Generative Grammar to the Analysis of Similes and Metaphors in Modern English" by Rosemarie Gläser from *Style* 5 (Fall 1971), 265–83. Reprinted by permission.

UNIVERSITY OF CALIFORNIA PRESS   For "The Five Key Terms of Dramatism." Reprinted from Kenneth Burke: *A Grammar of Motives,* pp. xv–xxiii (Berkeley and Los Angeles: University of California Press, 1969). Reprinted by permission of the author and publisher. And for excerpts from *Surprised by Sin: The Reader in Paradise Lost* by Stanley Fish. Originally published by the University of California Press, reprinted by permission of The Regents of the University of California.

THE VIKING PRESS   For an excerpt from "The Brides" from *Collected Poems* by A. D. Hope. Copyright © 1966 by The Viking Press. Reprinted by permission of The Viking Press, Inc.

A. P. WATT & SON   For an excerpt from "To a Friend Whose Work Has Come to Nothing" from *The Collected Poems of William Butler Yeats.* Reprinted by permission of M. B. Yeats, Miss Anne Yeats, and Macmillan Company of Canada.

Preface

Rhetoric has become a lively field in the last twenty years or so. It has developed many new theories concerning, attitudes toward, and answers to important questions about invention, style, form, pedagogy, the composing process, and other subjects. The concerns of rhetoric are not trivial; even the most practical and mundane theories of rhetoric bear not only on the teaching of composition but also on the theory of literature, for rhetoric concerns itself with the effects of language on an audience in specific situations, and, whatever else it may be, literature *is* language.

As the readings in this volume make clear, rhetoric has an extremely practical value for instructors of writing. But even if the field were all theory and had no practical application, it would still be worth pursuing for a curious but obvious reason. Any field is defined by the questions it asks: if the questions are not trivial, then the field is not trivial. And any field gains its substance through the theories it develops in the attempt to answer those questions. The study of literature as a scholarly discipline is engaging not only because the objects of its inquiry are engrossing but also because theories of literature are themselves richly worth thinking about. Such also is the case with rhetoric.

Contemporary Rhetoric has three purposes. First, it brings together some of the most significant recent work in the field of rhetoric. Second, it interprets that work. (And I like to think that in many instances the interpretation might almost be as valuable as the original work itself.) Third, it develops new theoretical material concerning invention, style, and form.

The essays and background discussions in this book achieve, I think, a balance between theory and practice, and they cover most of the important questions, even though they cannot provide all the answers.

The book is aimed at a broad and varied audience: composition students at all levels (who can use it as their reader and theoretical base); those who are in training to be instructors of writing at any level (who can use it as their textbook); students of rhetoric; and scholars in the field of rhetoric. It is my contention that classes in writing become more meaningful—and thus more effective—if students realize that there is theory behind what is happening. There are two kinds of knowing: knowing *about* and knowing *how to,* and I believe that instruction in the *how to* of writing can proceed most effectively in a context of knowing *about;* therefore, *Contemporary Rhetoric* is a book for students as well as teachers.

A friend of mine with a front stoop reviewed this project at its inception and said most encouraging and helpful things; I thank Professor Jenefer Giannasi of Northern Illinois University both for her help and for her infinite hospitality. I also thank William Dyckes and Katherine Kernan of Harcourt Brace Jovanovich for their careful editing and helpful suggestions.

To my sons, Jeff and Tony; to my mother, Henrietta Winterowd; and to my wife, Norma—just thanks, more thanks than I can ever express.

W.R.W.

Contents

Contemporary Rhetoric

A Conceptual Background with Readings

Introduction:
Some Remarks on Pedagogy

Conceptual Frameworks

A conceptual framework is a schema—sometimes diagrammatic—that serves two purposes. It allows one to organize a subject, and it automatically becomes an inventive heuristic for the discovery of subject matter. Let me give the most obvious example of what I mean. Here is a conceptual framework for rhetoric:

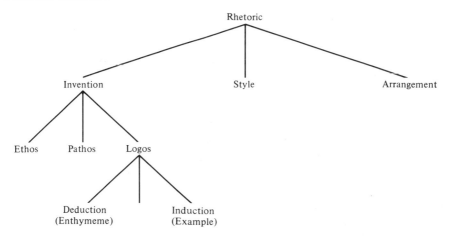

To state the obvious, the schema shows rhetoric to be a three-part subject. (Note that I have left out delivery and memory—two of the traditional parts of rhetoric.) Invention itself is a three-part subject, having to do with ethos (ethical appeal: "Is the discourser * a good person? Can he or she be

---

* In order to avoid the clumsiness of talking about "speaker or writer" or "speaker / writer," I will use the term *discourser*. A discourser is one who generates language sequences, either written or spoken.

1

trusted?"), pathos (pathetic appeal: "What is the nature of the audience? How can the discourser adjust the discourse to the audience?"), and logos (logical appeal: "What arguments for his case can the discourser discover?"), and so on. To comment more extensively on the traditional "departments" of rhetoric would be redundant, for, as a glance at the table of contents indicates, *Contemporary Rhetoric* deals with invention, style, and arrangement (as well as pedagogy).

All the strictly rhetorical matters dealt with in this book can be assigned to one of these three departments. Thus, the framework is an organizational schema. But it is also a heuristic in that it can be used to generate questions about a piece of discourse. Admittedly, it is not a very discriminating heuristic; it is, in fact, so gross as to be useless for most discoursers. However, this book also contains a great variety of subheuristics that will serve to generate information about invention, style, and arrangement.

As I hope will become apparent in *Contemporary Rhetoric,* conceptual frameworks are tremendously useful as devices for organization, even when they are theoretically trivial—which is not to say that all conceptual frameworks are theoretically trivial.

By way of demonstrating this usefulness and at the same time getting into the substance of this book, I would like to explain and use one conceptual framework in some detail. As will become apparent, the framework is not original with me, but, then, *Contemporary Rhetoric* is synthetic as well as exploratory.

A Conceptual Framework

According to my definition, rhetoric is the global art that develops theories concerning, and studies the manifestations of, all human discourse, not just persuasion. I will not defend that definition, nor will I elaborate upon it, but it is important, for it is the stipulation upon which the book is founded.

The definition is important here because the conceptual framework that I want to discuss deals with the whole universe of discourse, not just the suasory. (It is unnecessary, I suppose, to point out that most definitions of rhetoric have somehow focused primarily on the suasory.) In *Style in Language* (1960), a volume that has great historical and theoretical importance for rhetoric, Roman Jakobson developed a conceptual framework for the universe of discourse.[1] There is first an *addresser* (speaker/writer, discourser) and second an *addressee:* Third, the discourse has a *context,* or something referred to. The context is virtually synonymous with the term *referent,* as used by other theorists. Fourth, there is the *message* itself, and fifth, a *contact,* or "a physical channel and psychological connection between the addresser and the addressee, enabling both of them to enter and stay in communication."[2] Sixth, there must be a *code* that is at least partially comprehensible

---

[1] Roman Jakobson, "Linguistics and Politics," *Style in Language,* ed. Thomas A. Sebeok (Cambridge, Mass.: The MIT Press, 1960).
[2] Ibid., p. 353.

to both addresser and addressee. These, then, are the essential factors in the discourse situation. In his article Jakobson presented these factors in a simple and effective graphic form:

Context

Message

Addresser_____ _____Addressee

Contact

Code

Presenting a graphic representation of the framework does not, of course, fall into the area of legerdemain, but it does make for a memorable and fundamentally more useful schema.

The second point that Jakobson makes is more interesting and more central to what *Contemporary Rhetoric* is about, and we will come to it shortly.

First, I would like to make an extremely simple procedural point, so that my purpose in explaining Jakobson's concepts will be clear. Almost every mental or physical entity has a certain undifferentiated, massive quality about it until we discover a method to view it from different angles, to take it apart (mentally) and put it together again. Thus, the concept "vehicle" can be broken down into truck, bus, auto, and so on, or into two-wheeled, four-wheeled, six-wheeled, and so forth, or into diesel-powered, gas-powered, steam-powered, and so on. Each scheme of classification gives one a different perspective and results in different categorizations. If we view discourse in its undifferentiated massiveness, we have no place to begin to deal with it systematically. On the other hand, we recognize the dangers of starting at random with a small fragment or with only one factor and hoping on the basis of these to derive useful generalities away from the context of the whole.

Jakobson's schema is thus tremendously useful if for no other reason than that it gives us a place to begin our search for understanding. Furthermore, it relates parts to the whole. We can begin to ask questions about addresser, addressee, context, message, code, and so on. Notice, in fact, that Jakobson's schema serves as a heuristic to aid one in discovering the nature of discourse itself.

Suppose, for instance, that I am interested in the poetry of Allen Ginsberg —as indeed I am—and that I want a procedure that will yield me as complete an understanding of what he is doing as possible. I might well use the Jakobson schema as a heuristic to develop the information I am seeking. Each of the items in the schema can be turned into a question, the answering of which will yield data that is vital to my purpose. (The questions themselves are profound. The answers, of course, might be either trivial or profound, depending upon a variety of circumstances, not the least of which is the skill and intelligence of the person who answers them.) The following discussion lists the sorts of questions that develop from the Jakobson schema.

Addresser: Who wrote the works? The trivial answer is merely, "Allen Ginsberg wrote them." (In unattributed works, the answer to this question could involve a great deal of work.) But, of course, we are actually interested in the question "Who is Allen Ginsberg?" in its figurative sense, and that implies all of the subtleties of good biographical work. The biographer—from Boswell to Sandburg—is, after all, merely answering the question "Who is ＿＿＿?"

In literature, the questions concerning addresser also bring up the problem of personae. Who is speaking in *Gulliver's Travels?* Certainly not Swift.

Context: "What are the works about?" This question takes us into the real world "out there" to see how the works interpret reality as we see it, and "in there" into Ginsberg's mind. But we can only determine what is in Ginsberg's mind by understanding the fictive world that he presents in his works. I realize, of course, that I have backed myself into an apparently paradoxical corner. I will not try to wriggle my way out (for such a maneuver would take this discussion into bypaths), but will simply refer the reader to the emerging doctrines of phenomenological criticism and to my article "The Realms of Meaning: Text-Centered Criticism." [3]

Whenever we discuss the theme of a work, we are, of course, talking about its context, the information that it conveys. Among other things, Ginsberg's poetry is "about" the American counter-culture.

Message: "What is being said about the context?" Which is a different question from "What is the context?" "What is being said about the context?" brings up all exegetical work, from the baldest paraphrase of the text to the "readings" that have become so subtle and productive since New Criticism gave us a methodology.

Whenever we deal with form in a text, we are dealing with message. Furthermore, whenever we speak of aesthetic value, we are talking about message.

Contact: "What about the medium?" This question sends us off into the world of McLuhan, communication theorists, psychologists, and anthropologists, for it asks about the physical channel and psychological connection between addresser and addressee.

Code: "What is the nature of the code?" Linguists are beginning to develop a variety of interesting answers to this sort of question. But code, I take it, involves more than language, either natural or artificial (mathematics, Morse code, Fortran, etc.), and includes in poetry, for instance, the metrical code. Stretching Jakobson's meaning farther than perhaps he would want it stretched, the term *code* might be said to embrace all formal features of the message, at the level of the sentence and at global levels beyond the sentence, hence the whole complex business of coherence (about which *Contemporary Rhetoric* will have a good deal to say).

[3] W. Ross Winterowd, "The Realms of Meaning: Text-Centered Criticism," *College Composition and Communication* 23 (December 1972), 399–405.

Finally, *addressee:* "What is the effect of the message upon him?" To illustrate the implications of this question, I refer the reader to this quote from the preface of *Surprised by Sin: The Reader in Paradise Lost,* by Stanley E. Fish:

> In 1964, when I began to write *Surprised by Sin,* a certain timidity led me to construct a special argument for *Paradise Lost,* and more particularly for my subtitle. Since this poem tells the story of how its readers came to be the way they are, there is (I reasoned) some justification for an interpretation which follows the form of the reader's experience. I still believe in this argument, but not as a justification for talking about the reader. It *is* important to specify the peculiarly circular nature of the reader's relationship to this poem; but a justification is not necessary because it is the reader's relationship to any poem (or play or novel or essay) that is, or should be, our concern. [4]

In *Contemporary Rhetoric,* as I have conceived it, there is no place for a consideration of literature—and I therefore am going to quote another paragraph from Mr. Fish, partially to illustrate the importance of the addressee in the schema, but, more centrally, to give a hint about the relationship between rhetoric and literature. Mr. Fish continues:

> It is obvious that in saying this, I am courting the "affective fallacy." Indeed I am embracing it and going beyond it. The fear expressed by Wimsatt and Beardsley—that by focusing on the "psychological effects" of a work, there is danger "that the poem itself as an *object* of specifically critical judgment tends to disappear"—exactly defines my intention. That is, making the work disappear into the reader's experience of it is precisely what should happen in our criticism, because it is precisely what happens when we read. The lines of plot and argument, the beginnings, middles, and ends, the clusters of imagery, all the formal features that are observable when we step back from this reading experience, are, during the experience, components of a response; and the structure in which they are implicated is a structure of response. In other words, there is no necessary relationship between the visible form of a work and the form of the reader's experience—one is a complex of spatial, the other temporal, patterns—and since it is in the context of the latter that meaning occurs, a criticism which restricts itself to the poem as "object" will be inadequate to its pretensions. [5]

That is, criticism must deal with reader response, and the art that traditionally has dealt with reader/listener response is rhetoric, not literary criticism.

Up to now, we have dealt with the six factors in Jakobson's schema as if they were components, separate and discrete from one another. Indeed, it is one of the virtues of a conceptual framework that it can theoretically compartmentalize that which really is a unified whole. Without losing sight of Ginsberg's own self-expression, one can view *Kaddish* as an imaginative con-

[4] Stanley E. Fish, *Surprised by Sin: The Reader in Paradise Lost* (Berkeley, Los Angeles, and London: University of California Press, 1971).

[5] Ibid., pp. ix–x.

struct, as a report on the state of the world, as a linguistic artifact, and so on, when, in fact, the poem is all those elements working together in dynamic suspension. Therefore, we can borrow an idea and a term from Kenneth Burke and talk about *ratios* among factors.[6]

To get the proper "mix" of factors in the instance of *Kaddish* (Ginsberg's lament on the death of his mother), we need an addresser-context ratio, for the biographies of both Allen (addresser) and his mother (context) determine the message to a great extent—which is not to say that other factors do not influence the message. What I am saying, in effect, is that once the framework has been exhausted as a series of compartmentalized factors used to generate information (although the model is necessarily simplified for heuristic purposes), then the factors can be combined in ratios, and the investigator can begin to work back toward the holistic view that was so unmanageable originally.

This, then, shows something of how a conceptual framework becomes a heuristic. Now, on to Jakobson's second and more interesting point.

All we need to do is add a catalyst to Jakobson's schema, and it will transform itself so that it has uses other than those just discussed. Jakobson does add such a catalyst: purpose.

As a start toward the transformation, think of an expletive, for instance, the "damnit!" that I uttered when I cut my finger at noon today. If we orient the purpose of that utterance in relation to the schema, we will put it with the addresser. This is a way of pointing out that the expletive is oriented strictly toward the addresser in purpose. The expletive is self-expressive, or, in Jakobson's term, *emotive*. Stated in another way, the discourse is emotive if its purpose is related exclusively to the addresser.

It turns out that there is a purpose of discourse (and hence a kind of discourse) that is related to each item of the schema, but before we explore these, a disclaimer is in order. In real life it is difficult to find an instance of discourse in which the purpose is clear-cut and single, as in the case of the expletive. By using the conceptual framework, we will grossly oversimplify the nature of discourse (by schematizing it) so that we can better understand its complexities.

Related (according to function) to context is *referential* discourse. Its purpose is to convey information, and a clear-cut instance is this: "Lift receiver. Deposit coin. Listen for dial tone. Dial number." A scientific report is almost purely referential.

The purpose of message is *poetic*. That is, discourse is poetic if the message itself, with no reference to other factors, is its sole purpose. Or, poetic discourse is that in which the message itself is the overwhelmingly important element. Granted, it would be difficult to find a "pure" piece of poetry in this sense; perhaps pure poetry can exist only in the mind of God, for it tends to get

[6] Kenneth Burke, *A Grammar of Motives and a Rhetoric of Motives* (Cleveland and New York: The World Publishing Company, 1962), pp. xvii–xxv.

corrupted by social and persuasive purposes. Maybe the nearest thing to pure poetry is something like this: "Hickery dickery dock / The mouse ran up the clock / The clock struck one / And down he run / Hickery dickery dock."

The purpose of contact is *phatic,* keeping the lines open, as it were. I quote Jakobson:

> There are messages primarily serving to establish, to prolong, or to discontinue communication, to check whether the channel works ("Hello, do you hear me?"), to attract the attention of the interlocutor to confirm his continued attention ("Are you listening?" or in Shakespearean diction, "Lend me your ears!"—and on the other end of the wire "Um-hum!"). This set for contact . . . may be displayed by a profuse exchange of ritualized formulas, by entire dialogues with the mere purpose of prolonging communication. Dorothy Parker caught eloquent examples: " 'Well!' the young man said. 'Well!' she said. 'Well, here we are,' he said. 'Here we are,' she said, 'Aren't we?' 'I should say we were,' he said, 'Eeeyop! Here we are.' 'Well,' she said. 'Well!' he said, 'well.' " The endeavor to start and sustain communication is typical of talking birds; thus the phatic function of language is the only one they share with human beings. It is also the first verbal function acquired by infants; they are prone to communicate before being able to send or receive informative communication.[7]

The purpose related to code is *metalingual,* and metalanguage is language about language. Every definition is, then, metalingual in nature, as is a statement such as "What do you mean by that?" Grammars are metalingual, and transformational generative grammar is metalingual with a vengeance, having developed a metalanguage to talk about natural language.

The purpose related to addressee is what Jakobson calls *conative,* more traditionally termed "rhetorical." And thereby hangs a tale.

The best-known definition of rhetoric is "the art of finding the available means of persuasion in regard to any subject whatever." And from Aristotle on, most definitions have had the notion of persuasion built into them. The present discussion is not the place for a history of rhetoric, but without going into detail one can say that if the first connotation of rhetoric is "persuasion," the second is mendacity, and this pejoration of the term—which has been occurring since Plato's time—makes it an uncomfortable one to live with. A couple of years ago I was talking to an investment banker at a cocktail party. When he asked me what I did for a living, I told him that I taught at USC. And what were my scholarly interests? "Modern poetry and rhetoric," I replied. "Ah," he said, "I know what rhetoric is. That's where the truth stops and the B.S. begins." And that basically sums up the dilemma of the rhetorician.

I have solved the problem by purloining an idea from my friend James Kinneavy, author of *A Theory of Discourse.* I call myself a *discourse theorist* and take all of the modes to be my province—and notice that the Jakobson

7 Jakobson, pp. 355–56.

schema does indeed give us a modal classification that, in my view, is more useful than the traditional "narration-description-argumentation-exposition" classification.

The six Jakobsonian modes are, according to purpose:

Referential
[Context]

Poetic
[Message]

Emotive   Conative
[Addresser]_____[Addressee]

Phatic
[Contact]

Metalingual
[Code]

Varieties of Composition and Their Usefulness

Can we really teach composition, and what evidence is there that we can? And if we can, how?

If we accept Jakobson's schema as at least a working model, we find immediately that any act of composition will involve six major factors: an addresser, a context, a message, some sort of contact, a code, and an addressee. Any theory or practice in pedagogy, then, will have to take account somehow of all six factors.

As anyone who has been in the business of composition for very long knows, the winds of fashion waft theory and practice from one pole to another and back again. The advent of structural grammar and the subsequent coming of transformational generative grammar both had the effect of moving a great deal of instruction toward a code orientation. Only the foolish, of course, argued that a knowledge of grammar of any variety would aid the student in writing. (There is no necessary correlation between one's ability to describe the language and one's ability to use it.) The sensible argument—and one that I am in complete sympathy with—is that the study of language is a humane discipline; therefore, linguistics is a valid subject matter on which to base a writing course. (Just as we use literature for *subject matter* in courses in expository writing, not to teach students to become creative writers.) My twittering antennae tell me that the fervor for linguistics-based writing courses has died down considerably of late.

Any course that stresses argumentation is, of course, addressee-oriented, but in the twentieth century, or at least the last half of it, heavy stress on argumentation has been left pretty much to our colleagues across the hall in the Speech Department.

Certainly the dominant trend in the teaching of composition has been context-oriented—that is, the writing of expository essays—and even when fashion moved some courses into a study of language (code orientation), the final purpose was not to produce linguists but to train writers of exposition, who would use language as their subject matter during the course.

Any course in creative writing under the aegis of the composition program is message-oriented, and such courses have always been around and will continue to survive, simply because at their best they are a more intense and rewarding experience for students than the theme-a-week mixture of sociology and "well-supported" opinion about everything under the sun that makes up the normal—not the best—garden variety writing class.

Having thus quickly disposed of context, message, code, and addressee, I would like to spend a bit of time considering the implications of courses that are contact and addresser oriented.

Granted, McLuhan is already old hat. Nonetheless, he was the first prophet of a continuing major trend in compositional pedagogy, that is, contact, or media, orientation. McLuhanism can have two related manifestations in the composition course. First is the course that uses the media (television, cinema) as its subject matter, and second is the course that turns to composing in the media (making films and television tapes). For instance, an unstartling but extremely successful innovation at the University of Southern California is a cluster of freshman classes in which film is the subject matter for expository writing. More innovative is the course that interprets the word "composing" broadly and allows students to make their statements in writing, film, television, or other media.

Even English departments—in some cases the supreme instances of atavism—are moving vigorously into the study of film, if not of television. Basic textbooks, such as John Harrington's *The Rhetoric of Film,*[8] are appearing, and respected scholars in English, like John Ashmead of Haverford College, are turning their considerable talents toward the understanding of film as a *kind* of literature. In fact, Ashmead's 1972 distinguished lecture for NCTE was "New Theories of Film and Their Significance for the Seventies," and this lecture was published in a volume called *The Humanity of English.*[9]

Now this opening up of the concept of rhetoric and composition is one of two recent developments that are worth looking at carefully, for they both take us to some of the overwhelming questions that we must ask if we want to reside in the palace of theoretical and applied rhetoric.

The writing of expository essays (context orientation), which is overwhelmingly the major concern of composition classes taken as a whole, has at least two important justifications: expository writing gets the business of the world done (therefore one must learn to write exposition in order to be effective in the world), and expository writing develops significant ideas (therefore, when one learns to write exposition, one also learns to think). Both of

[8] John Harrington, *The Rhetoric of Film* (New York: Holt, Rinehart and Winston, 1973).

[9] *The Humanity of English* (Urbana, Ill.: NCTE, 1972).

these arguments are mirrored in the following, which is a typical statement from a freshman composition book:

> If it were possible to commission some omnipotent scientist to develop a pill that would make us all great writers, it would have three powers. It would give us the significant ideas that are at the core of all great writing. It would give us the ability to analyze those ideas and make them clear, interesting, and convincing. And it would provide us with the writing ability to fulfill that obligation. Fortunately or unfortunately, scientists have not yet provided us with pills for instant genius, and we must look elsewhere for all three powers.[10]

It is, however, doubtful that very many people who are involved in getting the business of the world done really need to write exposition of the sort that English instructors think of when they say the word, for these people, I suspect, have at the backs of their minds the kinds of things that appear in *Harper's, Atlantic Monthly,* and *Partisan Review;* certainly that is the sort of essay that populates the so-called freshman reader. Just run your eyes down the credit pages of any of these readers if you do not agree with my point. Nobody in the "real" world, however, needs to write essays in order to be effective or to survive. Engineers must write reports, physicians generally write nothing but prescriptions, college professors usually write technical essays based on their research, and so on. Essayists are a small and highly specialized group of craftsmen who exercise their skills for love and profit and for, I suspect, an increasingly small audience.

I am arguing that college students do not need to learn to write expository essays so that they can survive in the world. But, the counter-argument will run, almost everyone needs to learn to express himself or herself effectively, and the principles learned in the writing of expository essays will carry over into other modes of expression. Well, I answer, that is an untested premise, and it is not particularly attractive anyway. One could just as well argue that the prevalent mode of expression in our age is television; therefore, people should learn to express themselves in that medium, and the principles that they learn there will carry over into other modes of expression. The sheer pervasiveness of television makes that argument powerful:

> If any form of media deserves the modifier "mass," it is television. Virtually every individual in this country has access to a home television set and statistics show that we watch television an average of 45 hours a week. The average TV viewing time for preschoolers is 28½ hours per week. Children in the 6–11 age range watch almost 24 hours of TV weekly and teenagers about 20 hours a week.[11]

[10] Harry H. Crosby and George F. Estey, *College Writing: The Rhetorical Imperative* (New York: Harper and Row, 1968), p. 4.

[11] John F. Savage, "Jack, Janet, or Simon Barsinister," *Elementary English* 50 (January 1973), 133.

The argument that writing expository essays teaches the principles of sound thinking is analogous to the argument that learning Latin (or mathematics or whatever) is good in and of itself, for it builds intellectual muscles, in the way that jogging is good in and of itself because it conditions the cardio-vascular system. Why expository writing as a conditioner for gray matter? Why not some other discipline, say philosophy?

As far as I'm concerned, then, there is really no compelling reason for insisting that every student have a try at composing a series of expository essays, any more than one might argue that every student ought to have some skill at dentistry or any other *single* discipline. Notice the kinds of arguments that we might develop for insisting that all students take an introductory course in cavity filling. Not everyone intends to be a dentist; in fact, an extremely small proportion of the population will finally enter the profession. However, filling teeth gives one manual dexterity and practice in extremely detailed work and allows one to appreciate the responsibilities and rewards of a practitioner in the health sciences. Furthermore, we all have teeth and must use them in such basic activities as eating and speaking. Tooth-filling, therefore, expands one's physical, cognitive, and affective capabilities. (And that, of course, is more than one can say for composing expository essays, since in that process no physical skill is necessary.)

How seriously is the above paragraph meant? I take the Fifth and let the reader decide.

In any case, the contact orientation that came with the McLuhan revolution has expanded the meaning of composition to include composing for the media. This is not to say that many composition courses are producing films or TV shows; what is happening is that the product and the process of composing for the media are being studied.

Ashmead nicely states the importance of the new contact orientation for English departments:

> When I began teaching English some two decades ago my department chairman forbade the teaching of movies. And, in fact, I have come to movies obliquely, by way of linguistics and theory, hoping to achieve respectability, perhaps, by the familiar academic route of incomprehensibility.
>
> And yet I would say that movies today continue to be a living art, in contrast to modern poetry, drama, and other forms of literary crewelwork. We must not be misled by attendance figures which show a drop from 70–90 million patrons a week at the end of World War II to the present 15 million a week. Many movies now reach their bulk audiences on TV; a truism of TV is that any first-rate movie will knock down the ratings of all other competing programs.[12]

That is, the contact orientation that McLuhanism brought to composition programs simply put them nearer the real world.

[12] Ashmead, pp. 97–98.

Notice, however, that this argument is hedging and, in a sense, getting nowhere. Now ought to be the time to fish or cut bait; I really ought to be on the verge of recommending that composition courses become composition courses in the widest sense, that is, that they give students the opportunity to compose in a variety of media, including the scribal. (*Insist* that students compose in a variety of media? Assign not a theme a week, but a theme one week, a videotape the next, and a film the next?)

But I cannot make such a recommendation and remain consistent. Very few people need to compose *in any medium*—except in the hothouse atmosphere of the classroom. I am not arguing to take away the opportunity for anyone to learn to compose in any medium, including the scribal (confined to an expository theme a week, if that's what the student wants). I am simply questioning the sanity of requiring that everyone learn to (or try to learn to) compose in a given way. What, after all, are the uses of composition?

Well, it seems pretty obvious that most people—the vast majority of cultured, successful, effective citizens—do not need any great ability to compose. That is, writing in the English-department sense is useful to only a very few people.

Like any other art, composing (of any sort) has its own inherent satisfactions. It is an art—like playing a musical instrument or painting—that can bring richness to the life of the practitioner. One can argue, then, that learning to compose has this "use."

We will, however, discover the real usefulness of composing if we shift our focus from context and contact orientation to addresser orientation. And, in fact, it is just this shift that has been the most important development in theories and practices of composing for roughly the last seven years. Addresser-oriented discourse is, using Jakobson's term, emotive, but that particular word is not neutral enough for the purposes of this discussion; therefore, we will opt for *self-expressive*.

I have argued that very few people ever "use" writing for these purposes (to discuss ideas in exposition—context orientation; to create poetry—message orientation; merely for phatic purposes—contact orientation; to discuss language—code orientation; to persuade—addressee orientation) even though everyone uses most of them continually in speaking. It is also, I think, self-evident that almost no one ever uses writing self-expressively. That is, composing in the English-department sense of the word has little usefulness. (I realize that freshmen in the composition classes go on to write essays for history and research papers for psychology. But after they graduate, very few of them ever have need or occasion to compose in any real sense.)

Paradoxically, however, it may well be true that the *potentially* most useful sort of composing is the self-expressive. This point has never been more eloquently expressed than by Eldridge Cleaver in a widely quoted passage:

> After I returned to prison, I took a long look at myself and, for the first time in my life, admitted that I was wrong, that I had gone astray—astray

not so much from the white man's law as from being human, civilized—for I could not approve the act of rape. Even though I had some insight into my own motivations, I did not feel justified. I lost my self-respect. My pride as a man dissolved and my whole fragile moral structure seemed to collapse, completely shattered.

That is why I started to write. To save myself. I realized that no one could save me but myself. The prison authorities were both uninterested and unable to help me. I had to find out who I am and what I want to be, what type of man I should be, and what I could do to become the best of which I was capable. I understood that what had happened to me had also happened to countless other blacks and it would happen to many, many more.[13]

We can summarize what Cleaver is saying as follows: one "uses" self-expressive writing to adjust to the world. It is writing in which addresser and addressee become one. (As usual, the schema that I am using leads me to oversimplification, but that happens to be an excellent strategy for understanding a complex matter. Obviously, Cleaver is not *merely* expressing himself; in one sense, he merges addresser and addressee, but in another, there is an audience "out there" somewhere that he wants to reach. I trust that the reader will always keep in mind the fearful complexity of all discourse even while I—for reasons of strategy—am oversimplifying.)

As the selection from Cleaver indicates, self-expressive writing is not necessarily undisciplined. Indeed, consider two poets who are the antipodes of one another, but both of whom are "confessional" (i.e., self-expressive): Ginsberg and Lowell. By his own avowal, Ginsberg just lets language flow out and revises minimally, if at all. Lowell's tight craftsmanship needs no comment.

There is, interestingly enough, some evidence that self-expressive writing is more difficult for some people (and perhaps for most people) than simple exposition. In *The Composing Processes of Twelfth Graders*. Janet Emig draws a profile of a twelfth-grade writer named Lynn. What is an easy subject for Lynn and what does she find difficult to write about? The easy subject is one that is nonpersonal, "one that does not demand interacting with her feelings, one that is *not* reflexive [i.e., self-expressive]." [14] A paragraph from Emig's comments on Lynn is well worth pondering.

> The linguist Leon A. Jakobovits suggests that "stale art" is algorithmic—that is, it is produced by a known algorithm, "defined as a computational device that specifies the order and nature of the steps to be followed in the generation of a sequence." One could say that the major kind of essay too many students have been taught to write in American schools is algorithmic, or so mechanical that a computer could readily be programed to produce it: when a student is hurried or anxious, he simply reverts or regresses to the only program he knows, as if inserting a single card into his brain.[15]

[13] Eldridge Cleaver, *Soul on Ice* (New York: Dell Publishing Co., 1968), p. 15.
[14] Janet Emig, *The Composing Processes of Twelfth Graders* (Urbana, Ill.: NCTE, 1971), pp. 48–49.
[15] Ibid., pp. 50–53.

Jakobovits and Emig are undoubtedly correct, in at least the metaphorical sense. Therefore, it becomes apparent that self-expressive writing cannot be *taught* (if, indeed, any kind of writing can), for teaching must have to do with providing algorithms whereby students can get from beginning to end in a given mode of writing. The minute a student begins to work according to an externally imposed algorithm, his writing is no longer self-expressive. We can translate this notion into the following truism (which is nonetheless powerful in conceptual basis): *writing according to formula is hack writing*— which is exactly what most essays in composition classes are. The writer who opts for the self-expressive mode (might it not, in its purest form, be called the *idiosyncratic* mode?) enters into the jungle with no compass and no maps (no algorithms).

I am tempted at this point to rephrase a sentence from the last paragraph as if it were a law. Being inherently undogmatic, I will rephrase it in the form of a hypothesis, the testing of which ought to be one of the central concerns of every instructor of writing and every rhetorician:

> *Teaching [of writing] must have to do with providing algorithms whereby students can get from beginning to end in a given piece of writing.*

Our logic carries us inexorably to the conclusion that self-expressive writing cannot be taught; therefore, the composition instructor's only function is to provide the student with the opportunity for writing. But this conclusion is, of course, valid only in the hypothetical world of "pure" types. In actuality, self-expression as a pure type exists only in the emotive exclamation.

Dartmouth and After

Starting in about 1967 with the famous (or infamous) Dartmouth Conference, serious attention began to be paid to the value of writing as self-expression. The Dartmouth Conference is too well known and too thoroughly hashed and rehashed in the literature for me even to spend time outlining the nature of the meetings or their conclusions. But what I do want to spend a bit of time and energy on is an evaluation of the premises and the effects (or possible effects) of the Dartmouth Conference and other movements toward self-expressiveness.

It will be remembered that the present discussion substituted the term *self-expressive* for Jakobson's word *emotive* as the purpose of addressee-oriented discourse. So far, that substitution has served well, but now the schema must be retransformed; *emotive* must be put back in place of *self-expressive*, for the argument now demands positing that *all discourse is self-expressive*. Since it comes from the self, it can be expressive of nothing but self—unless, of course, one refers to aleatory sequences produced by computers or to committee efforts in which the self becomes so minimal as not to count.

Clinging to the Jakobson schema (which has served so well to this point), we can say that self-expression in discourse may take emotive (e.g., *de pro-fundis clamavi*), referential (e.g., an expository essay explaining socialism on the college campus), poetic (e.g., a poem or a short story), metalingual (e.g., a study of style), or conative (e.g., an argument directed to a given audience), or phatic forms. An example of the phatic form of discourse is the small talk that occurs when one tries to get conversation going at, say, the beginning of a cocktail party; all the talk about weather or, as in Los Angeles, about the freeways, is simply getting channels of communication working. But in what way is that self-expressive? It is virtually as pure a form of self-expression as emotive language is, isn't it?

I referred to the Jakobson schema once again and then went on to describe the spectrum of self-expression because only with this variety firmly in mind will we be able to evaluate the Dartmouth Movement fairly. I speak of the Dartmouth Movement, not the conference, because there is a strong trend toward self-expression represented by many who were not actually present at the Dartmouth Conference.

The Dartmouth Conference shifted the focus in the teaching of English toward self-expression. If one thinks about it, this shift is radical. And it must, finally, be salubrious.

The spirit of the Dartmouth Conference appears most eloquently in John Dixon's *Growth Through English,* a little book about language processes in elementary schools that, by extension, sets a tone for all writing classes.[16] (Dixon, however, talks about the whole spectrum of English activities; we are concerned only with writing.)

I am reluctant to deal with *Growth Through English* in detail, for it is widely known and readily accessible. A longish quote, however, will capture the spirit of both *Growth Through English* and the Dartmouth Conference.

> There is . . . a central paradox about language. It belongs to the public world, and an English classroom is a place where pupils meet to share experience of some importance, to talk about people and situations in the world as they know it, gathering experience into new wholes and enjoying the satisfaction and power that this gives. But in so doing each individual takes what he can from the shared store of experience and builds it into a world of his own.
>
> When sceptical teachers ask, "Isn't that diary [that Dixon quotes] an example of the work of the rare few: aren't drills the only thing for the rest?" we must look again at our human purposes in using language. Recalling experience, getting it clear, giving it shape and making connections, speculating and building theories, celebrating (or exorcizing) particular moments in our lives—these are some of the broad purposes that language serves and enables. For days we may not work much beyond the level of gossip in fulfilling these purposes, but inevitably the time comes when we need to

[16] John Dixon, *Growth Through English* (Reading, England: National Association for the Teaching of English, 1967).

invest a good deal of ourselves and our energy in them. It is the English teacher's responsibility to prepare for and work towards such times.[17]

From the above quotation, we might assume that the Dartmouth conferees had Jakobson's schema in the backs of their minds, and, in fairness, it must be said that by statement and by implication they were advocating what the present discussion has proposed: that writing of any kind equals self-expression, and that self-expression can have a variety of manifestations, from the emotive to the conative.

Furthermore, Dixon's book obviously deals with the problem of increasing the language abilities of children, but, as was perhaps inevitable, extrapolations were made, so that undiluted Dartmouthism is now invading the colleges and universities—without the corrective of realizing that self-expression involves more sorts of writing than the wryly personal.

This concludes our fairly extensive survey of the purposes of writing as they manifest themselves in the classroom. But I suppose that as an honest man I need to lay it on the line and make clear where I stand.

With the Dartmouthians and Eldridge Cleaver, I believe that the only real "use" of writing—except in extremely rare instances—is self-expression (which I take to be concomitant with self-discovery). Since self-expression is as various as the purposes of discourse, I think that the writing class should be a happy anarchy, giving students rich opportunities for any kind of composition that they feel they need, either for "real" uses or for self-expression.

Since it is axiomatic with me that—given physical and mental abilities—any student will master any language task that he or she really feels the need to master, I see no reason for a stress upon any one kind of writing in any composition class. The problem is, of course, that students may discover their need *after* they have passed through freshman English, but that is no excuse for using the freshman English class to prepare students to accomplish tasks that they may well never encounter. This means, of course, that the English department should staff writing labs, to help students at all levels with writing problems as those problems arise. When students need to write a research paper for history—if indeed they ever do—they can read Turabian, and if that does not suffice, they can come to the writing lab, where they will get help.

Speculations about Pedagogy

Contemporary Rhetoric is largely an attempt to bring together current knowledge on the state of the art. Let it be said now, however, that the state of our knowledge concerning the composing process is at best primitive. Therefore, no one can claim to have a well-founded theory of pedagogy. The basis for any teaching must finally be subjective and founded upon one's own estimate of results.

Consider what happens when anyone produces a stretch of writing. A discourser (addresser) involves himself in the mental and physical tasks of gen-

[17] Ibid., pp. 6–7.

erating ideas, arranging them, and putting them down in some fashion, usually with pen or typewriter. Consider that we are just now beginning to arrive at a precise understanding of the sentence as produced (but how it gets produced by the human mind is still a mystery), then multiply that ignorance by a quantum leap, and you will have some idea of how little we know about the processes whereby the discourser generates discourse. As Janet Emig puts it:

> Composing in writing is a common activity of literate persons. Yet descriptions of what occurs during this experience, not to mention attempts to explain or analyze, are highly unsatisfactory. An investigator who attempts to characterize the composing process fully and accurately finds that the sources available are too disheveled and contradictory to provide a coherent characterization.
>
> About the only unanimity among the data is the assumption, in the words of D. Gordon Rohman, that "writing is usefully described as a process, something which shows continuous change in time like growth in organic nature." [18]

Any view of the composing process that limits itself just to the discourser, however, is likely to be warped, for the discourse itself is shaped not only by the discourser's mental and kinetic abilities but also by other factors in the discourse complex. Aside from an addressee (or addressees) to be adjusted to, there are also the context of composing (the rhetorical situation, discussed below), the sort of contact that is established, and the limitations and possibilities of the code to be taken into account. Each of these factors is so complex as to defy accurate description. There can be no "Skinner box" studies of the composing process, for isolating the composer and limiting his or her activity to one segment of the whole process simply falsifies what actually goes on. This is not to say that experiments such as the one that Mellon conducted are not valuable.[19] It is to say, however, that an unfathomable amount of data from such microscopic studies as Mellon's must be assembled before anyone can claim with honesty and responsibility to understand the process of composing in any precise sense. And research is just beginning. True, in 1915 Rollo Walter Brown did his classic study *How the French Boy Learns to Write,* but that study was only a description of what happens; Brown made no theoretical contribution—which is not to belittle his considerable pioneering accomplishment.

Our understanding of the limits on composition that the code imposes is worth looking at, for surely in the last fifteen years or so we have gathered a mountain of precise data at the level of the sentence—that is, transformational generative grammar and other varieties of modern linguistics have made phenomenal progress.

It has become a truism that children enter school with a more or less complete "knowledge" of their native language; that is, they are *capable* of gen-

[18] Emig, p. 1.
[19] John C. Mellon, *Transformational Sentence-Combining* (Champaign, Ill.: NCTE, 1969).

erating sentences that contain pretty much the whole variety of structures that the language affords. In theory, then, a college freshman, say, should quite at will be able to learn to write like Mark Twain or William Faulkner, like Leslie Fiedler or Tom Wolfe. In theory, yes. However, as any instructor knows, there are interferences that always keep *performance* well below the level of *competence*. (It will be remembered that competence is a hypothetically global knowledge of the language, and performance is what the discourser produces.) Any theory of composition, then, will have to take account of the disjunction between competence and performance.

I propose the following model: *the college freshman enters the composition class with an intuitive mastery of his or her native dialect.* I am almost saying, but not quite, that students know everything there is to know about their native dialect; that is, they have complete competence in their own dialect, and undoubtedly have an almost total competence in other dialects as well. Certainly, in their college careers they will not encounter any writing in English that they cannot understand if they can grasp the concepts embodied in the writing. The language itself will not deter them from understanding anything that they read.

This is not to say that all prose is equally clear, nor is it to say that there is no such thing as virtually opaque prose. For instance, regardless of the concepts involved, a high degree of nominalization creates difficulty in reading—*for every reader.* Sentence *a* below is easier to read than sentence *b* simply because sentence *b* is highly nominalized:

> *a.* A grammar is made up of a finite series of rules that can generate an infinite number of sentences, a fact that explains why we can understand sentences that we have never seen before.
> *b.* A grammar's being made up of a finite series of rules that can generate an infinite number of sentences is the explanation for our understanding of sentences that we have never seen before.

The explanation of the difficulty of the second example is fairly straightforward. In reading a sentence, one looks for a predicate (or main word) around which the other terms can be organized. Notice that *c* makes immediate sense, while *d* does not:

> *c.* That my Redeemer liveth pleases me.
> *d.* * My Redeemer liveth pleases me.

The reason is that *c* begins with what I call the *perceptual that,* which automatically warns the reader to organize the sentence around "please," the main predicate, not around "liveth," the subordinate predicate. In *a,* the reader immediately grasps "is made up" as the point around which the rest of the sentence will be organized, but in *b,* the reader must hold a series of twenty-one words in suspension before he arrives at the organizational point, "explanation."

Something of the complexity of the reading task is intimated here, though the main purpose has been to give an example supporting the argument that some writing is inherently more difficult to read, not necessarily because of the concepts involved, and not because of the reader's defective "knowledge" of his language, but because some grammatical constructions create more perceptual difficulties than others.

If we can grant, then, that the college freshman has a complete knowledge of his or her own language—even though, to be sure, he or she does not know all 600,000 or so words that make up its lexicon—we must conclude that writing difficulties arise from the following three sources: the inability to generate ideas that language can carry; interferences, such as emotional or physical problems or the lack of a proper "scene" for writing; simple lack of experience in what Robert Zoellner, in his *College English* monograph "Talk-Write: A Behavioral Pedagogy for Composition," has called "the scribal mode."

We are now ready to come back to our questions: Can we really teach composition? What evidence is there that we can? If we can teach composition, how?

It has already been mentioned that, theoretically at least, every college writer has a complete competence in his or her native dialect. That is, the language itself will be no barrier to the understanding of any piece of discourse. Some concepts will be too difficult for the student to grasp, but these are independent of the language itself as a system. Competence is global. Performance—the ability to write or speak sentence sequences or even individual sentences—varies widely among individuals, and, in fact, no two people have exactly the same performance level.

It would seem, then, that the goal of teaching should be to move skills from the global area of competence into the area of performance. (This is exactly the purpose of the work done by Francis Christensen and John Mellon, as well as Frank O'Hare.) This point is so fundamental that I will state it again. Hypothetically, every adult user of a language has the ability to produce every kind of sentence that has ever been produced in the language. Since no user does or ever will produce every kind of sentence in a language, it can be concluded that competence is greater than performance. This idea is confirmed by the fact that users of a language can identify well-formed and ill-formed sequences in the language.

Insofar as pedagogy in writing is concerned *only* with sentence production —although, of course, it is concerned with a great deal more, though "mere" sentence production is not to be underestimated—it should be possible to activate competence, to bring it into the area of performance, by the use of systematic exercises such as those devised by Christensen, Mellon, and O'Hare. There are, however, a great many arguments against such "programing." The following two arguments are the ones that seem most important to me.

Our knowledge of the languaging process, while it has made great advances in the past fifteen years or so, is nonetheless minimal and primitive; we have only scant data and a variety of tenuous theories on which to proceed if we are to give students "programed" instruction. Furthermore, we know precious little about the "factors" of sentences in the language. As an example: surely the most extensive transformational-generative treatment of English syntax resulted from the so-called UCLA Syntax Project. Nevertheless, the authors have elected *not* to treat adverbials, for explaining them is beyond the present state of the art.[20] Startling as this may sound—after all, aren't adverbials among the most common and simple of sentence devices?—it is nonetheless the case, and it illustrates the limitations of our knowledge concerning the nature of the sentence.

These two factors—our ignorance concerning both the languaging process and the nature of the language—should deter anyone from great certainty in regard to the efficacy of any one pedagogical program. Now take into account the idiosyncrasy of each mind, and something of the complexity of teaching "mere" sentence structure begins to emerge. (And notice that we have taken into account only the addresser—sentence production—and the code—the nature of the sentence itself. We intentionally overlooked context, message, contact, and addressee.)

One can only conclude that writing is far too difficult a skill to be taught—and yet we do "teach" it. Or perhaps, at the very best, we provide opportunities for students to write, read, and get responses to their writing.

The following we do know with some certainty: (1) the "factors" involved in writing are overwhelmingly numerous and largely unknown; (2) by processes that are understood dimly if at all, the mind chooses devices, structures, and so on that it finds significant; and (3) in language learning, *feedback* is essential.

Working on the basis of what we do know, then, it is possible to say that the composition class should create as rich an environment as possible for scribal stimuli and scribal responses of all kinds. There are two functions in which instructors can be certain of usefulness. They can lead students to analyze various kinds of texts and provide detailed and immediate feedback to the writer.

This is not to say that other functions lack value. The point is that only in these two functions can the instructor feel certain of effectiveness.

The Context of Composing

It would seem that the classroom is the worst place in the world for composing to take place. According to popular dogma, the classroom is artificial; it is hermetically sealed from the "real" world. But then any given scene in which composition takes place is artificial and hermetically sealed. By this I mean that the act of composition is by its nature a lonely process, with the possible audience removed in time and distance from the discourser.

Lloyd Bitzer has said that the rhetorical situation—the gestalt in the real

[20] Robert P. Stockwell et al., *The Major Syntactic Structures of English* (New York: Holt, Rinehart and Winston, 1973), p. 26.

world that stimulates discourse—consists of three factors: (1) an exigence, that is, a need to discourse, (2) an audience, and (3) constraints.[21] This little rubric is useful to keep in mind when one is thinking about the context of composing. If the classroom is artificial in regard to composition, it is because the reasons for writing are frequently extrinsic rather than intrinsic; there is no real audience, and the constraints are specialized and frequently unrealistic.

A word about classroom exigence will suffice. A theme assignment is hardly exigent; it hardly creates the need to bring about change or action or sympathetic agreement. As John Dixon says, most classroom writing is in the nature of dry runs. One corrective for this tendency is to keep in mind the varied purposes for writing: emotive, referential, poetic, phatic, metalingual, and conative. In the classroom, writing is all too frequently limited to the referential and conative. Expanding the sorts of writing that students can do, and are encouraged to do, exponentially increases the possibility that the writers will feel some kind of real exigence.

And, to be briefly truistic, why should all classroom writing or even most classroom writing be done on the basis of rigid assignments? Every writer should be free to follow his or her own leads, into whatever subjects. The notion of the workshop is helpful here: a group of writers working on their own projects with an instructor to help them accomplish whatever it is they set out to do.

But there is a whole literature on "open" writing, and I do not intend to remap territory that Ken Macrorie, James Miller, D. Gordon Rohman, and others have already covered.

Everyone knows how stultifying it is for students, consciously or subconsciously, to aim their writing at the teacher. And creating a real audience is an easy thing. Essays can be reproduced and distributed to all members of the class, and there are other ways by which students can be convinced that they are writing for real people in the real world. If students have the freedom to do writing of their own choice, filling their own needs, they will automatically create audiences other than the instructor.

The factor in the context of composing that I would like to focus on is *constraints*. Every discourse situation is an intricately woven tapestry of opportunities and constraints, or, to use Melville's figure from *Moby Dick,* a mat in which the warp of necessity goes with the woof of free will to make up the whole fabric.

Constraints such as laws concerning obscenity, libel, and sedition are only the most obvious ones governing what can and cannot be said; in the public press there are also subtle and not-so-subtle economic pressures. In every social situation, there is the mystery that Kenneth Burke is so fascinated by, the isolation of me from you. There are language taboos that are by no means

[21] Lloyd F. Bitzer, "The Rhetorical Situation," *Philosophy and Rhetoric* 1 (January 1968), 1–14.

universal, but that strongly influence what can and cannot be said or written in a given situation.

Tracing the intricate patterns of constraints in discourse situations is fascinating and informative—a good exercise for student writers and instructors of writing alike; however, the classroom does impose some constraints that are unique and that ought to be of interest to anyone concerned with the process of composing.

Specifically, the classroom typically puts heavy stress on language constraints, or the sort of language that can be used. In general, instructors insist upon what might be called "handbook standard" or "Edited Standard English." This demand is justified by arguments such as the following: "Standard English is the language that educated men and women use in their written communications." Perhaps, but there is a wrongheadedness to this argument that ought to be apparent to anyone who thinks about the range of uses for language. We can turn right back to the Jakobsonian schema for our perspective on this problem.

Nothing in language usage is ever good or bad except in relation to a purpose. Dylan Thomas and e. e. cummings certainly did not use written standard English in their poetry, and assuredly Jerry Rubin did not in *Do It.*

So the first obvious and simple point is that we need to be completely relativistic in the classroom, judging language only on the basis of its effectiveness for a given purpose. And we also need a good deal more common sense than has been characteristic of English classrooms in the past.

Theorists are coming more firmly to the conclusion that language acquisition is not a function of intelligence. If this is in fact the case, then so-called language deficiencies (i.e., deviations from standard English in either speech or writing) are the result of cultural circumstances, not intellectual factors. Deviations from written standard English fall into the four general categories of vocabulary, spelling, punctuation, and "mechanics" (including such matters as verb agreement, as well as more fundamental syntactic gambits).

Vocabulary that deviates from standard English is not a matter of language as much as it is of culture. In the first place, given cultures have their unique stocks of words for certain uses, as in the phrase *"carry* me back to ole Virginie."* Another example is the various terms for carbonated soft drinks: soda, soda pop, pop, soda water, tonic, and so on. If a writer lacks the vocabulary to deal with a given subject, the problem is with his culture, not his dialect.

Spelling is, of course, a tremendous problem in American schools, for there is a great pressure from society at large for orthography. But how difficult a conceptual task is correct spelling? Every instructor of college composition has encountered (probably at least once a year) a problem speller who seemingly can never make the distinction between "principle" and "principal." The same student often, though, is successful in learning to speak French or grappling with modern physics or mastering the concepts of psychology. That is, the same student who "can't" spell is capable of other, extremely demanding conceptual tasks, and, on the other hand, students whose writing is simply vapid often spell with invariable correctness. One must conclude that *virtually everyone can learn to spell correctly if the motivation is there.*

Well, then, what about punctuation? In *Structural Essentials of English,* Harold Whitehall demonstrated, in some twenty-two pages, that punctuation in English is perfectly systematic and that the system is perfectly explicable.[22] Conventional punctuation is not a mystery or even a terribly intricate system, surely not as intricate as the transit, road, and freeway system in a major urban center such as Los Angeles. Though I realize that my analogy may not be completely valid, it nonetheless seems perfectly reasonable to me to say that anyone who can negotiate the complexities of getting around efficiently in a place such as Los Angeles certainly has the native intelligence to learn to punctuate. Once again, the whole question is one of motivation. (Perhaps I am oversimplifying, but I think not. On the basis of modern theory and on the basis of my own observation, I firmly believe that any "normal" person can master any dialect and any nicety of written English if he or she is sufficiently motivated.)

Deviations from standard English usage always concern fundamentally unimportant and minor shifts.

> Differences between standard and nonstandard English are not as sharp as our first impressions would lead us to think. Consider, for example, the socially stratified marker of "pronominal apposition"—the use of a dependent pronoun in such sentences as:
>
> > My oldest sister she worked at the bank.
>
> Though most of us recognize this as a nonstandard pattern, it is not always realized that the "nonstandard" aspect is merely a slight difference in intonation. A standard speaker frequently says the same thing, with a slight break after the subject: *My oldest sister—she works at the bank, and she finds it very profitable.* There are many ways in which a greater awareness of the standard colloquial forms would help teachers interpret the nonstandard forms. Not only do standard speakers use pronominal apposition with the break noted above, but in casual speech they can also bring object noun phrases to the front, "foregrounding" them. For example, one can say:
>
> > My oldest sister—she worked at the Citizens Bank in Passaic last year.
> >
> > The Citizens Bank, in Passaic—my oldest sister worked there last year.
> >
> > Passaic—my oldest sister worked at the Citizens Bank there last year.[23]

The urban black dialect has simplified the rules of grammar by merely deleting the genitive marker: *the lady's hat* equals *the lady hat.* Also in urban black, the unconjugated "be" is used to indicate durative quality, *He be here* meaning something like *He is usually here.*

---

[22] Harold Whitehall, *Structural Essentials of English* (New York: Harcourt Brace Jovanovich, 1951), pp. 119–33.

[23] William Labov, *The Study of Nonstandard English* (Urbana, Ill.: NCTE, n.d.), p. 14.

As for syntax, there are two kinds of deviations from the standard: those that result from mispunctuation and those that result from mixed up thinking. The first deviation is illustrated almost every time an instructor writes "frag" in the margin of a student paper, and the second is illustrated when neither the instructor nor the writer can explain exactly what a given sentence is intended to mean.

Here is an example of seventh-grade writing from an inner-city school:

The Space Man

Once about a time there was a green monster that	1
slap me in the face and then I ran and told my mother	2
about it and she told me to go to bed for lying. And	3
I got out of the house and got my gun and then I went	4
looking for him I said I am going to get him and then	5
I seen him get in his spaceship and then I went to my	6
airplane and I follow him to Mars and he had all his	7
friend after me and I ran very fast I hanged from a	8
star and I hit two Mars men in the face and then I	9
got the rest of them.	10

This passage contains every sort of "error" that an instructor of writing is likely to encounter, with the exception of misspellings, for the spelling in the passage has been regularized.

In the first line, the "about" in the formulaic "once *upon* a time" seems to be a mere slip of the ballpoint, but the unconjugated form "slap" (line 2) is characteristic of urban black dialect. The fused sentences in line five (". . . I went looking for him I said I am going to get him. . . .") might occur in the writing of any ethnic or socioeconomic group. The "seen" in line six as the past tense of "see" is a common feature of nonstandard English. The unconjugated "follow" in line seven is, once again, typical of urban black English, but note that it could possibly be interpreted as historical present, in which case the passage would contain a tactical, rhetorical error, not a mechanical error, for the shift from past to historical present would be jarring to most readers. In line eight there are fused sentences again (". . . very fast I hanged . . .").

The point of reproducing and commenting on this passage was to demonstrate that language deviance is always—viewed from the right perspective— a completely minor sort of thing. When teachers concentrate on "errors" in spelling, punctuation, usage, and syntax, they are referring invariably to superficial aspects of the whole composition—*and are creating artificial constraints that must, by their very nature, be destructive.*

I have said before that nothing in language is good or bad except in regard to purpose (and purpose, of course, encompasses audience). I have also said that virtually every student is capable of mastering any dialect as well as the niceties of Edited Standard English if he or she is properly motivated.

Almost every student can learn to write well enough to survive in the capitalist system if that student has a real purpose.

On the other hand, we are beginning to realize more and more clearly the devastation we wreak when we insist that students change dialects. James Sledd has said it better than anyone else:

> With his own eyes the arguer [Sledd himself] has seen British working people, and chicanos, and black Americans humiliated by contempt for their language and twisted by their own unhappy efforts to talk like their exploiters. An expert is no more needed to prove that such humiliation is damaging or such efforts an expense of spirit than a meteorologist is needed to warn of the dangers of urinating against the wind: but the weight of the argument rests mainly on the fact that if any man can be so shamed and bullied for so intimate a part of his being as language, then every man is fully subject to the unhampered tyrants of the materialist majority.[24]

Sledd, of course, is talking about spoken language, and the discussion here concerns written, but the principle remains the same: the damage done by insistence on written standard English is widespread and irreparable. If they want to, the students themselves will change both their written and spoken language. If they want to. If they do not want to, pressure can only create mental turmoil.

In any case, the argument has been that emotive (purely self-expressive) writing could well be the most important for the student, in which case there should be no constraints upon his language, for he is writing for himself.

In summary: the only constraints that should be imposed upon writing are those that come from genuine purpose. If students have a genuine purpose, they will want every feature of their writing to work toward their success. In many classrooms, the constraints imposed by demands that everyone write standard English loom so large that other, equally important and much more natural constraints are completely overshadowed.

A Theory of Composing

By way of a preliminary statement, my debt to Janet Emig will be obvious throughout this discussion. Giving credit where credit is due would merely create a garland of ibids.; therefore, it is recommended that everyone have the firsthand experience of reading *The Composing Process of Twelfth Graders,* Emig's excellent monograph.

Essays in the body of *Contemporary Rhetoric* will flesh out the discussion that follows, but this discussion will, it is hoped, show the coherence among several of the essays.

The composing process involves several levels of activities, all working at once, either in conjunction with or against one another. Now let it be said

[24] James Sledd, "Doublespeak: Dialectology in the Service of Big Brother," *College English* 33 (January 1972), 451.

from the beginning that I know precisely as little about the composing process as anyone. It is with diffidence and tentatively, then, that I embark on a speculative discussion that I hope will not sound dogmatic.

As I said, a variety of activities takes place as the mind simmers, bubbles, or steams along. One thing going on in the mind is the creation of propositions, that is, predicates and the various words, phrases, and constructions that relate to them.[25] These propositions might appear on the surface as, for instance, *intransitive sentences:*

George smokes.

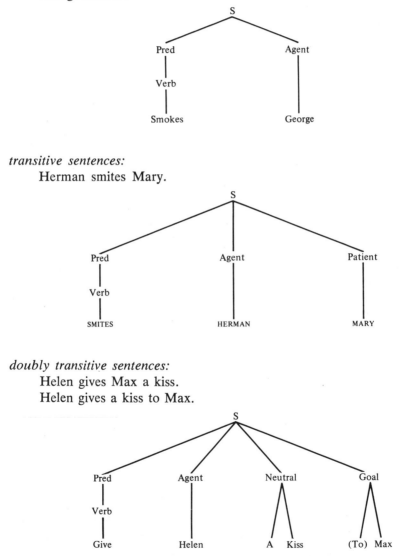

transitive sentences:
Herman smites Mary.

doubly transitive sentences:
Helen gives Max a kiss.
Helen gives a kiss to Max.

[25] Charles J. Fillmore, "The Case for Case," *Universals in Linguistic Theory,* ed. Emmon Bach and Robert T. Harms (New York: Holt, Rinehart and Winston, 1968).

predicate nominal sentences:
Norma is my wife.

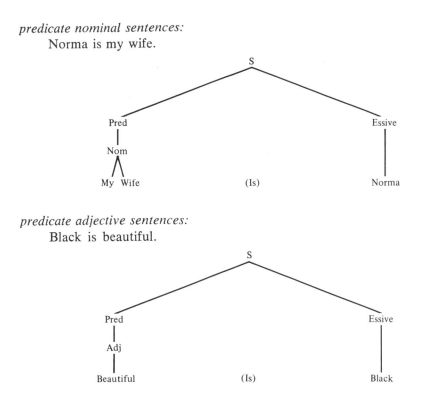

predicate adjective sentences:
Black is beautiful.

It seems to me that when we begin to represent the propositional nature of language we are getting as near as we possibly can to "pure" thought, the raw stuff of which discourse is made. At least, I see no way of getting farther back into the process, for as we go beyond the propositional nature of language, the tunnel becomes so dark that we can only grope.

I would speculate that all thought—and hence all composing—begins at the propositional level; therefore, I would also say that uniqueness in thought originates at the propositional level, and that uniqueness in thought is a function of intelligence.

Inexperienced writers tend to write series of propositions, as in the following piece:

My Baby Brother—Heui Ferguson III

(1) My baby brother was born Jan. 24, 1972. (2) He weighed 8 pounds. (3) Well, my mother went to the hospital at 12:30 on Jan. 23. (4) He was born that morning at 6 A.M. (5) My father called me and my grandmother at 8 o'clock. (6) I was asleep. (7) The phone rang. (8) I woke up and they told me it was a boy. (9) I really wanted a girl. (10) I had to take what I could get.

(11) On Jan. 26, my mother and brother came home. (12) My brother's name is Heui Ferguson III. (13) His nickname is He-He. (14) Well, now he's 9 months old and boy is he bad. (15) He cries all the time when he gets shots. (16) He's a spoiled brat. (17) He's always eating something off the ground. (18) He's a paper freak. (19) If he sees a paper bag, here comes

He-He. (20) And when you don't give him something he wants, he will bite you.

(21) Now he has six teeth and he bites the mess out of you. (22) He crawls all over the place and he now knows when it's time to eat. (23) When my father comes in to eat dinner He-He comes too. (24) He eats with everybody. (25) Everything I said about my brother is true, but I still love him, and that's my baby brother.

This piece, written by a seventh-grader, is utterly charming—a point that needs stressing—for even though it is syntactically threadbare, matter so exactly suits manner that the native charm of the propositions is not submerged in sophisticated syntax. In other situations, of course, the manner might not be suited to the matter, and the result would be disastrous for the writer.

To delineate the nature of prose that does not use the major devices of proposition combining, we might examine each of the sentences in the piece quoted above. The arithmetic of the passage is that there are 1.75 propositions per sentence (43 propositions in all, if one does not construe "baby" in "baby brother" as an adjective). I will analyze the sentences that contain more than one proposition.

(5) Coordinate noun phrases. The deep structure propositions are *My father called me at 8 o'clock* and *My father called my grandmother at 8 o'clock*.

(8) Coordinate clauses and a noun phrase complement. Deep structure propositions: *I woke up* and *They told me (something)* and *It was a boy*.

(10) Base clause and noun phrase complement. Deep structure propositions: *I had to take (something)* and *I could get (something)*.

(11) Coordinate noun phrases. Deep structure propositions: *On Jan. 26, my mother came home* and *On Jan. 26, my brother came home*.

(14) Coordinate clauses.

(15) Main clause and adverb clause.

(19) Main clause and adverb clause.

(20) Main clause, adverb clause, adjective clause. Deep structure propositions: *He will bite you* and *When you don't give him something* and *He wants (something)*.

(21) Coordinate clauses.

(22) Coordinate clauses and noun phrase complement: *He crawls all over the place* and *He knows (something)* and *It's time to eat (sometime)*.

(23) Main clause, adverb clause, infinitive complement: *He-He comes too* and *When my father comes in* and *(my father) to eat dinner*.

(25) Three coordinate clauses and an adjective clause: *Everything is true* and *I still love him* and *That's my baby brother* and *I said (everything) about my brother*.

This survey demonstrates how threadbare the writer's syntactic performance is. She relies overwhelmingly on coordination and adverb clauses, for some reason avoiding a wide variety of verbal constructions, nominalizations, absolutes, relatives, and complements that would amount to syntactic fluency. If the writer does not have this fluency, she needs to acquire it.

The arithmetic of proposition combining has a magical quality about it, for one plus one make not two, but three; that is, combining propositions generates meaning. Take the two propositions *The Lone Ranger rode a horse* and *The horse saved his life* and combine them thus: *The Lone Ranger rode a horse that saved his life.* The result is that one preserves the meaning of each proposition and creates their new, relational meaning. Ergo, one and one make three.

Nor is the creation of meaning through embedding a trivial quality, but rather one of the great creative powers that the language confers upon its users: the power to express relationships through a finite series of recursive devices.

To sum up: the composing process obviously involves the generation of propositions. That is the absolute minimum that we can think of when we speak of composition. The composing process also involves using the syntactic devices of the language to put propositions within propositions. That is:

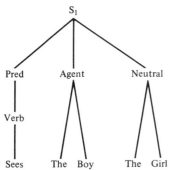
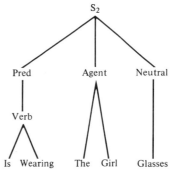

Combining these simple propositions creates:

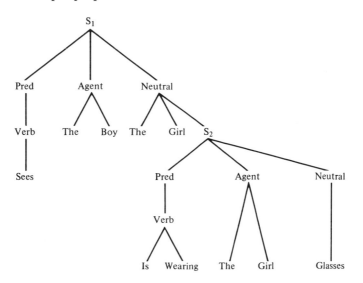

which can result in a variety of surface forms, among them:

> The boy sees the girl who is wearing glasses.
> The boy sees the girl wearing glasses.
> The girl who is wearing glasses is seen by the boy.
> The girl wearing glasses is seen by the boy.

This ability to combine propositions into syntactic units is certainly one of the most powerful mental accomplishments that the individual ever achieves, and on the basis of admittedly slim evidence and a good deal of subjectivity, I would like to discuss it briefly.

If students can develop what John Mellon calls "syntactic fluency," that is, the ability to embed propositions using the syntactic devices of the language, they have acquired, it seems to me, a real generative capability—the ability to put "kernel" ideas together rationally so that their mutual significance is recognizable. In my experience, I have never encountered a student with a high degree of syntactic fluency who was not also able to handle the elements of composition that transcend the sentence: to construct larger units, such as paragraphs, to adjust discourse to an audience, to grapple with sophisticated ideas. It is, of course, illogical to say that students can handle larger pieces well simply because they can handle sentences; perhaps syntactic fluency is not antecedent to other skills in writing, but is simply concurrent with them. And yet I feel that if students develop syntactic fluency, the other skills that they need will somehow develop. Therefore, the matter of style in composition classes is of central importance, not merely because style is the dress of ideas, but because style viewed as the resources of language is the means whereby ideas are expressed. A person who has limited stylistic resources also has limited resources for conceptualizing.

A variety of the articles in *Contemporary Rhetoric* deal with this whole question; however, the book has nothing to sell—except the notion that both students and instructors should understand the concepts underlying the activity they are both engaged in. Therefore, I can only say that before anyone can speak with a great deal of certainty about composition—either doing it or teaching it—we need much more knowledge than we have now.

Finally, in the composing process, structures beyond the sentence are generated. While modern grammar provides detailed and theoretically stimulating models with which we can speculate about the generation of sentences, our knowledge concerning structures beyond the sentence is scant and frustratingly vague. The articles assembled in *Contemporary Rhetoric* on concepts of form represent a good survey of both the theoretical and the practical sides of the question.

Because we know so pitifully little about structures beyond the sentence and even less about how the mind apprehends structures even at the sentence level, we, as students and instructors of composition, are left in the starlit forest of a dimly understood mystery, and we have only the most hazy maps of that forest. What all of this means is that a programmatic system of teaching structures beyond the sentence—either how to produce them or how to analyze them—must rely on the ability of the apprehending mind to sort out those factors that are meaningful. There is no more efficient way of teaching students to write long stretches of discourse than to immerse them in the close analysis of examples, using the exegetical techniques that have been so successful in literary criticism, but never forgetting that this exegesis is a hit-or-miss affair, basically unmethodical, although it may have the appearance of method.

In short, instructors of composition have two functions: in a variety of systematic ways, they can increase the students' syntactic fluency and they can also act as guides for close reading. This pretty much sums up the major activities in the "teaching" of writing, at least if one assumes that close reading will bring one to ask the proper questions concerning form, rhetorical stance, validity of arguments, and so on.

The Composing Process: A Model Adapted from Emig

One of the most faddish words in the composition business at present is "prewriting." Something happens in the mind of the composer before the ballpoint or the typewriter starts spewing out words. Whatever it is that happens is called "prewriting." In one sense, prewriting of anything starts at the moment of birth (or at the moment of conception), when the organism begins to gather itself together as a unique entity, and, in another sense, prewriting is only that fraction of a second between the generation of a specific idea (whatever that process might be like) and the putting down of that idea on paper.

In order to begin examining the nature of the composing process, we will use the example of a mythical novelist writing a hypothetical novel.

Novelist Faulkway feels the progressively more severe itching that warns him it is time to begin work on his next novel. But he has no plot in mind, not even characters. So he sits down at the typewriter and describes Character X, a man standing on a streetcorner. Now some action must take place, so Faulkway has Character Y, a voluptuous lady, walk past X. X whistles, and Y reacts in a given way—and the novel is off. It will generate and program itself as Faulkway proceeds with it, for actions and motifs that appear, as if by magic, will open certain possibilities for other actions and motifs and preclude certain others. Faulkway's writing is nearer to being automatic than we like to think, and it turns out that *Hypothetical,* as Faulkway chooses to call his novel, is a great success; it sells more copies than *Jonathan Livingston Seagull* and is a greater critical success than *Catch 22.* And all of this automatically! Well, not quite.

Recently, I heard a panel of screen writers discussing their techniques of composition. Gloria Katz and Willard Huyck (*American Graffiti*) said that they did extensive preplanning before they even began to write the script, recording ideas on three-by-five cards and then arranging the cards in meaningful sequences. David Ward (*The Sting*) claimed that he worked the complete plot out in his mind, constructing a detailed "map" of the whole script, but putting nothing down in writing until he was ready to begin composing. John Milius (*Dirty Harry*) begins with a scene or a character and works from there; he claims that the final result is always a complete surprise to him. Katz and Huyck revise extensively, producing five or six versions of the script before they are satisfied; Ward and Milius claim that they seldom revise. Perhaps these three examples represent the whole spectrum of the relationship between prewriting and composing.

In any case, there is an automatic, generative quality to composition that is almost magical. For instance, as I look back over the stack of pages that I have written for this book, I realize that the larger design was carefully planned and outlined, resulted, as a matter of fact, from notes for a lecture that I have given repeatedly. But as I look at the individual paragraphs, as I think about my own writing, I am filled almost with a sense of awe concerning what happened and what is happening at this very moment as I type. How in the world does this stuff get generated?

The following quote begins to illustrate the complexity of the mysterious process whereby language is generated.

> When a person knows a language, what does he know? What information does he have in his head, somewhere in the neurophysiology of his brain? A set of sentences from which he chooses the right one when he wants to say something? The meaning of a set of sentences from which he chooses the right interpretation for the sentences he hears? Even if the sets of sentences and interpretations were enormous, they would still be inadequate. Outside of a small and unimportant list of greetings like *Good morning,* clichés like *My, it's hot today,* and routinized statements like proverbs, few sentences are spoken or heard more than once. Each spoken sentence must be constructed anew to express and communicate particular meanings to particular individuals —oneself or others.
>
> The heart of human language capability is creativity in expressing and understanding meanings, "free from control of external stimuli, and appropriate to new and ever-changing situations" (N. Chomsky, [*Form and Meaning in Natural Language*], n.d., p. 66). It can be explained only if what we know in common with other members of our language community is a finite set of rules. These rules express the relationships that hold between meaning and sound in our particular language, and they channel our creativity within the limits of intelligibility and appropriateness for our speech community.[26]

Furthermore, "By a rough, but conservative calculation, there are at least 10^{20} sentences 20 words long, and if a child were to learn only these it would take him something on the order of 1,000 times the estimated age of the earth just to listen to them."[27] Now add complexity to complexity by realizing that there

[26] Courtney B. Cazden, *Child, Language, and Education* (New York: Holt, Rinehart and Winston, 1972), p. 6.

[27] George A. Miller, "Some Preliminaries to Psycholinguistics," *Psycholinguistics and Reading,* ed. Frank Smith (New York: Holt, Rinehart and Winston, 1973), p. 18.

is no theoretical limit to the length of a sentence in a natural language and hence no limit to the number of sentences that the language can produce, and something of the difficulty of understanding the process of composition begins to emerge.

Confronted by this fearful complexity, by a process about which we know so little, it is no wonder that we feel intimidated. Somehow, by processes that we understand dimly if at all, meaningful language sequences do get generated. Letters, essays, reports, poems do get written.

Whenever one is thinking about the process of composing, a good method of forming reliable insights is honest introspection. If the linguist can be guided by his intuition, there is no reason why the rhetorician cannot follow the same procedure. This leads to a practical and important bit of advice for instructors and students of writing.

Most frequently, the writing produced for classes is viewed as product: discussion centers around the produced essay (or poem, or whatever). Equal emphasis should be placed on the process. How did the piece of discourse get produced? How did the writer generate his ideas? The description of a course planned for a summer institute in the composing process at the University of Southern California states the notion succinctly:

> This is a course in creative writing, but it is adapted for the Institute in that the focus will be on process, not product. Participants will engage in extensive examination of how their writings came to be and through introspection and discussion will gain practical insight into the problem of composing.

In fact, such a procedure can generate writing, for students might well keep detailed journals in which they record the processes whereby other writing comes into being.

In any case, the current interest in prewriting—a relatively new development in textbooks and classroom practices—is surely one of the healthiest movements in our field.

What goes into the planning of a piece of writing? Once some ideas have been gathered, how does the writer begin to put those ideas into shape?

Since 1962, I have been asking my students if they tended to outline before they began to write. Although I do not have exact figures, I can say that only a small minority of these hundreds of students relied on an outline in their planning. However, as I write this introduction, I am following a one-page, single-spaced outline that I have developed over a period of a year or so. In fact, I have thought through this schema so often that it is familiar to me, and I have discussed the ideas that it raises so frequently that I pause, backtrack, or stumble infrequently.

Writing is not only the exposition of ideas, but also the working out of ideas. Often we really don't know what we want to say until we've said it.

As in most aspects of the composing process, our knowledge of what actually takes place during the planning stage is hazy at best, but our uncertainty tends to generate dogmatic pronouncements about how one ought to plan. The following is one of the less heinous examples:

> While you are deciding how you will use your material in developing your subject, you will also be thinking about how you will organize your paper. Grouping related material into blocks and then arranging these blocks in a sensible order constitutes the fourth stage in writing. From this stage should emerge a plan for the paper—whether in your mind or in scribbled notes or in a formally prepared outline.[28]

The reason for our dogmatic approach to the planning of compositions is more interesting, of course, than the dogmas themselves. Until very recently, rhetorical theories concerning written composition were an unexamined tradition, and notions perpetuated themselves from one textbook-writer to the next. Not only was the tradition unexamined, the very process of composition was not closely scrutinized. In her study, Janet Emig delineates the situation:

> The purpose of this inquiry is to examine the composing process of twelfth-grade writers, using a case study method. Case study has scarcely been employed as a technique for securing data about the composing process of students, although so basic a means of systematically collecting information seems not only inherently interesting but requisite to most sorts of future empirical investigations in this unexamined field.
>
> Case study has long been a mode of inquiry within the physical, biological, and social sciences: powerful modern instances can be cited, for example, from psychiatry and from education. From his earliest papers Freud built his theory of personality upon the foundation of case study. In contemporary psychiatry, Bruno Bettelheim uses a combined method of introspection and case study within such accounts of normal and deviant behavior as *Love Is Not Enough, The Informed Heart,* and *The Empty Fortress.*[29]

The paragraphs from Emig are a totally accurate comment on the procedures we have used for investigating our field and a good explanation of why most pronouncements concerning planning come from the tradition, not from observations of the ways in which successful writers actually do plan.

In regard to reformulation or revision, one of my students made an apposite and telling comment: "Once I discovered *on my own* that I could use paste and scissors, half of my problems with revision were solved." This statement is worth pondering briefly, for it says a good deal about deficiencies in the teaching of writing and also about the nature of revising. I would ask the reader to answer for himself, "What *does* the quotation tell us about the teaching of composition and the nature of revision?"

Since there is no discussion of revision or reformulation in the body of the book, the subject is worth investigating briefly at this point.

[28] Porter G. Perrin, *Writer's Guide and Index to English,* 4th ed., rev. Karl W. Dykema and Wilma R. Ebbitt (Chicago: Scott, Foresman, 1965), p. 47.
[29] Emig, pp. 1–2.

What sorts of operations does reformulation involve? Here as elsewhere, the sentence is a good model from which to extrapolate. In reformulating a sentence, one can *delete:*

> The gurgling that was in the kitchen was the dishwasher.
> The gurgling in the kitchen was the dishwasher.

One can *reorder:*

> Writing is difficult because it demands total concentration.
> Because it demands total concentration, writing is difficult.

One can *substitute:*

> Tonto rides a horse.
> Tonto rides a pinto.

One can *embed:*

> John Wayne often plays the good guy in movies. He is a great American idol.
> John Wayne, a great American idol, often plays the good guy in movies.

And it seems to me that these four operations also classify all the sorts of things that can be done in reformulation beyond the sentence, although the entities involved would be more extensive than words, phrases, or clauses.

The notion that any revision can be classed either as deletion (crossing out), reordering, substitution, or embedding may seem trivial at first glance, but such insights have great value for instructors and students of writing. The four items serve as a conceptual framework that will help the student and instructor understand what actually goes on when revision takes place, and, furthermore, they can generate the kind of practical advice that instructors need to know how to give students. That is, the instructor can use the four-item list as inventive topics for helping students achieve success with writing.

The business of reformulation is, of course, just as complex as other aspects of the composing process, and it would be a mistake to think that the writer reformulates all at once at a given stage; as anyone who has ever written anything knows, reformulation is a constant process, part of the generative nature of the act of writing.

To conclude the discussion of reformulation, I am tempted to give a detailed account of various changes that I made in this manuscript as I wrote it. Some of these changes were major (for instance, I shifted two large sections), and others were minor; the sum total of the reformulation was enormous. And yet, this morning as I read it over, I realize that I don't really want to make a great many changes beyond the ones made while writing. And so, rather than discuss the changes made in my manuscript, I would like to suggest that everyone closely examine his or her own process of reformulation. Again, there is a great deal to be learned about the composing process through introspection.

And now to the last stage of the composing process and, fittingly, to the last notion that this long introduction will discuss: *stopping*. I want to be completely anecdotal in dealing with stopping, and my anecdote will constitute a parable, the meaning of which I will leave the reader to unravel.

Not too long ago, I spoke to the distinguished faculty of a renowned English department in a great university. In fact, I discussed the composing process, and many of the ideas that have appeared in this introduction were mentioned in my talk. When I had nearly reached the end of my discussion, I introduced the concept of stopping, or closure. And I asked this question: "What do we mean by stopping in the composing process?" There was a moment of silence, and then someone said, "But that's a simple-minded question." I rejoined, "And we humanists hate simple questions; we deal with eternal verities like truth and beauty. And yet can you specify with any precision what you mean when you tell a student, 'This piece is inconclusive' or 'This ending is good'?"

And perhaps the best conclusion that I can think of for this introduction is the following, from *Child Language and Education*, by Courtney B. Cazden:

Creativity and Rules

The notion that behavior is systematic and rule-governed suggests that children's "errors" are often clues to child thought. Children take the problems we pose and deal with them in their own ways. Researchers and teachers either measure how well the children have learned to see the world "our" way or they try to discover how children see it for themselves. To Piaget, "errors" are an important source of information on qualitative changes in intelligence as the child's mind develops (Ginsberg and Opper [*Piaget's Theory of Intellectual Development: An Introduction* (Englewood Cliffs, N.J.: Prentice-Hall)], 1969). Clinchey and Rosenthal ([*"Analysis of Children's Errors,"* in *Psychology and Educational Practice,* ed. G. S. Lesser (Glenview, Ill.: Scott,Foresman)], 1971) suggest how classroom teachers can learn from children's errors, too.

Finally, the creative quality of human language is one aspect of creative intelligence. Noam Chomsky speaks directly to educators:

There are strong pressures to make use of new educational technology and to design curriculum and teaching methods in the light of the latest scientific advances. In itself, this is not objectionable. It is important, nevertheless, to remain alert to a very real danger: that new knowledge and technique will define the nature of what is taught and how it is taught, rather than contributing to the realization of educational goals that are set on other grounds and in other terms. Let me be concrete. Technique and even technology is available for rapid and efficient inculcation of skilled behavior, in language teaching, teaching of arithmetic, and other domains. There is, consequently, a real temptation to reconstruct curriculum in the terms defined by the new technology. And it is not too difficult to invent a rationale, making use of the concepts of "controlling behavior," enhancing skills, and so on. Nor is it difficult to construct objective tests that are sure to demonstrate the effectiveness of such methods in reaching certain goals that are incorporated in these tests. But successes of this sort will not demonstrate that it is important to concentrate on developing skilled behavior in the student. What little we know about human intelligence would at least suggest something quite different: that by diminishing the range and complexity of materials presented to the inquiring mind, by setting behavior in fixed patterns, these methods may harm and distort the normal development of creative abilities (N. Chomsky [*Form and Meaning in Natural Language* (Amsterdam: North-Holland)], n.d., pp. 66–67).

A truly educative environment is one from which the child is most likely to learn the regularities, patterns, or rules that make this creativity possible. Maybe the child is such a powerful consumer that the nature of the environment matters little as long as certain ingredients are present; maybe teaching specific primitive responses will even ultimately retard the development of more advanced processes. . . .[30]

If *Contemporary Rhetoric* brings up the important questions regarding composition, then it will have served its purpose, for it will have acted as a heuristic. My friend Richard Young of the University of Michigan once said to me, "Rhetoric is a fascinating discipline precisely because *everything* remains to be done."

Let's get on with the task, then.

[30] Cazden, pp. 27–28.

Invention

The modern term for it is "prewriting," but traditionally rhetoric has called it "invention": the process whereby a writer discovers ideas to write about.

The looky-feely-smelly school of invention turns students on to their own senses, making them aware that they are continually bombarded by sense impressions and that these can flesh out essays. So young writers look at pictures, listen to sounds, and smell limburger, and then translate these experiences into prose. And although my tone is cynical, I know how important—and how exciting—such exercises can be.

We live in a world of ideas, as well as physical sensations, however, and the looky-feely-smelly approach does not help much when young writers are confronted with the problem of, say, reacting in prose to a work of literature. So the largest part of this section on invention will explore ways to help writers work with ideas.

One of the most interesting (and certainly one of the most neglected) aspects of rhetoric is the notion of topics or places of invention. Throughout the more recent history of rhetoric, the importance of topics for invention has been either minimized or overlooked.

But topics need to be reconsidered from both the theoretical and the pedagogical points of view. The purpose of this discussion will be (a) to point out that all topics fall into one of four categories, according to the nature of their operation, and (b) to attempt to revitalize the concept of topics in rhetorical theory and in pedagogy. The first purpose of the discussion will clarify the nature of all topics, and among the expert witnesses who

This introduction is a revision of " 'Topics' and Levels in the Composing Process," College English 34 (February 1973), 701–09.

would testify concerning the desirability of the second purpose is Richard McKeon:

> We need a new art of invention and discovery in which places are used as means by which to light up modes and meanings of works of art and natural occurrences and to open up aspects and connections in existence and possibility. The data and qualifications of existence are made by attention and interest; and discoveries made in a book or a work of art should provide places by which to perceive creatively what might otherwise not be experienced in the existent world we constitute. It is a long time since topics have been used as an art of invention in rhetoric. . . . A reconstituted verbal art of invention, adapted to our circumstances and arts, might be used to shadow forth the methods and principles of an architectonic productive art generalized from invention in language to discovery in existence.[1]

In agreement with at least one school of modern linguistics, I assume that the composing process involves putting meanings into structures or saturating structures with meanings, although, to be sure, the mechanisms whereby this process takes place are not known, and, in fact, the assumption that something of the kind takes place is really just an explanatory metaphor adopted to get theorists over the barricades of some extremely difficult questions. What I am saying—although I do not intend to argue the point—is that there is, in some sense, both form and meaning, even though separating the two is next to impossible if one takes into consideration all the various opinions concerning and definitions of form and content.[2]

Central to the composing process is "invention," the means whereby the writer discovers subject matter. And the concept of "topics" or "commonplaces" is the very heart of invention in the classical theory of Aristotle. It will be recalled that topics are, in effect, probes or a series of questions that one might ask about a subject in order to discover things to say about that subject. They are general and apply to all subject matter; they are not, as it were, subject-specific. So that Aristotle's topics can generate arguments for, say, negotiating any peace, not just peace in a given war.

For example, the first of the twenty-eight demonstrative topics that Aristotle lists is the argument from opposites:

> If, now, it is not fair to grow enraged when evil doers injure us unwittingly, then neither do we owe a grain of thanks to him who does us good when forced to do it.

[1] Richard McKeon, "The Uses of Rhetoric in a Technological Age," *The Prospect of Rhetoric,* ed. Lloyd F. Bitzer and Edwin Black (Englewood Cliffs, N.J.: Prentice-Hall, 1971), p. 55.

[2] Roland Barthes goes so far as to say that, ". . . we can no longer see a text as a binary structure of Content and Form; the text is not double but multiple; within it there are only forms, or more exactly, the text in its entirety is only a multiplicity of forms without content. We can say metaphorically that the literary text is a stereography: neither melody, nor harmony (or at least not unrelieved harmony), it is resolutely contrapuntal; it mixes voices in a volume, not in a line, not even a double line." ("Style and Image," *Literary Style: A Symposium,* ed. Seymour Chatman [London and New York: Oxford University Press, 1971], p. 6.)

Another of the topics is *a fortiori* (from degrees of more and less):

> If it behooves each citizen among you to care for the reputation of your
> city, it behooves you all as a city to care for the glory of Greece.[3]

There is no better comment on the topics than Kenneth Burke's: "The so-
called 'commonplaces' or 'topics' in Aristotle's *Art of Rhetoric* . . . are a
quick survey of opinion. . . ."[4] Burke goes on to say that in the topics
Aristotle "catalogues" the available means of persuasion, and it is to the kinds
of cataloguing that we will turn first, and then to the sorts of things that are
catalogued. It will become apparent that, classed according to system of cataloguing and things catalogued, there are only four possible kinds of topics.

First, simply but significantly, it is apparent that topics can be either *finite*
or *nonfinite* lists.

Perhaps the most common sorts of topics that one encounters (and in
many ways the least interesting, although useful) are what are generally called
"methods of paragraph development." These are so commonly encountered
that I will not go into detail concerning them, but such a list would typically
contain items like the following: data, enumeration, analogy, anecdote, cause
and effect, comparison and contrast, definition, description, metaphor, restatement, and so on. Now it is perfectly obvious that this list could be extended
almost indefinitely, for it might contain all the sorts of things that can go
into paragraphs, which ultimately implies classification in some way of all the
sorts of things in the universe. That is, methods of paragraph development
as topics are characteristically nonfinite lists. Aristotle's topics are also just
as obviously a nonfinite list.

But we can conceive of, find in great abundance, and invent for ourselves
topics that constitute finite lists. Burke's Pentad is nothing more than a
finite set of topics, as Burke himself avows:

> What is involved, when we say what people are doing and why they are
> doing it? An answer to that question is the subject of this book. The book is
> concerned with the basic forms of thought which, in accordance with the
> nature of the world as all men necessarily experience it, are exemplified in
> the attributing of motives. . . . any complete statement about motives will
> offer *some kind of* answers to these five questions: what was done (act),
> where or when was it done (scene), who did it (agent), how he did it
> (agency), and why (purpose).[5]

(The Pentad is particularly useful, of course, in generating subject matter
concerning any piece of discourse, either written or spoken, either literary
or nonliterary. But my purpose at the moment is not to demonstrate the usefulness—or lack thereof—of any set of topics.)

---

[3] *The Rhetoric of Aristotle,* trans. Lane Cooper (New York: Appleton-Century-Crofts,
1960). The twenty-eight demonstrative topics are on pp. 159–72.

[4] Kenneth Burke, *A Grammar of Motives and A Rhetoric of Motives* (New York:
World Publishing Company, 1962), p. 580.

[5] Kenneth Burke, *A Grammar of Motives,* p. xvii.

It follows from the nature of a finite list of topics that it must not allow for any questions that are not covered by the items of the set. That is, if one can ask questions, *within the terms set down for the Pentad,* which cannot be classed under one of the items of the Pentad, then the Pentad is *faulty* as a finite set of topics. (I personally do not feel that the Pentad is faulty, but that question is beside the point in this discussion.)

A faulty set of topics, used here as an example (and reproduced completely in this section), will clarify this problem. A five-item set emerged from the National Developmental Project on Rhetoric. In a severely abbreviated (but not, I think, unfair) form, this is the set:

(1) The social reality of the present movement may be viewed in terms of the resources for innovation or the defense of tradition. . . . what are the social conditions and resources available to the inventing person?

(2) A second set of questions: what are the materials and perspectives upon facts out of which invention may be fashioned? What technologies may be harnessed in making a car, what facts or interpretations of facts may be spoken. . . ?

(3) What about the *persons* who will participate in the invention—and the drives which make them vital or retarding factors in the process. . . ?

(4) What is the *deep structure* of the invention. . . ?

(5) Finally, what *presentational form* is adopted for the thing invented. . . ?[6]

For this provocative and useful set of topics, the authors make the following unfortunate claim: "These five aspects may be considered as a generative frame, *an ordering of all the relevant aspects of any invented, innovative, or novel creation.* As such they provide a place of places, a frame of frames, an account of the origin or creation of all things novel, including rhetorical artifacts." [7] One question generated by another set of topics that we will be dealing with shortly (that developed by Young, Becker, and Pike) demonstrates the faultiness of the above as a finite set. "How is the subject under consideration changing?" This question does not fit any of the topics in the set (and one can find other questions that do not fit); therefore, the set is faulty.

If rhetorical theory is to have the integrity that only precision and logical consistency can bring to it, then nonfinite sets of topics must not masquerade as finite sets. We have here something of the dilemma faced by grammarians who worked under the assumption that "A noun is the name of a person, place, or thing" or that "A sentence is the expression of a complete idea." These definitions were theoretically destructive and had only marginal value

[6] *The Prospect of Rhetoric,* pp. 228–36.

[7] Robert L. Scott, James R. Andrews, Howard H. Martin, J. Richard McNally, William F. Nelson, Michael M. Osborn, Arthur L. Smith, Harold Zyskind are the authors. *The Prospect of Rhetoric,* pp. 232–33. Italics mine.

—if any—in pedagogy, since they precipitated the whole logomachy of what a "thing" or a "complete idea" is.

Sets of topics can be, then, either finite or nonfinite lists. They can also be *content-oriented* or *form-oriented*.

For one example of a set of form-oriented topics, I refer to my own "The Grammar of Coherence," a set that, according to my claim, will generate structures at the paragraph level and beyond.[8] (In brief, my argument is that six and only six relationships prevail in coherent discourse beyond the sentence, or, more precisely, beyond the transformational unit. If this is indeed the case, as I believe it is, then these relationships will serve as topics that will "automatically" generate paragraphs or, for that matter, essays.)

A further example: in an article that has received far too little attention, Alton L. Becker developed a schema to analyze and describe the structure of paragraphs.[9] What has not been generally recognized is that this schema can be used as a finite set of form-oriented topics. It happens that the schema is brief enough to serve as an example in the present context.

Becker claims that empirical investigation reveals that expository paragraphs invariably have the following elements in various combinations and permutations (the details of which I will ignore):

T opic
R estriction
I llustration

P roblem
S olution

Q uestion
A nswer

That is, TRIPSQA will describe the form of any expository paragraph. A paragraph that Becker analyzes will serve as an example of what he is getting at.

> (P) How obsolete is Hearn's judgment? (S_1) (T) On the surface the five gentlemen of Japan do not themselves seem to be throttled by this rigid society of their ancestors. (R) Their world is in fact far looser in its demands upon them than it once was. (I) Industrialization and the influence of the West have progressively softened the texture of the web. Defeat in war badly strained it. A military occupation, committed to producing a democratic Japan, pulled and tore at it. (S_2) (T) But it has not disappeared. (R) It is still the invisible adhesive that seals the nationhood of the Japanese. (I) Shimizu, Sanada, Yamazaki, Kisel, and Hirohito were all born within

[8] W. Ross Winterowd, "The Grammar of Coherence," *College English* 31 (May 1970), 828–35.

[9] Alton L. Becker, "A Tagmemic Approach to Paragraph Analysis," *The Sentence and the Paragraph* (Champaign, Ill.: NCTE, 1966), p. 33.

its bonds. Despite their individual work, surroundings and opinions, they have lived most of their lives as cogs geared into a group society. . . .[10]

It is easy to see how TRIQAPS—and note that I have acronymized the system —can serve as a set of form-oriented topics.

> *Write a topic sentence.*
> As one ages, one learns that all vices are pleasant.
> *Restrict it.*
> But most vices are unhealthy.
> *Illustrate.*
> Smoking causes cancer.
> Drinking causes cirrhosis.
> Even the caffeine in coffee has been found to increase the process of aging.

Admittedly, depending on one's vantage point, TRIQAPS can be viewed as either a form-oriented or a content-oriented set of topics. Perhaps the best known example of a set of purely form-oriented topics is the set that constitutes what Francis Christensen called "free modifiers." Christensen did not view his modifiers as topics, but, in effect, they are precisely that, for they can be used to generate sentences. That is, to a sentence base one can add a variety of structures (noun clusters, verb clusters, absolutes, and so on). In deciding to add a structure, one must search for subject matter to "fill" that structure. I will illustrate the process:

> *Write a base.*
> The little girl skated.
> *Add an absolute.*
> Her pigtails flying, the little girl skated.
> *Add a verb cluster.*
> Her pigtails flying, the little girl skated, effortlessly gliding down the sidewalk.
> *Add a relative clause.*
> Her pigtails flying, the little girl, who every Saturday morning came to my house for popcorn, skated, effortlessly gliding down the sidewalk.

And so on. Note that the instructions specify the addition of structures, not of content. Adding a structure must generate content for the structure.

In my opinion, the most interesting and productive set of content-oriented topics is that developed by Richard E. Young, Alton L. Becker, and Kenneth L. Pike.[11] To summarize it here would distort its complexity, but what Young, Becker, and Pike claim is (a) that to know anything, we must

---

[10] From Frank Gibney, *Five Gentlemen of Japan,* quoted in Becker.
[11] Richard E. Young, Alton L. Becker, and Kenneth L. Pike, *Rhetoric: Discovery and Change* (New York: Harcourt Brace Jovanovich, 1970).

know how it differs from everything else, how much it can change and still be itself, and how it fits into hierarchies of larger systems; and (b) that we can view anything from three perspectives, that of particle, that of wave, and that of field. The juxtaposition of these two concepts creates a nine-item set of content-oriented topics.

Now then, we can recapitulate and systematize.

Content-oriented nonfinite sets of topics.
Aristotle's topics, methods of paragraph development, and so on.
Content-oriented finite sets of topics.
Young, Becker, and Pike's topics; from one point of view, TRIQAPS; Burke's Pentad; the parts of the classical oration, and so on.
Form-oriented finite sets of topics.
From one point of view, TRIQAPS; the set outlined in "The Grammar of Coherence"; Christensen's free modifiers, and so on.

Regarding the fourth category, *form-oriented nonfinite sets of topics,* a theoretical problem of considerable dimensions arises. It is that any set of topics that is nonfinite and form oriented must be faulty (according to the definition of "faulty" developed in this discussion), for it is impossible that formal relationships regarding any level of discourse can be infinite in number. The same argument that demonstrates the finite nature of a grammar can be applied to demonstrate the finite nature of relationships beyond those handled by the grammar of a language. The validity of this argument seems self-evident. Therefore, a form-oriented set of topics that is nonfinite must be merely incomplete and hence faulty. One example is lists of figures of grammar—from Peacham to Lanham [12]—for these lists are sets of topics; another example is methods of organization discussed in rhetorics.

The conceptual framework for theories of topics is, then, clear-cut, but what of topics in pedagogy?

One way of conceptualizing the process of composition is to assume that it involves a three-level hierarchy. The first level is that of the proposition. Following the model developed by Charles Fillmore, I would argue that a *core,* or *kernel,* sentence is made up of a modality plus a proposition.[13] The modality contains such elements as auxiliary, yes/no question, negation, and so on. The proposition is the predicate and the variety of "roles" that relate to it and to one another. Thus, schematically:

Modality   *Proposition*
present tense   Predicate (kiss): Agent (George), Patient (Mary)

George kisses Mary.
Mary is kissed by George.

[12] Richard A. Lanham, *A Handlist of Rhetorical Terms* (Berkeley and Los Angeles: University of California Press, 1968).
[13] Charles Fillmore, "The Case for Case," *Universals in Linguistic Theory,* ed. Emmon Bach and Robert Harms (New York: Holt, Rinehart and Winston, 1968), pp. 1–88.

The instructor cannot, it seems to me, intervene at this level. If the student is incapable of generating these core sentences, there is obviously some dysfunction that is beyond the reach of mere pedagogy, that demands therapy.

The next level is that of interpropositional connections, which might be called the level of *syntax*.

> George, who is a neurotic, chews gum.
> George, a neurotic, chews gum.
> A neurotic, George chews gum. (ambiguous?)

In his work, Francis Christensen demonstrates that the instructor can intervene at this level in the composing process, indeed with dramatic results. In *Transformational Sentence-Combining*,[14] John Mellon also demonstrates that the instructor can help the student at the level of syntax, as does Frank O'Hare in his monograph.[15] Since one of the great intellectual powers one can attain is the ability to combine predications, the work of Christensen, Mellon, and O'Hare is not to be ignored or to be written off lightly.

But in this discussion of topics, we are most concerned with the third level in the composing process, which I shall call the level of the *transition,* since it has to do with units such as paragraphs and essays. It is at this level that the concept of topics becomes tremendously important.

The purpose of topics is not to supply verbiage in lieu of real subject matter but to generate ideas concerning the subject. In this sense, topics are devices for problem-solving; they are heuristics. Young, Becker, and Pike explain heuristics and, in the process, give an admirable explanation of how topics function:

> A heuristic procedure . . . provides a series of questions or operations that guides inquiry and increases the chances of discovering a workable solution. More specifically, it serves three functions:
>
> (1) It aids the investigator in retrieving relevant information that he has stored in his mind. (When we have a problem, we generally know more that is relevant to it than we think we do, but we often have difficulty in retrieving the relevant information and bringing it to bear on the problem.)
>
> (2) It draws attention to important information that the investigator does not possess but can acquire by direct observation, reading, experimentation, and so on.
>
> (3) It prepares the investigator's mind for the intuition of an ordering principle or hypothesis.[16]

[14] John C. Mellon, *Transformational Sentence-Combining* (Champaign, Ill.: NCTE, 1969).

[15] Frank O'Hare, *Sentence Combining: Improving Student Writing Without Formal Grammar Instruction* (Urbana, Ill.: NCTE, 1973).

[16] Richard E. Young, Alton L. Becker, and Kenneth L. Pike, *Rhetoric: Discovery and Change*, p. 120.

In this sense, everyone uses "topics" more or less systematically all the time; most of us unconsciously have developed a variety of sets of topics that we apply quite automatically in all kinds of circumstances.

The concept of topics, then, is not trivial, although, to be sure, there are trivial or faulty sets of topics. But what about topics in the classroom as a pedagogical device?

The future of the profession holds a great deal of promise; we are well into the era of "technical breakthrough"; we are at the point where we have the "software" and "hardware" to do a much more effective job than we have in the past. As briefly as possible, I would like to explain why it is conceivable that instruction in writing can now be more effective than it ever was in the past.

First—an important point that is connected with my thesis, but that would take us far afield if we pursued it—we are at the point where we can say, with the eloquence and passion of James Sledd, "Leave your language alone!" We are ready to allow youngsters to function in their own dialects, and hence we will not wreak the spiritual devastation that a "purist" attitude inevitably brings about.

At the level of syntax, we are beginning to get theories and materials—such as those of Francis Christensen, John Mellon, and Frank O'Hare—that enable the teacher to be of significant help in the student's quest for the ability to put idea within idea within idea. . . . That is, for the first time, we now have the means actually to help students systematically attain syntactic fluency, and surely that fluency is one of the significant intellectual accomplishments.

Finally, it is time to revitalize the concept of topics. The reasons for this are clear enough to anyone who has ever taught writing at any level. As Charlie Brown learned when his teacher said, "Write a five-hundred word essay on what you did during your summer vacation," one of the most intransigent problems for inexperienced (and experienced!) writers is invention, and what I am suggesting is that topics as they have developed and as they are developing provide the best devices of invention.

This is not to say that students are robots, who automatically turn to this or that set of topics before they write, but that they are alert and aware, and that they know what sort of help is available to them when they must solve the problem implied by the question "What can I say about this subject?" I am also claiming that some work with sets of topics will introduce students to techniques that they can use to develop their own problem-solving devices, their own heuristics.

I must plead guilty to the charge that I sound unhumanistic, for I *am* profoundly unhumanistic in the normal English-department sense of that word, but I do avow that I am not suggesting students should be deprived of their marvelous, chaotic freedom, for I love both chaos and freedom. But what I am suggesting is that there are more efficient "programs" for enabling students to gain the *freedom* to express themselves than the old by-guess-and-by-golly method that is so tremendously humanistic. The object is not syntax for its own sake or random ideas to fill empty egg crates; rather, the quest of the English instructor should be for every means whereby the student can most efficiently gain the liberation that self-expression gives him or her.

Now my final comment about the theory of topics can be made. Composition is obviously a total process, a whole fabric, that can be "taken apart" only schematically and for theoretical purposes, so that when I claim there are three levels in the process of composition, I do not mean to imply that in practice the writer works first on one level and then on the other. (In fact, I know just as little about the act of composition as anyone else.) Viewing the compositional process from the standpoint of topics allows us to conceptualize it in a more unified way than the *points d'appui* taken by most theories. What I mean is this: if one views theories of form and theories of style merely as sets of topics—which in most instances they are—then the whole process of composition is unified under the auspices of invention, generally conceived to be the least mechanical and most "creative" of the departments of rhetoric.

And this viewpoint is a healthy corrective to the tendency that creeps into textbooks and classrooms: namely, to "do" a "unit" on the sentence and then a unit on the paragraph, and so on. Thus, the theory developed in this discussion could, ultimately, lead to a change in classroom practice, and it seems to me that change is badly needed.

Topics should not shackle the mind. They should liberate.

Suggestions for Further Reading

Bilsky, Manuel, et al. "Looking for an Argument." *College English* 55 (January 1953), 210–16.

Brockriede, Wayne E. and Douglas Ehninger. "Toulmin on Argument: An Interpretation and Application." *Quarterly Journal of Speech* 46 (February 1960), 44–53.

D'Angelo, Frank J. "Imitation and Style." *College Composition and Communication* 24 (October 1973), 283–90.

English, Hubert M., Jr. "Linguistic Theory as an Aid to Invention." *College Composition and Communication* 15 (October 1964), 136–40.

Hallie, Philip B. "Models, Burglary, and Philosophy." *Philosophy and Rhetoric* 4 (Fall 1971), 215–29.

Harrington, Elbert W. *Rhetoric and the Scientific Method of Inquiry, a Study of Invention.* Boulder, Colo. University of Colorado, 1948.

Infante, Dominic. "The Influence of a Topical System on the Discovery of Arguments." *Speech Monographs* 38 (June 1971), 125–28.

Karrfalt, David H. "The Generation of Paragraphs and Larger Units." *College Composition and Communication* 19 (October 1968), 211–17.

Larson, Richard L. "Invention Once More: A Role for Rhetorical Analysis." *College English* 32 (March 1971), 665–72.

———. "Problem-Solving, Composing, and Liberal Education." *College English* 33 (March 1972), 628–35.

Manicas, Peter T. "On Toulmin's Contribution to Logic and Argumentation." *Journal of the American Forensic Association* 3 (September 1966), 83–94.

Odell, Lee. "Piaget, Problem-Solving, and Freshman Composition." *College Composition and Communication* 24 (February 1973), 36–42.

Rothenberg, Albert. "Inspiration, Insight, and the Creative Process in Poetry." *College English* 32 (November 1970), 172–83.

The March 1972 issue of *College English* (Vol. 33) has a cluster of articles on problem solving and invention. Also highly recommended: the chapter on "Models" in Abraham Kaplan, *The Conduct of Inquiry* (Scranton, Pa.: Chandler, 1964).

The Composing Process: Review of the Literature

Janet Emig

Nothing in our strange profession is odder than our consistent failure to make systematic examinations of the process we are dealing with— that of composing—and the means whereby we go about teaching the skill. Only three studies come immediately to mind (though others have been done): Rollo Walter Brown's How the French Boy Learns to Write *(1915), Albert R. Kitzhaber's* Themes, Theories, and Therapy *(1963), and Janet Emig's* The Composing Processes of Twelfth Graders *(1971). Emig's study— which is discussed in the introduction to this book—is unique and common- sensical (one is tempted to say, "because of its common sense"):*

> *The purpose of this inquiry is to examine the composing process of twelfth- grade writers, using a case study method. Case study has scarcely been employed as a technique for securing data about the composing process of students, although so basic a means of systematically collecting information seems not only inherently interesting but requisite to most sorts of future empirical investigations in the examined field.*

The subjects for case studies have always been at hand, but, as teachers of writing, we have too often relied on tradition, ignoring the writers that we are working with. Typically, as Zoellner has pointed out, we give a theme *assignment, turn the student loose to complete the assignment as best he or she can, and then respond to the efforts with red squiggles in the margins of the composition.* We rely on fruitless dicta about outlining, treat revision as if it were not an ongoing process, and tell the student that writers must have a thesis clearly in mind before they begin to write. In the meantime, real writers do complete real themes that are more or less successful, and we have no idea if these writers follow our advice or if their actual composing process has any relation to what we tell them to do and what we assume that they do.*

Emig's review of the literature is an excellent source for descriptions of and theories concerning the composing process. It is relatively complete, and it is admirably balanced. It seems obvious to me that every teacher of composition should have read Emig's monograph.

Most of the data about the composing process occur as three broad types. First there are accounts concerning established writers, chiefly of imaginative, but also of factual, works such as the scientific essay and the historical monograph. These accounts take three forms: (a) description by a writer of his own methods of working; (b) dialogue, usually in the form of correspondence, between a writer and a highly attuned respondent, such as a fellow writer or a gifted editor; and (c) analysis by professional critics or fellow writers of the evolution of a given piece of writing, from sources tapped to revision undertaken and completed. Second, there are dicta and directives about writing by authors and editors of rhetoric and composition texts and handbooks. Third, there is research dealing with the whole or some part of what has been called, globally, "the creative process"; or with a particular kind of creative behavior—the act of writing among adolescents.

These descriptions of the composing process present certain difficulties as sources of data. (1) The data are unsystematic: they do not deal with part or all of the composing process according to any shared set of strategies. (2) The statements provided by different sources of data contradict one another—more, they are often unique, even idiosyncratic. (3) Very few of the sources deal in adequate theoretical or empirical depth with how students of school age write. They answer very few of the following major and interesting questions about students as writers:

> If the context of student writing—that is, community milieu, school, family—affects the composing process, in what ways does it do so, and why?
> What are the resources students bring to the act of writing?
> If there are specifiable elements, moments, and stages in the composing process of students, what are these? If they can be differentiated, how? Can certain portions be usefully designated by traditional nomenclature,

---

* Robert Zoellner, "Talk-Write: A Behavioral Pedagogy for Composition," *College English* 30 (January 1969), 267–320.

such as planning, writing, and revising? Are elements organized linearly in the writing process? recursively? in some other manner? How do these elements, moments, and stages in the composing process relate to one another?

If there is a phenomenon "prewriting," how can it be characterized?

What is a plan for a piece of writing? When and why do students have or not have a plan?

Under what conditions—physical, psychic—do students start to write?

If writing is essentially a selection among certain sorts of options—lexical, syntactic, rhetorical—what governs the choices students make?

What psychological factors affect or accompany portions of the writing process? What effects do they have? What is a block in writing (other than dysgraphia)? When and why do students have blocks? How can they be overcome?

Under what conditions do students stop work on a given piece of writing? If all, or certain kinds of, writing within schools differs from all, or certain kinds of, writing outside schools, how do they differ and why?

If there are modes of school writing, how can these be differentiated? If the mode in which a piece is written affects the process of writing, or the process the mode, how?

What is the press of such variables as the reading of others' writing and the personal intervention of others upon any portion or upon the totality of the writing process?

Accounts by and about Established Writers

On the established writer as a useful source of data about writing, an investigator can say simply with the novelist Peter de Vries, "Don't ask the cow to analyze milk"; [1] or he can examine this source.

If he does, he finds that writers' comments on how they write assume many modes. Occasionally, prose writers and poets write about their writing within their novels, short stories and poems: James Joyce in *Portrait of the Artist as a Young Man,* Thomas Mann in "Tonio Kröger," and Wordsworth in "The Prelude" are examples. In addition, they write about their own writing in diaries, journals, notebooks, letters, prefaces to their own and to others' works, essays, full-length critical studies, autobiographical sketches and full-length self-studies, and interviews recorded in print, on record, and on film.[2]

[1] Peter de Vries, Interview from *Counterpoint,* compiled and edited by Roy Newquist, p. 147

[2] Exemplars of writers' accounts in these modes, in the order mentioned in the text, are: Virginia Woolf, *A Writer's Diary, Being Extracts from the Diary of Virginia Woolf,* ed. Leonard Woolf; Katherine Mansfield, *Journal of Katherine Mansfield,* ed. J. Middleton Murry; Gerard Manley Hopkins, *The Note-books and Papers of Gerard Manley Hopkins,* ed. Humphry House; John Keats, *The Selected Letters of John Keats,* ed. Lionel Trilling; Henry James, *The Art of the Novel, Critical Prefaces by Henry James,* ed. Richard P. Blackmur; Elizabeth Bowen, "Notes on Making a Novel," *Collected Impressions;* E. M. Forster, *Aspects of the Novel;* F. Scott Fitzgerald, *The Crack-Up,* ed. Edmund Wilson, pp. 69–84; J. Paul Sartre, *The Words,* trans. Bernard Frechtman; *Writers at Work: The Paris Review Interviews,* I, ed. Malcolm Cowley; Dylan Thomas, "An Evening with Dylan Thomas," Caedmon Recording No. 1157; "Creative Person, W. H. Auden," National Educational Television (NET) telecast, April 17, 1967.

As the range of modes chosen suggests, writers describe their methods of working and their attitudes toward writing for different reasons. With modes where the writer's audience is initially and perhaps ultimately himself—as in diaries, journals, and notebooks not written for publication, and in certain kinds of letters—the writer is usually concerned with working out a specific problem in the evolution of a specific piece of writing. These modes are expressive: they represent a private forum where, to paraphrase E. M. Forster, a writer can discover how he thinks or feels about a matter by seeing what he has said. Self-discovery, compression or partiality of expression, immediacy, and uniqueness of stimulus characterize descriptions in these modes.

With modes such as the critical essay and the extended autobiography, an audience other than oneself must be acknowledged. Consequently, amenities aiding an audience are observed: accounts are more formal in diction and in organization, and more elaborated. These accounts also tend to be retrospective affairs, and consequently reportorial in approach.

By their quite different natures, these two basic sets of modes present different kinds of difficulty as data. Descriptions in the expressive mode are frankly idiosyncratic: they purport to be true only for an N of 1—a single writer who is pursuing, particularly if he is a major writer, a unique problem. Perhaps the most powerful contemporary expression of the problem of uniqueness are these lines from "East Coker" by T. S. Eliot:

> So here I am, in the middle way, having had twenty years—
> Twenty years largely wasted, the years of *l'entre deux guerres*—
> Trying to learn to use words, and every attempt
> Is a wholly new start, and a different kind of failure
> Because one has only learnt to get the better of words
>
> .   .   .   .   .   .
>
> . . . a new beginning, a raid on the inarticulate
>
> .   .   .   .   .   .
>
> In the general mess of imprecision of feeling,
> Undisciplined squads of emotion.[3]

Descriptions in modes involving an audience other than oneself present other kinds of difficulties. Since these accounts are retrospective, a possible difficulty with such data is the high probability of the inaccuracy of the account, incurred in part by the time-lag between the writing and the description of that writing.

A second, related difficulty is that not only are accounts *post hoc* affairs, most of those published are by writers who work almost exclusively in the imaginative modes and who have been rewarded by publisher and public for their fictive endeavors. One thinks of D. H. Lawrence's comment in *Studies in Classic American Literature* that all of the old American artists were hopeless liars: that only their art-speech was to be trusted as an accurate revela-

---

[3] T. S. Eliot, "East Coker," *Four Quartets*. Copyright 1943 by Harcourt Brace Jovanovich, Inc. and Faber and Faber Ltd.

tion of their thoughts and feelings; and he wonders if the observation may not justly be extended to imaginative writers of all nationalities and all eras when they talk about their methods of writing.[4]

In a recent interview the poet-critic John Ciardi speaks directly of this matter:

> *N* [Roy Newquist, the interviewer]: If you would, I'd like you to read a few of your poems and comment on them—how they happened to be written, perhaps, or what you were driving at.
>
> *Ciardi:* You're asking for lies. It's inevitable. I've been asked to do this over and over again, and lies come out.
>
> Let me put it this way. The least a poem can be is an act of skill. An act of skill is one in which you have to do more things at one time than you have time to think about. Riding a bike is an act of skill. If you stop to think of what you're doing at each of the balances, you'd fall off the bike. Then someone would come along and ask you to rationalize what you thought you were doing. Well, you write a poem. And somebody comes along and asks you to rationalize what you thought you were doing. You pick out a theme and you're hung with trying to be consistent with the theme you've chosen. You have to doubt every explanation.
>
> Nobody has worked harder than Valéry, the French poet, in trying to explain how he produced certain poems. He answers with every qualification in the world—touching this and that but ultimately lying. You have to end up lying. You know that you had something in your mind, but you can never get it straight.[5]

In addition to unintentional lies, some writers very openly admit they try to throw interviewer and public off the scent, usually because they fear any conscious, explicit probing into their methods of work will, to use Hemingway's verb, "spook" their writing. In the recorded interviews granted by such writers they are usually quite frank about their reluctance to discuss their actual methods of work.

Finally, both kinds of accounts share a difficulty: they focus upon the feelings of writers about the difficulties of writing—or not writing—almost to the exclusion of an examination of the act itself. A very wide survey of writers' accounts reveals this preoccupation: Nelson Algren, Arnold Bennett, Joseph Conrad, Simone de Beauvoir, Guy de Maupassant, F. Scott Fitzgerald, E. M. Forster, Andre Gide, John Keats, Norman Mailer, Katherine Mansfield, Jean Paul Sartre, Robert Louis Stevenson, Leo Tolstoi, Mark Van Doren, H. G. Wells, and Virginia Woolf are but some of the writers for whom this generalization holds true.[6]

[4] D. H. Lawrence, *Studies in Classic American Literature,* p. 11.

[5] John Ciardi, Interview from *Counterpoint,* compiled and edited by Roy Newquist, pp. 122–23. Copyright 1964 by Rand McNally & Company.

[6] H. E. F. Donohue, *Conversations with Nelson Algren; The Journals of Arnold Bennett,* ed. Frank Swinnerton; Joseph Conrad, *The Mirror of the Sea* and *A Personal Record,* ed. Morton Dauwen Zabel; Simone de Beauvoir, *The Prime of Life,* trans. Peter

Perhaps one of the best-known and dramatic examples of this preoccupation with writing difficulties is Virginia Woolf in *A Writer's Diary*. Although she makes occasional allusion to formal problems in her novels and even in the diary itself, she writes constantly about her feelings, usually negative, about the evolution of her works and about their critical reception by a coterie of friends-and-critics. She finds sustaining her energies after beginning her novels an especial source of difficulty. Here, for example, are excerpts describing her struggles with *Jacob's Room:*

> My mind turned by anxiety, or other cause, from its scrutiny of blank paper, is like a lost child—wandering the house, sitting on the bottom step to cry.
>
> (December 5, 1919) [7]

and

> It is worth mentioning, for future reference, that the creative power which bubbles so pleasantly in beginning a new book quiets down after a time, and one goes on more steadily. Doubts creep in. Then one becomes resigned. Determination not to give in, and the sense of an impending shape keep one at it more than anything. I'm a little anxious. How am I to bring off this conception? Directly one gets to work one is like a person walking, who has seen the country stretching out before. I want to write nothing in this book that I don't enjoy writing. Yet writing is always difficult.
>
> (May 29, 1923) [8]

The limitation in referring to these forms of data exclusively, then, is that they focus on partial phenomena. They often describe brilliantly the context, the affective milieu of the writing act; but the act itself remains undescribed.

Dialogue between Writer and Attuned Respondent

A second form of data about the composing process is the dialogue, usually in the form of correspondence about an imaginative work in progress, between a writer and a highly attuned respondent, such as a fellow artist or a skilled editor. In the first category, possibly one of the best-known technical correspondences is that between Gerard Manley Hopkins and Robert Bridges during the second half of the nineteenth century. Their letters, written over a period of twenty-four years from 1865 to 1889, often deal with formal problems each encountered in individual poems, with technical criticism of each

Green; Guy de Maupassant, "Preface to *Pierre et Jean*," *The Life Work of Henry René Guy de Maupassant;* F. Scott Fitzgerald, *The Crack-Up;* E. M. Forster, *Writers at Work: The Paris Review Interviews,* II; Andre Gide, *The Journals of Andre Gide,* trans. Justin O'Brien; John Keats, *Selected Letters;* Norman Mailer, *Advertisements for Myself;* Katherine Mansfield, *Journal;* Jean Paul Sartre, *The Words;* Robert Louis Stevenson, *Essays in the Art of Writing;* Leo Tolstoi, *Talks with Tolstoi: Tolstoi and His Problems,* trans. Aylmer Maude; Mark Van Doren, *Autobiography;* H. G. Wells, *Experiments in Autobiography; Discoveries and Conclusions of a Very Ordinary Brain (Since 1866)*.
[7] Virginia Woolf, *A Writer's Diary,* ed. Leonard Woolf, p. 21.
[8] Ibid., p. 25.

other's poetry, and with their evolving theories of rhythm and versification.[9]

Understandably, correspondence between a writer and his editor, when not mercantile, is usually technical. In American letters perhaps the best-known correspondence in this category is that between the novelist Thomas Wolfe and Maxwell Perkins, his editor at Charles Scribner's publishing house.[10] A second, more recent example is the correspondence between the critic Malcolm Cowley and William Faulkner detailing the history of the Viking Portable Library edition of Faulkner's works.[11]

Inherently interesting as this form of data is, it, too, has limited value for a full inquiry into writing because it does not deal with the total process; rather, it focuses on only one part of the process, the revision specific to a given piece of work—for example, Hopkins' problems with "The Wreck of the Deutschland," or Wolfe's, with *Look Homeward, Angel*. Indeed, this specificity may be its major limitation in that the observations on these acts of revision may therefore be imperfectly generalizable.

Analyses by Others of Evolutions of Certain Pieces of Writing

Another form of data about writing is analysis of the evolution of a piece of writing by someone other than the author. Sometimes the analysts are fellow writers, as with Henry James's study of Hawthorne or John Berryman's of Stephen Crane. Sometimes the analysts are critics, as with Josephine Bennett's study, *The Evolution of "The Faerie Queene,"* and Butt and Tillotson's study, *Dickens at Work*.

These analysts focus upon different moments in the evolution of certain pieces. For some, focus is upon the early stages—sources read and recorded in notebooks and other accounts by the writer that later resonate in a work; for others, focus is upon the later stages—upon revisions, changes the writer makes in drafts that lead to, or even follow, initial publication.

Perhaps the best-known example of focus upon the early, upon what might even be called the prewriting, activities of the writer, is *The Road to Xanadu* by John Livingston Lowes, in which Lowes traces the sources through Coleridge's labyrinthine and cryptic notebook allusions to his reading for every aspect of "Kubla Khan" and "The Rime of the Ancient Mariner," from individual word choice to total thematic organization.

Although there is probably no one analysis of a prose work that holds the critical esteem of Lowes's analysis, a representative study is Jerome Beaty's *Middlemarch, From Notebook to Novel*. Focussing on chapter 81 as exemplar, Beaty juxtaposes his own direct analyses of Eliot's process of composing with accounts by her husband, John Cross; her publisher, John Blackwood; a biographer, Joan Bennett; and by the author herself. He finds a dissonance between his analyses and all other accounts which state or imply that Eliot

[9] *The Letters of Gerard Manley Hopkins to Robert Bridges,* ed. Claude Colleer Abbott.
[10] *The Letters of Thomas Wolfe,* ed. Maxwell Perkins.
[11] Malcolm Cowley, *The Faulkner-Cowley File: Letters and Memories, 1944–1962.*

wrote the scene between Dorothea and Rosamond in a "stroke of creative genius" with little prefiguring and less revision.[12]

Beaty's analyses of Eliot's notebook entries reveal that she planned for this chapter as she planned for other chapters in the novel:

> The plans for Chapter 81 are not particularly detailed—there was no attempt to sketch the stages of the conversation or the form of the dialogue—but then no chapter in *Middlemarch* was planned in that manner; it was not George Eliot's way. But it *was* planned for. All the motives and events, for example, are in the notebook that Dorothea has returned out of pity. That Rosamond is "wrought upon" by this pity of love, and that she tells Dorothea that it is Dorothea Will loves.[13]

His studies of the manuscript also reveal that not only was chapter 81 revised, "this chapter was more heavily revised than most of the others in *Middlemarch,* and revised in almost all its aspects: timing, content, point of view, characterization, tone, and outcome." [14]

Beaty concludes his analysis of chapter 81:

> Writing, to George Eliot, was not an unpremeditated outpouring; neither was it a mechanical following of detailed blueprint. It was a process of evolution and of discovery.[15]

Whatever the motivation behind George Eliot's statements, the discrepancies between her description and Beaty's findings also serve to make suspect yet another writer's account as a valid source of data about his own process of writing, while at the same time suggesting the value of direct analysis of writers' notebooks and drafts as sources of information about the writing process.

Other analysts have been interested instead in the process of revision or the transmutation of elements in original or early drafts into the burnished rightness of the final form. An early example in poetry criticism is M. R. Ridley's detailed examination of the drafts of certain poems by John Keats— specifically, "The Eve of St. Agnes" and the four major odes. More recent is *W. B. Yeats: The Later Poetry* by Thomas Parkinson, specifically chapter two, "Vestiges of Creation," and chapter four, "The Passionate Syntax." Studies of the revisions of prose works include Rudolf Arnheim's *Poets at Work* and an interesting casebook *Word for Word,* prepared by Wallace Hildick, in which are set forth for student examination "authors' alterations"

---

[12] Beaty attributes the statements, at least by Cross and Eliot herself, to a shared belief in the Romantic notion of inspiration prevalent in the nineteenth century, even into the Victorian period:

"Their best work . . . was written without premedation, in a frenzy of inspiration. Therefore it follows that revision and hard work are the signs of those who are less than geniuses." [Jerome Beaty, *Middlemarch, From Notebook to Novel: A Study of George Eliot's Creative Method.* Copyright 1960 by University of Illinois.]

[13] Ibid., pp. 110–11.

[14] Ibid., p. 123.

[15] Ibid., p. 125.

by T. S. Eliot, D. H. Lawrence, Alexander Pope, Samuel Butler, Thomas Hardy, William Wordsworth, Henry James, William Blake, and Virginia Woolf.[16]

Literary critics have always studied style; in recent years scholars of style have made increasing use of linguistic analysis, often employing a computer. At times their cluster of techniques has been applied to works of disputed or shared authorship. Frederick Mosteller and David Wallace, for example, examined the Federalist Papers to ascertain whether John Jay or James Madison was the author of disputed passages, as well as what part Thomas Jefferson played in the revisions. In 1963, Bernard O'Donnell examined Stephen Crane's posthumously published novel, *The O'Ruddy,* to ascertain what parts of the work were actually written by Crane and what parts by the reporter who completed the novel.

Computer analysis of style has also been employed to make a comparative examination of grammatical and lexical elements in authors' styles. J. B. Carroll, for example, attempted by factor analysis to delineate "the basic dimensions on which style varied"; and he demonstrated that the style of Mickey Spillane and F. Scott Fitzgerald varied along certain specifiable dimensions. Boder showed that the verb-adjective quotient was a significant index of stylistic differences among professional and student writers. There are certain general computer programs for handling language data, such as Iker and Harway's work with content analysis, and Stone and Boles's *General Inquirer Program.*

Although in these linguistic studies the process of writing is sometimes purportedly under scrutiny, to this writer's knowledge none of the investigators has yet attempted to develop generalizations from their studies of specific works and authors. They have not attempted, in other words, to delineate

---

[16] Certain themes emerge from a reading of these studies. One is the primacy of artifact over nature as stimulus to imaginative writing. What the writer has read seems more crucial than whatever is meant by direct confrontations with nature and other kinds of experience. This thesis has also been propounded for painters and other artists by Andre Malraux in Les Voix du Silence.

A second awareness is the validity of a distinction made by Stephen Spender in his essay "The Making of a Poem" between Mozartians and Beethovians. In her essay "The Uses of the Unconscious in Composing," this investigator elaborated Spender's distinction:

> The Mozartian is one who can instantaneously arrange encounters with his unconscious; he is one in whom the creative self leads a constant and uninterrupted life of its own, serene to surface disturbances, oblivious of full upper activity—coach-riding, concert-giving, bill-paying. The Mozartian can "plunge the greatest depths of his own experience by the tremendous effort of a moment" and surface every time with a finished pearl—a Cosi Fan Tutte, a Piano Concerto in C Major.
> The Beethovian, on the other hand, is the agonizer, the evolutionizer. Scholars studying his first notes to a quartet or a symphony, as Spender points out, are astounded by their embryonic clumsiness. The creative self in a Beethovian is not a plummeting diver, but a plodding miner who seems at times to scoop south with his bare hands. To change the metaphor, for the Beethovian, composing is not unlike eating an artichoke—pricks and inadequate rewards in our tedious leaf-by-leaf spiraling toward the delectable heart. [Janet Emig, "The Uses of the Unconscious in Composing," *College Composition and Communication* (February 1964), 11.]

the, even *a,* writing process or to ascertain whether the process has constant characteristics across writers. Rather, they have been concerned with product —rather than process—centered research.

Rhetoric and Composition Texts and Handbooks

Another possible source of data about the composing process is the rhetoric or composition text which gives students dicta and directives about how to speak and write. The best-known classical rhetorics are of course Plato, Aristotle, Cicero, and Quintilian. These have provided the models for theory, and applications, down the centuries. Contemporary examples of rhetoric texts include Francis X. Connolly's *A Rhetoric Casebook,* Leo Rockas's *Models of Rhetoric,* and Martin, Ohmann and Wheatley's *The Logic and Rhetoric of Exposition.*

Composition handbooks—a more recent development—also give dicta and directives; but, unlike most of the rhetoric texts, they cite no substantiation for them. (See, for example, Warriner's handbook.) The authors and editors of these texts neither state nor imply that they have tapped any of the following possible sources of data, if not substantiation: (a) introspection into their own processes of writing; (b) accounts by and about professional writers; and (c) accounts of and about secondary students, the audience to whom their advice is purportedly directed.

In America, beginning probably with John Walker's *A Teacher's Assistant in English Composition* (1803), composition texts served a different audience from that of rhetoric texts: whereas the rhetoric text was designed to help prepare young men of the upper classes for the pulpit, bar, and public forum, the composition text was designed to help younger students of both sexes in the middle and lower classes achieve a basic written literacy. In his survey of the rhetorical tradition Edward P. J. Corbett notes these differences in the two approaches to teaching writing:

> Rhetoric courses in the schools gradually assumed a new orientation—the study of the four forms of discourse: exposition, argumentation, description, and narration. The virtues that were stressed in this approach to composition were unity, coherence, and emphasis. Style continued to engage some attention, but the focus shifted from the schemes and tropes to a concern for diction (which gradually deteriorated into a neurotic concern for "correct usage") and for syntax (which, under the popular handbooks, became a rather negative approach to "correct grammar"). The study of the paragraph concentrated on the topic sentence and the various ways of developing the topic sentence to achieve maximum unity, coherence, and emphasis.[17]

The characterization these texts convey of the composing process is of a quite conscious, wholly rational—at times, even mechanical—affair with many of the components for a piece of discourse extrinsic to the speaker or writer.

---

[17] From *Classical Rhetoric for the Modern Student* by Edward P. J. Corbett, p. 566. Copyright © 1965 by Oxford University Press.

For example, *inventio,* the first *division* of classical rhetoric, does not refer to the writer's finding within his own experience the sources of his discourse; it refers rather to discovering, in the universe outside, the *topoi,* or "the set of sources available . . . in my argument." [18] The organization of a piece of writing, particularly a speech, is, if one believes Cicero and others, fixed by a traditional schema consisting of six parts: exordium, narrative, partition, confirmation, repetition, peroration. A speaker or writer does not evolve a mode of organization that is indigenous to a specific content: he follows instead the six-part outline.

How the writer feels about the subject matter and how his feelings may influence what he writes—the affective dimension—are not really considered in these texts. The notion that there might be a press of personality upon all components of the process is not present. This is not a criticism of the classical texts; it is an historical comment. The rhetorical tradition is simply, in its major works, significantly prior to the development of psychology with its interests in introspection and theories of personality development. Because they do not consider the possible effect of a writer's personality upon the process, however, rhetoric and composition texts are not a useful source of data for most of the questions posed earlier in this chapter.

Theory of the Creative Process

Research is a third source of data that might provide a theoretical base or a methodological model for this inquiry. The two modes examined in this section are (1) theoretical studies of what is called, globally, "the creative process," and (2) pieces of empirical research dealing with the writing of adolescents.

In *The Art of Thought* (1926) Graham Wallas typologizes creative thought as a four-stage process—a delineation that persists, with occasional shifts and changes of terms and categories, into the present literature. Wallas credits Helmholtz, the German physicist, with first describing three stages in the process; the fourth Wallas adds along with descriptive terms for all four stages:

> We can . . . roughly dissect out a continuous process, with a beginning and a middle and an end of its own. . . . Helmholtz, . . . speaking in 1891 at a banquet on his seventieth birthday, described the way in which his most important new thoughts had come to him. He said that after previous investigation of the problem "in all directions . . . happy ideas come unexpectedly without effort, like an inspiration. So far as I am concerned, they have never come to me when my mind was fatigued, or when I was at my working table. . . . They came particularly readily during the slow ascent of wooded hills on a sunny day." Helmholtz here gives us three stages in the formation of a new thought. The first in time I shall call Preparation, the stage during which the problem was "investigated . . . in all directions";

[18] *Essays on Rhetoric,* ed. Dudley Bailey, p. 82.

the second is the stage during which he was not consciously thinking about the problem, which I shall call Incubation; the third, consisting of the appearance of the "happy idea" together with the psychological events which immediately preceded and accompanied that appearance, I shall call Illumination.

And I shall add a fourth stage, of Verification, which Helmholtz does not here mention . . . in which both the validity of the idea was tested, and the idea itself was reduced to exact form.[19]

Many students of creativity as well as creators across modes—painting, composing—share this view of the creative process. Writing, for example, which can be regarded as a species of creative behavior, is often described in quite similar terms. In his introduction to *Writers at Work: The Paris Review Interviews,* Malcolm Cowley describes the composing process shared by the short-story writers and novelists interviewed:

There would seem to be four stages in the composition of a story. First comes the germ of the story, then the period of more or less conscious meditation, then the first draft, and finally the revision, which may be simply "pencil work," as John O'Hara calls it—that is, minor changes in wording—or may lead to writing several drafts and what amounts to a new work.[20]

In the process of writing, revision seems to occupy the same place that verification holds in scientific and mathematical inquiries.

Another view of the specific poetic process as a sequence of *five* (perhaps six) aligned stages is presented by the psychologist R. N. Wilson in his essay "Poetic Creativity, Process and Personality":

A rough paradigm of the stages of poetic creativity would include at least the following elements: the selective perception of the environment; the acquisition of technique; the envisioning of combinations and distillations; elucidation of the vision; and the end of the poem and its meaning to the poet.[21]

This sequence differs from Wallas's chiefly in regarding the acquisition of technique as an element in the process (it is probable the acquisition of technique is regarded instead as a requisite *to* the process by Wallas and others); and in its concern with the end of the process, a later element than "elucidation" which for Wilson includes revision, Wallas's fourth stage, and the contemplation of the product.

In the literature there are perhaps only two markedly different characterizations of creation as something other than a process of several aligned stages. One characterization represents it as the tension generated between a single

[19] Graham Wallas, *The Art of Thought,* pp. 79–81. Copyright 1926 by Harcourt Brace Jovanovich.

[20] Malcolm Cowley, *Writers at Work, The Paris Review Interviews.* Copyright 1961 by the Viking Press, Inc. and Martin Secker & Warburg Limited.

[21] R. N. Wilson, "Poetic Creativity, Process and Personality," *Psychiatry* (1954), 163–76.

or multiple set of opposing variables; the second, as the point or moment of intersection between two disparate modes or fields of endeavor.

The earliest description of creation as the tension generated between a single set of polarities is probably Plato's dialogue *Ion,* with the movement of the artist between frenzy (divine inspiration) and formulation. The best-known is perhaps Freud's interpretation of creativity, in "The Relation of the Poet to Day-Dreaming" (1908) and "Leonardo da Vinci and a Memory of His Childhood" (1910), as the tension between the unconscious and conscious activities of the mind. In *Neurotic Distortion of the Creative Process,* L. S. Kubie also dichotomizes the activities of the mind during creation; but he suggests that creative behaviors emanate from the preconscious rather than the unconscious portion of the mind. Kubie describes the distinctive features of preconscious processes as

> their automatic and subtle recordings of multiple perceptions, their automatic recall, their multiple analogic and overlapping linkages, and their direct connections to the autonomic processes which underlie affective states.[22]

In his essay "The Conditions of Creativity" (1962), Jerome Bruner describes creation as the tension produced among a multiple set of "antimonies." [23] These are detachment and commitment, passion and decorum, freedom from and domination by the artifact, deferral and immediacy, and conflicting identities within the creator. Creators are at once "disengaged from that which exists conventionally" and "engaged deeply in what they construct to replace it"; urgently vital in artistic impulse and courteous and formal in artistic expression; separated from the object and bored enough by creating it to put off completion until the psychologically appropriate time; and involved through their creation in "working out of conflict and coalition within the set of identities that compose" their personality.[24]

Another markedly different characterization of creativity is proffered by Arthur Koestler in his massive study, *The Act of Creation* (1964). Koestler describes creation, not as the outcome of a series of aligned stages nor as the result of tension between "antimonies," but rather as the intersection of two disparate "matrices." "Matrix" he defines as "any ability, habit, or skill, any pattern of ordered behavior governed by a *'code'* of fixed rules." [25] In Koestler's view, creation is "bisociative"; that is, the creator perceives "a situation or event in two habitually incompatible associative contexts." [26] Humor, literary creation, and scientific discovery are examples Koestler gives of bisociative activity.

Viewed singly, these three delineations of creation may seem descriptions of fact. Juxtaposed, however, they reveal their hypothetical nature. That there

[22] L. S. Kubie, *Neurotic Distortion of the Creative Process,* pp. 44–45.
[23] Jerome Bruner, "The Conditions of Creativity," *On Knowing: Essays for the Left Hand.*
[24] Ibid.
[25] Arthur Koestler, *The Act of Creation,* p. 38.
[26] Ibid., p. 95.

are data supporting all three sets of hypotheses suggests there may be process*es* of creation with quite different profiles or typographies. Indeed, there is the strong possibility that other delineations are equally valid.

Empirical Research about Adolescent Writing

Most pieces of empirical research on the adolescent writer focus upon the product(s) rather than upon the process(es) of their writing and, consequently, do not provide an appropriate methodology for a process-centered inquiry. Of the 504 studies written before 1963 that are cited in the bibliography of *Research in Written Composition,* only two deal even indirectly with the process of writing among adolescents.[27]

Two recent American studies which focus upon process rather than upon product of composition are "The Sound of Writing" by Anthony Tovatt and Ebert L. Miller and *Pre-Writing: The Construction and Application of Models for Concept Formation in Writing* by D. Gordon Rohman and Albert O. Wiecke.

Tovatt's study proceeds from the premise that "we write with our ears" and that if students can "hear" what they are writing, they can transmute satisfactory patterns of written discourse. In the first experimental year of the study (1964–65) thirty ninth-grade students, matched with a control class, were given the OAV (oral-aural-visual) stimuli approach to writing. As one of the two most significant—or at least unique—features of the experiment, the students used tape recorders equipped with audio-active headsets so that they could hear themselves electronically as they composed. A second was that the teacher provided a constant role-model as writer by composing in the presence of the experimental class until they "eventually accept[ed] the fact [that] good writing is achieved through sustained labor in three basic stages: prewriting, writing, and rewriting." [28]

Tovatt reports these findings:

> The OAV stimuli procedures demonstrated in the first year a general superiority over a conventional approach in increasing student abilities in writing, reading, listening, and language usage. However, rating of compositions from

[27] These are the unpublished dissertations, "Proposals for the Conduct of Written Composition Activities in the Secondary School Inherent in an Analysis of the Language Composition Act" by Lester Angene and "Factors Affecting Regularity of the Flow of Words during Written Composition" by John A. Van Bruggen. Angene looks only at finished student themes: any examples and statements involving the process of writing he draws from a sample of professional writers and from analysis of the writing act in one composition handbook, written by his advisor. Van Bruggen's emphasis, as the title of his study makes clear, is the physical rate at which a sample of eighty-four junior high school students write—more specifically, how often and how fast they actually place pen to paper (actually stylus to electric disc) in the production of their themes. The process of writing, beyond this series of physical contacts between pen and paper, remains unexamined.

[28] Anthony Tovatt and Ebert L. Miller, "The Sound of Writing," *Research in the Teaching of English* (Fall 1967), 182–83.

the control and experimental classes was inconclusive in establishing the superiority of either approach.[29]

In the study by Rohman and Wiecke, the investigators divide the writing process into three stages: "prewriting," "writing," and "rewriting." They focus upon prewriting—which they define as "the stage of discovery in process when a person assimilates "his subject' to himself"—because prewriting "is crucial to the success of any writing that occurs later" and "is seldom given the attention it consequently deserves."[30]

In a project involving three sections of a sophomore-level course in expository writing at Michigan State University in 1964, the investigators sought "(1) to isolate and describe the principle of this assimilation and (2) to devise a course that would allow students to imitate its dynamics."[31]

The principle of the assimilation, they decided, is the conversion of an "event" into an "experience," to use the words of novelist Dorothy S. Sayers. The three means they employed were (1) the keeping of a journal, (2) the practice of some principles derived from the religious meditation, and (3) the use of the analogy. The essays produced after a one-semester course with the emphasis on assimilation "showed a statistically significant superiority [one set, at the .05 level; one set, at the .01 level] to essays produced in control sections."[32]

Both the Tovatt-Miller and the Rohman-Wiecke studies are experiments in instruction: that is, systematic group interventions are introduced to effect a change in students' behavior as they write. The purpose of the present inquiry, on the other hand, is to attempt to describe how student writers usually or typically behave as they write with minimal direct intervention by the investigator. In other words, the Tovatt-Miller and the Rohman-Wiecke studies are efforts to instruct or teach; this inquiry is an effort to describe. Nevertheless, as two of the few serious efforts extant to examine writing in process for adolescent writers, they deserve acknowledgment and explication.

Conflicting Data

Among these three major sources of data there is often disagreement. Writers' accounts and composition texts, for example, present a powerful instance of the phenomenon noted at the beginning of this chapter—one set of sources that contradict or are often directly contradicted by another. Here, for example, are two accounts of how the writing process proceeds:

> (1) A good writer puts words together in correct, smooth sentences, according to the rules of standard usage. He puts sentences together to make paragraphs that are clear and effective, unified and well developed. Finally,

[29] Ibid., pp. 187–88.
[30] D. Gordon Rohman and Albert O. Wiecke, *Pre-Writing: The Construction and Application of Models for Concept Formation in Writing,* Michigan State University, 1964, USOE Cooperative Research Project No. 2174, p. 103.
[31] Ibid., p. 30.
[32] Ibid., p. 181.

he puts paragraphs together into larger forms of writing—essays, letters, stories, research papers.

In practice, as you know from your own experience, a writer begins with a general plan and ends with details of wording, sentence structure, and grammar. First, he chooses the *subject* of his composition. Second, he tackles the *preparation* of his material, from rough ideas to final outline. Third, he undertakes the writing itself, once again beginning with a rough form (the first draft) and ending with a finished form (the final draft) that is as nearly perfect as he can make it.

These three basic stages of composition are almost always the same for any form of writing. Each of the three stages proceeds according to certain definite steps, listed below in order.

a. Choosing and limiting the subject	1. Subject
b. Assembling materials	
c. Organizing materials	2. Preparation
d. Outlining	
e. Writing the first draft	3. Writing
f. Revising	
g. Writing the final draft [33]	

(2) You will write . . . if you will write without thinking of the result in terms of a result, but think of the writing in terms of discovery, which is to say the creation must take place between the pen and the paper, not before in a thought, or afterwards in a recasting. Yes, before in a thought, but not in careful thinking. It will come if it is there and if you will let it come, and if you have anything you will get a sudden creative recognition. You won't know how it was, even what it is, but it will be creation if it came out of the pen and out of you and not out of an architectural drawing of the thing you are doing . . . I can tell how important it is to have that creative recognition. You cannot go into the womb to form the child; it is there and makes itself and comes forth whole—and there it is and you have made it and felt it, but it has come itself—and that is creative recognition. Of course you have a little more control over your writing than that; you have to know what you want to get; but when you know that, let it take you and if it seems to take you off the track don't hold back, because that is perhaps where instinctively you want to be and if you hold back and try to be always where you have been before, you will go dry.[34]

The first of these comes from Warriner's *English Grammar and Composition,* 11, one volume of a very widely used series of composition handbooks. The second is by the writer Gertrude Stein. Clearly, the statements are almost antithetical: according to Stein, writing is an act of discovery emanating "out of the pen and out of you" while Warriner's suggests writing is a tidy, accre-

[33] John E. Warriner, Joseph Mersand, and Francis Griffith, *English Grammar and Composition,* 11, pp. 379–80. Copyright 1958 by Harcourt Brace Jovanovich.
[34] John Hyde Preston, "A Conversation," *Atlantic Monthly* (August 1935), 189. Copyright 1935 by John Hyde Preston.

tive affair that proceeds by elaborating a fully pre-conceived and formulated plan.

Statements in composition texts and handbooks also differ from those of established writers in discussion of what might be called specific components in the writing process. Take this same matter of planning, for example. The quotation above from Warriner's handbook unequivocally states that a writer always makes an outline before "writing," regardless of the mode of writing.

In 1964 this investigator collected data from professional writers regarding their planning practices. Responding to a questionnaire about their planning practices were the following professional and academic writers: Max Bluestone, Reuben Brower, Jerome Bruner, John B. Carroll, John Ciardi, Kenneth Lynn, Raven I. McDavid, Harold Martin, Theodore Morrison, Henry Olds, James K. Robinson, Israel Scheffler, Clifford Shipton, B. F. Skinner, Priscilla Tyler, and Mark Van Doren.[35]

The data from these questionnaires belie the textbook generalization that all writers make written outlines for all forms of writing they do. Indeed, the data suggest there is great diversity and individuality in planning practices, at least among this sample of writers.

In the sample four of the sixteen writers—J. B. Carroll, James K. Robinson, Israel Scheffler, and B. F. Skinner—proceed as the texts state all writers do. That is, they make a rough outline, then an elaborated one complete with full sentences, indentations, and numbering and lettering of items. For these writers the outline seems to represent the major act in the writing process, as B. F. Skinner makes clear:

> When I begin to think of a developed paper or a book, I turn almost immediately to outlines. These grow in detail, almost to the point of producing the final prose.

And James K. Robinson notes the usefulness of the elaborated outline not only for himself but also for his students:

> I found both for myself and for students whom I have had in Freshman English that the sentence outline is most satisfactory since it forces one to make definite statements that will enable one to test logical relationships or developments in the paper to be written. It goes a step beyond words or phrases in planning.

Israel Scheffler also produces an outline that structures, as well as fully pre-figures, the final piece of writing:

---

[35] Respondents to a questionnaire devised and distributed July 1964 by Janet Emig were: Max Bluestone, University of Massachusetts, Boston; Reuben Brower, Harvard University; Jerome Bruner, Harvard University; John B. Carroll, Harvard University; John Ciardi, poet, Poetry Editor, *Saturday Review;* Kenneth Lynn, Harvard University; Raven I. McDavid, University of Chicago; Harold Martin, President, Union College; Theodore Morrison, novelist, Harvard University; Henry Olds, Harvard Graduate School of Education; James K. Robinson, University of Cincinnati; Israel Scheffler, Harvard University; Clifford Shipton, Director, American Antiquarian Society, Worcester, Massachusetts; B. F. Skinner, Harvard University; Priscilla Tyler, Harvard University; Mark Van Doren, poet, Columbia University.

. . . The outline is as detailed as I can make it, with different systems of numbering and lettering, plus indentation, to reveal subordination and other relationships among the items. The main items I try to spell out as full sentences or short paragraphs, the subordinate items as sentences, clauses, or simply tags to indicate examples or other points. I worry about parallelism of items with parallel position in the outline, as well as subordination of other items.

Normally, the outline does not cover all the details of the eventual draft, but I do want it to give the main structure of the whole in as explicit form as I can get it at the beginning.

The majority in the group take what might be called a middle position toward planning—that is, they make some kind of informal outline adapted to their individual styles of working and to the mode of the piece involved. Kenneth Lynn jots down in phrase form a sequence of items he plans to use, observing some system of indentation. Harold Martin sets down phrases without any particular order, then groups these "for meaningful relationships," and finally marks "1–2–3 for order": he finds no value to "IA, la." Theodore Morrison calls the plan he makes for his novels "a quick conspectus": he uses "heads as a reminder of where I am going."

Members of this middle group seem to be against any plan that totally pre-figures a piece of writing. Their shared reason is aptly set forth by Max Bluestone:

The rough scheme [his form of plan] is a map to the territory of my thoughts. The map is never precise, first because the territory has not been thoroughly explored and second because writing is in itself the discovery of new territory. I usually anticipate discovery in the act of composition.

Contradicting another statement in Warriner's, writers in the sample who work in more than one mode proceed differently in different genres. Poetry seems to be a genre for which no outlines or elaborated plans are ever made, at least by the writers of poetry in this sample—Max Bluestone, John Ciardi, and Mark Van Doren.

Max Bluestone, Theodore Morrison, and Mark Van Doren, novelists and short story writers in the sample, also note for these modes they seldom make elaborate written outlines. They would seem to agree with the novelist Eileen Bassing about the use of the outline in fiction.

N [Roy Newquist]: Could you outline your working procedures? Perhaps it's best to refer directly—if only roughly—to the production of *Home before Dark* and *Where's Annie?*

Bassing: I'm glad you said "roughly" because I don't think I could give you a precise outline of any particular thing I write. I very much admire writers who can work from a neat, orderly outline, and I always feel that my method can only be called "chaotic." The complete outline isn't for me.

I do have a shadowy outline in my mind—as I did in *Home before Dark,* for example. I knew what I wanted to say, and I knew a great deal about my central character. Once you have the character you're pretty well started, . . .

. . . The outline, again [with her novel *Where's Annie?*] was very shadowy—I had the beginning, a kind of middle, a scene here and there, and maybe the end. . . .

N: In other words you don't really work from an outline at the beginning. You work from an idea, or some characters, and write a first draft—then make an outline and write it again. Is that right?

Bassing: Yes.

N: Isn't that a very unusual way of working?

Bassing: Is it? I don't think so.[36]

The single mode of exposition then is the only mode cited by this sample for which outlines are produced with any degree of regularity, and then only by *some* of these writers.

The data from the questionnaire also suggest that a second generalization of rhetoric texts and manuals about planning is not valid, at least for this sample of writers—that is, all planning precedes all writing as all writing precedes all revising. The metaphor implied in these accounts about the writing process is linear: each "stage" is monolithic and holds a fixed position in a lock-step chronological process. There are, in other words, no major recursive features in the writing process.

All writers in the sample state they do engage in some form of planning prior to the production of a piece of sustained discourse: for Reuben Brower and Jerome Bruner this takes the form of conversation with friends. They also state or imply, however, that they continue to plan and to adapt and revise previously written plans as the piece evolves. Theodore Morrison makes a conspectus "at such times as seem necessary or seem to offer help." Some of the writers even make written plans or outlines as part of their revising. Max Bluestone states that if he is revising "something that has lain fallow," he might make a revised outline as well, one that "usually has to do with compression and elaboration of the version before me." Clearly, for these authors the so-called "stages" of writing are not fixed in an inexorable sequence. Rather, they occur and reoccur throughout the process. These data then make suspect the straight line which rhetoric texts imply as an appropriate metaphor for the writing process.[37]

---

[36] Eileen Bassing, Interview from *Counterpoint,* compiled and edited by Roy Newquist. Copyright 1964 by Rand McNally & Company.

[37] An aside: there is almost perfect unanimity among authors in the sample that whatever training in formal outlining they received in school has no influence on their current planning practices. Mark Van Doren and Jerome Bruner put it mildly: "Formal training seemed artificial and didn't interest me."

Others react more strongly: "Such procedures have helped me not at all." (Kenneth Lynn) "It was forced upon me and I did what I had to do, but I resist such outlining as a destruction. It seems to imply that one may complete his thought process in the outline and then merely go for 'style' in the writing. Nonsense. The writing and the thinking are inseperable [*sic*]. Any other assumption can only produce hack-work." (John Ciardi)

This discrepancy then between these two forms of data—the statements made about writing in composition texts and handbooks and statements by professional writers—make suspect the validity of one form, if not both forms, of data.

Another dissonance occurs between the statements made about the practice and value of outlining in composition texts, manuals, and textbooks and the actual practices of able secondary students as examined by empirical research. Modern rhetoric and composition texts, as the quotation above from Warriner's handbook suggests, present the formal outline as a customary prelude to student writing, at least in the mode of exposition.

In a pilot study conducted in 1964, this investigator examined two assumptions behind the generalization on outlining presented in Warriner's handbook. The first assumption is descriptive: student writers do organize by outlining. The second is normative: to assure the most skillfully organized theme, student writers should organize by formal outlining. These assumptions were treated as hypotheses and examined in the following ways.

If assumption one is true, if student writers do organize by outlining, it seemed logical to believe that superior student writers would use outlining in organizing a group of expository themes whether they were directed to or not. The only data that would yield such information were the total written evolutions of a number of student themes, from first recorded act through final submitted draft. To acquire such data, the investigator asked an eleventh-grade high honors English class of twenty-five students to save and to submit, with the final drafts of all expository themes written during an eight-week period, all written actions they performed in the course of writing these themes.

The students were given no directives about how these themes were to be organized. When one student asked, during the explanation about saving all materials, if the investigator expected to find outlines with every theme, the investigator said she had no set expectations about what she would find; she

Table 1

Types of Outlines Accompanying 109 Expository Themes Written by 25 Eleventh Grade Students

Theme Assignment	Total Number of Expository Themes Written	Total Number of Outlines	Number of Informal Outlines	Number of Formal Outlines
1.	25	15	9	6
2.	14	6	6	0
3.	23	6	5	1
4.	22	4	3	1
5.	25	9	8	1
Total	109	40	31	9

wanted only to have everything produced in the course of writing them, whatever these materials happened to be.

During the eight-week period the students submitted (as part or all of five writing assignments) 109 expository themes together with all written actions that preceded the final drafts. Of these, 40 themes (or 36.7 percent) were accompanied by a plan, defined here as any schema related to the composition of the theme, prior to that theme. Of these plans, nine (or 8.3 percent) qualified as formal outlines by what are, conventionally, the minimal criteria for formality: numbers or letters precede the items, and there is at least one level of indentation. The remaining 91.7 percent were atypical according to the generalization set forth in Warriner's handbook. To conclude from these very scant data that the students from whom these themes were collected typically or customarily do not outline formally for more than eight percent of the themes they write, much more that *all* secondary students do not, is, of course, unwarranted. These data however shed additional doubt upon the validity of the generalization in the rhetoric and composition texts.

The second assumption in the teaching of the outline, that the writing of a formal outline assures a more successfully organized theme, was examined in the following way: perhaps the most common means of determining the success of organization of a theme is by teacher evaluation, specifically, by the grade given the theme. If the writing of an outline prior to the writing of the theme assures superior organization, it would seem to follow that the student theme which had been preceded by an outline would rank higher by teacher evaluation than the theme which had not.

To test this hypothesis, three independent judges who were experienced teachers of English were asked to grade, from the total of 109 themes submitted, a sample of 20; 9 of which had been accompanied by outlines—4 formal, 5 informal—and 11 of which had not. The judges were not told to what category any theme belonged. They were asked to evaluate each theme solely on the basis of its organization.[38]

After the three judges evaluated all 20 themes and submitted their grades, the grades were coded according to whether that theme was accompanied by a formal outline, by an informal outline, or by no outline at all. These data, analyzed by a program of covariant analysis, revealed no correlation between the presence or absence of any outline and the grade a student receives evaluating how well organized that theme is.

Conclusion

Some of the data presented in this chapter contribute either useful methodological or theoretical models for this inquiry.

---

[38] To assure that the judges would be evaluating what constituted good organization according to the same set of criteria, the investigator asked them to draw up a list on which they all agreed and on which they would base their grades. What constituted to each of them an *A, B,* and *C* was also informally discussed, and the judges agreed that an *A* should represent fulfillment of all criteria; *B* most of them; and *C,* some.

The technique of the interview found in the accounts of professional writers is scarcely unique to this form of data; but as one helpful means for eliciting information from student writers, it will also be employed in this inquiry. The provocative and rich responses to certain kinds of questions, especially those posed in the *Paris Review* interviews, recommend such questions as those on prewriting be asked in this study as well.

Although, as the brief review of rhetoric and composition texts revealed, these data do not provide generative category-systems, several of the theories of creativity do. Examples include the attenuation of the poetic or creative process suggested by R. N. Wilson, particularly the notions that the "selective perception of the environment" and the contemplation of a product and its "meaning" represent components to describe if they apply to the composing process of students. The four-stage description of the process delineated by Helmholtz, Wallas, and Cowley will serve as the center of the delineation of the writing process in this study.

The Rhetorical Stance

Wayne C. Booth

Booth's article on the rhetorical stance has become a classic of sorts. It is an intelligent, nontechnical discussion of one of the most important concepts in rhetoric.

Classical rhetoric, of course, divided the "proofs" into three categories: logos, *concerning substance;* ethos, *concerning the speaker; and* pathos, *concerning the audience. Rhetorical stance has to do with* ethos *and* pathos, *adjusting one's manner of delivery to the audience being addressed.*

*As speech-act theory has shown, it is possible to discuss promising, threatening, stating, and so on, in extremely specific terms as rule-governed behavior. That is, for instance, a promise has been made when certain conditions have been fulfilled.**

Take the following example of a request. Husband (H) and Wife (W) are at a party, and the hour is growing late. The wife makes the simple declarative statement, "It's getting late," and the husband replies, "Yes, I'll take you home

* John Searle, *Speech Acts: An Essay in the Philosophy of Language* (Cambridge, England: The University Press, 1969), *passim*.

now." The husband has obviously interpreted the statement as a request, and we can follow Searle * in stating very precisely the conditions for that interpretation. Namely, four constitutive rules have operated. Propositional: *H has interpreted the sentence as predicating a future act of H.* Preparatory: *H is able to do A, W believes that H is able to do A, and it is not obvious to both H and W that H will do A in the normal course of events.* Sincerity: *W wants H to do A.* Essential: *The sentence counts as an attempt to get H to do A.*

But why does it count as such? Obviously content is appropriate. Note that in the situation outlined, all of the following have the same content: It's getting late / Let's go home / Take me home / I'm getting awfully tired / Don't you think we've worn out our welcome? Therefore, rhetorical stance has, first, to do with the style in which the content is embodied, and, second, with tone of voice, whether shrill, whining, or seductive.

Producing English sentences is clearly rule-governed behavior, as is stating, requesting, begging, threatening, and so on. Producing effects is subject to rules only in the sense that writing poems is, and such rules cannot be stated in any systematic way. Adjusting discourse to the audience through style and tone is simply a matter of intuition and practice.

Booth's statement goes just about as far as possible without getting down to the close analysis of a given piece of discourse produced for a given audience.

In conjunction with Booth's article, which sets the stage for an understanding of the concept of adjusting to an audience, one should read Karl R. Wallace's "Topoi and the Problem of Invention," for in this piece, Wallace outlines a set of topics that students can use as a "checklist" in their attempts to adjust their writing to a given audience.

Booth's essay was an important landmark, setting off discussion of rhetorical stance in English departments. However, Booth recently published two books which "flesh out" and elaborate suggestions that the article adumbrates. Those books—both published in 1974—are The Rhetoric of Irony *(University of Chicago) and* Modern Dogma and the Rhetoric of Assent *(Notre Dame University). See also Booth's* Now Don't Try to Reason with Me: Essays and Ironies for a Credulous Age *(University of Chicago, 1972).*

Last fall I had an advanced graduate student, bright, energetic, well-informed, whose papers were almost unreadable. He managed to be pretentious, dull, and disorganized in his paper on *Emma,* and pretentious, dull, and disorganized on *Madame Bovary.* On *The Golden Bowl* he was all these and obscure as well. Then one day, toward the end of term, he cornered me after class and said, "You know, I think you were all wrong about Robbe-Grillet's

* Ibid., p. 66.

Jealousy today." We didn't have time to discuss it, so I suggested that he write me a note about it. Five hours later I found in my faculty box a four-page polemic, unpretentious, stimulating, organized, convincing. Here was a man who had taught freshman composition for several years and who was incapable of committing any of the more obvious errors that we think of as characteristic of bad writing. Yet he could not write a decent sentence, paragraph, or paper until his rhetorical problem was solved—until, that is, he had found a definition of his audience, his argument, and his own proper tone of voice.

The word "rhetoric" is one of those catch-all terms that can easily raise trouble when our backs are turned. As it regains a popularity that it once seemed permanently to have lost, its meanings seem to range all the way from something like "the whole art of writing on any subject," as in Kenneth Burke's *The Rhetoric of Religion,* through "the special arts of persuasion," on down to fairly narrow notions about rhetorical figures and devices. And of course we still have with us the meaning of "empty bombast," as in the phrase "merely rhetorical."

I suppose that the question of the role of rhetoric in the English course is meaningless if we think of rhetoric in either its broadest or its narrowest meanings. No English course could avoid dealing with rhetoric in Burke's sense, under whatever name, and on the other hand nobody would ever advocate anything so questionable as teaching "mere rhetoric." But if we settle on the following, traditional, definition, some real questions are raised: "Rhetoric is the art of finding and employing the most effective means of persuasion on any subject, considered independently of intellectual mastery of that subject." As the students say, "Prof. X knows his stuff but he doesn't know how to put it across." If rhetoric is thought of as the art of "putting it across," considered as quite distinct from mastering an "it" in the first place, we are immediately landed in a bramble bush of controversy. Is there such an art? If so, what does it consist of? Does it have a content of its own? Can it be taught? Should it be taught? If it should, how do we go about it, head on or obliquely?

Obviously it would be foolish to try to deal with many of these issues in twenty minutes. But I wish that there were more signs of our taking all of them seriously. I wish that along with our new passion for structural linguistics, for example, we could point to the development of a rhetorical theory that would show just how knowledge of structural linguistics can be useful to anyone interested in the art of persuasion. I wish there were more freshman texts that related every principle and every rule to functional principles of rhetoric, or, where this proves impossible, I wish one found more systematic discussion of why it is impossible. But for today, I must content myself with a brief look at the charge that there is nothing distinctive and teachable about the art of rhetoric.

The case against the isolability and teachability of rhetoric may look at first like a good one. Nobody writes rhetoric, just as nobody ever writes writing. What we write and speak is always *this* discussion of the decline of rail-roading and *that* discussion of Pope's couplets and the other argument for abolishing the poll-tax or for getting rhetoric back into English studies.

We can also admit that like all the arts, the art of rhetoric is at best very chancy, only partly amenable to systematic teaching; as we are all painfully aware when our 1:00 section goes miserably and our 2:00 section of the same course is a delight, our own rhetoric is not entirely under control. Successful rhetoricians are to some extent like poets, born, not made. They are also dependent on years of practice and experience. And we can finally admit that even the firmest of principles about writing cannot be taught in the same sense that elementary logic or arithmetic or French can be taught. In my first year of teaching, I had a student who started his first two essays with a swear word. When I suggested that perhaps the third paper ought to start with something else, he protested that his high school teacher had taught him always to catch the reader's attention. Now the teacher was right, but the application of even such a firm principle requires reserves of tact that were somewhat beyond my freshman.

But with all of the reservations made, surely the charge that the art of persuasion cannot in any sense be taught is baseless. I cannot think that any-one who has ever read Aristotle's *Rhetoric* or, say, Whateley's *Elements of Rhetoric* could seriously make the charge. There is more than enough in these and the other traditional rhetorics to provide structure and content for a year-long course. I believe that such a course, when planned and carried through with intelligence and flexibility, can be one of the most important of all educational experiences. But it seems obvious that the arts of persuasion cannot be learned in one year, that a good teacher will continue to teach them regardless of his subject matter, and that we as English teachers have a special responsibility at all levels to get certain basic rhetorical principles into all of our writing assignments. When I think back over the experiences which have had any actual effect on my writing, I find the great good fortune of a splendid freshman course, taught by a man who believed in what he was doing, but I also find a collection of other experiences quite unconnected with a specific writing course. I remember the instructor in psychology who pen-cilled one word after a peculiarly pretentious paper of mine: *bull*. I remember the day when P. A. Christensen talked with me about my Chaucer paper, and made me understand that my failure to use effective transitions was not simply a technical fault but a fundamental block in my effort to get him to see my meaning. His off-the-cuff pronouncement that I should never let myself write a sentence that was not in some way explicitly attached to preceding and fol-lowing sentences meant far more to me at that moment, when I had some-thing I wanted to say, than it could have meant as part of a pattern of such rules offered in a writing course. Similarly, I can remember the devastating lessons about my bad writing that Ronald Crane could teach with a simple question mark on a graduate seminar paper, or a pencilled "Evidence for this?" or "Why this section here?" or "Everybody says so. Is it true?"

Such experiences are not, I like to think, simply the result of my being a late bloomer. At least I find my colleagues saying such things as "I didn't learn to write until I became a newspaper reporter," or "The most important training in writing I had was doing a dissertation under old *Blank*." Sometimes they go on to say that the freshman course was useless; sometimes they say that it was an indispensable preparation for the later experience. The diversity of such replies is so great as to suggest that before we try to reorganize the freshman course, with or without explicit confrontations with rhetorical categories, we ought to look for whatever there is in common among our experiences, both of good writing and of good writing instruction. Whatever we discover in such an enterprise ought to be useful to us at any level of our teaching. It will not, presumably, decide once and for all what should be the content of the freshman course, if there should be such a course. But it might serve as a guideline for the development of widely different programs in the widely different institutional circumstances in which we must work.

The common ingredient that I find in all of the writing I admire—excluding for now novels, plays and poems—is something that I shall reluctantly call the rhetorical stance, a stance which depends on discovering and maintaining in any writing situation a proper balance among the three elements that are at work in any communicative effort: the available arguments about the subject itself, the interests and peculiarities of the audience, and the voice, the implied character, of the speaker. I should like to suggest that it is this balance, this rhetorical stance, difficult as it is to describe, that is our main goal as teachers of rhetoric. Our ideal graduate will strike this balance automatically in any writing that he considers finished. Though he may never come to the point of finding the balance easily, he will know that it is what makes the difference between effective communication and mere wasted effort.

What I mean by the true rhetorician's stance can perhaps best be seen by contrasting it with two or three corruptions, unbalanced stances often assumed by people who think they are practicing the arts of persuasion.

The first I'll call the pedant's stance; it consists of ignoring or underplaying the personal relationship of speaker and audience and depending entirely on statements about a subject—that is, the notion of a job to be done for a particular audience is left out. It is a virtue, of course, to respect the bare truth of one's subject, and there may even be some subjects which in their very nature define an audience and a rhetorical purpose so that adequacy to the subject can be the whole art of presentation. For example, an article on "The relation of the ontological and teleological proofs," in a recent *Journal of Religion,* requires a minimum of adaptation of argument to audience. But most subjects do not in themselves imply in any necessary way a purpose and an audience and hence a speaker's tone. The writer who assumes that it is enough merely to write an exposition of what he happens to know on the subject will produce the kind of essay that soils our scholarly journals, written not for readers but for bibliographies.

In my first year of teaching I taught a whole unit on "exposition" without ever suggesting, so far as I can remember, that the students ask themselves what their expositions were *for*. So they wrote expositions like this one—I've saved it, to teach me toleration of my colleagues: the title is "Family relations in More's *Utopia*." "In this theme I would like to discuss some of the relationships with the family which Thomas More elaborates and sets forth in his book, *Utopia*. The first thing that I would like to discuss about family relations is that overpopulation, according to More, is a just cause of war." And so on. Can you hear that student sneering at me, in this opening? What he is saying is something like "you ask for a meaningless paper, I give you a meaningless paper." He knows that he has no audience except me. He knows that I don't want to read his summary of family relations in *Utopia*, and he knows that I know that he therefore has no rhetorical purpose. Because he has not been led to see a question which he considers worth answering, or an audience that could possibly care one way or the other, the paper is worse than no paper at all, even though it has no grammatical or spelling errors and is organized right down the line, one, two, three.

An extreme case, you may say. Most of us would never allow ourselves that kind of empty fencing? Perhaps. But if some carefree foundation is willing to finance a statistical study, I'm willing to wager a month's salary that we'd find at least half of the suggested topics in our freshman texts as pointless as mine was. And we'd find a good deal more than half of the discussions of grammar, punctuation, spelling, and style totally divorced from any notion that rhetorical purpose to some degree controls all such matters. We can offer objective descriptions of levels of usage from now until graduation, but unless the student discovers a desire to say something to somebody and learns to control his diction for a purpose, we've gained very little. I once gave an assignment asking students to describe the same classroom in three different statements, one for each level of usage. They were obedient, but the only ones who got anything from the assignment were those who intuitively imported the rhetorical instructions I had overlooked—such purposes as "Make fun of your scholarly surroundings by describing this classroom in extremely elevated style," or "Imagine a kid from the slums accidentally trapped in these surroundings and forced to write a description of this room." A little thought might have shown me how to give the whole assignment some human point, and therefore some educative value.

Just how confused we can allow ourselves to be about such matters is shown in a recent publication of the Educational Testing Service, called "Factors in Judgments of Writing Ability." In order to isolate those factors which affect differences in grading standards, ETS set six groups of readers —businessmen, writers and editors, lawyers, and teachers of English, social science and natural science—to reading the same batch of papers. Then ETS did a hundred-page "factor analysis" of the amount of agreement and disagreement, and of the elements which different kinds of graders emphasized. The authors of the report express a certain amount of shock at the discovery that the median correlation was only .31 and that 94% of the papers received either 7, 8, or 9 of the 9 possible grades.

But what *could* they have expected? In the first place, the students were given no purpose and no audience when the essays were assigned. And then all these editors and businessmen and academics were asked to judge the papers in a complete vacuum, using only whatever intuitive standards they cared to use. I'm surprised that there was any correlation at all. Lacking instructions, some of the students undoubtedly wrote polemical essays, suitable for the popular press; others no doubt imagined an audience, say, of *Reader's Digest* readers, and others wrote with the English teachers as implied audience; an occasional student with real philosophical bent would no doubt do a careful analysis of the pros and cons of the case. This would be graded low, of course, by the magazine editors, even though they would have graded it high if asked to judge it as a speculative contribution to the analysis of the problem. Similarly, a creative student who has been getting A's for his personal essays will write an amusing colorful piece, failed by all the social scientists present, though they would have graded it high if asked to judge it for what it was. I find it shocking that tens of thousands of dollars and endless hours should have been spent by students, graders, and professional testers analyzing essays and grading results totally abstracted from any notion of purposeful human communication. Did nobody protest? One might as well assemble a group of citizens to judge students' capacity to throw balls, say, without telling the students or the graders whether altitude, speed, accuracy or form was to be judged. The judges would be drawn from football coaches, hai-lai experts, lawyers, and English teachers, and asked to apply whatever standards they intuitively apply to ball throwing. Then we could express astonishment that the judgments did not correlate very well, and we could do a factor analysis to discover, lo and behold, that some readers concentrated on altitude, some on speed, some on accuracy, some on form—and the English teachers were simply confused.

One effective way to combat the pedantic stance is to arrange for weekly confrontations of groups of students over their own papers. We have done far too little experimenting with arrangements for providing a genuine audience in this way. Short of such developments, it remains true that a good teacher can convince his students that he is a true audience, if his comments on the papers show that some sort of dialogue is taking place. As Jacques Barzun says in *Teacher in America,* students should be made to feel that unless they have said something to someone, they have failed; to bore the teacher is a worse form of failure than to anger him. From this point of view we can see that the charts of grading symbols that mar even the best freshman texts are not the innocent time savers that we pretend. Plausible as it may seem to arrange for more corrections with less time, they inevitably reduce the student's sense of purpose in writing. When he sees innumerable W13's and P19's in the margin, he cannot possibly feel that the art of persuasion is as important to his instructor as when he reads personal comments, however few.

This first perversion, then, springs from ignoring the audience or over-reliance on the pure subject. The second, which might be called the advertiser's stance, comes from *under*valuing the subject and overvaluing pure effect: how to win friends and influence people.

Some of our best freshman texts—Sheridan Baker's *The Practical Stylist,* for example—allow themselves on occasion to suggest that to be controversial or argumentative, to stir up an audience is an end in itself. Sharpen the controversial edge, one of them says, and the clear implication is that one should do so even if the truth of the subject is honed off in the process. This perversion is probably in the long run a more serious threat in our society than the danger of ignoring the audience. In the time of audience-reaction meters and pre-tested plays and novels, it is not easy to convince students of the old Platonic truth that good persuasion is honest persuasion, or even of the old Aristotelian truth that the good rhetorician must be master of his subject, no matter how dishonest he may decide ultimately to be. Having told them that good writers always to some degree accommodate their arguments to the audience, it is hard to explain the difference between justified accommodation —say changing *point one* to the final position—and the kind of accommodation that fills our popular magazines, in which the very substance of what is said is accommodated to some preconception of what will sell. "The publication of *Eros* [magazine] represents a major breakthrough in the battle for the liberation of the human spirit."

At a dinner about a month ago I sat between the wife of a famous civil rights lawyer and an advertising consultant. "I saw the article on your book yesterday in the Daily News," she said, "but I didn't even finish it. The title of your book scared me off. Why did you ever choose such a terrible title? Nobody would buy a book with a title like that." The man on my right, whom I'll call Mr. Kinches, overhearing my feeble reply, plunged into a conversation with her, over my torn and bleeding corpse. "Now with my *last* book," he said, "I listed 20 possible titles and then tested them out on 400 businessmen. The one I chose was voted for by 90 percent of the businessmen." "That's what I was just saying to Mr. Booth," she said. "A book title ought to grab you, and *rhetoric* is not going to grab anybody." "Right," he said. "My *last* book sold 50,000 copies already; I don't know how this one will do, but I polled 200 businessmen on the table of contents, and . . ."

At one point I did manage to ask him whether the title he chose really fit the book. "Not quite as well as one or two of the others," he admitted, "but that doesn't matter, you know. If the book is designed right, so that the first chapter pulls them in, and you *keep* 'em in, who's going to gripe about a little inaccuracy in the title?"

Well, rhetoric is the art of persuading, not the art seeming to persuade by giving everything away at the start. It presupposes that one has a purpose concerning a subject which itself cannot be fundamentally modified by the desire to persuade. If Edmund Burke had decided that he could win more votes in Parliament by choosing the other side—as he most certainly could have done—we would hardly hail this party-switch as a master stroke of rhetoric. If Churchill had offered the British "peace in our time," with some laughs thrown in, because opinion polls had shown that more Britishers were "grabbed" by these than by blood, sweat, and tears, we could hardly call his decision a sign of rhetorical skill.

One could easily discover other perversions of the rhetorician's balance— most obviously what might be called the entertainer's stance—the willingness to sacrifice substance to personality and charm. I admire Walker Gibson's efforts to startle us out of dry pedantry, but I know from experience that his exhortations to find and develop the speaker's voice can lead to empty color-fulness. A student once said to me, complaining about a colleague, "I soon learned that all I had to do to get an A was imitate Thurber."

But perhaps this is more than enough about the perversions of the rhetorical stance. Balance itself is always harder to describe than the clumsy poses that result when it is destroyed. But we all experience the balance whenever we find an author who succeeds in changing our minds. He can do so only if he knows more about the subject than we do, and if he then engages us in the process of thinking—and feeling—it through. What makes the rhetoric of Milton and Burke and Churchill great is that each presents us with the spectacle of a man passionately involved in thinking an important question through, in the company of an audience. Though each of them did every-thing in his power to make his point persuasive, including a pervasive use of the many emotional appeals that have been falsely scorned by many a freshman composition text, none would have allowed himself the advertiser's stance; none would have polled the audience in advance to discover which position would get the votes. Nor is the highly individual personality that springs out at us from their speeches and essays present for the sake of selling itself. The rhetorical balance among speakers, audience, and argument is with all three men habitual, as we see if we look at their non-political writings. Burke's work on the Sublime and Beautiful is a relatively unimpassioned philosophical treatise, but one finds there again a delicate balance: though the implied author of this work is a far different person, far less obtrusive, far more objective, than the man who later cried *sursum corda* to the British Parliament, he permeates with his philosophical personality his philosophical work. And though the signs of his awareness of his audience are far more subdued, they are still here: every effort is made to involve the *proper* audi-ence, the audience of philosophical minds, in a fundamentally interesting inquiry, and to lead them through to the end. In short, because he was a man engaged with men in the effort to solve a human problem, one could never call what he wrote dull, however difficult or abstruse.

Now obviously the habit of seeking this balance is not the only thing we have to teach under the heading of rhetoric. But I think that everything worth teaching under that heading finds its justification finally in that balance. Much of what is now considered irrelevant or dull can, in fact, be brought to life when teachers and students know what they are seeking. Churchill reports that the most valuable training he ever received in rhetoric was in the diagraming of sentences. Think of it! Yet the diagraming of a sentence, regardless of the grammatical system, can be a live subject as soon as one asks not simply "How is this sentence put together?" but rather "Why is it put together in this way?" or "Could the rhetorical balance and hence the desired persuasion be better achieved by writing it differently?"

As a nation we are reputed to write very badly. As a nation, I would say, we are more inclined to the perversions of rhetoric than to the rhetorical balance. Regardless of what we do about this or that course in the curriculum, our mandate would seem to be, then, to lead more of our students than we now do to care about and practice the true arts of persuasion.

Heuristics and Composition

Janice Lauer

Lauer argues that theorizers concerning freshman English need to break out of the ghetto created by the shallowness of the theory that has been available for them to work with. As I have said elsewhere, modern linguistics has provided an exciting "way out" and enlivened rhetorical inquiry —on the English-department side of the hall at least.

Lauer's article—with its extensive bibliography—suggests another way of opening the field up: through studying the work done with heuristics by psychologists.

To her list, I would like to add The Conduct of Inquiry, *by Abraham Kaplan (Scranton, Pa.: Chandler, 1964). Kaplan's subtitle is "Methodology for Behavioral Science," but his book is not behaviorist in orientation. Composing is undeniably behavior, and from such works as Kaplan's, the rhetorical theorist can gain a whole new perspective on the process of composition and upon his intervention as a teacher in that process. Of particular value, it seems to me, is Kaplan's chapter on models.*

Freshman English will never reach the status of a respectable intellectual discipline unless both its theorizers and its practitioners break out of the ghetto. Endless breastbeating, exchanges of despair, or scrambles after rhetorical gimmicks can result in little more than an ostrich solution. Advertisers engaged "seriously" in the art of communication quickly learned the necessity of lifting their heads to seek the insights of such fields as psychology, sociology, and economics. Unless both the textmakers and the teachers of composition investigate beyond the field of English, beyond even the area of rhetorical studies for the solution to the composition problem, they will find themselves wandering in an endless maze.

A few rhetoricians have begun their exodus from the ghetto. In their examination of the rhetorical malaise, they isolated the dead art of invention as a major cause of the writing problem. Harrington diagnosed: "Most teachers know that rhetoric has always lost life and respect to the degree that invention has not had a significant and meaningful role." [1] Then began the faint call for the reinstatement of the lost art of invention—the art of discovering "what to say," of making original judgments on experience, of discovering means of communicating this unique insight with a particular voice to a particular ear, of deciding between nonsynonymous utterances. But a call for invention is not enough. What *ars inveniendi* is needed? The Topics? Has invention remained static since its Ramian exile from rhetoric? Booth suggests that it has: "I find it interesting, incidentally, that with all our modern passion for inventing new studies with proper labels we do not even have words in our language for the sciences of invention and arrangement or for the study of emotional and ethical appeals." [2]

If Booth is looking at rhetorical theory, he will not find such a label. But in other disciplines, a study of the art of discovery is being made under the label "heuristics." In 1957, Polya, a mathematician, described the history of heuristics: "Heuristics, or *ars inveniendi,* was the name of a certain branch of study, not very clearly circumscribed, belonging to logic, or to philosophy or to psychology, often outlined, seldom presented in detail, and as good as forgotten today. The aim of heuristics is to study the methods and rules of discovery and invention. . . . Heuristic reasoning is reasoning not regarded as final and strict but as provisional and plausible only, whose purpose is to discover the solution of the present problem." [3] One discipline which has recently been giving considerable attention to heuristics is psychology. A number of psychologists, interested in the area of creative problem solving, are analyzing the elusive and complex experience of creativity. They have discovered that creative people have developed an effective set of heuristic procedures. Psychologists, therefore, have been trying to identify the general

---

[1] Elbert Harrington, "A Modern Approach to Invention," *Quarterly Journal of Speech* 48 (December 1962), 373.
[2] Wayne Booth, "The Revival of Rhetoric," *New Rhetorics,* ed. Martin Steinmann (New York: Charles Scribner's Sons, 1967), p. 11.
[3] G. Polya, *How to Solve It* (New York: Doubleday Anchor, 1957), p. 113.

features of these heuristic procedures. Their findings should be invaluable for the teacher who is dealing with the creative process of composition.

These findings should be even more beneficial for those rhetoricians who are formulating new theories of invention. Steinmann called for a metatheory of rhetoric which would, among other things, "specify . . . what methods of discovery and verification it [rhetoric] must use." [4] The sources for a metatheory of rhetoric cannot be found in rhetoric itself. If methods of invention are formulated blindly in an effort to reinstate invention or to advertise a textbook in which "prewriting is stressed throughout," without any criteria against which to measure these methods of invention, then such techniques are likely to meet the fate of other transient composition solutions such as semantics, linguistics, anthologies, etc.

Psychologists' work in creative problem solving has been a struggle, grappling with unmanageable complexities of variables, battling with strict behaviorists. The bibliography here is a record of that struggle. It includes pioneers such as Duncker and Wallas, who were interested in identifying the stages of creativity, defining heuristics and locating its place in the creative process. Differing approaches such as Skinner's and Miller, Galanter, and Pribram's describe heuristics, discussing specific heuristic procedures. Most psychologists have experimented on a single procedure, e.g., direction, fluent and flexible generation, or goal-sensitivity selection. Guilford has factored creativity into a number of sub-abilities. Other psychologists, including Maltzman, are demonstrating the "trainability" of heuristic procedures. One of the latest modes of studying creative problem solving is that of the information theorists, Newell, Simon, and Shaw, whose computer work enabled them to control some of the complexity of creativity.

For both the theorist and the teacher of composition, the bibliography below presents the current work of psychology in the area of heuristics. Since education in rhetorical theory has been, up to now, mainly a question of self-education, the presentation of a bibliography is an extension of that tradition based upon the hope that, in fact, such an education is taking place. Without it, the creation of a potent contemporary rhetoric is a pious wish.

Psychological Bibliography on Heuristics

Ammons, R., and C. Ammons. "Rational Evaluation of the 'Standard Anagram Task' as a Laboratory Analogue of 'Real Life' Problem Solving," *Psychological Report* 5 (1959), 718–20.

Anderson, Harold (ed.). *Creativity and Its Cultivation.* New York: Harper and Brothers Publishers, 1959.

Anderson, Maxwell, Rhya Carpenter, and Roy Harris. *The Bases of Artistic Creation.* New Brunswick: Rutgers University Press, 1942.

---

[4] Martin Steinmann, "Rhetorical Research," *New Rhetorics,* ed. Martin Steinmann (New York: Charles Scribner's Sons, 1967), p. 27.

Anthony, W. S. "Working Backward and Working Forward in Problem Solving," *British Journal of Psychology* 57 (1966), 53–59.

Arnheim, R. "Perceptual Abstraction and Art," *Psychological Review* 54 (1947), 66–82.

Asher, James. "Toward a Neo-Field Theory of Problem Solving," *Journal of General Psychology* 68 (1963), 3–8.

Barron, Frank. "The Psychology of Creativity," *New Directions in Psychology II.* New York: Holt, Rinehart and Winston, 1965.

Bentley, Arthur. *Inquiry into Inquiries.* Boston: The Beacon Press, 1954.

Berayaev, Nicholas. *The Meaning of the Creative Act.* Translated by Donald Lawrie. New York: Collier Books, 1962.

Berlo, David. *The Process of Communication.* New York: Holt, Rinehart and Winston, 1960.

Berlyne, D. E. *Structure and Direction in Thinking.* New York: John Wiley, 1965.

Bloom, B. S., and L. J. Broder. *Problem Solving Processes of College Students.* (Supplementary Educational Monographs, No. 73.) University of Chicago, 1950.

Boas, George. *The Inquiring Mind.* La Salle, Illinois: Open Court Publishing Co., 1959.

Brassecu, Sabert. "Creativity and the Dimensions of Consciousness," *Humanitas* 4 (1968), 133–44.

———. "The Psychology of Imagination," *Scientific American* 199 (1958), 150–70.

Brilhart, John, and Lurene Jachem. "Effects of Different Patterns and Outcomes of Problem Solving: Discussion," *Journal of Applied Psychology* 48 (1964), 175–79.

Bronowski, Jacob, Henry Commager, Gordon Allport, and Paul Buck. *Imagination in the University.* Canada: University of Toronto Press, 1964.

Bruner, Jerome. "Going Beyond the Information Given," *Contemporary Approaches to Cognition.* (A Symposium Held at the University of Colorado.) Cambridge: Harvard University Press, 1957.

———. "Inhelder and Piaget's 'The Growth of Logical Thinking': A Psychologist's Viewpoint," *British Journal of Psychology* 50 (1959), 363–70.

———. *On Knowing.* Cambridge: The Belknap Press of Harvard University Press, 1963.

———. "The Act of Discovery," *Readings in the Psychology of Cognition.* Edited by Richard Anderson and David H. Ausubel. New York: Holt, Rinehart and Winston, Inc., 1966.

———. *The Process of Education.* New York: Vintage Books, 1960.

Bruner, Jerome, Jacquelin J. Goodnow, and George A. Austin. *A Study of Thinking.* New York: John Wiley and Sons, Inc., 1956.

Bruner, Jerome, R. Olicer, Pat Greenfield, et al. *Studies in Cognitive Growth.* New York: John Wiley and Sons, Inc., 1966.

Burack, B. "The Nature and Efficiency of Methods of Attack on Reasoning Problems," *Psychological Monographs* 64, No. 313 (1950).

Burke, Ronald, and Norman Maier. "Attempts to Predict Success on an Insight Problem," *Psychological Reports* 17 (1965), 303–10.

Burke, Ronald, Norman Maier, and Richard Hoffman. "Functions of Hints in Individual Problem-Solving," *American Journal of Psychology* 79 (1966), 389–99.

Burt, Cyril. "The Structure of the Mind, II," *British Journal of Educational Psychology* 19 (1949), 176–99.

Buswell, C. T. "Patterns of Thinking in Solving Problems," *University of California Public Education* 12 (1956), 63–148.

Campbell, D. T. "Blind Variations and Selective Retentions in Creative Thought as in Other Human Knowledge Processes," *Psychological Review* 67 (1960), 380–400.

Carroll, John. *Language and Thought.* Englewood Cliffs, New Jersey: Prentice-Hall, Inc., 1964.

Chomsky, Noam. "Preexamination Stress, Information Schedules, and Learning," *Journal of General Psychology* 63 (1960), 219–28.

Contemporary Approaches to Cognition. (A Symposium Held at University of Colorado.) Cambridge: Harvard University Press, 1957.

Corcoran, D. W. "Serial and Parallel Classification," *British Journal of Psychology* 58 (1967), 197–203.

Cormon, Bernard. "The Effects of Varying Amounts and Kinds of Information as Guidance in Problem Solving," *Psychological Monographs* 71, No. 431 (1957).

Daniels, Philip Bliss. *Strategies to Facilitate Problem Solving.* (Cooperative Research Project Number 1816.) Provo, Utah: Brigham Young University, 1964.

Davis, Daniel. "An Examination of Human Strategies for Acquiring Information," *Dissertation Abstracts* 26 (1966), 7454–55.

Davis, Gary. "Current Status of Research and Theory in Human Problem Solving," *Psychological Bulletin* 66 (1966), 36–54.

Davis, Gary, and Mary Manske. "An Instructional Method for Increasing Originality," *Psychonomic Science* 6 (1966), 73–74.

Dewey, J. *Art as Experience.* New York: Minton, 1934.

Dreistadt, Roy. "The Use of Analogies and Incubation in Obtaining Insights in Creative Problem Solving," *Journal of Psychology* 71 (1969), 159–75.

———. *How We Think.* Boston: Heath and Co., 1933.

Duncan, Carl. "Effect of Instruction and Information in Problem Solving," *Journal of Experimental Psychology* 65 (1963), 321–27.

Duncan, C. P. "Recent Research on Human Problem Solving," *Psychological Bulletin* 56 (1959), 397–429.

Duncker, K. "A Qualitative (Experimental and Theoretical) Study of Productive Thinking," *Journal of Genetic Psychology* 33 (1926), 642–708.

———. "On Problem Solving," *Psychological Monographs* 59, No. 270 (1945).

Eagleson, O. W. "A Study of Puzzle-Solving," *Journal of Psychology* 9 (1940), 259–68.

Edwards, M. O. "A Survey of Problem-Solving Courses," *Journal of Creative Behavior* 2 (1968), 33–51.

Eindhoven, J., and W. E. Vinacke. "Creative Processes in Painting," *Journal of General Psychology* 47 (1952), 150–58.

Eisenman, Russell, and Nancy Robinson. "Generality of Some Complexity-Simplicity Measures Related to Creativity," Proceedings of the 76th Annual Convention of the American Psychological Association, 1968, 441–42.

Eisenstadt, Marvin. "Problem-Solving Ability of Creative and Non-Creative Students," Journal of Consulting Psychology 30 (1966), 81–83.

Ewart, P. H., and J. F. Lambert. "The Effect of Verbal Instructions Upon the Formation of a Concept," Journal of General Psychology 6 (1932), 400–13.

Fergenbaum, Edward, and J. Feldman (eds.). Computers and Thought. New York: McGraw-Hill, 1963.

Flanagan, Marie, and Howard T. Gallup. "Creativity Training," Psychological Reports 21 (1967), 934.

Fraiberg, Louis. "New Views of Art and the Creative Process in Psychoanalytic Ego Psychology," The Creative Imagination. Edited by Hendrick Ruetenbeek. Chicago: Quadrangle Books, 1965.

Freedman, Jonathan. "Increasing Creativity by Free Association Training," Journal of Experimental Psychology 69 (1965), 89–91.

Gagne, Robert. Conditions of Learning. New York: Holt, Rinehart and Winston, 1965.

———. "Problem Solving and Thinking," Annual Review of Psychology 10 (1959), 147–72.

Gall, Meredith, and Gerald Mendelsohn. "Effects of Factor Technique and Subject-Experimenter Interaction on Creative Problem Solving," Journal of Personal and Social Psychology 5 (1967), 211–16.

Gallup, H. "Originality in Free and Controlled Association Response," Psychological Reports 13 (1963), 923–29.

Ghiselin, Brewster (ed.). The Creative Process. New York: A Mentor Book, 1952.

Golann, Stuart. "Psychological Study of Creativity," Psychological Bulletin 60 (1963), 548–65.

Goldner, R. H. "Individual Differences in Whole-Part Approach and Flexibility-Rigidity in Problem Solving," Psychological Monographs 71, No. 450 (1957).

Gordon, William. Synetics: The Development of Creative Capacity. New York: Harper, 1961.

Greenwald, Anthony. "Behavior Change Following a Persuasive Communication," Journal of Personal and Social Psychology 33 (1965), 370–91.

Gruber, Howard, Glenn Terrell, and Nicholas Werthermer (eds.). Contemporary Approaches to Creative Thinking. New York: Atherton Press, 1962.

Guilford, J. P. "Creativity," American Psychologist 5 (1950), 444–54.

———. "Creativity: Yesterday, Today, and Tomorrow," Journal of Creative Behavior 1 (1967), 3–14.

———. "Factors in Problem Solving," A.R.T.C. Instruction Journal 4 (1954), 197–204.

———. "Factors that Aid and Hinder Creativity," Teachers College Record 63 (1962), 380–91.

———. "Potentiality for Creativity," Gifted Child Quarterly 6 (1952), 87–90.

———. "The Structure of the Intellect," Psychological Bulletin 53 (1956), 267–93.

Hadamard, J. The Psychology of Invention in the Mathematical Field. Princeton: Princeton University Press, 1945.

Hall, Mary. "The Generality of Cognitive Complexity-Simplicity," *Dissertation Abstracts* 27 (1966), 1607.

Hallman, Ralph. "Aesthetic Pleasure and the Creative Process," *Journal of Humanistic Psychology* 6 (1966), 141–47.

Haygood, R. C., and L. E. Bourne. "Attribute and Rule-Learning Aspects of Conceptual Behavior," *Psychological Review* 72 (1965), 175–95.

Heidbreder, E. "Problem Solving in Children and Adults," *Journal of Genetic Psychology* 35 (1928), 522–45.

Helson, H. "Some Common Features of Concrete and Abstract Thinking," *American Journal of Psychology* 59 (1946), 468–72.

Hildreth, C. "Puzzle Solving with and without Understanding," *Journal of Educational Psychology* 33 (1942), 595–609.

Hilgard, E. R. *Theories of Learning.* New York: Appleton-Century-Crofts, 1948.

Hitt, William. "Toward a Two-Factor Theory of Creativity," *Psychological Record* 15 (1965), 127–32.

Hoffman, Richard. "Conditions for Creative Problem Solving," *Journal of Psychology* 52 (1961), 429–44.

Hunt, Earl. *Concept Learning: An Information Processing Problem.* New York: John Wiley and Sons, 1962.

Hutchinson, Eliot. *How to Think Creatively.* New York: Abingdon, 1949.

Huttenlocker, Janellen. "Constructing Spatial Images: A Strategy in Reasoning," *Psychological Review* 75 (1968), 550–60.

———. "Materials for the Study of Creative Thinking," *Psychological Bulletin* 28 (1931), 392–410.

Inhelder, Barbel, and Jean Piaget. *The Growth of Logical Thinking.* France: Basic Books, Inc., 1958.

Israeli, Nathan. "Set Theory Models for Research Concerning Creative Thinking and Imagining," *Journal of General Psychology* 60 (1959), 63–96.

John, E. R. "Contributions to the Study of the Problem-Solving Process," *Psychological Monographs* 7, No. 477 (1957).

John, E. R., and H. J. Rimoldi. "Sequential Observation of Complex Reasoning," *The American Psychologist* 10 (1955), 470.

Johnson, D. "A Modern Account of Problem Solving," *Psychological Bulletin* 41 (1944), 201–29.

Johnson, D., R. Lincoln, and E. Hall. "Amount of Material and Time of Preparation for Solving Problems," *Journal of Psychology* 51 (1961), 457–71.

Johnson, Edward. "An Information-Processing Model of One Kind of Problem Solving," *Psychological Monographs* 78 (1964).

Karlins, Marian, Thomas Coffman, Helmut Lamm, and Harold Schroder. "The Effect of Conceptual Complexity on Information Search in a Complex Problem-Solving Task," *Psychonomic Science* 7 (1967), 137–38.

Karlins, Marvin, Robert Lee, and Harold Schroder. "Creativity and Information Search in a Problem-Solving Context," *Psychonomic Science* 8 (1967), 165–66.

Kettner, N., J. Guilford, and P. Christensen. "A Factor Analytic Study Across Domains of Reasoning, Creativity, and Evaluation," *Psychological Monographs* 73, No. 479 (1959).

Kleinmuntz, Benjamin (ed.). *Problem Solving: Research, Method and Theory.* New York: John Wiley and Sons, Inc., 1966.

Kneller, George. *The Art and Science of Creativity.* New York: Holt, Rinehart, and Winston, 1965.

Koestler, Arthur. *The Act of Creation.* London: Hutchinson, 1964.

Kohler, W. *Gestalt Psychology.* New York: Liveright, 1947.

Kohn, P. "Serendipity on the Move: Toward a Measure of Intellectual Motivation," *Canadian Psychologist* 6 (1965), 20–31.

Kolers, P. A. "Subliminal Stimulation in Problem Solving," *American Journal of Psychology* 70 (1957), 437–44.

Kretschmer, Ernst. *The Psychology of Men of Genius.* New York: Harcourt, Brace and Co., 1931.

Langfield, H. S. *The Aesthetic Attitude.* New York: Harcourt, Brace and Co., 1920.

Laughery, K. R., and I. W. Gregg. "Simulation of Human Problem-Solving Behavior," *Psychometrika* 27 (1961), 265–82.

Lehman, Harvey. *Age and Achievement.* New Jersey: Princeton University Press, 1953.

Ling, B. C. "The Solving of Problem Situations by the Pre-School Child," *Journal of Genetic Psychology* 68 (1946), 3–28.

Linker, Eugene. "An Analysis of Human Pattern-Alternator Problem Solving," *Dissertation Abstracts* 22 (1961), 1724–25.

Luchins, C. "Mechanization in Problem Solving," *Psychological Monographs* 56, No. 248 (1942).

Lynch, Mervin, and Eleanor Swink. "Some Effects of Priming, Incubation and Creative Aptitude on Journalism Performance," *Journal of Communication* 17 (1967), 372–82.

Mackley, Bernard, and Franklin Shontz. "Creativity: Theoretical and Methodological Considerations," *Psychological Record* 15 (1965), 217–38.

Mackworth, Norman. "Originality," *American Psychologist* 20 (1965), 51–66.

Maier, Norman. "Maximizing Personal Creativity Through Better Problem Solving," *Personnel Administration* 27 (1964), 14–18.

———. "Reasoning in Humans," *Journal of Comparative Psychology* 10 (1939), 115–43.

Maier, Norman, and Ronald Burke. "Test of Concept of Availability of Functions in Problem Solving," *Psychological Reports* 19 (1966), 119–25.

Maltzman, Irving. "On the Training of Originality," *Psychological Review* 67 (1960), 229–42.

Maltzman, Irving, Marigold Belloni, and Martin Fishbein. "Experimental Studies of the Associative Variables in Originality," *Psychological Monographs* 78, No. 580 (1964).

Maltzman, Irving, W. Bogartz, and L. Breger. "A Procedure for Increasing Word Association Originality and Its Transfer Effects," *Journal of Experimental Psychology* 56 (1958), 392–98.

Mandler, J., and G. Mandler (eds.). *Thinking: From Association to Gestalt.* New York: John Wiley and Sons, Inc., 1964.

Meadow, Arnold, and Sidney Parnes. "Evaluation of Training in Creative Problem Solving," *Journal of Applied Psychology* 43 (1959), 189–94.

Mednick, Sarnoff. "The Associative Bases of the Creative Process," *Human Learning.* Edited by Arthur Stoots. New York: Holt, Rinehart and Winston, Inc., 1964.

————. "The Associative Bases of the Creative Process," *Psychological Review* 69 (1962), 220–32.

Mednick, Martha, Sarnoff Mednick, and Edward Mednick. "Incubation of Creative Performance and Specific Associative Priming," *Journal of Abnormal and Social Psychology* 69 (1964), 84–88.

Melton, A. (ed.). *Categories of Human Learning*. New York: Academic Press, 1964.

Merrifield, P. R., J. P. Guilford, P. R. Christensen, and J. W. Frick. "The Role of Intellectual Factors in Problem Solving," *Psychological Monographs* 76, No. 529 (1962).

Miller, George. *Language and Communication*. New York: McGraw-Hill, 1963.

Miller, George A., Eugene Galanter, and Karl N. Pribram. *Plans and the Structure of Behavior*. New York: Holt, Rinehart and Winston, Inc., 1960.

Monoghan, Robert. "A Systematic Way of Being Creative," *Journal of Communication* 18 (1968), 47–56.

Murphy, G. *Personality*. New York: Harper, 1947.

MacKinnon, Donald. "The Nature and Nurture of Creative Talent," *The American Psychologist* 17 (1962), 484–95.

McKellar, Peter. *Imagination and Thinking*. New York: Basic Books, Inc., 1957.

McPherson, J. H. "The People, the Problem and the Problem Solving Methods," *Journal of Creative Behavior* 2 (1968), 103–10.

Newell, A., J. C. Shaw, and Herbert Simon. "Elements of a Theory of Human Problem Solving," *Psychological Review* 65 (1958), 151–69.

————. "The Processes of Creative Thinking," *Contemporary Approaches to Creative Thinking*. Edited by Howard H. Gruber, Glenn Terrell, and Michael Wertheimer. New York: Atherton Press, 1962.

Newton, Joseph. "An Investigation of Intuitive and Analytical Thinking," *Dissertation Abstracts* 25 (1965), 616–17.

Nicholson, Patrick. "An Experimental Investigation of the Effects of Training upon Creativity," *Dissertation Abstracts* 20 (1959), 1071.

Northrop, F. S. C. *The Logic of the Sciences and the Humanities*. New York: Macmillan Co., 1947.

Osborn, Alexander. *Applied Imagination*. New York: Charles Scribner's Sons, 1953.

Parida, G. "Thinking as Problem Solving: A Gestalt Point of View," *Indiana Journal of Psychology* 33 (1958), 157–63.

Parnes, Sidney J. "Can Creativity Be Increased?" *Personnel Administration* 25 (1962), 2–9.

————. "The Literature of Creativity, Part II," *The Journal of Creative Behavior* I (Spring 1967), 191–240.

Parnes, Sidney J., and Eugene A. Brunelle. "The Literature of Creativity, Part I," *The Journal of Creative Behavior* I (Winter, 1967), 32–109.

Parnes, Sidney J., and A. Meadows. "Effects of Brainstorming Instructions on Creative Problem Solving by Trained and Untrained Subjects," *Journal of Educational Psychology* 50 (1959), 171–76.

Patrick, C. "Creative Thought in Poets," *Archives of Psychology* 26 (1935), 1–74.

————. "Creative Thought in Artists," *Journal of Psychology* 4 (1937), 35–73.

————. "Scientific Thought," *Journal of Psychology* 5 (1938), 55–83.

Sargent, S. S. "Thinking Processes at Various Levels of Difficulty," *Archives of Psychology,* No. 249 (1940).

Saugstad, P., and K. Raaheim. "Problem-Solving, Past Experience and Availability of Functions," *British Journal of Psychology* 51 (1960), 97–104.

Schaefer-Simmern, H. *The Unfolding of Artistic Activity.* Berkeley, California: University of California Press, 1948.

Schum, David. "Inferences on the Basis of Conditionally Nonindependent Data," *Journal of Experimental Psychology* 72 (1966), 401–09.

Seidenfeld, Jack. "Creativity and Cognitive Functioning," *Dissertation Abstracts* 27 (1966), 1630–31.

Sharnol, Thomas. *Originality.* London: T. Werner Laurie, 1917.

Sheerer, Martin. "Problem-Solving," *Scientific American* 208 (1963), 118–28.

Simon, Herbert, and Peter Simon. "Trial and Error Search in Solving Different Problems: Evidence from the Game of Chess," *Behavioral Science* 7 (1962), 425–29.

Skinner, B. F. "An Operant Analysis of Problem Solving," *Problem Solving: Research Method, Theory.* Edited by Benjamin Kleinmuntz. New York: John Wiley and Sons, 1966.

Smith, Paul (ed.). *Creativity: Report on the Third Communications Conference of the Art Directors Club of New York.* New York: Hastings House, 1959.

Spence, Janet. "Effects of Verbal Reinforcement Combinations and Instructional Conditions on Performance of a Problem-Solving Task," *Journal of Personal and Social Psychology* 3 (1966), 163–70.

Staats, Arthur (ed.). *Human Learning.* New York: Holt, Rinehart and Winston, Inc., 1964.

Staats, Arthur, and C. R. Staats. *Complex Human Behavior.* New York: Holt, Rinehart and Winston, 1963.

Stein, M., and Shirley Heinze. *Creativity and the Individual.* Glencoe, Illinois: Free Press, 1960.

Stein, Morris. *Survey of the Psychological Literature in the Area of Creativity with a View Toward Needed Research.* (Cooperative Research Project No. E3.) New York: New York University, 1962.

Stimmel, David. "The Effects of Past Experiences upon Problem-Solving Task Require the Use of Heuristic Procedures," *Dissertation Abstracts* 24 (1963), 1715.

Stubbings, John. "A Comparison of Torrance Tests of Creative Thinking and Guilford's Measures of Creative Ability on Sex, Cognitive, and Personality Variables," *Dissertation Abstracts* 28 (1968), 4496–97.

Suedford, Peter. "Information Processing: The Effects of Differential Pattern Components and Input Rate," *Psychonomic Science* 6 (1966), 249–50.

Szekely, L. "Productive Processes in Learning and Thinking," *Acta Psychologica* 7 (1950), 388–407.

———. "The Dynamics of Thought-Motivation," *American Journal of Psychology* 56 (1943), 100–04.

Taton, R. *Reason and Chance in Scientific Discovery.* New York: Science Editions, 1962.

Taylor, Calvin (ed.). *Creativity: Progress and Potential.* New York: McGraw-Hill Book Co., 1964.

———— (ed.). *Instructional Media and Creativity.* New York: John Wiley and Sons, 1966.

———— (ed.). *Widening Horizons in Creativity.* New York: John Wiley and Sons, Inc., 1964.

Taylor, Calvin W., and Frank Barron (eds.). *Scientific Creativity: Its Recognition and Development.* New York: John Wiley and Sons, Inc., 1964.

Thompson, R. *The Psychology of Thinking.* Hammondsworth: Penguin Books, 1959.

Thurstone, L. L. "A Psychologist Discusses the Mechanism of Thinking," *The Nature of Creative Thinking.* (Industrial Research Institute.) New York: New York University Press, 1957.

Torrance, Paul E. *Guiding Creative Talent.* New Jersey: Prentice-Hall, Inc., 1962.

————. "Current Research on the Nature of Creative Talent," *Journal of Counseling Psychology* 6 (1959), 309–15.

Torrance, Paul E., and Ethel Hansen. "The Question-Asking Behaviors of Highly Creative and Less Creative Basic Business Teachers," *Psychological Reports* 17 (1965), 815–18.

Tresselt, M. E., and M. S. Mayzner. "Switching Behavior in a Problem-Solving Task," *Journal of Psychology* 50 (1960), 349–54.

True, Herbert. "Creativity as a Function of Idea Fluency, Practicability, and Specific Training," *Dissertation Abstracts* 17 (1957), 401–02.

Underwood, B. J. "An Orientation for Research in Thinking," *Psychological Review* 59 (1952), 209–20.

Vinacki, W. Edgar. *The Psychology of Thinking.* New York: McGraw-Hill Book Co., 1952.

Walkup, Lewis. "Creativity in Science Through Visualization," *Journal of Creative Behavior* 1 (1967), 283–90.

————. "Creativity in Science Through Visualization," *Perceptual and Motor Skills* 21 (1965), 35–41.

Wallas, G. *The Art of Thought.* New York: Harcourt, Brace and Co., 1926.

Weaver, H. E., and E. H. Madden. "Direction in Problem Solving," *Journal of Psychology* 27 (1949), 331–45.

Weinberg, Gerald. "Experiments in Problem Solving," Unpublished Master's thesis, University of Michigan, 1965.

Weir, Morton. "Developmental Changes in Problem-Solving Strategies," *Psychological Review* 71 (1964), 473–90.

Welch, Livingston. "Recombination of Ideas in Creative Thinking," *Journal of Applied Psychology* 30 (1964), 638–43.

Wells, Herbert, and Daniel Watson. "Strategy Training and Practice in Disjunctive Concept Attainment," *Psychological Reports* 17 (1965), 925–26.

Wertheimer, M. *Productive Thinking.* New York: Harper and Brothers, 1945.

Westcott, Malcolm. "On the Measurement of Intuitive Leaps," *Psychological Reports* 9 (1961), 267–74.

Westcott, Malcolm, and Jane Ronzoni. "Correlation of Intuitive Thinking," *Psychological Reports* 12 (1963), 595–613.

Wild, D. W. *Intuition.* Cambridge: University Press, 1938.

Wilner, A. "An Experimental Analysis of Analogical Reasoning," *Psychological Reports* 15 (1964), 479–94.

Wilson, R. C., J. P. Guilford, P. R. Christensen, and D. J. Lewis. "A Factor-Analytic Study of Creative-Thinking Abilities," *Psychometrika* 19 (1954), 297–311.

Young, Marguerite L. "Modification of Problem-Solving Strategies," *Perceptual and Motor Skills* 21 (1968), 127–34.

The Problem of Problem Solving

Ann E. Berthoff

Berthoff's discussion serves as a corrective to implications that might arise from Lauer's essay; however, Berthoff's argument against heuristics is perilous. As my introduction to this volume should have made clear, I can envision no "technology" of composition, no effective programing of students for efficiency in learning to write—nor would most composition teachers want such efficiency. From my point of view, "efficient" exercises in sentence building, for instance, are downright morbid because they miss the point concerning the creative act of producing meaningful language in a rhetorical situation.

Berthoff says, "The concept of problem solving serves the belief that the school's function is to prepare citizens for life in a technological society." But any educational methodology can well serve that function—and lack of methodology is surely a method or at least a dogma.

The concept of problem solving (or topics or heuristics) is totally neutral; problem solving can solve the problems of a technological society, but it can also (possibly) solve the problem of the student who is isolated within his or her selfhood, unable to bridge the gap between the self and others simply because he or she does not know what to say. All heuristics are nothing more than ways whereby the writer can "walk around" a subject, viewing it from different angles, taking it apart in various ways, probing it. In the process, the student presumably develops new perspectives. Such activity could well be subversive of the goals of a technological society. And, in any case, society is technological. Surely it is the composition teacher's duty to help the student cope with this fact.

Two other points need to be made. First, composition teachers are in the ghetto simply because they have not done their homework in the way that literature teachers have. There is a body of theory that adds depth and intellectual fascination to the study of literature. In our self-made ghetto, compositionists have neglected theory, opting to concern ourselves with the prag-

matics of day-to-day teaching. The shallowness of our field has alienated the best people in English departments and has left us with very little to talk about, except what works in certain circumstances.

Second, we have a bias that often makes us recoil from modes of conceptualization that are not sanctioned by the humanistic tradition, for most of us have exactly the same training as our colleagues in literature have, all of us function within English departments, and everyone who has functioned within an English department knows where its values lie. In effect, the very strength of literary studies as a humane discipline is also the basis of the weakness that keeps composition teachers who are trained in literature from escaping their ghetto.

Unless both the textmakers and the teachers of composition investigate beyond the field of English, beyond even the area of rhetorical studies for the solution to the compositional problem, they will find themselves wandering in an endless maze.

—Janice Lauer, *CCC,* December, 1970

Composition courses should be eliminated, not improved: eliminated because they help to support an oppressive system.

—Louis Kampf, *CCC,* October, 1970

Those who set themselves the problem of what to do in English composition very often proceed by way of converting English composition itself to a problem. Sister Janice Lauer considers "the composition problem" beyond the competence of English teachers to solve; unless we seek the help of psychologists who have studied problem-solving, we will not solve ours. Even for Professor Kampf, "composition courses" are a problem, if only because they might prove difficult to get rid of; there is no question, however, that they should be abolished since they manifest and support that system which exploits and enthralls every one of us.

It would be worthwhile to employ each of these arguments in developing a critique of the other: every issue in public life has mutually defining psychological and political aspects, the exact relationship of which it is a primary and continuing intellectual task to discover. Such an analysis might at least reveal certain shortcomings in the articles from which I have quoted above. If Kampf fails to raise in any helpful way the truly revolutionary question ("What then is to be done?") because he does not consider learning in its psychological aspects, Sister Janice Lauer, with her narrow understanding of heuristics, virtually precludes from consideration all approaches but those sanctified by the technologists of learning; approaches which are politically not above suspicion. Indeed, each of these arguments can be faulted on psycholcgical and political grounds, separately considered, but the important point is, I think, that neither Professor Kampf nor Sister Janice Lauer considers the crucial interdependency of psychological and political factors. In radical critics of education, from Jane Addams and Maria Montessori to I. A. Richards and Paulo Freire, what we may chiefly value is not their prescriptions but their understanding of this juncture, the necessary point of departure for any philosophy of education being the account offered of the relationship of society and knowledge.

In the remarks that follow I will address myself to the somewhat more limited topic of the psychological inadequacies and political dangers of problem-solving as a pedagogical concept.

If "problem-solving" is only jargon for the process of raising and formulating questions, then it is, of course, a primary operation of mind. Insofar as it refers to those acts of naming and judgment by which abstraction is accomplished, problem-solving is of central importance to a student of language and literature, to any student of anything. But as a concept developed by educational psychologists, "problem-solving" may well be considered merely that mental operation which, because it is the most easily tested, is the one psychologists know most about.

If studying "the problem of composition" leads us to consider the use of metaphor, the logic of analogy, the various means by which we come to know our knowledge and hence ourselves, then it can be enormously beneficial. If, for instance, we follow such heuristic procedures as those set forth by W. J. J. Gordon, whose *Synectics* is listed in Sister Janice Lauer's bibliography, and by John Wilson and Edward De Bono, whose *Thinking with Concepts* and *New Think: The Use of Lateral Thinking in the Generation of New Ideas* she does not include, then we English teachers will be playing on our home ice; for this approach to problem-solving is consonant with what we may know of poetics and the grammar and rhetoric of motives. But, more usually, "problem-solving" provides no such pedagogical grist. Several afternoons spent sampling Sister Janice Lauer's bibliography convinces me that the guides she recommends are, for the most part perhaps, themselves perplexed. Accepting their guidance, we would be led from our English maze only to be abandoned among task definitions, communication frames, nonverbal processes and all the other features of a strangely familiar landscape. It is familiar because it is the scene of the derailment of the Dartmouth Conference. The Anglo-American Conference on the Teaching of English sought guidance from precisely those quarters to which Sister Janice Lauer is recommending that we turn. In trying to solve the problem of what "English" is, the Dartmouth conferees failed to undertake the real job of formulating working concepts which of course requires that the purposes of education be considered: that is a political act, and it was avoided.[1] Instead, the Conference concluded that "English" is somehow involved with "intellectual" and "crea-

---

[1] See Wayne O'Neil's damning assessment of the Dartmouth Conference, *Harvard Educational Review,* Spring, 1969.

tive" uses of language, that what we teach is "communication" and "expression." "The intellectual uses of language" were identified with problem-solving and then posited as the polar opposite of "creativity." This spurious opposition (it is not a logical antithesis) of the "creative" and the "intellectual" has been the primary contribution of the psychologists of learning to the field of the teaching of English. The harm it has caused is scarcely calculable.

Teachers studying heuristics as understood by Sister Janice Lauer will soon discover that a theory of learning as problem-solving requires a view of language as signal code, a notion that converts meaning to "information," form to "medium," interpretation to "decoding," etc. By thus misconceiving of the human use of language, communication theory or, rather, pedagogy deriving from it falsely defines the forms of knowing. There is a fundamental failure to recognize that "the linguistic adult," in the current phrase, who comes to school is an *animal symbolicum*.

The best argument I have read against information theory as the basis for a philosophy of language is set forth by I. A. Richards in several essays reprinted in *So Much Nearer* (New York, 1968) which along with his earlier *Speculative Instruments* (New York, 1955) provides an important line of defense against the influence of psychologists and linguistic scientists operating outside the field of their competence. A careful reading of these books would sound the warning that a receptivity to many of the notions encouraged by the technicians on Sister Janice Lauer's list precludes an interest in the symbolic nature of language, the purposes of literature and in what Richards calls "the self-ordering growth of mind."

Psychologists have recently noted that the rules for meaningful learning may be different from the rules for nonsense learning: it is a discovery which could have been hastened by abandoning the theory that language functions like a signal code and we can hope that others like it will be made with increasing frequency. Meanwhile, back in their maze, English teachers should dare to raise their own fresh questions about the nature of learning and knowing and should dare, furthermore, to answer some of those questions which have been thought to lie in the province of the problem-solvers, that protectorate of educational psychology.

A psychology of learning, no matter how carefully researched or how liberal its assumptions, can be politically dangerous unless it is conceived in the context of a sound sociology of knowledge. I have been suggesting that "heuristics" as conceived by Sister Janice Lauer's problem-solvers is philosophically shallow, but the real trouble with problem-solving as a pedagogical concept is that it constitutes a clear and present political danger. The case can easily be made that problem-solving, as conceived by educational psychologists, is the concept of learning our bureaucratized society needs in order to realize the philosophy of education that is most in keeping with its institutional biases. The concept of problem-solving serves the belief that the school's function is to prepare citizens for life in a technological society. Here is a recent formulation: "It is no longer possible for our society to operate effectively without a substantially greater capacity for scientific thinking on the part of average people than has heretofore been necessary. . . . Science is essentially problem solving." [2] But of course a critical recognition of the alliance between the needs of commercial interests and what the American public schools offer is nothing new. For instance, Jane Addams observed in 1907 that "it is possible that the business men, whom we in America so tremendously admire, have really been dictating the curriculum of our public schools, in spite of the conventions of the educators and the suggestions of university professors." The problems of American education which Jane Addams defined in *Democracy and Social Ethics* have not been alleviated in any fundamental respect; indeed, it might be claimed that matters are worse since "educators" and "university professors" nowadays agree with the business community, insofar as they support a cheapened philosophy of education with their notion that problem-solving is central to the learning process.

Since in many respects Jane Addams' analysis would surely be enthusiastically endorsed by Louis Kampf and other radical critics I have read, it might be pertinent to point out that her conclusions differ as much from the despairing counsel of those for whom abolition of the schools—or at least of English—seems the most rational and humane option as they do from the service-oriented, enriched learning programs of modern educators. She considered that history and art, a sense of continuity and sharpened perceptions were the only means to that social consciousness which is alone truly humanizing. Jane Addams did not preach to those who came to night classes at Hull House. She did not simply encourage them to "feel free to fret about themselves and their surroundings," as Kampf would have it; she set about to teach them how to be free. She did it in many ways, explaining how to avoid exploitative merchants (consumer education) and how to organize locally for adequate garbage collection (community control); she taught them how to be free by making literature available to them as a form of knowledge in which they could discover themselves.[3]

For Jane Addams, making the cultural revolution was profoundly connected with the development and cultivation of literacy. Though early in his article Kampf states that "writing might be one way for students to begin the arduous task of discovering themselves and the world around them," he does not return to this notion in calling for a cultural revolution. The problem, he writes, is "not how we might improve composition courses but whether we can change the social context within which they are taught." Yes: and what are the classroom implications of that aim? The vital question for teachers, it seems to me, is this: Can we change the social context in which

[2] This statement is to be found in an introductory essay in *Learning about Learning,* a U.S. government conference report edited by Jerome Bruner (OE-12019; 1966). It is patently absurd: the chief cultural significance of the technological revolution is, precisely, that fewer people have to be concerned with any kind of thinking at all. And whatever science is "essentially," it is not problem-solving. Such unquestioned assumptions are a feature of contemporary educational theory, as it is represented in this report.

[3] She read George Eliot aloud to them after a long day's night in the sweat shops. In this respect, she is the forerunner of such teachers as Dan Fader, who has remarked that many of today's youngsters will have no sense of identity, no sense of dignity, unless they get it from books.

English composition is taught by the way we teach English composition? And that is a question that neither the problem-solvers nor the theoretical revolutionaries can help us answer.

When we make problem-solving central to a philosophy of education we effectively separate learning from knowing: the results are philosophically disastrous and politically dangerous. If we are to make the cultural revolution, I believe we must attend to the tired slogan, "Begin with where they are." And if we begin with our students as problem-solvers then we will have cut ourselves and them off from the possibility of discovering the natural resources of mind. The social context of English composition courses cannot be defined in either political or psychological terms unless it is understood in philosophical terms and that means asking where it is indeed that our students are, not assuming that they are "nonverbal," as was the custom a few years ago, or that they are "linguistic adults," meaning not "language animals" but well-programmed encoders. Finding a place for literature and composition in the curriculum means finding a place for reading and writing in our students' lives, creating a social context for such study. It means that we have to define the common ground of all school work, of all disciplines, an undertaking that is philosophical precisely because it is concerned with that juncture of the public and personal, the social and individual, the political and the psychological.

We need all the help we can get. We need to learn from great teachers like Montessori, who began with the child not as a communicator or problem-solver, bifurcated into a sometime-creator, but with the child as a form-finder and form-creator; with the child as a human person, not a machine or super-pigeon. Sylvia Ashton-Warner has asked, "What might come of infant teachers visiting the university and professors visiting the infant room?" What indeed! For one thing, we could learn from her how the words of the "key vocabulary" —those words charged with meaning—are "the captions of the dynamic life itself." There are a dozen points of departure for us in *Teacher,* which despite its lush prose, is more valuable than three dozen articles in the psychology journals. We need "to investigate beyond the field of English," as Sister Janice Lauer has said. The revolutionary intellectual discoveries of our time which bear most importantly on the psychology of learning are that the unconscious is linguistic and that implicit in the act of knowing is the potentiality for social change: but neither Lévi-Strauss nor Paulo Freire will find a place on a list of problem-solvers.

An attentive reading of Paulo Freire would be, I think, of immediate heuristic value for English teachers; the challenges of teaching Brazilian peasants to read and write and of teaching the American disadvantaged and disenchanted to read and write have a great deal in common.[4] If instead of problem-solving we encourage what Paulo Freire calls "problematizing the existen-

[4] Two long essays have appeared in *Harvard Educational Review* (May and August 1970): "The Adult Literacy Process as Cultural Action for Freedom" and "Cultural Action and Conscientization." Freire's *Pedagogy of the Oppressed* (New York, 1970) sets forth a sociology of knowledge which brilliantly defines the political potentialities of the awakened imagination.

tial situation" we will be undertaking revolutionary tasks indeed. For English teachers it means that we join our students in the rediscovery of the reality of our common lives; the critical assessment of the language which builds our knowledge of the world is the primary step in the transformation of that reality. With his assumption about the role of language in creating the world in which we live, Freire can say that "teaching men to read and write is no longer a matter of . . . memorizing an alienated word, but a difficult apprenticeship in naming the world." Naming the world means learning to see and hear, learning to listen, perhaps even to "flowery apostrophes to Nature" with which Kampf is so impatient. Learning to see what you're looking at—rubbish in the playground, drunkards on the subway, nouns in a stanza, flowers in a field—and to hear what's being said—lies in official pronouncements, truth in the language of the streets—wins knowledge that can liberate. No "learning experience," no matter what the "learning environment," can liberate if the act of naming does not become an act of knowing. "Know your knowledge" was Coleridge's advice to the young. It is still a revolutionary precept.

I offer in conclusion some observations and comments which I have found to have heuristic value.

> A discussion of the reasons for the choice of words . . . can become an introduction to the theory of all choices.   —I. A. Richards

> Plato has said that "questioning and answering each other in discourse" is our only access to the world of "idea."   —Ernst Cassirer

> Though all organisms are critics in the sense that they interpret the signs about them, the experimental, speculative technique made available by speech would seem to single out the human species as the only one possessing an equipment for going beyond the criticism of experience to a criticism of criticism. We not only interpret the characters of events (manifesting in our responses all the graduations of fear, apprehension, expectation, assurance, for which there are rough behavioristic counterparts in animals)—we may also interpret our interpretations.   —Kenneth Burke

> Thought is like all behavior. The child does not adapt himself right away to the new realities he is discovering and gradually constructing for himself. He must start by laboriously incorporating them within himself and into his own activity. This egocentric assimilation characterizes the beginnings of thought just as it characterizes the process of socialization.   —Jean Piaget

> The recognition of structure gives the mind its ability to find meaning.
> —Susanne K. Langer

> Man, disciplined through liberty, begins to desire the true and only prize which will never belittle or disappoint him—the birth of human power and liberty within that inner life of his from which his activities must spring.
> —Maria Montessori

> For every one pupil who needs to be guarded from a weak excess of sensibility there are three who need to be awakened from the slumber of cold

vulgarity. The task of the modern educator is not to cut down jungles but to irrigate deserts. The right defense against false sentiments is to inculcate just sentiments. By starving the sensibility of our pupils we only make them easier prey to the propagandist when he comes. For famished nature will be avenged and a hard heart is no infallible protection against a soft head.—C. S. Lewis

The untrained mind, wearied with meaningless detail, when it gets an opportunity to make its demand heard, asks for general philosophy and background.
—Jane Addams

No child ever asked for a Janet or a John costume.—Sylvia Ashton-Warner

Speaking the word is not a true act if it is not at the same time associated with the right of self-expression and world expression, of creating and recreating, of deciding and choosing and ultimately participating in society's historical process. . . . As an event calling forth the critical reflection of both the learners and educators, the literacy process must relate speaking the word to transforming reality and to man's role in this transformation.—Paulo Freire

Languages are created by the poor who then go on renewing them forever.
—The Schoolboys of Barbiana

Response to Ann E. Berthoff, "The Problem of Problem Solving"

Janice Lauer

Although I feel that Ann Berthoff's criticism of work on heuristic procedures by psychologists is misdirected and unsupported, I do agree with her comments on heuristics, finding them in no way incompatible with work in psychology. I especially agree with her remarks on Paulo Freire's "problematizing the existential situation." In fact, this conception of "problem" comes close to my understanding of the term and paraphrases well the notion of "creative problem solving" held by a number of psychologists. In addition, her closing "heuristic" nuggets give authority and pungent formulation to some of the ideas on heuristic procedures that are being identified as powerful forces in creativity by those, including psychologists, who are examining heuristics theoretically.

However, recent work by cognitive psychologists should lead us to expect that readers will interpret what they read in terms of their own categories;

hence I was not surprised to find my discussion on "Heuristics and Composition" translated by Ann Berthoff into "Problem Solving and Composition." But her conception of problem solving as limited to a narrow area of educational psychology-problem solving-learning is not the one held by the majority of psychologists in my bibliography. Evidently Ann Berthoff's "several afternoons of sampling" my two hundred item bibliography did not enable her to realize that most of the psychologists working on heuristics are doing so in the context of creativity or, as some of them label it: "creative problem solving." They see a sense of the problematic as the impetus for creativity. When a person becomes aware that elements in his universe are incompatible, when he has a need that cannot be fulfilled, his complacency is disturbed enough to create—to find a solution, a reordering, a fulfillment.

Problem solving as Ann Berthoff conceives of it is aimed at finding the right solution, the correct answer, in a finite number of steps governed by explicit rules. Problem solving as creativity seeks only reasonable answers and is open-ended. Problem solving as creativity uses not sets of rules but heuristic procedures, systematic but flexible guides to effective guessing. It is this second kind of activity that is relevant to composition. These distinctions and much broader ones were evidently not detected in the sampling which led Ann Berthoff to label all those psychologists as "the technicians." A careful reading would have distinguished between behaviorists, gestaltists, factor-analysts, and information-theorists—each with different starting points, methods, and conclusions. They would hardly be happy with the following description of their research: "This spurious opposition (it is not a logical antithesis) of the 'creative' and the 'intellectual' has been the primary contribution of the psychologists of learning to the field of the teaching of English" (93).

A thorough study of the items on the bibliography might also have revealed that work in psychology on heuristics and creativity is still quite recent and exploratory. Some psychologists are still defending the psychological legitimacy of their studies on creativity against those who accuse them of swimming in waters too complex and uncontrollable. Many are still experimenting to find methodology better suited to the study of creativity. Most studies deal with only small segments of this complex behavior. Is Ann Berthoff suggesting that psychologists have no right to study this area? Is she objecting to the tentative nature of the variety of insights that are emerging from these heterogenous studies? Is she asking that we wait until psychology furnishes a conclusive explanation of heuristics before we examine its work? All of these might be possible objections to raise, but none of them are made. Instead her quarrels rest on the false assumption that psychology has *one* contribution to make, a contribution which she identifies with an overly narrow conception of problem solving. This assumption leads her to assert such extreme consequences as:

> Teachers studying heuristics as understood by Janice Lauer will soon discover that a theory of learning as problem solving requires a view of language as

signal code, a notion that converts meaning to "information," form to "medium," interpretation to "decoding," etc. (93).

or

A receptivity to many of the notions [which?] encouraged by the technicians on Janice Lauer's list precludes an interest in the symbolic nature of language (93).

In addition, Ann Berthoff laments the psychologists' polarizing of the creative and the intellectual, but she indulges in a few polarities herself which are as unsubstantiated as is her own accusation:

(1) psychology / creativity (93)
(2) psychologists: information theorists: linguistic scientists / those interested in the symbolic nature of language (93)
(3) problem-solving learning / knowing (95)
(4) problem-solving / discovery of the natural resources of the mind (95)
(5) child (using problem solving) as machine and super pigeon / child as form finder and form creator (95)
(6) articles in *Teacher* / three dozen articles in psychology journals (95)
(7) problem solving / problematizing the existential situation (95).

Dichotomizing, especially unsubstantiated polarization, rarely leads to understanding the complexity of human experience. At the same time, failure to make distinctions (not necessarily oppositions) and to reason logically often lead to cloudy conclusions. In one section, Ann Berthoff shackles "problem solving, as conceived by educational psychology" to "preparation for life in a technological society." She states her argument in the following passage in which she quotes, and misuses, Jerome Bruner's argument:

The case can easily be made that problem solving, as conceived by educational psychologists, is the concept of learning our bureau-critized [sic] society needs in order to realize the philosophy of education that is most in keeping with its institutional biases. The concept of problem solving serves the belief that the school's function is to prepare citizens for life in a technological society. Here is a recent formulation [Jerome Bruner's]: "It is no longer possible for our society to operate effectively without a substantially greater capacity for scientific thinking on the part of average people that has heretofore been necessary. . . . Science is essentially problem solving."

Here Ann Berthoff has failed to distinguish between Bruner's term, "science," and her own term, "technology." Secondly, she has assumed that if scientific thinking is essentially problem solving, therefore problem solving is essentially scientific thinking. Hence her ability to conclude that if psychologists advocate problem solving, they are thereby narrowing learning to scientific thinking. *Non sequitur.*

This misinterpretation of Bruner as well as of my bibliography springs, I believe, from a sense of threat which is widespread—the fear of many humanists that they and their values will be gobbled up by the "scientists." Such a fear creates an atmosphere inimical to the changes needed to solve our very real educational problems. The effect of being too critical too soon of hypotheses is no hypotheses at all; it discourages potentially useful insights. I might have left out of the bibliography the information theorists, Newell, Simon, and Shaw, as being less obviously useful, than, say, the gestaltists, but they have contributions to make, or at least it is too soon to conclude that they don't. When confronted with difficult problems, as is the English teacher today, it is unwise to close off any sources of solution; not unless we enjoy the problems.

I would like to argue for pluralism in our thinking. Those working seriously on heuristics are dealing with studies in psychology, philosophy, mathematics, and rhetoric as they must, since this is where the important theoretical work is being done. I would hope that Ann Berthoff's tolerance would extend beyond those pragmatic works such as Gordon's *Synectics,* which has immediate practical application to composition and to the rest of the items on the bibliography, mainly pure research and theory, which require the creative cooperation of both the theorist and the teacher of composition if they are to affect the quality of our instruction.

I would like to conclude by removing the red flag from the discussion of "Heuristics and Composition" by rephrasing my statement which has caused so much concern:

> Unless both the textmakers and the teachers of composition investigate beyond the field of English, beyond even the area of rhetorical studies for insight into the nature of the creative process of composition, "the process of naming the world," they will find themselves wandering in an endless maze.

I would hope that Ann Berthoff would now remove the red herring.

Response to Janice Lauer, "Counterstatement"

Ann E. Berthoff

Janice Lauer has genially removed "the red flag"—the term "problem solving"—but our disagreement over the alleged benefit to English teachers of research in "heuristics" as defined by psychologists is rather more than a quibble; it is a matter of concepts and premises and not of words only. Adding "creative" to "problem solving" doesn't really solve the problem of problem solving which is, as I see it, that those who reduce and limit the operation of imagination in this way—psychologists who undertake to study "mentation" or problem solving or concept formation or creativity—leave out, in order to accumulate "meaningful data" and quantifiable results, the very factors which we as English teachers should be concerned with. The principle of these is the nature of language itself as an organ of growth, a speculative instrument, our means of creating and discovering those forms which are the bearers of meaning.

English teachers who turn to psychologists for their pedagogical concepts and their epistemology, as they did at the Dartmouth Conference, tend to develop assumptions about language which are diverting: they lead away from the questions of how the formative powers of language can be made available to our students. I have discussed the hazards of those assumptions in a recent article in *College English* ("From Problem-solving to a Theory of Imagination," March, 1972) and will not repeat my argument here; instead, I offer the following quotation from a psychologist who is considering the "fundamentally psychological problem of how individuals attain concepts and how these concepts are related to word meanings." John B. Carrol writes: "There is a gap between the findings of psychologists on the conditions under which very simple 'concepts' are learned in the psychological laboratory and the experiences of teachers in teaching the 'for real' concepts that are contained in the curricula of the schools. It is not self-evident that there is any continuity at all between learning 'DAX' as the name of a certain geometrical shape of a certain color and learning the meaning of the word 'longitude.' Even if such a continuity exists, it is not clear how the relative difficulty or complexity of concepts can be assessed" ("Words, Meanings and Concepts," *Harvard Educational Review*, Spring, 1964). This gap—and it is the same as that which obtains between "problem solving tasks" or "information processing" and the uses of English—cannot be closed so long as language is conceived of as a kind of signal code, a refinement of the "symbol system" a bee uses to indicate to his fellows where the flowers are.

The philosophical issues involved in assessing the contributions of psychology to an understanding of what we do when we compose are complex. I would urge anyone who wishes to understand them to read Chapter Two of Susanne K. Langer's *Mind: An Essay on Human Feeling* (Baltimore, 1967). There she examines those "idols of the laboratory"—Physicalism, Methodology, Jargon, Objectivity, Mathematization—which have meant that psychology has not developed "the powerful and freely negotiable concepts in terms of which to handle the central subject matter, which is human mentality— properly, and not foolishly, called 'mind.' "

But shall we come to cases? Let me pose some questions which I am certain Janice Lauer would agree are of interest both to teachers of English and to educational psychologists: How do creative people learn? How is creating related to questioning? How are the forms of notation related to one another? Is there a relationship between the sketch and a painting comparable to that between a draft and a finished composition? What are the different ways in which an artist chooses what is "right"? What does he mean when he says it "feels right"? How does a dancer revise a dance? How does a musician correct an interpretation? How does a poet revise his poem? Is "what comes first?" a question all creators recognize as a really tough one? How do they pose the question? When do they discover that they've decided it? How do artists get started on a work? One scientist has said that he "gets a hunch" and then goes about collecting facts that support it, discarding those that don't fit: how is this comparable to what we do when we compose?

These are all questions which I believe we can ask pretty much on our own. By choosing judiciously from Janice Lauer's bibliography and by looking again at those writers we happen to admire; by reading the notebooks and journals of artists and thinkers (Leonardo, Delacroix, Klee, G. M. Hopkins, Coleridge, Thoreau, et al.) and by talking with present-day artists and artisans, we can learn anew the sources and modes of the creative imagination. This kind of inquiry is not the special province of "experts" in the field of psychology; it is the principal legacy of the Romantic Movement. English teachers have access to knowledge concerning the form-creating powers of "the prime agent of all human perception," as well as the form-creating powers of the Secondary Imagination, whenever we remember where to look.

Now here are two statements from creative persons: "There are some enterprises in which a careful disorderliness is the true method." That's Herman Melville. Here's Alfred North Whitehead: "There is a state of imaginative, muddled suspense which precedes any successful inductive generalization." I believe that speculation taking these two wise sayings as a point of departure could lead us to understand, for instance, why the Formal Outline is properly the last step and not the first in composing; why it is so useful to keep options open, to keep freedom of choice alive, especially at first, by writing phrases, images, sets of oppositions, by thoughtful doodling instead of depending on the concoction of topic sentences; why it is that "pre-writing" is so painful for those who have not learned the uses of chaos; how it is that naming and re-naming, developing analogies and metaphors can lead us to discover "the shape of content"; it could help us to understand what Paul Klee means when he notes: "I begin with chaos; it is the most natural start. In so doing, I feel at rest because I may, at first, be chaos myself." And so on.

If we make use of the knowledge we have as teachers of English, we can pursue such speculation fruitfully, without the guidance of psychologists who are studying the "area" of "creativity." For creativity is not an *area;* it is the heart of the matter and the matter is using the mind to create images and models by means of language. The "creative problem solving" we develop as we learn to compose is called *thinking;* and thinking is something other than "effective guessing," which is what Janice Lauer tells us the psychologists mean by *heuristics*. Anything pedagogically useful that can be said about thinking (remembering that artists use their minds; they don't just emote) will also be true of the process of composing. If composition is conceived as the expression of thinking about experience—the experience of ideas, of events, of what is happening, of problems, of feelings, of words, poems, stories —then practice can develop certain capacities: to relate the particular example to the general concept; to develop analogies; to set up limits (including grammatical and syntactical limits); to discover contexts and how they change according to need and purpose, consciously and unconsciously; to balance the concrete and the abstract; to frame definitions and revise them; to keep in mind both the example and the general law, precept, or principle illustrated; to conceptualize by means of metaphor, to define with imagery; to relate cause and effect, and I and the Other, Now and Then—past and future. In this frame of reference, critical writing is necessarily creative and creative writing will be critical; such practice in composition is *heuristic* in the sense in which philosophers use the term: it exercises the means by which we come to discover and to understand.

My aim in the rather polemical article to which Janice Lauer has responded patiently was to reject the notion that English teachers are amateurs in the field of understanding the activity of the mind. They can develop a serviceable, relevant, politically sound and philosophically coherent pedagogy on the basis of what they understand about the nature of the imagination. They do not have to seek guidance from "experts" who have studied such matters as "goal-sensitivity selection" and "product pleasure" and "the sensitization and activation of cognitive skills." The psychologists factor "creativity" into sub-abilities so that they can state laws about trivial coding and sign recognition; to think that they are dealing with imagination is a delusion.

I. A. Richards urged in *The Philosophy of Rhetoric* that rhetoric should be rehabilitated as "an inquiry into how words work." He argued that rhetoric "must take charge of the criticism of its own assumptions and not accept them, more than it can help, ready-made from other studies. How words mean, is not a question to which we can safely accept an answer either as an inheritance from common sense . . . or as something vouched for by another science, by psychology, say—since other sciences use words themselves and not least delusively when they address themselves to these questions." The advice and the warning of 1936 remain cogent.

Report of the Committee on the
Nature of Rhetorical Invention

In 1970 two conferences on rhetoric, sponsored by the Speech Communication Association and funded by the National Endowment for the Humanities, generated a group of papers concerning rhetoric, and these were published in The Prospect of Rhetoric. *Members of the committee that prepared the report on invention were Robert L. Scott, James R. Andrews, Howard H. Martin, J. Richard McNally, William F. Nelson, Michael M. Osborn, Arthur L. Smith, and Harold Zyskind.*

Elsewhere—Philosophy and Rhetoric (Winter 1973)—I have published a detailed reaction to the conferences and in particular to the report of the committee on invention. Most readers of this report will see that it contains a great many problems.

There are, however, two respects in which the report is valuable for teachers of composition. First, the set of topics outlined is interesting and usable. Second, the recommendations at the end of the report are themselves a kind of set of topics which the teacher can use to explore the problem of invention.

Granted, the topics in the report are too complicated for unsophisticated students, but the teacher can easily transform them into a relatively simple set. This transformation will largely be making the topics more direct and less jargonistic. Here is one way in which these topics might be transformed:

(1) What relationship does the subject have to the present? For example: What are the relationships between the drug culture and current society? Or: Why is Hamlet *meaningful to readers in the 1970s?*

(2) What are the components of the subject? For example: What are the bases for a decision to "drop out" of society? Or: What would be the ideal components of a rapid transit system for the Los Angeles basin?

(3) What is the effect of the subject upon people?

(4) What is the "system" that underlies the subject? For example: What is the structure of Hamlet? *Or: How does an urban transit system work?*

(5) What form does the subject have? This amounts to delineating the features that make the subject what it physically is.

I am not suggesting that this is the only or the best transformation of the set of topics outlined in the report. What I am trying to demonstrate is that these topics can be changed so that they will be useful to students—and also that one set of topics can generate another set.

Man's Rhetorical Environment

We begin with the assumption that a vital aspect of man's experience is rhetorical. By this we mean that every man will find himself in circumstances in which he cannot act alone, in which he must seek to act cooperatively with others, or in which others will seek to make him act cooperatively.

From his interactions with others, man finds that his ability to share symbols gives him the power to meet his rhetorical needs with rhetorical materials. Because of compelling social realities man's consciousness of his rhetorical environment is expanding. The technological revolution in media and in traditional forms of persuasion have significantly extended man's inventive needs and potentialities. These changes are critical to his ability to share and perceive symbols.

In the pages that follow, we understand that the old concepts of *speaker* and *audience* or the newer concepts of *source* and *receiver* only point vaguely to the varied nature of the roles of interacting communicators. Likewise, the old term *message* is scarcely adequate to contain the shifting reality of current discourse and of non-discursive forms.

The General Nature of Rhetorical Invention

Rhetoric's traditional involvement with persuasion about probabilities links it inevitably with invention. The subjects about which men persuade do not by themselves mandate an order to discourses. Invention, in sum, is not a product of necessity. It depends on an action of the mind. In more limited terms, so far as rhetoric is an art of communication among people, rhetorical invention is that aspect of the art which constructs its subject matter. It is important, in an age in which fixed forms—whether in metaphysics, art, politics, cultural patterns, and so forth—are under attack, to look at the world from the perspective of invention, taken as the generation of something new. In this sense discovery, invention, creativity are overlapping processes, or aspects of the process of generating the new. Invention (used now as the generic term) becomes in this context a productive human thrust into the unknown.

This view requires an expansion of most conventional treatments of rhetorical invention. Conventionally it has to do with the making of arguments by a speaker for an audience for the purpose of gaining assent to a predetermined proposition. The major shortcomings of this approach to invention are three: (1) It tends to rob the inventional process of its dynamic character and to substitute a static relationship among the fixed entities of source, facts, receiver, and goal; (2) it tends to describe the inventional process as though its energies were expended by a single unit, the speaker, in a single direction, the hearer's psyche; (3) and finally, it tends to assume that the inventional process is more the recovery of already existing facts than the actual discovery of facts and creative solutions.

In the conventional view the process of invention comes into play only after the speaker has decided upon the proposition he will advocate. He makes that prior decision on the basis of ethical values and ratiocination; *then* he invents arguments to make it appealing to the audience.

What is recognized in the revitalized conception we seek is the fact that even the ethical values and logic, which the speaker employs prior to "normal" invention, were themselves once discovered. All concepts and even all things in man's world were once—were first—discoveries. Thereafter they move towards the status of tradition. In any event, they continue to exist and exert influence in man's world only so far as men's minds and beliefs sustain them. From this perspective the core social process turns on the coming-to-be, the nourishment, and the evolution or replacement of inventions. Life may thus be looked at in terms of the processes of change and habituation which constitute it.

To create a description of the process of rhetorical invention consonant with this perspective, we need to ask ourselves the crucial question: What is required to explain the coming-to-be of the novel, the new, the "invented," and to explain it in such fashion as to aid one not only in understanding but also in participating in the process?

In the tradition of rhetoric we seek a perspective, overview, or promptuary scheme with which to examine this process. It should serve as a generative theory of rhetoric. The development of such a scheme is in fact a primary task of rhetoric today. We suggest two such schemes below. They are offered as suggestive. More important, we indicate here the criteria to be satisfied by them. First, the scheme should be such as to provide a place for—indeed to invite—not only specific topics but whole systems of invention. Second, the scheme should itself accommodate the interplay among systems of invention. It ought to provide a basis for communication among them. Third, it would even allow for—indeed provide intellectual space for—their respective efforts at self-aggrandizement—that is, efforts to take over the field. The scheme should provide a marketplace of ideas in competition, in accordance with the honored practice in rhetoric of determining outcomes in fair and free contests to win the assent of men. Finally, the scheme should treat its systems from the standpoint of their instrumental or other value in the processes of invention—that is, as invention-functional.

One such scheme offered as satisfying these criteria has three descriptions: (a) *formally,* as a kind of process; (b) *conceptually,* as an orientation or point of view; and (c) *analytically,* as involving separate constituents of invention.

(a) As a kind of process, invention takes place in a field of persons interacting, each necessarily from his own perspective at any moment, by communications. What agent or speaker or audience or subject matter or other terms mean is derived from their roles and interactions in this process. This conception borders the generative explanation not only of particular communications addressed to immediate practical issues; it explains general theories as well. Indeed, in its frame a general theory is also a particular—for even such a theory can emerge in the communication process as something discovered by an individual, from his own perspective, and "transmitted" to others in a particular context at a given moment.

Moreover, we should especially note that the rigidity of the distinction between speaker and audience loses its sacredness. Not only does the feedback process undermine this distinction, but also the interplay of various points of view is often more generative than a single person's efforts. Even when that is not the case—even in conventional speaker-audience situations —the "acceptance" by the audience of a proposition must often depend on the audience's reinventing the communication for itself, however subvocally. The distinction between the audience as active and as passive acquires a profound meaning when thus conceived as a distinction between the process of reinventing and the process of merely "soaking up" a communication; and it becomes significant also for learning theory. Being an audience—not just being a speaker—is also involved in the process of generating and regenerating one's self, one's beliefs, and one's actional stances.

(b) The world comprehended from the viewpoint of this process consists of: whatever creations from the past are influencing the present moment, that moment itself as the field of co-existing cultures and power, and the future as projectible and inventible. What we are suggesting here is a rhetorical way of looking at history—rhetorical insofar as the past exists for us only in its vital influences upon us. The past exists through the action of minds interpreting, applying, or rebelling against live reinventions of historical records and remains.

Ortega's concept of "the generation" is useful here in describing the "world" of rhetoric. Indeed, the very ambiguousness of the term "generation" is suggestive in considering the process of invention. Ortega conceived of each generation as an intersection of past and future, and as unique in its traditions and its purposes. Although different generations may possess many of the same ideas or symbol systems, the earlier generations possessed as innovations what later generations possess as traditions. The difference is crucial, not only psychologically, but also to the very meaning and force of the idea or symbol. The rhetorical world is just such a dynamic stream of influence in constant interplay and reformation, and accordingly inventional theory would have to comport with this dynamic quality. To adopt a determinant and structured theory would be arbitrarily to exclude too much, to be false to history, and to cut ourselves off from the infinite potentialities latent in the world of rhetoric.

(c) Having treated the generative framework formally as a process and conceptually as a viewpoint, we may now consider it analytically as a set of fundamental frames. The constituents of invention are: social conditions and resources, perspectives on facts, persons, deep structures, and presentational forms.

(1) The social reality of the present moment may be viewed in terms of the resources for innovation or the defense of tradition. One can explain the

coming-to-be of a new event or object, whether a speech, a new model of automobile, or a decision to expand a war in Asia, by considering the creation in terms of the question: what are the social conditions and resources available to the inventing person? For example, what uses are automobiles put to in society, what conventions govern the uttering of messages, what understandings does a nation have about the character of Asians or the events of war and peace?

(2) A second set of questions: What are the materials and perspectives upon facts out of which invention may be fashioned? What technologies may be harnessed in making a car, what facts or interpretations of facts may be spoken, what political or military conditions may be used to ground or justify the invasion decision?

The levels of generality here are not restricted. At one extreme we would note the way in which a traditionalist and a revolutionary perspective would determine the configurations in which whole social "movements" appear. For them perspectives need not always be value-laden, even in normally rhetorical terms. They may rather be such as to make facts appear determinate and necessary or contingent and optional.

(3) What about the *persons* who will participate in the innovation—and the drives which make them vital or retarding factors in the process? Who will make, sell, use the car; create, challenge, assent to the speech; announce, administer, implement the invasion? Questions of such specificity may be broadened to consideration of such creative emotions as Bergson describes by which some persons generate fundamental insights into the nature of man.

(4) What is the *deep-structure* of the invention? What are the underlying relationships between motor, transmission, steering, and so forth, of the car? How are the parts, conceptions, and relations embodied in the speech? What are the reasons, methods, and results of the invasion decision?

(5) Finally, what *presentational form* is adopted for the thing invented? What stylistic features shall the car exhibit? How shall the speech be arranged, phrased, transmitted? In what manner will the decision be offered to those affected? One feature of this topic is that it views "style" as itself inventive. But "style" should not be taken narrowly. The relation between this traditional rhetorical rubric and today's "life style" must be considered. What happens to the concept of life when it is viewed under such rubric? The critical point about this rubric is that it sees what is invented as a manifest object which can pass concretely in fact or appearance from one person to another. Finally, symbolic systems *as* symbolic (e.g., Burke's logology) would fall under this topic, since the relevant characteristic of a symbol in communication is that it is the object which actually passes between the parties.

These five aspects may be considered as a generative frame, an ordering of all the relevant aspects of any invented, innovative, or novel creation. As such they provide a place of places, a frame of frames, an account of the origin or creation of all things novel, including rhetorical artifacts.

A major advantage and value of this scheme is that, while it is at a level of reflection above the construction of, say, a communication on a political policy, yet it does not put us as theorists in a different world looking out on the world of rhetoric as different from that in which we view it. The use of the frame of frames, or even thought about it, is "rhetorical." It treats each of the constituents in the form they have *as* influences in the process of invention and it uses them to find places for systems as well as for particulars.

In brief we have here a set of topics comprehensive and neutral enough to qualify as the place of places for a generative rhetoric.

A Way of Conceptualizing a Dynamic Notion of Invention

Let us consider now another overview of invention which we believe helpful. Undoubtedly it is not the only way of conceptualizing invention consistent with our desire for a dynamic, open view.

Let us conceive of a universe of arguments and persuasive tactics, and of galaxies within the universe which are formed by relationships and clusterings among the rhetorical materials. These galaxies have centers, which may be called world-views or stances or originating positions. One such galaxy may center about the Burkeian notion of root metaphor; for example, "Man is a brick," "Man is a machine," "Man is an animal," "Man is the Son of God." Another may concern the individual's perceived relationship with the social, economic, political world about him: "Others are trying to destroy our world" (conformity and identification) or "The world is trying to destroy me" (alienation). Still another may center in a political system's view of the individual: "Government is the servant of the individual" or "Government is the master of the individual." And so on. There is no effort here to chart all the galaxies within the universe of rhetorical possibilities.

The point and the assumption of this perspective is that inventional resources may vary radically from one galaxy to another. There may also be important elements of commonality or similarity, such as recurrent patterns of reasoning and symbolizing. These resources will include: (1) alternatives for symbolic roles for communicators, (2) alternatives for forming or transforming an audience role, (3) a broad spectrum of verbal and non-verbal tactics (including premises for reasoned argument, ritualized gestures, God and Devil symbols and so on), all intended for maintaining and stabilizing the world view and audience-rhetor roles within that view, or for courting and proselytizing adherents. The "age" of the galaxy will be an essential shaping factor: whether the world view is coming to birth, is developing in popularity, is dominating its population, is decaying in influence, and so on.

The discussion thus far may raise the question of the relation of this kind of overview and the frame of frames. For one answer, the following might be considered.

A man with a system of organizing frames, operating within a galaxy, will undoubtedly have strong commitments. From his world view the fundamental frames become instruments for rhetorical invention. The question arises, however, how do galaxies shift? How do new centers of commitment come into being? The frame of frames may provide a focus beyond existing galaxies, helping to bring new world views into being. Conversely in the perspective of a world view, the frame of frames may be treated as partial and, therefore, censurable. The critical point is the peculiar function and power of each. A world view is something lived in and by; the other frame is (ideally) a comprehensive set of neutral instruments or checkpoints for invention.

The point of departure herein discussed obviously does not provide an inventional system. What it should provide are "places for the places" in a kind of organizing or at least encompassing and perhaps even generating view. Inventional systems as such will result only from programs of research which will examine and illuminate the rhetorical resources peculiar to and common to world views. We anticipate that the procedures of both criticism and experimentation may prove useful within these programs.

We ought to recognize that the universe-galaxy metaphor can carry us only so far. Given the flexibility of view which we hope would be suggested by the figure, a person may "join" and "withdraw" from various conceptual frames during the course of a lifetime, and may "belong" to various world views simultaneously without contradiction. In each, however, insofar as he has a consequential commitment to its perspective, he may profit from an inventory of the basic rhetorical resources available to it.

Insofar as we are dealing with an infinite and "expanding" universe, and galaxies beyond enumeration at this Conference, our research must be selective and continuing. We must ask, just what are the most fundamental ways of looking at human experience, commitment to which results in significant variation in life style and social organization.

If a revitalized conception of rhetorical invention takes on form and substance, its pedagogical impact and its promise for instructional improvement should prove considerable. It should open perspectives on the rhetorical dynamic operating not simply in public address, but in history, literature, philosophy, and other disciplines. It should sensitize the critic to the rhetorical presence within these dimensions, and sharpen his perceptions and evaluations of such presence.

Conference Recommendations

The following recommendations, submitted by the Committee on the Nature of Rhetorical Invention, were adopted by the Conference. These should be regarded as proposals for inquiry rather than as "action recommendations" in the usual sense. They indicate lines of research and frameworks in terms of which valuable scholarship in inventional theory might be pursued.

1. That research be undertaken on the nature of invention in nonwestern cultures; and, further, that the interactions between cultures and inventional processes be explored.

2. That the parameters, levels, and functions of diverse topical schemes be investigated with a view toward finding an architectonic overview—a place

of places—and that the concept of an architectonic overview itself be investigated; that the parameters, levels, and functions of diverse topical schemes be investigated with a view toward finding their generative potentialities.

3. The study of classical schemes of invention and the study of historical movements with a focus on inventional forces accompanying innovation and change should be re-examined in terms of the dynamic conception of rhetoric as discussed in the report of the Committee on Rhetorical Invention.

4. That inquiry be made into the problem of "producing" rather than "discovering" the universal audience or audiences.

> Perelman's concept of a universal audience is obviously important in the search for rapport or at least operational agreement among diverse groups. However, efforts directed to finding this audience or to describing it fail to take account of the pervasive importance of invention. Rather, (a) audiences are made, not given; (b) there is no *a priori* reason that there may not be many universal audiences, although not in a single situation; and (c) most important, the task is not, as often assumed, to address *either* a particular audience or a universal audience, but in the process of persuasion to adjust to and then to transform the particularities of an audience into universal dimensions.

5. That research be encouraged on the inventional role of language in the process of transforming world views into argument.

> The choice of language may be to a significant extent determined by the world view of the communication source and, further, may reflect the source's conception of the world view of the receiver. Language choices, accordingly, may be one indicator of the congruity or lack of congruity between the world views of participating members.

6. That the relationships between rhetorical and aesthetic invention be explored; that, further, those who wish to develop rhetoric's function as an architectonic art explore the modes of discovery in all areas, taking upon themselves the task of systematizing these modes, their respective values, and their transferability from one area to another.

7. That programs of research be encouraged which will examine the rhetorical resources peculiar to and common to world views. Priority should be assigned to investigating the connection between different life styles and social organizations on the one hand, and different world views on the other.

8. We endorse the concept of further interdisciplinary conferences exploring such relationships as those between rhetoric and philosophy, rhetoric and literature, and rhetoric and film, journalism and television. Further, we urge that the Speech Communication Association and regional associations sponsor periodically joint discussions between scholars whose work employs chiefly experimental methodologies and scholars whose work employs chiefly critical methodologies on theoretical issues common to the disciplines of rhetoric and speech communication.

9. That research efforts be devoted to the development of a theory of the structures of inquiring, deciding, and choosing.

10. That departments be encouraged to develop courses embodying a revitalized concept of invention as described in the report of the Committee on Rhetorical Invention.

Such courses will confront students at a time when they are most eager to establish identities and are perhaps most vulnerable to the blandishments of competing world views which offer identity as a concomitant of commitment. The courses should assist students in decisions to embrace or to reject world views; once commitments are made, such courses should assist students in relating to and becoming effective rhetorical participants within the styles of life implied by variant views. The courses should confront students with the implications of their choices and should make choice more responsible. Insofar as commonality exists among world views, such courses should assist students in understanding and tolerating other life styles, in identifying to the extent possible with the humanity shared by all men.

11. That we re-examine the relationship between "rhetorical invention" and "creativity."

Topoi and the Problem of Invention

Karl R. Wallace

Wallace's essay has several values. It contains a brief, but useful, outline of Perelman's theory of invention and an intelligent statement about the whole problem of invention; most interesting, it contains Wallace's own set of topics based on the classical notion of proofs: logos, ethos, *and* pathos.

The topics concerning logos *("Topoi of the Subject") and* ethos *("Topoi of the Speaker") are less interesting than those concerning* pathos *("Topoi of the Audience"). In fact, many heuristics, including the one developed by Young, Becker, and Pike, will serve as better probes than Wallace's topics concerning the subject, and almost any handbook of English can serve better for ethical arguments than Wallace's article, for the ethical argument in writing boils down, finally, to style and tone.*

Before the writer can adjust to an audience, however, he needs to form a concept of that audience, and it seems to me that Wallace's topics concerning the audience constitute an admirable survey. They are practical because students who typically write in a vacuum can easily use them to get a "picture" of the person or groups for whom they are writing.

In effect, Wallace's essay is a supplement to Booth's "The Rhetorical Stance."

A significant result of the National Developmental Conference on Rhetoric was the call for a rhetorical theory which emphasizes the content and substance of discourse rather than structures and techniques. The primacy of substance leads to the study of invention, to a fresh examination of systematic ways through which persons engaged in communication may be directed to the sources of information and argument and to modes of perception, interpretation, and judgment. So rhetoricians on the national scene propose to examine invention anew, with the intention of producing modern systems of *topoi*. I want to encourage the national endeavor, but I want also to invite rhetoricians to examine the task most critically. To see what the problems are I shall first direct attention to the way Perelman's *New Rhetoric* handles invention. His system is both practical and philosophical, without being overly philosophical, and thus it sets the stage for my attempt to get at the nature of invention and to present a set of *topoi* that seems to be specifically rhetorical and teachable.

1

Chaim Perelman asserts that "the new rhetoric is a theory of argumentation." [1] I suppose that every rhetorician knows that the new rhetoric and Perelman's new argumentation are not coextensive; nevertheless, Perelman is among the leaders of those who are moving toward a substantive rhetoric. In keeping with other logicians and philosophers, such as Max Black, Stephen Toulmin, and Gidon Gottlieb, he doubts whether formal logic has little, if any, use in ordinary discourse. Rhetoricians are directed again to field-dependent argument as that which constitutes the center of rhetorical discourse. They are reminded that argument is always saying something; it is meaningful; its symbols are not empty. It is not improper, then, to describe Perelman's new book as a survey of the places to which one turns when he wants to discover arguments. [2] It is a scholarly treatment of invention, of the basic sources of ideas and meanings that enter into discourse. I am not intimating that

[1] "The New Rhetoric: A Theory of Practical Reasoning," in *The Great Ideas Today 1970* (Chicago: Encyclopaedia Britannica, 1970), p. 281.

[2] The new book, of course, is that by Chaim Perelman and L. Olbrechts-Tyteca, *The New Rhetoric: A Treatise on Argumentation,* trans. John Wilkinson and Purcell Weaver (Notre Dame and London: Univ. of Notre Dame Press, 1969). Helpful in obtaining a general view of Perelman's chief writings is Ray D. Dearin's "The Philosophical Basis of Chaim Perelman's Theory of Rhetoric," *QJS* 55 (Oct. 1969), 213–24; see also the review article of *The New Rhetoric* by Carroll Arnold, *QJS* 56 (Feb. 1970), 87–92.

Perelman holds the key, the only key, to the house of invention; rather, he indicates what houses may be entered and occupied with profit, and he implies what houses may be contemplated and left alone.

For my purposes it is not necessary to describe Perelman's entire topical system. I trust it will be sufficient to present the main categories of his system, together with some explication, example, and comment along the way.

The first major category is called the Starting Points of Argument. These reflect the premises on which contending parties are in agreement. The first subclass is labeled, Facts and Truths. By facts Perelman means "objects of precise, limited agreement," such as the data acceptable in a given case. By truths he means statements that emerge from systems of thought, such as the statements that embody the laws or principles of a science or an art. The reference here to scientific knowledge merits inquiry. If rhetorical discourse by its nature is concerned with people in general rather than with people as specialists, one wonders whether scientific knowledge, particularly that represented by the hard sciences, physics and chemistry, can logically find a place in a system of modern *topoi*. If there are clusters of scientific generalities that should be the property of all men, what are they and who selects them? By refusing to acknowledge the validity of this problem, the scientists doomed the general education movement in this country. They poohpoohed the efforts of generalists to decide upon ideas and materials that should enter into general communication.

The second subclass Perelman calls Presumptions. Examples: Most people respect the truth; the quality of an act reveals the quality of the actor; the world of reality is preferable to the world of appearances. Such statements represent normalities of behavior for the population in which they are current. They are modes, not averages.

The next two subclasses are values and hierarchies of values. Perelman distinguishes between abstract and concrete values, the abstract being values like justice and truth, the concrete being values attached to persons rather than things, such as obligation, duty, and loyalty. He astutely observes that truth and justice are abstract ideals which are associated with revolutions, whereas the more concrete values, like obligation and duty, are associated with the preservation of the status quo. The notion of hierarchy, Perelman observes, underlies the structuring and ordering of values, and the notion of order in turn underlies what people regard as better and worse, superior and inferior, more or less. It is obvious that here he is dealing with *preferences* and with the ancient topic of degree; it may be less obvious that preferences sometimes are expressed as widely-held presumptions. For example: justice is superior to utility; ends are superior to means; values tied to persons are superior to values tied to things.

Perelman's last subclass of the Starting Points of Argument is entitled Loci. There are five kinds of loci: loci of quantity and quality; loci of order, loci of the existent, and loci of essence. In indicating what Perelman has in mind, a few examples will have to do. The topic of quantity, based on the idea of the norm, yields the belief that the rare and unusual is preferable to the common; and the topic of quality, based on the idea of the unique, yields the opinion, the judgment of a single wise man is worth more than the opinions of a hundred fools. Such statements as the end is superior to the means, the cause is more important than the effect, spring from valuations based on our notions of order.

When the rhetorician considers the use of the classical lists of loci—the places of invention—as he searches for modern *topoi,* it is instructive to observe Perelman's tactic. The ten categories called the predicaments and the five classes of assertion called the predicables are rejected as too impractical and metaphysical. Guided by the third book of Aristotle's *Topics,* Perelman selected kinds of loci that apply to values whenever they appear as preferences and whenever we justify our preferences through argument. As Perelman says, his loci are the loci of the preferable.[3]

The second major category of Perelman's *topoi* is called Quasi-Arguments. These are arguments, says Perelman, that "lay claim to a certain power of conviction, in the degree that they [appear] to be similar to the formal reasoning of logic or mathematics." [4] The locus of the power lies chiefly in the structure of the argument rather than in its content. One kind of structure is that drawn from dialectical compatibles and incompatibles. If A is regarded as "equal" to B, then A should be treated like B. The structure of the argument is thus set. The structure, perceived, implies the development of the argument, for the arguer is impelled to define A in a way that shows his equality with B.

Human beings, says Perelman, build concepts out of their experience. Each concept is a cluster of related experiences constructed and held together through associations which become habitual. Perelman leans heavily on association as the basis for another category of topics that reflect connections between experience and the real world. Within this category, one set of topics points to the *structure* of reality. As human beings, we all see the real world, for example, as wholes and parts of wholes. This habit is the basis of classifying objects, and in human experience is always evident in deductive structures. We see the world, too, as things in sequence. This habit is the basis of such linkages as cause-and-effect, and end-means. We perceive reality, also, as things and events that occur simultaneously, that coexist. The relation, for example, between a person's character and his acts is that of coexistence; so too is the relation between a person's character and the group to which he belongs. Another set of topics pointing to reality reflects our desire to regard the real world as something established and firm, as we do when we base a statement on example or on analogy. We behave thus, also, when we appeal to models as objects to be imitated or emulated, or to be avoided.

Without doing excessive violence to his scheme of things, it may be said that Perelman sees two chief directions of argument, the positive or construc-

---

[3] *Great Ideas,* p. 288.
[4] *New Rhetoric,* p. 193.

tive, and the negative or refutative. Our exposition so far has been dealing with the topics of constructive argument. It is time now to take a swift glance at the topics of refutation.

There are many such topics. Informing all of them is the principle of habitual association. But whereas the topics of constructive argument work to strengthen associations located in the materials and frames of human experience, the topics of refutation work to disassociate customary bonds.

Disassociation works something like this: Human experience consists in building concepts of various kinds, dimensions, and complexity. Each concept is a cluster of "elements," or what I prefer to call meanings. Disassociation is the process of breaking the connections between concepts, that is, between an element of one concept and the element of another concept. By way of illustration, here are a few topics:

> My meaning does not correspond with yours.
> The meaning of the word does not refer to the object being talked about; or the meaning does not fit the situation.
> The meaning has changed in some way, for it does not correspond with present usage.
> There are many meanings, or variables, and we do not know which one to apply.

Topics like these, it should be observed, demand elaboration through deductive structures whose content and language are the outcome of definitions.

The apparatus for finding topics of disassociation is through the application of what Perelman labels "philosophical pairs." I present a few of his pairs:

> Appearance / reality
> Means / end
> Individual / group
> Symbol / thing
> Verbal / real
> Fictitious / genuine
> Spirit / letter

Take the pair, appearance/reality. It is a prototype of all conceptual disassociation, says Perelman, for all our sensations are responses to an object world. Appearances are the immediately given; reality is that which is independent of experience. As a rule, people attach a higher value to reality than to appearance. The outcome is a master topic of argument: Appearances differ, but reality is fixed. Related to this topic are others: The real is preferable to the verbal; the genuine is better than the copy; deeds are preferable to words (or mere rhetoric). To break up these associations Perelman offers these topics: The real is constructed by man; knowledge of the real is indirect, even impossible; the real is uncommunicable in any satisfactory way. The end/means pair operates similarly to produce topics of argument.

It should be noted that conceptual pairs like these come from a philosophical approach to the topics of argument. They probe for ultimate, final origins of argument in a highly developed culture; they necessarily reflect man's epistemological and ontological views. The philosophical approach to argument is powerful and fascinating, of course; but we must realize, I think, that it may have limited application if we aim to construct a system of topics that is teachable to unsophisticated learners. In saying this I am not intending to denigrate Perelman's work; in fact, it is both stimulating and profitable, as I hope I have been able to suggest.

2

Now to look closely at the task of finding a set, or sets, of modern *topoi*. Here one deals with inventing as a process or activity and considers it in ways that will aid a communicator find materials and arguments and will help a listener and critic to understand and evaluate messages. The first problem: Is it possible to state precisely what is meant by inventive activity and what is not meant? Are we not dealing with *what* is said in discourse, with the content or subject matter of discourse, with ideas and meanings that enter into discourse, when people respond to communicative situations and must therefore be concerned with commonalities of belief and action? More precisely, are we not also referring to a certain *kind of mental activity,* the kind that prompts the recovery of meanings that have become symbolized in the language of speaker, writer, and audience? And if we are concerned with a promptuary scheme or system, how are the *topoi* expected to function? Are they to function as instruments of recall and recollection? Are they also to stimulate inquiry by revealing sources of ignorance and pointing in the direction of new information? Can they serve both purposes equally well?

If *topoi* are to yield the content of discourse, how far do rhetorical analysts extend their notion of content? Does it extend to images and to figures of speech? And if to figures of speech, do they rule out the class of figures called *schemes,* and include *tropes,* such as metaphor, because tropes as compared with schemes are more contentful, more substantial? In brief, should *topoi* as prompters of inventive activity be capable of producing images and metaphors? In raising this question, I am pointing to another problem, perhaps the most profound of all: Is creative activity, such as that revealed by imagery, different from inventive activity, such as that revealed by statement and argument?

Doubtless, then, in searching for modern *topoi,* rhetoricians are concerned with the content or subject matter of discourse, that is, with the experience, or those portions of experience, that people draw upon whenever they communicate with one another. But experience consists of more than subject matter; it embodies the forms, structures, or patterns of language behavior. I have in mind the basic patterns of statements and of argument that constitute units of thought. Of statement, there are the forms that are assertive, and that involve contrasts and similarities. Of argument, there are the frames called deduction, generalization, analogy, and the like. Topics, then, should have the power to call up appropriate linguistic structures, as well as subject matter. One of the lessons to be drawn from Perelman is that his work, like the treatises of the great classical rhetoricians, pays heed to both the content and form of argument, for in searching activity one looks either to a *place* (for materials) or to *structure* (for arguments).

Inventors of *topoi* cannot forget the receivers of messages. Central to the ready recall of experience that communication requires is memory. Classical rhetoric emphasized the memory of the speaker. Should not modern *topoi* assist the audience as well as the speaker? And will the topics useful to the communicator be as useful to the receiver? A respondent is both perceiver and judge, and the demands of the communicative situation, especially the tasks imposed by the unpredictables of impromptu, informal situations, levy upon his experience and memory as well as upon the speaker's.

3

Probably rhetoricians agree that *topoi* ought to prompt recall and inquiry and that they should be useful to both originators and receivers of communications. It is time now to turn to some practical matters. I shall raise some questions, which will overlap somewhat, and offer some opinions.

First, how general in nature, how broad and sweeping, should rhetorical topics be? Members of the national committee on the nature of rhetorical invention have advanced suggestions. They want inquiry into what is going on in the minds and imaginations, the souls and bodies, of "interacting communicators." They want something truly "generative," something so powerful and far-reaching that it would breed not one system of topics, but many; indeed, it should have the power of modifying and correcting topics from generation to generation, age to age. If such a vision is attractive, where would it lead? We would certainly need the best help of metaphysicians, psychologists, and learning theorists, which would be welcome; but in pursuit of the vision scholars would probably find themselves having to work through, and somehow in the end surmount, the systems of predicaments, pre-predicaments, post-predicaments, and predicables of the medieval schoolmen.

Yet, as the ancients recognized, a system of topics if it is to be workable must be sufficiently general to cut across a number of subject matters, particularly those in the social sciences and history. But the problem is, how general? Certainly there are places to start. Roget's classification of all knowledge is suggestive. So is the method of classification employed in making the index of the Great Books, called by its authors, Mortimer Adler and his associates, the Syntopican. Wilson and Arnold, in their textbook, *Public Speaking as a Liberal Art,* have come up with sixteen topics, very general in nature.[5] An

---

[5] These topics are found in the Second Edition (Boston: Allyn and Bacon, 1968), p. 115. Eleven topics appear under the heading, *Attributes:* Existence, Degree, Space, Time,

article in *College English,* written by Richard Weaver and three of his associates, makes a good case for including in any list of modern *topoi,* the categories of genus and definition, consequence, likeness and difference, testimony and authority.[6] The use of these categories in finding things to say is certainly teachable, as the authors demonstrate. A certain well-known textbook, in its fourth edition, carries a classification of values. The broadest categories are three: the desirable, the obligatory, and the commendable. The list is the result of examining modern ethics and value theory.[7] Vincent Bevilacqua has called to my attention some of the broad categories used by the eighteenth-century empiricists, including both philosophers and rhetoricians. Some of the topics are similarity, dissimilarity, variety, uniformity, and part-whole—whole-part relationships. Doubtless Stephen Toulmin's notion of inference-warrants suggests a topical system built around ideas that are field invariant vs. field variant. Indeed, Toulmin may have shown what it is to give the old medieval *topoi* a new interpretation and fresh application.[8] Richard L. Larson has used some of the old topics in producing a list of questions designed to prompt rhetorical invention in the composition class.[9] Kenneth Burke, in his *Grammar of Motives,* may well be preoccupied with a classification of motives from the rhetorical point of view. And Burke's pentad admirably shows the adaptability of Aristotle's four causes to the kind of creative inventiveness required to produce plots and their development.

It seems to me that the rhetorical theorist who reviews topical schemes comes to recognize what underlies them all. They all reveal points of view toward knowing and learning and toward using what is known and learned. A modern system of rhetorical topics, then, will reflect what is considered necessary to the acquisition of that knowledge which is productive of ready and effective communication. Or put more simply, we are concerned with the systematic acquisition of knowledge *for* communication and with its reappearance in some form or other *in* communications. This, accordingly, is our focus; this defines our special, our technical task. We are to dwell on the conditions of rhetorical invention, not of invention in general. We are not directly concerned with knowing and remembering, unqualified. This is the task of the psychologist who specializes in the conditions of learning and in memory.

Motion, Form, Substance, Capacity to Change, Potency, Desirability, Feasibility. Under the heading, *Basic Relationships,* five topics are listed: Causality, Correlation, Genus-species, Similarity or dissimilarity, Possibility or impossibility.

  [6] Manuel Bilsky, McCrea Hazlett, Robert E. Streeter, and Richard M. Weaver, "Looking for an Argument," *College English* 55 (Jan. 1953), 210–16. The authors remark that the notion of *substance* underlies all categories and all argument, and that the categories for the interpretation of substance are *being, cause,* and *similarity.* In the *Ethics of Rhetoric,* Weaver recognizes another category, *circumstance.*

  [7] Donald C. Bryant and Karl R. Wallace, *Fundamentals of Public Speaking,* 4th ed. (New York: Appleton-Century-Crofts, 1969), pp. 36–39.

  [8] See Otto Bird, "The Re-discovery of the Topics," *Mind* 70 (July 1961), 534–39.

  [9] "Discovery Through Questioning: A Plan for Teaching Rhetorical Invention," *College English* 70 (Nov. 1968), 126–34.

I do not mean that rhetoricians as inventors of an inventive system will not profit from knowing as much as possible about the processes of knowing and remembering, their natures and conditions. No field of study grows if it is content with its own stuff. It seems promising, for example, to look into a new treatment of attention and memory by Donald A. Norman.[10] Even its subtitle is inviting: An Introduction to Human Information Processing. I only remark now that if a topical system is to be firmly stored in the memory of a communicator, it should be an organized whole, the better organized the better. Integrated bits of information and schemata appear to be fundamental to long-term memory, especially in recall as distinguished from recognition. The kind of unit most tightly organized may be that which depends upon logical classification. William Nelson has reminded us that *topoi* represent a high order of abstract organization; he thinks of topics as "labels for super-ordinate structures of human cognition."[11] He has demonstrated, further-more, the usefulness of superordinate concepts in the recall of materials assigned for reading in the public speaking class. Rhetoricians will need help in the search for *topoi*, wherever they can find it.

I shall mention but one other fundamental matter. What is the relation of inventiveness to creativeness? If the two processes overlap, do rhetoricians deal with both of them? I think they have to, for the two concepts illuminate each other. Let me but allude to the advantage to be gained. Some probing into the literature on creativity would certainly take the investigator into imagery, into its nature and its sources. He would be led to consider anew the springs of poetic and dramatic discourse, and through them into the nature and kinds of imaginative activity. He would encounter again the dis-tinctions between imagination free and unfettered, save for the restraints of intelligibility, as manifest in the imagery of *Kubla Khan* and in modern sym-bolistic literature, and the imagination constrained by the boundaries set by human notions of the possible and the probable, as manifest in argument and persuasion. If it should turn out that there are differences that rhetoricians, in their search for *topoi*, think it prudent to maintain, the examination would at least point directly to matters of mutual concern to poetic and rhetoric; these are the conditions of metaphor and analogy. Aristotle specified some of the places of metaphor.[12]

4

The National Committee expects, quite rightly, that rhetoricians will pro-duce not one scheme of *topoi*, but many. As an example I present the out-line of my topical scheme.

Topoi *of the Subject:* Sources of information
    Facts, as found in things and persons

---

[10] *Memory and Attention: An Introduction to Human Information* (New York: John Wiley and Sons, 1969). Norman is aware of, and respects, the classical rhetoricians' treatment of memory.
[11] "*Topoi:* Functional in Human Recall," *Speech Monograph* 37 (June 1970), 121–26.
[12] *The Poetics*, Ch. 21.

Classification: naming and identifying facts and experience
  What is, and what is not, as revealed by modes of definition
  Like and unlike
  The unique
Causation: the facts involved in process and change
  The end or product as cause
  Means to end
    Materials
    Method of combining materials
Disagreement encountered, as revealed by
  Cicero's survey for issues
  Dewey's survey of the problem presented
  Special state of the audience situation as cause of a speaker's position

Topoi *of the Audience*
  General condition
  Values
    In general
      The desirable
      The obligatory
      The commendable
    In the chief rhetorical genre
      Deliberative
      Judicial
      Epideictic
  Value hierarchies
    Group and institutional
    Age
    Individual
  Economic
  Educational
  Affective states: emotions, motives, feelings
  Political preferences
    Ideals as determined by kinds of states
    Ideals professed by political parties
  The probable and possible, as revealed in
    Probabilities: assumptions and presumptions
    Habitual patterns of thought
      Deduction
      Generalization and example
      Analogy
      Correlation and causation

Topoi *of the Speaker*
  Character traits held desirable by audiences:
    ethos
  Signs of personality esteemed by audiences:
    the sensory [13]

---

[13] Subheads in the list I expand in the freshman classroom as extensively as seems practical. The modes of definition are named and illustrated; like and unlike are handled

When one contemplates this scheme, it will be observed, in the first place, that it relates directly to the communicative situation. It presumes that ideas and arguments spring from situations to which communicators must respond, or are invited to respond, with appropriate visual signs and verbalizations. The situations will vary from the highly utilitarian, such as "Pass me the bread," to aspects of socially pragmatic problems, such as those presented by the Women's Liberation Movement. It presumes, also, to be *primarily* an inventive scheme. So as a spur to inventive activity, it is intended to produce utterances that are felt to be *new* by both producer and receiver. In fact, it is originalness that marks an utterance—or any product—as creative.

It will be observed, secondly, that the scheme differs from systems of *topoi* that are few in number. These are bound to be very general and abstract in nature. Witness the old scheme of ten categories, or predicaments, and the five (or six) predicables. Witness, too, the Wilson and Arnold list, previously referred to. When one puzzles over such lists as they occur in the history of dialectic and logic, one wonders how practical they are whenever the questions we face are rhetorical in nature, rather than dialectical and philosophical. The puzzlement is not reduced for us moderns when Nelson demonstrates that a list few in number and abstract in nature is useful in recall.

Aids to invention, I think, differ from aids to memory, although the two kinds of stimulators will overlap. There is a problem here that rhetoricians must deal with. Do we need two kinds of *topoi,* one intended to help learners systematize their experience through at least the years of formal education, the other intended to provoke search and inquiry into what may be said? The first kind of topics would put the study of communication at the center of the citizen's education, where it should belong; every student would build up an index of his learning. The second kind of topics would indicate the abiding interest of rhetoricians in creative activity and would ally communication and rhetoric with psychology and the arts.

That inventive activity is something different from memorative activity can be indicated by looking at the first great system of rhetorical topics, that of Aristotle's. It is well known that Books I and II of the *Rhetoric* are for the most part a system of invention. Aristotle's famous definition of rhetoric sets the system, for rhetorical activity comes down to finding and applying the available means of persuasion. Over and over Aristotle insists that the endeavor is to discover the units of argument: enthymemes, and arguments from example. The kind of mental activity involved he indicated by analogy. When one is to fit a customer for a pair of shoes, there's a difference, he said, between drawing upon a stock of shoes already made up and designing and making a pair from scratch. In the first case one is depending chiefly upon

as underpinning for types of analogy and metaphor; values (commendable) are expanded as virtues, named and defined; the deliberative genre gives rise to subtopics concerning the good and degrees thereof, the judicial to the topics of justice and modes of justification. Emotions are named and defined in terms of stimulus conditions (circumstances); motives are links with considerations touching the choices inherent in the occasion for speaker and listener. And so forth.

memory; in the second he is drawing upon his skill in selecting and forming his materials for the end intended, namely, a particular pair of shoes. The distinction led Aristotle to condemn the commonplace passage, complete in idea and form, and to commend what the communicator could make from his own resources. At stake in inventive activity were units of meaningful utterance produced under the pressure of communicative urgency and involving the operations of selection, combination, and inquiry (when needed), the operations being dominated by the intended meaning and effect. That Aristotle was not centrally concerned with memory in the *Rhetoric* is indicated by his treatment of memory and its conditions in a separate treatise.[14]

I conclude by observing that inventing is at the heart of all communicative behavior. It is true that in communicating man is perceiving, defining, interpreting, judging, evaluating, criticizing, and arguing. It is true, also, that central to these operations is a process we call searching, in which we are directing attention goalwards, either in the expectation of something or in anticipation of something. What the parties to communication, both producers and respondents, search is their experience and the experience of others. It is true, moreover, that in producing utterances they intend to make sense rather than nonsense; hence meaning dominates the searching. It is true, furthermore, that being meaningful entails as the first condition, being orderly rather than chaotic. A system of *topoi,* then, is an orderly way of searching for meaningful utterances.

[14] *De Memoria et Reminiscentia,* trans. J. I. Beare, Easily available in *The Basic Works of Aristotle,* ed. Richard McKeon (New York: Random House, 1941).

Toward a Modern Theory of Rhetoric: A Tagmemic Contribution

Richard E. Young and Alton L. Becker

Alton Becker and Richard Young, along with Kenneth Pike, are associated with a movement in rhetoric which developed from a linguistic theory called "tagmemics." The article below adequately defines the goals and meth-

This article was in part supported by the Center for Research on Language and Language Behavior, University of Michigan, under Contract OE 5-14036, U.S. Office of Education.

ods of tagmemics, so that nothing more needs to be said about the theory here.

In a sense, it is unfair to tagmemics and to Becker and Young to reprint an article that is now more than a decade old, for work with tagmemic rhetoric has been progressing rapidly. Young, Becker, and Pike have since published a highly influential text, and in conjunction with the psychologist Frank Koen, Young has just published a detailed investigation of how his theories actually work when they are applied in the classroom.

However, the article appearing here remains the best short statement of tagmemic assumptions concerning rhetoric. And if it is not complete and thoroughgoing, it is nonetheless provocative and insightful.

A word about the tagmemic theory of invention is in order here. Tagmemicists believe that in order for anyone to know a thing, three aspects of that thing's existence must be perceived: (1) how it differs from everything else, (2) how much it can change and still be itself, and (3) how it fits into larger systems of which it is a part. Tagmemic theory also tells us that we can view anything (concrete or abstract) from three perspectives: (1) as a particle, (2) as a wave, and (3) as a field. Taken together, these six items obviously give us a nine-item heuristic (which, in fact, Young, Becker, and Pike put into a framework in Rhetoric: Discovery and Change).

This heuristic is so interesting and so productive that I would like to outline it here, for it is central to tagmemic theory, and it is not completely developed in the article below.

Suppose that students are faced with the problem of understanding a poem. First, they can view it as a particle, as a discrete entity. They will ask what its features are, i.e., describe it (contrast). *Next they can ask about its range of variation. How does it differ from others in its class? How much can it change and still be itself? They can ask about its* distribution: *How does it fit into and relate to the larger system of which it is a part? (This brings up the whole question of literature.)*

Now the poem can be viewed as a wave, a process. At first, this perspective might seem strange—until one realizes that the poem on the page is merely black squiggles against a white background (or white squiggles against a black background). What we call the poem actually grows in the reader's mind, i.e., it is quite literally a process. On the other hand, the poem can be viewed as the creation of a poet, as in The Road to Xanadu, *a study of a poem from the standpoint of the process whereby it came into being.* Contrast: *In what respects is the poem a process? What are the features of that process?* Variation: *How does the process in this poem differ from the processes in other similar works?* Distribution: *How does this poem as process fit into the process of literature?*

Finally, the poem can be viewed from the standpoint of field, *as a system.* Contrast: *How do the parts of the poem work together? We might mean stanzas here, but we might also mean imagery and idea, and so on.* Variation: *How does the poem as a system work in contrast to other pieces of literature as systems?* Distribution: *How does the poem as a system relate to the larger system of which it is a part, namely, literature?*

Be it said that this short example does not even begin to do justice to the richness of the heuristic.

I have talked extensively with Young about his ideas, and he insists that to gain maximum usefulness, the user must become completely familiar with the heuristic, applying it again and again to a variety of subjects, letting it become almost an intuitive method of problem solving. In this I suspect that Young is correct. Though the heuristic itself is fairly simple to understand, its elegance does not become obvious until one has used it again and again.

In any case, this heuristic—as well as other work of the tagmemicists— most certainly represents an important step in the revitalization of rhetoric.

> Our discussion will be adequate if it has as much clearness as the subject-matter admits of, for precision is not to be sought for alike in all discussions. . . . We must be content . . . in speaking of such subjects and with such premises to indicate the truth roughly and in outline, and in speaking about things which are only for the most part true and with premises of the same kind to reach conclusions that are no better. In the same spirit, therefore, should each type of statement be *received;* for it is the mark of an educated man to look for precision in each class of things just so far as the nature of the subject admits; it is evidently equally foolish to accept probable reasoning from a mathematician and to demand from a rhetorician scientific proofs.
>
> Aristotle, *Nichomachean Ethics* i.3.1094b 12–28.
> Trans. W. D. Ross

I

Years ago, the heart of a liberal education was the trivium of grammar, logic, and rhetoric. Modern linguistics has come to encompass more and more of this trivium, and has in the process become transformed. Traditional grammar is no longer anathema to the linguist, and linguistic description has adopted many of the techniques of logical analysis. Furthermore, linguistics is becoming increasingly interested in the analysis and description of verbal structures beyond the sentence, traditionally a rhetorical concern. It seems fitting, therefore, to explore the relationships of linguistics and rhetoric—discovering, hopefully, just what contributions a theory of language can make to a modern theory of rhetoric.

As Aristotle states in the quotation given above, the nature of the subject matter imposes some constraints on the statements we make about it. It is our intention, therefore, to define the subject matter of rhetoric as it has been understood traditionally, and then to illustrate how aspects of one modern linguistic theory—tagmemics—can form the basis for a new approach to rhetorical problems. The field is broad and there are many points of contact between linguistics and rhetoric which will be passed over here. Nor can we hope to consider all linguistic points of view, each with important contributions to make. We will limit ourselves to a description of three traditional stages in the rhetorical process—invention, arrangement, and style—and then approach the problems of each stage via tagmemic theory.

There are four rhetorical traditions which, taken together, constitute the history of rhetoric. There is sophistic rhetoric, which has as its goal the effective manipulation of language without regard to truth and logic. This tradition continues in modern propaganda and in advertising techniques. There is Platonic anti-rhetoric, which stresses not the art of writing but the quality of the writer in his adherence to truth and virtue: a good writer is a good man writing. There is the rhetoric of literary criticism, which applies the categories and techniques of rhetoric to the analysis and evaluation of poetry, drama, and narration. And finally, there is Aristotelian rhetoric, which had its origins in the law courts of early Greece and which was expanded, systematized, and given a philosophic foundation by Aristotle. After being brought to perfection by Cicero and Quintilian, it constituted a basic, and at times *the* basic, discipline in Western education for fifteen hundred years. It survives today, but with greatly diminished influence. Because this is still the most complete rhetoric ever developed and because it best defines what traditionally has been the scope of rhetoric, we shall focus our attention almost exclusively on the Aristotelian tradition.

For Aristotle, rhetoric was "the faculty of observing in any given case the available means of persuasion." [1] Its immediate end was to persuade a popular audience of what is true and just; its ultimate end was to secure the cooperation necessary for a civilized society. The classical art of rhetoric consisted of five separate arts which together embraced the entire process of developing and presenting a persuasive discourse: invention, arrangement, style, memory, and delivery. As the last two concern speaking rather than writing (which has become the principal concern of modern rhetoric), we shall consider only the first three: invention, arrangement, and style.

"Invention," wrote Cicero, "is the discovery of valid or seemingly valid arguments to render one's cause plausible." [2] Rhetoricians distinguished two kinds of arguments: extrinsic arguments, which came ready-made to the writer (e.g., eyewitness testimony, documents, confessions), and intrinsic arguments. The latter were of special interest to rhetoricians because they were subject to discovery by means of a system of topics. These topics were a kind of checklist of mental acts one could use when investigating and collecting arguments on a subject (e.g., definition by genus and differentia, comparison and

---

[1] Aristotle, *Rhetoric*, i.2.1355b 26–27, trans. W. D. Ross, in *The Basic Works of Aristotle*, ed. Richard McKeon (New York: Random House, 1941), p. 1329.
[2] Quoted in Wilbur S. Howell, *Logic and Rhetoric in England, 1500–1700* (Princeton, N.J.: Princeton University Press, 1956), p. 66.

contrast, cause and effect). Certain of these topics—the "common" topics—were appropriate to all three types of speech studied in the classical system: forensic, political, or ceremonial; others—the "special" topics—could be used with only one of the three.

Use of the topics presupposed wide learning since they were primarily a method for putting the writer in contact with knowledge which already existed. Edward Corbett has remarked that Mortimer Adler's *Syntopicon* of Great Ideas of the Western World would have been an ideal reference work for the ancient rhetorician.[3] It was the art of invention which made rhetoric the core of humanistic education until the late Renaissance.

During the Renaissance, under the influence of Bacon and Descartes, logic increasingly came to be seen not as the art of learned discourse, as it had been since Greek times, but as an instrument of inquiry. Rhetoric gradually enlarged its boundaries to include the arts of both learned and popular discourse. The process was finally completed in the nineteenth century in the work of John Stuart Mill; commenting on the proper domains of logic and rhetoric, Mill remarked that

> the sole object of Logic is the guidance of one's own thoughts: the communication of those thoughts to others falls under the consideration of Rhetoric, in the large sense in which that art was conceived by the ancients. . . .[4]

This spirit of modern science which was modifying the nature of logic and the scope of rhetoric also had its effect on the art of invention. Since the seventeenth century, we have increasingly regarded facts and experimental evidence as the basis for sound argument, rather than relying—as did our ancestors—on the wisdom of the past. That is, we have increasingly put our faith in extrinsic arguments. We have become much more interested in techniques for discovering what is unknown than in techniques for bringing old beliefs to bear on new problems. Thus the classical art of invention has diminished in importance while the modern art of experimental inquiry has expanded immensely. But this art of inquiry is no longer a part of modern rhetoric—each academic discipline having developed its own discovery procedures. The strength and worth of rhetoric seem, however, to be tied to the art of invention; rhetoric tends to become a superficial and marginal concern when it is separated from systematic methods of inquiry and problems of content.

The second art in classical rhetoric was that of arrangement. Rhetoricians developed persuasive patterns for organizing their materials—flexible systems of slots into which appropriate categories of subject matter were fitted. One common arrangement, the Ciceronian, had six slots: the exordium; the narrative, or exposition of the problem's history; the proposition; the demonstration; the refutation of alternative propositions; and the peroration. The func-

---

[3] Edward P. J. Corbett, *Classical Rhetoric for the Modern Student* (New York: Oxford University Press, 1965), p. 171.

[4] Quoted in Howell, p. 350.

tions and structures of each of these slots were systematically developed and described. Arrangement was the art of distributing within this pattern the subject matter gathered in the process of invention; arrangement also involved modifying the pattern by expanding, omitting, or reorganizing the various steps to meet the needs of the audience, speaker, and subject matter. The pattern was employed in all three types of speech: forensic, political, and ceremonial.

Since rhetoric was the art of persuasion, patterns for other modes of discourse (e.g., description, exposition) were given little attention. In the seventeenth century, however, developments in science led to an increasing interest in expository prose, a movement which parallels the shift from intrinsic to extrinsic argument. Other developments, such as the decline in the power of the aristocracy and the growing importance of evangelical religion, led to a rejection of elaborate patterning and the development of simpler, more manageable rhetorical forms, though none was described in the same detail as were the classical patterns.

Implicit in classical theory was a dualistic conception of discourse. Form was treated as independent of both the subject matter and the writer. Since the Renaissance, there has been a tendency to see form as the product of a particular mind or as discoverable within the subject matter itself. In the latter case, the form of a discourse is not separable from the content—the discourse is seen as having an organic unity. In either case, the form of a work is not predictable. If form is a personal matter, or is implicit in the subject matter, the rhetorician can make fewer generalizations about arrangement. Classical rhetoric was a rhetoric of precept; in modern times it has become, for the most part, a rhetoric of practice.

Style, the third of the rhetorical arts in classical rhetoric, was largely the technique of framing effective sentences. Its function was to give clarity, force, and beauty to ideas. Although grammar was its foundation, style was clearly a separate art, concerned with the effective use of language rather than simply with the correct use. Both, however, were concerned with language at the sentence level.

Aristotle justified the study of style on practical grounds. Ideally, rational argument alone should be sufficient to persuade. Since experience suggests that this is often not sufficient, the art of style must be employed if wisdom is to be persuasive. The art of style tended, however, to become an end in itself, at times preempting the entire field of rhetoric, possibly—as in the classical conception of arrangement—because of a dualistic view in which content and style were separable.

In the classical tradition, good style was a deliberate departure from the speech of everyday life. Renaissance classicists ingeniously isolated and systematized figures of speech. Henry Peacham's *Garden of Eloquence* (1577), for example, lists 184 schemes and tropes—artistic departures from ordinary syntax and word meanings. Clarity and appropriateness became less frequent constraints than elegance and ingenuity. As a result, "rhetoric" gained its pejorative connotation of elegant but empty verbosity.

As with the other rhetorical arts, there was a reaction against this concept of style; rhetoricians now sought a norm closer to the speech of everyday life. In the eighteenth century, the dualistic conception of style and content began to compete with monistic conceptions. Style came to mean either the characteristic expression of a particular personality (*Le style c'est l'homme même*) or the mode of expression organically a part of the subject matter itself.

Since the eighteenth century, the analysis of style has become almost exclusively the concern of literary criticism. In rhetoric courses today, style is still seen by and large as the art of framing effective sentences; but the art is much simpler, less systematic, and considerably more intuitive than it was in classical rhetoric.

The classical art of rhetoric has a number of weaknesses which make it inadequate for our time. Without involving ourselves directly in a criticism of the philosophical assumptions upon which classical rhetoric is based, we can note, in general, four major problems. First, the classical art of invention stresses authoritative confirmation of present beliefs, while modern modes of inquiry stress imaginative discovery of new facts and relationships. Second, the art of arrangement includes only patterns of persuasion, and neglects considerations of form in other important rhetorical modes such as description, narration, and exposition. Third, both the art of arrangement and the art of style divorce form from content, failing to consider the importance of the act of discovery in the shaping of form. And finally, the art of style is concerned primarily with embellishing, clarifying, and giving point to sentences, an approach which neglects both the deeper personal roots of style and the ways in which style is manifested in patterns beyond the sentences.

In recent years, numerous rhetoricians have been seeking a new rhetoric which would be as effective on a practical level and as stimulating and coherent on a theoretical level as is classical rhetoric. As Daniel Fogarty puts it, there are numerous "roots for a new rhetoric." [5] While other members of the trivium have changed greatly from their earlier forms (witness the revolution in Mill's *System of Logic,* the later changes in symbolic logic, and the recent revolution in grammatical theory) there has as yet been no comparable change in rhetoric. That is, there has been no change which includes both a complete theory and an explicit practical method. Rhetoric is still in the midst of a chaotic transition period. I. A. Richards is right, unfortunately, when he describes the general state of rhetoric today as

> the dreariest and least profitable part of the waste that the unfortunate travel through in Freshman English! So low has Rhetoric sunk that we would do better just to dismiss it to Limbo than to trouble ourselves with it—unless we

[5] Daniel Fogarty, *Roots for a New Rhetoric* (New York: Bureau of Publications, Teachers College, Columbia University, 1959).

can find reason for believing that it can become a study that will minister successfully to important needs.[6]

II

The tagmemic approach to language analysis and description, developed primarily by Kenneth L. Pike and his associates in the Summer Institute of Linguistics,[7] has for many years been concerned with problems which have traditionally been within the scope of rhetoric. This concern results, in part, from the strong motivation which such a model gives for moving beyond the specification of well-made sentences. In tagmemic theory, any linguistic unit is assumed to be well defined only when three aspects of the unit are specified: its contrastive features, its range of variation, and its distribution in sequence and ordered classes. This constraint on grammatical description (defined as a description necessary and sufficient to include all relevant aspects of any linguistic unit) has meant that a complete description of sentences for example, should include a specification of their distribution in paragraphs and other larger units of discourse.

This concern with problems which traditionally have been a part of rhetoric also results from the desire of many who use the tagmemic model to provide a means for producing extended discourse, primarily biblical translation. Translators frequently encounter instances of grammatical constraints extending beyond the sentence. In some Philippine languages, for example, there is a system of focus somewhat like active and passive voice in English though vastly more complex. To produce understandable discourse in these languages apparently requires a marked correlation between situational roles (actor, goal, instrument, setting, etc.) and grammatical roles (subject, predicate, object, locative, etc.) in a sequence of sentences.[8]

As the linguist moves beyond the sentence, he finds himself asking questions which have long concerned rhetoricians. The description of the structure of a sentence and the description of the structure of an expository paragraph, extended argument, or novel are not sharply different kinds of activity, for all involve selecting and ordering language in a significant way. The traditional separation of grammar, logic, rhetoric, and poetics begins to break down.

Selecting and ordering language, however, has two aspects. One sort of

---

[6] I. A. Richards, *The Philosophy of Rhetoric* (New York: Oxford University Press, 1936), p. 3. Kenneth Burke and S. I. Hayakawa have both developed extremely interesting theories of rhetoric and must be mentioned, along with Richards, as having made notable contributions to the development of a new rhetoric.

[7] The basic source of tagmemic theory is Kenneth L. Pike, *Language* (*in Relation to a Unified Theory of the Structure of Human Behavior*) (Glendale, Calif.: Summer Institute of Linguistics, Part I, 1951; Part II, 1955; Part III, 1960). A new edition, to be published by Mouton, is in preparation. [Humanities Press, 1967] Pike applies tagmemic theory to problems of rhetoric in "Beyond the Sentence," *College Composition and Communication*, XV, No. 3 (October 1964), and "Discourse Analysis and Tagmeme Matrices," *Oceanic Linguistics* (April 1965).

[8] Kenneth L. Pike, "A Syntactic Paradigm," *Language*, XXXIX (April–June 1963), 216–30. See also "Discourse Analysis and Tagmeme Matrices," footnote 7.

inquiry into the selection and ordering of language leads us deeply into the mental activity of the writer and into questions which are difficult, perhaps impossible, to answer except intuitively. Can we specify in detail why a writer chooses to write "John loves Mary" rather than "John is in love with Mary"? Probably not; we can only describe the choices he does make, the characteristic features of his style. Another sort of inquiry, however, leads us to the conventions which constrain the writer. We can specify the reasons why "Love John is Mary in" does not make sense to us except in rather farfetched ways. In the same way, we believe we can specify why the following sequence of sentences does not make sense:

> The trees are budding. Coal is a form of carbon. He has been singing for three hours now. The world used to be round. It seems enough.

If we were to prod the reader, insisting that the above "sentence" and "paragraph" do have meaning, he could probably find some sense in them, as many have in Chomsky's "Colorless green ideas sleep furiously." In each case one "discovers" meaning by imposing conventional formal patterns on the deviant sequences.

Both the process of imposing pattern on (or discovering pattern in) apparently meaningless utterances and the process of describing the conventions of language are important to the linguist. In the former process, he uses some sort of discovery procedure; in the latter, he employs a descriptive model which specifies the structures of conventional utterances. Although the act of discovery is in part intuitive, the model does provide both a method for finding significant linguistic patterns and a taxonomy of the sort of patterns the analyst is likely to find—the still tentative universals of language. Discovery procedures are not mechanical; there is as yet no completely systematic way of analyzing a language, just as there is no algorithm for planning an effective literary composition. But there are important guides to the processes: one can learn to analyze a language and he can learn a great deal about how to write an essay or a novel.

We believe that the procedures the linguist uses in analyzing and describing a language are in some important ways like the procedures a writer uses in planning and writing a composition, and hence that tagmemic theory can provide the basis for a new approach to rhetoric. Tagmemic discovery procedures can provide a heuristic comparable to the Aristotelian system of invention; the tagmemic descriptive model can give us a vehicle for describing conventional rhetorical patterns. If our beliefs are sound, this approach will provide a bridge between the traditionally separate disciplines of grammar and rhetoric.

A heuristic is a method of solving problems, a series of steps or questions which are likely to lead an intelligent analyst to a reasonable solution of a problem. There are two different (though related) kinds of heuristic: a taxonomy of the sorts of solutions that have been found in the past; and an epistemological heuristic, a method of inquiry based on assumptions about how we come to know something. Bacon's statement of the distinction is worth quoting:

> The invention of speech or argument is not properly an invention: for to invent is to discover that we know not, and not to recover or resummon that which we already know; and the use of this invention is no other but *out of the knowledge whereof our mind is already possessed, to draw forth or call before us that which may be pertinent to the purpose which we take into our consideration.* So as, to speak truly, it is no *Invention,* but a *Remembrance* or *Suggestion,* with an application; which is the cause why the schools do place it after judgment, as subsequent and not precedent. Nevertheless, because we do account it a Chase as well of deer in an inclosed park as in a forest at large, and that it hath already obtained the name, let it be called invention: so as it be perceived and discerned, that the scope and end of this invention is readiness and present use of our knowledge, and not addition or amplification thereof.[9]

Aristotelian rhetoric provides a taxonomy of effective rhetorical arguments which a speaker can use to attain specific ends with specific audiences. Tagmemic theory, on the other hand, provides an epistemological heuristic.

Tagmemic epistemology is based largely on two principles, though other principles are necessary for a complete statement of the theory. These two principles emphasize the active role of the observer in discovering pattern, and hence meaning, in the world around him. The first principle contrasts external and internal views of human behavior—in tagmemic jargon, *etic* and *emic* views. This distinction can be seen in the differences between phonetic and phonemic contrasts in linguistic phonology. A phonetic inventory provides a systematic statement of the overt phonological distinctions which occur in various human languages, while a phonemic description provides a systematic statement of the *significant* phonological distinctions in a particular language. A distinction is judged significant, and hence phonemic, if it signals a difference in the lexical meaning of linguistic units. Though there is much controversy about how phonological signals are to be described, the basic distinction remains valid: the contrast, for example, between aspirated and unaspirated consonants is lexically significant for a native speaker of Hindi or Burmese but not for a native speaker of English, who has difficulty in learning to hear this contrast.

The distinction is especially important when two emic systems come in contact, as when the speaker of English is learning to speak Hindi and is forced to recognize that his native distinctions are emic and not necessarily universal. Likewise, one who finds himself in a different culture must learn to distinguish universals of human behavior from particular customs and mores which taken together comprise the emic distinctions of a culture. The ways of treating time and space, for example, vary throughout the world, and one must learn these ways if he wishes to communicate and cooperate outside his own culture.

[9] Quoted in Howell, p. 367.

Though it is interesting to envision a universal etics of rhetoric—an orderly classification of the rhetorical forms found throughout the world—our present concern must be with the writer of English who is writing for readers of English. Even with this restriction one confronts frequent clashes of emic systems, for if a writer has anything new to say, his image of the world must be in some way different from that of his reader. It is at this point of difference that his message lies. He may seek to expand or clarify some feature of the reader's image, thus making it more nearly like his own, or he may seek to replace some feature of the reader's image. In the first instance he would be informing; in the second, persuading.

Before developing this discussion of rhetorical intention further, we must introduce the second major principle in tagmemic epistemology. This principle asserts that a complete analysis of a problem necessitates a trimodal perspective. After the trimodal principle had been worked out in tagmemic theory and the so-called *feature, manifestation,* and *distribution* modes had been defined, Pike noted a striking similarity between these modes and the triple perspectives of modern physics—the complementary views of physical phenomena as involving particles, waves, and fields; as a consequence, Pike decided to adopt this second set of terms for his behavioral model.[10]

Language phenomena—and presumably all human behavior—can be viewed in terms of particles (discrete contrastive bits), waves (unsegmentable physical continua), or fields (orderly systems of relationships). For example, a sentence can be viewed as a sequence of separate words or morphemes; as a physical continuum consisting of acoustic waveforms; or as a system of interrelationships manifesting the grammatical, lexical, and phonological rules of English. Tagmemic theory asserts that only by this complementarity of perspectives is a complete analysis of language structure possible.

The principle of trimodalism gives the analyst both a procedure for approaching new problems and a safeguard against a too limited view of the data. Only when he has described his data from all three perspectives can he be reasonably sure that his analysis is complete. The writer, likewise, can use the principle as an aid in discovering a wide range of features in his topic. Though a writer often emphasizes one mode in a particular work, he should be aware of the other possibilities, particularly if his readers customarily emphasize a different mode. Let us consider a simple example. A particle description of a flower emphasizes those features which make it distinctive from other flowers. A wave description emphasizes the flower as a moment in a process from seed to final decay (even this is only a peak in a larger wave) or as merging into a scene. A field description may partition a flower into its functional parts or classify it in a taxonomical system. The flower may also be seen metaphorically or symbolically, in which case it is conceived as part of a new conceptual field (religious, say, or geometric), where certain of its features (its beauty or its shape) are hypostatized, allowing it to manifest a category

---

[10] Kenneth L. Pike, "Language as Particle, Wave, and Field," *The Texas Quarterly,* II (Summer 1959), 37–54.

in a new field. One can view any topic trimodally and soon discover a wide range of significant perspectives.[11] The process is broad, flexible, and intuitive, though the intuition is guided by what has proved to be a very fruitful principle. It is especially useful since it is not limited to a particular subject matter. In this sense, it is similar to the "common" topics of classical rhetoric. A generally applicable approach helps to free us from the built-in limitations of a conventional, specialized approach. Thus the discovery procedure has a corrective function also.

This heuristic procedure—based on the emic-etic distinction and trimodal perspective—both helps the writer explore his topic and generates a set of questions which he can use to analyze his reader's preconceptions, that is, his reader's emic system:

1) What are the distinctive features of the reader's conception of the topic? What characteristics does it have that lead him to contrast it with similar things? (Particle view)

2) How are the reader's views on this topic part of a mental process, a phase in the continual development of his system of values and assumptions? (Wave view)

3) How does the reader partition the topic? What are its functional elements for him? How does he classify it? (Field view)

The answers to these questions provide criteria for selecting and ordering the writer's subject matter as he develops his discourse.

The missionary linguist in the field seeks to translate his message into the language and cultural conventions of the people, not to teach them English and his own emic conventions. He does not seek to replace their emic system with his own, but to modify their image after finding within it their motivations for receiving his message.[12] For he realizes that change is most effective and enduring when it occurs within the emic system of those he is trying to convince. Unlike traditional rhetoric which sought to persuade people by confirming authoritative attitudes, modern rhetoric, we believe, must seek identification. That is, the writer must seek to have his readers identify his message with their emic system.

Because it seeks identification rather than persuasion, and because this assumption often leads the writer to modify his own position, modern rhetoric—still in the process of development—is characterized by Kenneth Burke and others as "discussion rhetoric." The basis for a rhetoric of this sort has been developed by Anatol Rapaport in his book *Fights, Games, and Debates,* where it is called Rogerian debate—its assumptions having been derived from the methods of the psychotherapist Carl Rogers.[13] This principle

---

[11] For further illustrations of the use of tagmemic discovery procedures in rhetorical invention, see Hubert English, "Linguistics as an Aid to Invention," *College Composition and Communication,* XV, No. 3 (October 1964).

[12] Our conception of the image here is drawn in large part from Kenneth Boulding, *The Image* (Ann Arbor: University of Michigan Press, 1956), and from William Angus Sinclair, *Conditions of Knowing* (London: Routledge and Kegan Paul, 1951).

[13] Anatol Rapaport, *Fights, Games, and Debates* (Ann Arbor: University of Michigan Press, 1961).

of identification of the writer with his audience points toward a rhetoric not of opposition but of mutual respect.

A comparison of emic systems—different systems of selecting and grouping followed by writer and reader—leads the writer to find what he shares with his reader in his conception of the topic and what he does not share. One of the assumptions of tagmemics is that change can occur only over the bridge of a shared element. There can be no action at a distance. The key to understanding language change, for example, is the identification of the shared features of the initial state and the subsequent altered state. The writer's message is an unshared item in the comparison, while the shared items, insofar as they are relevant to the message, provide the means by which the reader can identify—and identify with—the message. Shared items are the potential bridges over which change can take place. These bridges may be broad cultural conventions or more specific things such as common social roles, problems, or philosophical assumptions. Among the most important of these shared items is a common language—a common set of patterns and rules governing selection and grouping of words or morphemes within a sentence, and of sentences and paragraphs within still larger units of discourse. It is here that the linguist can make his unique contribution to a new theory of rhetoric, especially as he broadens his focus to include units larger than the sentence.

So far we have dealt chiefly with what might be called prewriting problems, problems of discovery. We believe, as did Aristotle and Cicero, that a complete theory of rhetoric must include the entire sequence of acts which result in the finished discourse, beginning with the initial act of mental exploration. We have offered two principles of tagmemic heuristic as an indication, hardly an exhaustive one, of how linguistics can contribute to this aspect of rhetorical theory. We now turn to a description of rhetorical patterns beyond the sentence, extending techniques which have been used in the past in the description of lower-level patterns.

Early tagmemics was essentially, but not entirely, a slot-and-substitution grammar, describing linguistic patterns as sequences of functional slots which are filled, or manifested, by a class of fillers. These slots are seen as functional parts of a pattern and may be stated in a formula such as the following simplified formula for an English transitive sentence:

+ Subject + Verb + Object ± Manner ± Locative ± Temporal

(He walked the dog slowly around the block yesterday.) Some of these slots are obligatory (+), some optional (±). Each may be manifested by one of a set of filler constructions; thus the subject slot can be filled by a noun phrase, a pronoun, an adjective phrase, a verbal phrase, a clause, etc. More fully represented, the subject slot in the formula above would be:

+ Subject: np,p,ap,vp, . . . c

Tagmemics assumes that language is composed of interlocking lexical, phonological, and grammatical hierarchies. Here, the internal surface structure of the fillers of the subject slot of the sentence are described at the clause, phrase, word, and morpheme levels of the grammatical hierarchy.

In at least two important ways, however, recent tagmemic grammar goes beyond the surface-level descriptions of other slot-and-substitution grammars.[14] First, tagmemic grammars go on to represent the filler class of a functional slot as a multidimensionally ordered set, or, in tagmemic jargon, a matrix. The categories of these ordered sets indicate relationships of concord between one tagmeme and another; thus, the filler class of the subject tagmeme is ordered into categories such as singular-plural and human-nonhuman in concord with these same categories in the predicate, so that, for example, a singular, nonhuman subject specifies the selection of a singular, nonhuman verb, preventing such collocations as "the tree jump fences."

Second, and more important for our present discussion, tagmemic grammars specify in addition to the surface structure of patterns an ordered set of operations to be carried out on the patterns. These include ordered reading rules by which all possible readings of a formula are generated. Then each reading is reordered according to permutation rules. Finally, in each reading and its permuted variants, the tagmeme symbols are replaced by each of the possible filler constructions according to a set of exponence rules. These operations are carried out repeatedly until only morphemes or symbols for morpheme classes manifest the formulas, which are then terminal grammatical strings, not yet sentences until phonological and lexical specifications have been met.

Though a description of English will not specify sentences such as the one mentioned earlier, "Love John is Mary in," it so far contains no constraints to prevent it from accepting a sequence of sentences of this type:

> The trees are budding. Coal is a form of carbon. He has been singing for three hours now. The world used to be round. It seems enough.

This is not a paragraph because there is no formal connection between the sentences. We can discern no conventional pattern relating them, as we can, for example, in this pair of sentences:

> What is John doing?
> He's washing his face.

This second sequence manifests a conventional rhetorical pattern—Question-Answer. The question is marked by three formal features: the word order, the question word *what,* and (in writing) the punctuation. The second sentence is recognized as an answer to the question by: the pronoun reference (*he* has to be a substitute for *John* here); the parallel grammatical structure, in which the functional slots of the question words in the first sentence

---

[14] A full description of tagmemic grammatical theory can be found in Robert Longacre, *Grammar Discovery Procedures* (The Hague: Mouton, 1964). Tagmemics is contrasted with transformational and other models in Longacre, "Some Fundamental Insights of Tagmemics," *Language,* XLI, No. 1 (January–March 1965), 65–76.

(What . . . doing) are filled in the second (washing his face); the parallelism of verb form (is—ing); the fact that *washing* is a possible lexical equivalent for *doing;* and (in writing) the period. Question-Answer is a formal pattern illustrating a number of formal constraints which extend beyond the sentence.

The relationship of these two sentences can be described in numerous ways (probably most simply by seeing the first as a permutation of the second), but the sentences can only be described as a *sequence* by positing the larger Question-Answer pattern, and by specifying the formal ways in which the two functional slots in this larger pattern are related, just as we specify the relationship between subject and predicate in a sentence. A number of these relatively simple two-part patterns can be described, including greetings, cause and result (hypothesis), topic and illustration, topic and partition, disjunction, and so forth. These patterns can be manifested by a single sentence or by two or more sentences. A large number of higher-level units of discourse can be described as chains of these simple two-part patterns.

As we move on to larger rhetorical patterns, the complexity increases. Formal signals become redundant: for example, we can identify the Answer in the Question-Answer pattern above by five of its contrastive features. Further, lexical and semantic features become increasingly important in recognizing patterns: in the example above we recognize *washing* as a lexical equivalent of *doing.* Lexical equivalence chains are probably the most important markers of higher-level patterns.[15] We can illustrate some of this complexity by attempting to describe the paragraph as a formal structure, limiting ourselves here to only one rather simple pattern.

We believe that written paragraphs are emically definable units—not just groups of sentences isolated by rather arbitrary indentations—and that this fact can be demonstrated. We are presently carrying out controlled testing of the recognition of these units in collaboration with psychologists at the Center for Research on Language and Language Behavior, University of Michigan. Informal investigation has shown that readers, given a text in which all paragraph indentations have been removed, can successfully mark paragraph breaks, with only limited indeterminacy at predictable points. In addition, the readers are able to recognize a number of recurring paragraph patterns and to partition these patterns in predictable ways.

One of the most common of these patterns is the one we have labelled TRI (topic-restriction-illustration) or more formally,

$$+ \, T^2 \pm R + I^n.$$

(The raised numbers indicate that in reading the formula, T may be read twice; R, once; and I, *n* number of times recursively.) This is the Topic-Illustration pattern with an optional intermediary slot in which the topic is restricted in some way (e.g., by definition, classification, or partition). The following paragraph illustrates this pattern:

---

[15] The concept of lexical equivalence chains is derived in large part from Zellig S. Harris, *Discourse Analysis Reprints* (The Hague: Mouton, 1963), pp. 7–10.

(T) The English Constitution—that indescribable entity—is a living thing, growing with the growth of men, and assuming ever-varying forms in accordance with the subtle and complex laws of human character. (R) It is the child of wisdom and chance. (I) The wise men of 1688 moulded it into the shape we know, but the chance that George I could not speak English gave it one of its essential peculiarities—the system of a Cabinet independent of the Crown and subordinate to the Prime Minister. The wisdom of Lord Grey saved it from petrification and set it upon the path of democracy. Then chance intervened once more. A female sovereign happened to marry an able and pertinacious man, and it seemed likely that an element which had been quiescent within it for years—the element of irresponsible administrative power—was about to become its predominant characteristic and change completely the direction of its growth. But what chance gave, chance took away. The Consort perished in his prime, and the English Constitution, dropping the dead limb with hardly a tremor, continued its mysterious life as if he had never been.[16]

The slots in this tripartite pattern are marked by lexical equivalence classes, two of which have extended domains: 1) English Constitution, indescribable entity, living thing, It, child, . . . English Constitution; 2) men, human character, wise men of 1688, George I, Lord Grey, . . . Consort. Note that the domain of the first chain is the entire paragraph, while that of the second chain is the I slot. Chains can thereby be ranked as head and attribute chains, each paragraph including a head chain and one or more attribute chains.

The slots are also marked by: grammatical parallelism (first and second sentences, third and fourth sentences); tense shift (shift to past in the I slot); pronoun domains; determiners; and transitional function words (then, but).

The TRI pattern has a number of variant forms which can be specified by the reading, permutation, and exponence rules. Only a few of these variants will be illustrated. Since R is optional, the pattern can be read as: $+ T + I$. For example, a paragraph by Marchette Chute:

(T) The only safe way to study contemporary testimony is to bear constantly in mind this possibility of prejudice and to put almost as much attention on the writer himself as on what he has written. (I) For instance, Sir Anthony Weldon's description of the Court of King James is lively enough and often used as source material; but a note from the publisher admits that the pamphlet was issued as a warning to anyone who wished to "side with this bloody house" of Stuart. The publisher, at any rate, did not consider Weldon an impartial witness. At about the same time Arthur Wilson published his history of Great Britain, which contained an irresistibly vivid account of the agonized death of the Countess of Somerset. Wilson sounds reasonably impartial; but his patron was the Earl of Essex, who had good reason to hate that particular countess, and there is evidence that he invented the whole scene to gratify his patron.[17]

[16] Lytton Strachey, *Queen Victoria* (New York: Harcourt Brace Jovanovich, Inc., 1921), pp. 300–01.
[17] Marchette Chute, "Getting at the Truth," *The Saturday Review*, Sept. 19, 1953, p. 12.

If I is read a number of times, the pattern may be broken by indentation into more than one paragraph, although it remains a single emic unit. Indentation, like line ends in poetry, can either correspond to formal junctures or, for various reasons, can interrupt the structure in a way somewhat similar to poetic *enjambement*.

The TRI pattern can be permuted to IRT, producing the so-called funnel effect or inductive structure. This is comparable to such permutations at the sentence level as "Home is the sailor" from "The sailor is home." Another illustration by Marchette Chute:

> (I) The reason Alice had so much trouble with her flamingo is that the average flamingo does not wish to be used as a croquet mallet. It has other purposes in view. The same thing is true of a fact, which can be just as self-willed as a flamingo and has its own kind of stubborn integrity. (R) To try to force a series of facts into a previously desired arrangement is a form of misuse to which no self-respecting fact will willingly submit itself. (T) The best and only way to treat it is to leave it alone and be willing to follow where it leads, rather than to press your own wishes upon it.[18]

This permutation is frequently used to begin or end discourse, probably because it imparts a greater sense of closure than the more open-ended TRI order.

Other permutations include TIRI, ITR, and TRIT, to list only the most common. Following exponence rules, slots in paragraph patterns may be filled by other rhetorical patterns. In the following example by Bernard Iddings Bell, the Answer slot in the Question-Answer pattern which we discussed earlier is filled by a TRI pattern, producing a compound paragraph structure:

> (Q) Is the United States a nation composed chiefly of people who have not grown up, who think and act with the impulsiveness of adolescents? (A-T) Many shrewd observers of the American scene, both abroad and here at home, are saying that this is indeed the case. (R) They intentionally disturb our patriotic complacency. (I) They bid us view with alarm cultural immaturity revealed by current trends in journalism, by the radio, by the motion picture, by magazines and best-selling books, by mass response to emotionalized propaganda—political and otherwise; by a patent decay of good manners, by the spread of divorce and by other manifestations of parental irresponsibility; by all the various aspects of behavior which indicate to a student of human affairs the health or sickness of a civilization.[19]

Tagmemic matrix theory provides further insight into another traditional problem of rhetoric. We said earlier that form and idea are seen by many as organically unified, a view that we share. The literary statement contains within itself its own dimensions of development. It constitutes a semantic field

---

[18] *Ibid.,* p. 44.
[19] Bernard Iddings Bell, "We are Indicted for 'Immaturity,'" *New York Times Magazine,* July 20, 1947, p. 8.

which is clearly perceived when we try to extend it. The relevant categories of the English Constitution paragraph discussed above can be displayed in the rows and columns of an emic paragraph matrix (see table below).

If we were to extend the paragraph, we would be obliged to supply a still more recent illustration of the effect of wisdom on the Constitution. It should be possible from a study of a large number of paragraph matrices to generalize further about various types of paragraph development. The investigation of paragraphs as semantic fields is as yet only beginning.

A writer's style, we believe, is the characteristic route he takes through all the choices presented in both the writing and prewriting stages. It is the manifestation of his conception of the topic, modified by his audience, situation, and intention—what we might call his "universe of discourse." These variables directly affect selecting and grouping in all three linguistic hierarchies: grammatical, phonological, and lexical. An analysis and description of style involves the specification of the writer's characteristic choices at all points in the writing process, although usually only the final choices are directly accessible to the analyst.

Forces Shaping the English Constitution

historical manifestations	wisdom	chance
(1688)	The wise men . . . molded it into the shape we know.	
(1714)		George I . . . gave it . . . the system of a Cabinet independent of the Crown and subordinate to the Prime Minister.
(1832)	Lord Grey saved it from petrification and set it upon the path of democracy.	
(1840)		[Victoria's marriage made it seem likely that a quiescent element] was about to become its predominant characteristic and change . . . the direction of its growth.
(1861)		[With the death of the Consort] the English Constitution . . . continued its mysterious life as if he had never been.

The classical conception of style has a number of limitations. To see style as an addition to the message, an affective layer imposed on conventional language, ignores the close connection between language and idea. Seeing it as essentially a matter of sentences ignores stylistic patterns beyond the sentence. In addition, the theory grew out of a very specialized sort of practice—formal public speaking in the courts and legislatures and at ceremonial gatherings. As a result it has a limited range of applicability. Seventeenth century critics were right in saying that its generalizations were inappropriate to a wide range of important topics, audiences, and situations. Finally, the highly normative approach of classical rhetoric tends to ignore the individuality of the writer, describing *a style* rather than *style* itself.

To consider style, however (as do some modern rhetoricians), to be the expression of a particular personality lays too much stress on one variable in the universe of discourse and too little on the others. Some stylistic features of a work inevitably remain unexplained if one commits himself to this definition strictly. To see style as a vision of the topic also has limitations; it ignores the influence of situation and audience on choice. It assumes that the act of writing is essentially expressive, not communicative. Both of these views inhibit systematic theorizing about style; when style is seen as something highly personal, generalization becomes difficult.

To see style in the way many linguists do today—as deviation from conventional language—leads to the difficulty of defining conventional language. Somehow, the deviations must be separated from the corpus, perhaps by measuring the frequencies of patterns. However it is done, it leaves conventional language as a styleless language. This view, like the classical view, tends to conceive of style as an embellishment, an added affective layer. Though very unconventional styles can be identified as linguistic deviations, there are "conventional" styles which this approach does not explain. These include the different styles we all use in various situations, with various audiences, and in writing with various intents on various topics.

It seems to us that a full discussion of style must include the prewriting process if it is to interpret the formal manifestations on the written page—the purely linguistic choices that the writer has made. Without the context of a linguistic unit—the universe of discourse—we are able to describe stylistic features only in a fairly trivial way. With the context provided, there is the possibility of explaining the writer's choices. In a complete theory, then, a particular style is a characteristic series of choices throughout the entire process of writing, including both discovery (invention) and linguistic selection and grouping (arrangement).

We have presented what we believe to be the traditional problems of rhetoric and have suggested how a linguistic model which includes both a discovery procedure and a descriptive technique may provide the base for a new approach to rhetoric, a bridge between the humanities and the sciences.

A tagmemic rhetoric stands somewhere between the rigorous theories of science and the almost purely intuitive theories of the humanities. We see no reason to reject the insights of either the former or the latter, believing that all new knowledge—like the process of writing itself—involves both intuitive analogy and formal precision.

Suggestions for Further Reading

Under a grant from the National Endowment for the Humanities, Richard E. Young and Frank M. Koen completed a study of tagmemic discovery procedures: *The Tagmemic Discovery Procedure: An Evaluation of Its Uses in the Teaching of Rhetoric* (Ann Arbor: The University of Michigan, 1973). The following bibliography is taken from that work.

(Key: *CCC—College Composition and Communication; CE—College English; SLLB—Studies in Language and Language Behavior*)

1964

English, Hubert M. "Linguistic Theory as an Aid to Invention." *CCC* 15 (Oct.), 136–40.

Howes, Alan B. "A Linguistic Analogy in Literary Criticism." *CCC* 15 (Oct.), 141–44.

Pike, Kenneth L. "A Linguistic Contribution to the Teaching of Composition." *CCC* 15 (May), 82–88.

1965

Becker, Alton L. "A Tagmemic Approach to Paragraph Analysis." *CCC* 16 (Dec.), 238–42.

Pike, Kenneth L. "Language: Where Science and Poetry Meet." *CE* 26 (Jan.), 283–92.

Young, Richard E., and Alton L. Becker. "Toward a Modern Theory of Rhetoric: A Tagmemic Contribution." *Harvard Educational Review* 35 (Fall), 450–68. (Reprinted in *Language and Learning*, J. Emig, ed. New York: Harcourt Brace Jovanovich, Inc., 1966; *Teaching Freshman Composition*, G. Tate and E. P. J. Corbett, eds. New York: Oxford, 1967; *New Rhetorics*, M. Steinmann, Jr., ed. New York: Scribners, 1967.)

1966

Becker, Alton L. In "Symposium on the Paragraph." *CCC* 17 (May), 67–72.

Becker, Alton L., and Richard E. Young. "The Role of Lexical and Grammatical Cues in Paragraph Recognition." *SLLB* 2 (Feb.), Center for Research on Language and Language Behavior, Univ. of Michigan, Ann Arbor, 1–6.

1967

Becker, Alton L. "Images of Man and the Persuasive Style: Writing in the Elementary School," in *The Craft of Teaching and the Schooling of Teachers*, Paul Olson, ed., First National Conference, U.S. Office of Education Tri-

University Project in Elementary Education (Sept., 18–20), Denver, Colorado.

Holtz, William. "Field Theory and Literature." *The Centennial Review,* 532–48.

Koen, Frank, Alton L. Becker, and Richard E. Young. "The Psychological Reality of the Paragraph." Part I, *SLLB,* Center for Research on Language and Language Behavior, Univ. of Michigan, Ann Arbor, 526–38.

Lauer, Janice Marie. *Invention in Contemporary Rhetoric: Heuristic Procedures,* unpublished dissertation, University of Michigan, Ann Arbor.

Pike, Kenneth L. *Language in Relation to a Unified Theory of the Structure of Human Behavior.* The Hague: Mouton.

1968

Houle, Sister M. Sheila. "Kenneth L. Pike's Behavioremic Theory as Model for Explicating the Imagery in Joseph Conrad's 'Heart of Darkness,' " unpublished dissertation, University of Iowa, Iowa City.

Koen, Frank, Alton L. Becker, and Richard E. Young. "The Psychological Reality of the Paragraph." Part II, *SLLB* (Feb.), Center for Research on Language and Language Behavior, Univ. of Michigan, Ann Arbor, 482–98.

Young, Richard E. "Notions of 'Generation' in Rhetorical Studies." *SLLB* (Feb.), 546–56.

———. "Discovery Procedures in Tagmemic Rhetoric: An Exercise in Problem Solving." *SLLB* (Sept.), 187–203.

1969

Becker, Alton L., and Sybil Stanton. "Programed Instruction in Sentence Sequencing." *SLLB* (Feb.), 621–34.

Koen, Frank, Alton L. Becker, and Richard E. Young. "The Psychological Reality of the Paragraph." *Journal of Verbal Learning and Verbal Behavior* 8 (Feb.), 49–53.

Young, Richard E. "Problems and the Process of Writing." *SLLB* (Feb.), 494–502.

1970

Klammer, Thomas P., and Carol J. Compton. "Some Recent Contributions to Tagmemic Analysis of Discourse." *Glossa* 8:2, 212–22.

Odell, Camillus Lee. "Discovery Procedures for Contemporary Rhetoric: A Study of the Usefulness of the Tagmemic Heuristic Model in Teaching Composition," unpublished dissertation, University of Michigan, Ann Arbor.

Young, Richard E., Alton L. Becker, and Kenneth L. Pike. *Rhetoric: Discovery and Change.* New York: Harcourt Brace Jovanovich, Inc.

1971

Klammer, Thomas P. "Multihierarchical Structure in a Middle English Breton Lay—A Tagmemic Analysis." *Language and Style* 4, 3–23.

———. "The Structure of Dialogue Paragraphs in Written English Dramatic and Narrative Discourse," unpublished dissertation, University of Michigan, Ann Arbor.

Discovery Through Questioning: A Plan for Teaching Rhetorical Invention

Richard L. Larson

Theoretically, Larson's article has the virtue of "placing" rhetorical invention in the context of the modern composition class. In a practical sense, Larson's set of topics constitutes a useful and simple device that students can use to generate ideas.

I feel that sets of topics such as Larson's ultimately will not yield as much as heuristics such as Young, Becker, and Pike's. A good heuristic gives one a new way to approach subject matter, a questioning procedure that becomes automatic, almost intuitive. Therefore, the best heuristic will have all of the elegant simplicity of a profound mathematical formula. One, after all, is not interested in the formula but in what it will yield. On the other hand, a study that Young completed demonstrates that one needs sophistication and practice if the heuristic is to be productive. Larson's set of topics is almost immediately available to the beginner. Its virtue lies in its simplicity and practicality.

One point that Larson makes needs underscoring: the general public is convinced that nothing very profound goes on in English classes—some spelling drills, a few exercises in punctuation, a little cleaning up of the "errors" in prose. In fact, that is what goes on in all too many English classes. But—in spite of popular opinion and the perversions that characterize many composition classes—we teachers of writing deal with fundamental concerns, two of which are the traditional "departments," style and invention. Unfortunately, we have too often in the past oversimplified the concept of style so that we concentrated almost exclusively on editing, neglecting the more fundamental concern of activating students' competence to embody ideas in structures. As for invention—until very recently we have done little to help the student. When we awakened to the simple notion that we needed to help the student gain ideas, we resorted too often to what I call the "smelly-looky-feely" gimmicks that were based on the notion that if students could be brought alive to the sensual world around them, they would have things to say. Which was right, as far as it went. But rhetorical invention has a profounder meaning than awakening students to their senses and having them produce haikus about autumn leaves, sandpaper, and limburger cheese. We live not only in a sensual world but in a world of ideas and concepts, and it is to this world that rhetorical invention addresses itself.

If there is one crucial difference between the treatment of "invention" by classical rhetoricians and by the authors of texts on "rhetoric" today, it is this: for the classical rhetoricians "invention" is one step in what Aristotle called "finding the available means of persuasion in a given case," while for present-day writers of textbooks invention is finding something—anything—to say about any chosen subject. Aristotle, Cicero, and their followers trained students to argue for a particular proposition of fact or of value or of policy—these may correspond roughly to forensic, epideictic, and deliberative discourse, respectively—that had already been securely determined. They evidently assumed that if the exact proposition to argue was in doubt, the speaker knew what were the propositions that might be argued, and had only to decide which proposition best fitted the facts. Either the client was guilty of murder, for example, or the homicide was accidental, or the client acted in self-defense. Either the dead warrior deserved honor for his humane treatment of captives, or he was a coward and a weakling for failing to punish captured enemies ruthlessly. Either the state should make war on its enemies until it wins, or the state should negotiate with its enemies. After he had chosen his ground, the speaker could draw on his knowledge of rhetoric to help him defend it.

To be sure, as Richard Hughes points out, "argument" for Aristotle is "discovered judgment" on questions such as those listed above; "the rhetorician . . . discovers a judgment in an area where experience is still flexible enough to take many shapes" ("The Contemporaneity of Classical Rhetoric," *College Composition and Communication,* October, 1965, p. 158). But what is discovered is still a judgment (presumably on an issue that admits of alternative resolutions), and the judgments (propositions) from which the speaker had to choose were suggested to him almost immediately by his data. Once he had discovered his judgment, his task became that of adapting his arguments, the design of his discourse, and his mode of expression to his audience and the occasion for speaking. Or, as Professor Hughes puts it a few sentences later in the article just cited, the speaker's task was to propagate "that realized judgment in whatever structures [would] lead to a duplication of his discovery in the mind of his audience."

The authors of current texts on rhetoric (particularly the rhetoric of written communication), however, do not assume that young writers and speakers who will use their books have in hand a proposition (or more than one) ready to be argued. These students are a long way, it seems, from being ready to argue propositions of fact, value, or policy. Confronting the task of writing an essay, most students are barren of ideas, our text-writers tell us, or they are inclined to prefer unworkably broad subjects (e.g., "heroes in Dickens"), or they have many undeveloped ideas—none of them well-formed propositions that can be argued in an essay. When they discuss invention, our text-writers apparently seek no more than to get students to write something specific—it seems not to matter what—about some subject—it seems not to matter which. (In "Teaching Students the Art of Discovery," *College Composition and Communication,* February, 1968, David Harrington demonstrates the fuzziness and relative emptiness of the advice about invention in many current texts.) Writing and speaking are simply chores assigned by teachers of English and Speech, rather than means for putting across an author's convictions vividly to readers or listeners so that author and audience may approach a meeting of minds (what Kenneth Burke calls "identification").

Granting that the treatment of invention in many current "rhetoric" texts is superficial, these books may be quite correct in assuming that in teaching invention we face a task which the rhetoricians of Greece and Rome evidently did not try to address. That is the task of helping students decide what experiences, or parts of experiences, *should* be discussed. To state the point differently, the task is to help students see what is of interest and value in their experiences, to enable them to recognize when something they see or read or feel warrants a response from them, in other words to stimulate active inquiry into what is happening around them in place of the indifference or passivity with which they often face other than their most dramatic experiences. Of course some students often have convictions to express (propositions to argue) and most students have such convictions sometimes. So teaching "invention" as the classical rhetoricians perceived it is by no means irrelevant, although we might wish our students to think of rhetoric, and therefore of invention, not as a means of persuasion (which can be achieved unfairly) but as the art of writing so as to win the reader's respect for their convictions in every case, and his assent wherever assent can be fairly won. What is needed for the teaching of invention today, therefore, is a plan that will help the student explore his experiences to discover when it is important to speak out, and that will help him speak out effectively on those occasions. We need a plan that draws attention first to the experience and then to the task of communicating effectively.

One source of help in finding this plan may be the psychologists who have studied the phenomenon of "creativity," as Gordon Rohman demonstrated in the report of his experiments with "prewriting" exercises a few years ago in writing classes at Michigan State University, which were based in part on theories by Rollo May and Arthur Koestler about the process of creating.[1]

[1] Useful discussions of the psychology of creativity appear in Calbin Taylor and Frank Williams, eds., *Instructional Media and Creativity* (New York, 1966), especially in the papers by J. P. Guilford and Malcolm Provus.

These writers argue that if a student is to create, to "bring [something new] into birth" (Rollo May's words), he must learn to understand thoroughly his experiences, the data he has to work with—what May calls his "world." He must become intimately familiar with the details of those experiences, the possible relationships among facts, and the possible implications of those facts. He must then be willing to transform, reformulate, or recombine those experiences into new imagined forms. As May puts it, the creative person (including, presumably, a student seeking new ideas) must engage in an intense "encounter," voluntarily or involuntarily, with his experiences or what he sees around him. "Genuine creativity is characterized by an intensity of awareness, a heightened consciousness. . . . The creative act is an encounter characterized by a high degree of consciousness" ("The Nature of Creativity," *Etc.: a Review of General Semantics,* Spring, 1959, pp. 264–265, 268). "Creating," as the psychologists use the term, can surely be thought of as another name for "invention."

I propose therefore, that in our teaching of "invention" we make a persistent effort to force students to become as familiar as possible with the facts, and possible relationships among the facts, about experiences on which they might write, and also that we force them to examine the facts underlying concepts they consider important and the content of propositions on which they may want to write. I use the term "fact," in reference to concepts, to designate linguistic or semantic experiences that help form a concept (the encounters that a person has had with believers and churches, for example, help establish the concept of "religion"). When speaking of the "content" of a proposition, I refer to the range of possible statements the words used in that proposition might make, the premises it takes for granted, the judgments it may imply, the feelings it may stir, and so on. I propose that students come to this thorough knowledge of their experiences, concepts, and propositions through a process of systematic questioning—questioning which students engage in mostly by themselves, rather than questioning conducted for them by the teacher. The teacher may demonstrate the technique of systematic questioning, but the students must apply the technique for themselves if they are really to learn its usefulness.

I have, accordingly, prepared an outline of questions that teachers of rhetoric might train students to use. The questions are divided into seven groups; I think that most of the writing assignments we give, or better still, most of the occasions a student might find for writing, can be classified in one of the seven groups. Occasions for writing about literature (including intellectual prose) and history, for example, fall into group IB or ID. Occasions for writing about objects or events that we have directly observed (including personal experiences) fall into IA or IB. If the student is examining more than one event, the activity falls into group ID.

Using Robert Gorrell's terms, I suggest that the kinds of subjects enumerated in Group I are "topics requiring comment." The study of propositions, or "topics with comment already supplied," is dealt with in Part II. The study of questions, which are topics on which the writer has yet to choose among possible comments, is also included under Part II. The central inventive questions under Part II, of course, are those dealing with how the proposition can be supported, that is, how the writer can induce his reader to believe, or at least respect, the proposition. Almost equally important are the questions that invite the student to consider fully what he is saying: What do all the words in context—not just the subjects and verbs, but the adverbs, adjectives, prepositions, and the very order of parts in the sentence—*say* to the reader? Invention under Part II consists of discovering what needs to be said in order to cause the reader to believe all of the important assertions contained in the proposition.

In compiling the questions, I have drawn freely on the work of logicians, rhetoricians, and theorists of language. Use of logical techniques of division and classification is encouraged in many of the questions. Paul Rodgers' suggestions about training students to observe objects precisely (in "Breaching the Abstraction Barrier," *College Composition and Communication,* February, 1966) were especially helpful. So were some concepts (such as "range of variation") introduced by the tagmemic theorists. Applying perspectives from different sources, I am convinced, can call attention to the importance of data that may at first seem insignificant, and can suggest ways of restructuring a body of data so as to disclose features of an experience that had not been recognized but that are well worth writing about. This construction of new patterns and frameworks, what Professor Guilford in *Instructional Media and Creativity* calls "system-building," is an important step in the process of creation.

> One of the most neglected processes in present creative-training procedures, and yet one of the most important of the common creative processes found in the very productive creator, is the construction of systems. Most descriptions of what creative persons do mention that relatively early in the total sequence of events some kind of system appears, whether it be a theme, a story plot, a motif, or some other kind of outline affair. This is the backbone, the skeleton, or framework of the major production to come. Within the total framework, subsystems are also developed . . . (p. 91)

For the student who applies rigorously the questions I have listed, then, invention may indeed become synonymous with "creation" or "discovery." Use of these questions may help to alter his entire way of perceiving experiences, both inside and outside of the English composition class.

This design for questioning is of value, of course, only if students know how to apply it rigorously. When a teacher assigns a subject for writing, he can direct students in use of these questions by helping them see the class into which the subject falls and then asking them deliberately to apply all of the questions that pertain to it. In class discussion the first, tentative answers to many of the questions listed may lead to other questions—such as about the nature and value of the observations or other evidence used in those first answers, possible sources of data that have been overlooked, possible analogies between what has been observed and what can be remembered from the past, and so on. Not all of the questions, of course, will produce useful answers for every subject, and the student should learn which questions provide valuable ideas on which subjects and which ones are comparatively fruitless on those subjects. To learn this skill of discriminating among questions will help the student to discover more rapidly how to find out what matters in the data before him.

The process of questioning can also be carried on silently by the student himself once he has mastered the questions, or, perhaps more promising, it can be carried on by students working in small groups. Use of such study groups would turn over the responsibility of learning to the students themselves, and would encourage students to help teach each other—both of them practices increasingly favored by innovative classroom teachers.

Invention of matter for discussion does not, of course, follow immediately and automatically upon rigorous application of questions to possible subjects for composing. Students have still to evaluate the details and perspectives turned up by the questions. There are at least three sorts of evaluations that can help stimulate the desire to write. The first, which Gordon Rohman emphasized in his experiments at Michigan State, is the discovery that the subject being studied can be compared in some way to another subject or to a remembered experience, and that the analogy may hint toward a generalization (a statement of the discovery that the same characteristic may be attributed to many items). Much of the literary analysis performed by scholars (and by students as well) relies on this sort of evaluation. So does the study, for example, of a particular work of art or architecture, when the identification of the details of that object calls to mind similar details in other works already studied and encourages generalizations about an artist, a subject, or a period.

The second kind of evaluation is simply personal response: "I like a thing" or "I don't like it"; "I believe this thing or event is good or is not good or is dangerous." Of course, some students make personal judgments freely, and we want them to do so; students who refuse to commit themselves frequently write banal papers. But we also want their judgments to be informed by knowledge of the facts. Detailed questioning turns up the facts and may bring into focus the standards for making judgments, both of them necessary for responsible writing—as opposed to capricious writing—about personal judgments.

The third kind of evaluation, perhaps the most useful, is the detection of conflict, inconsistency, or inexplicability in the answers to the questions. If the student analyzing a subject can discover in his analysis a problem that matters to him, he is on his way to informative exploration of the subject and toward something worth saying in a piece of writing. To suspect that what happens at the end of a novel is not adequately accounted for by what we know about the principal characters puts the student on the road toward either a more thorough understanding of that novel or a reasoned assessment of that novel. To discover that the actions of a group, or even a whole society, are in conflict with its ostensible goals, for example, is to find an occasion for warning the members of that group and for proposing different actions. One stimulus to writing is puzzlement or discomfort, as Richard Whately implied when he identified introductions "inquisitive," "paradoxical," and "corrective" as common in rhetorical discourse. One of the jobs of a teacher of writing may be to induce creative puzzlement in his students; to resolve the puzzle they may want to search and to write.

These three sources of the impulse to write come, as I have said, from the study of topics for which comments have not already been supplied. The impulse to write, I have implied, comes from the discovery of a comment that seems worth making. The process of invention need not stop, however, when comment has been added to topic. For adding comment to topic gives the writer a proposition, and most propositions can be understood better by applying to them the questions listed in Part II of my outline. Though a comment supplied by a student after he has asked numerous questions about a body of data may not require as much further effort at invention as a comment handed to the student cold for discussion, even those comments that have been generated by a student (or a professional writer) after an analysis of data and a search for ways of resolving his puzzles merit systematic analysis. If the writer has arrived at a conviction, he still has the task of leading his reader to respect that conviction. To do so, he must be sure that he knows what points in his comment need elaboration, explanation, clarification, illustration, and what support his comment obligates him to provide. What he cannot elaborate usefully he may need to drop. What he cannot support he may need to reconsider and perhaps to alter. Those underlying, unstated assumptions which the reader must accept before he can respect the writer's opinions may themselves need support, and the search for support may disclose the need for further examination of data, perhaps even for a change in the comment. When Loren Eiseley writes, for example, that ". . . we are all potential fossils still carrying within our bodies the crudities of former existences, the marks of a world in which living creatures flew with little more consistency than clouds from age to age" (*The Immense Journey* [New York, 1957], p. 6), he accepts the obligation to discover materials that will make clear what he means by this judgment about human evolution, to present data that will illustrate and substantiate his claim, to reveal what he is assuming about the course of evolution, and perhaps to demonstrate why this perception is important enough for a reader to ponder.

In short, once a possible comment has been discovered, it can be evaluated, perhaps revised. The invention of a comment for the writer's topic is not a process that is quickly finished; it continues with testing and revision of possible assertions until the comment that best suits the writer's data is found. Finding a suitable way of stating one's comment on a topic, then, is often itself a problem for which the writer must find a solution; he must identify alternative statements and test them to see whether they are workable.

I have emphasized here the discovery of the content for a piece of writing, and I have not discussed the discovery of a form for ordering that content nor of language for the presentation of that content. Teachers of composition spend a great deal of time talking about ways of arranging data, about outlines, plans of organization, rhetorical strategies, usage, diction, figures of speech, and punctuation. Though doubtless important, these techniques ought always to be the servants of an idea, not its masters, which is what they sometimes seem to be. If there is nothing to say, there is no reason to spend much energy on how to say it. Students know this, even if their teachers do not seem to, and they act on the knowledge. This fact—I hesitate to call it a discovery—calls, I think, for considerable refocusing of our efforts as teachers, as theorists of rhetoric, away from the formal, stylistic, and even logical difficulties of a completed utterance to the process by which a writer comes to have something to say in the first place. If we can help the student find something to say that matters, he may reciprocate by expending a little energy on the form and language with which he says it. But even if he doesn't, he may still write with conviction and excite our interest as readers—something that no empty utterance, however perfect its form, can do.

Our curricula in composition and rhetoric, in fact, might be organized to give students practice in analyzing, by means of questions such as those listed here, a succession of increasingly complex experiences. Such a plan would be quite as legitimate as one that uses rhetorical techniques or great issues as an organizing principle. The course in composition might then become a course in discovering what is worth writing about in the successive experiences. Discussions of ways to organize papers and of "voices" to adopt might follow, and be subordinate to, efforts at this kind of discovery. The course in rhetoric might regain some of its lost dignity if instructors insisted first of all upon the worth and importance of what their students said.

One further point. Leaders of professional organizations of English teachers warn that the profession has failed to convince the American public that what it does for its students is important enough to warrant continued support and encouragement—from Congress, from the U.S. Office of Education, from foundations. I apologize for adding such a pragmatic argument to a discussion of pedagogy, which of course should be unsullied by crass motives, but if English teaching is having trouble with its "image," the reason may be its seeming preoccupation with form and expression at the expense of ideas. The student's ability to discover ways of talking about his observations and experiences, though no more important to the teacher of English than his ability to arrange and state ideas, may be what is most valuable to him outside his English classroom in his later role as professional man and citizen. To decide that we will help students to discover and perfect ideas may be one way to define for ourselves a role that adult citizens can applaud. And, the highest of tributes, even our students may esteem more than they do now our courses in composition.

A Plan for Teaching Rhetorical Invention

I. "Topics" That Invite Comment

    A. *Writing about Single Items* (*in present existence*)

        What are its precise physical characteristics (shape, dimensions, composition, etc.)?

        How does it differ from things that resemble it?

        What is its "range of variation" (how much can we change it and still identify it as the thing we started with)?

        Does it call to mind other objects we have observed earlier in our lives? why? in what respects?

        From what points of view can it be examined?

        What sort of structure does it have?

        How do the parts of it work together?

        How are the parts put together?

        How are the parts proportioned in relation to each other?

        To what structure (class or sequence of items) does it belong?

        Who or what produced it in this form? Why?

        Who needs it?

        Who uses it? for what?

        What purposes might it serve?

        How can it be evaluated, for these purposes?

    B. *Writing about Single Completed Events, or Parts of an Ongoing Process* (*These questions can apply to scenes and pictures, as well as to works of fiction and drama.*)

        Exactly what happened? (Tell the precise sequence: who? what? when? how? why? Who did what to whom? why? What did what to what? how?)

        What were the circumstances in which the event occurred? What did they contribute to its happening?

        How was the event like or unlike similar events?

        What were its causes?

        What were its consequences?

        What does its occurrence imply? What action (if any) is called for?

        What was affected (indirectly) by it?

        What, if anything, does it reveal or emphasize about some general condition?

        To what group or class might it be assigned?

        Is it (in general) good or bad? by what standard? How do we arrive at the standard?

How do we know about it? What is the authority for our information?
How reliable is the authority? How do we know it to be reliable? (or
unreliable?)
How might the event have been changed or avoided?
To what other events was it connected? how?
To what kinds of structure (if any) can it be assigned? On what basis?

C. *Writing about Abstract Concepts* (*e.g., "religion," "socialism"*)

To what specific items, groups of items, events, or groups of events, does
the word or words connect, in your experience or imagination?
What characteristics must an item or event have before the name of the
concept can apply to it?
How do the referents of that concept differ from the things we name with
similar concepts (e.g., "democracy" and "socialism")?
How has the term been used by writers whom you have read? How have
they implicitly defined it?
Does the word have "persuasive" value? Does the use of it in connection
with another concept seem to praise or condemn the other concept?
Are you favorably disposed to all things included in the concept? Why or
why not?

D. *Writing about Collections of Items* (*in present existence*) [These questions
are in addition to the questions about single items, which can presumably
be asked of each item in the group.]

What, exactly, do the items have in common?
If they have features in common, how do they differ?
How are the items related to each other, if not by common characteristics?
What is revealed about them by the possibility of grouping them in this
way?
How may the group be divided? What bases for division can be found?
What correlations, if any, may be found among the various possible sub-
groups? Is anything disclosed by the study of these correlations?
Into what class, if any, can the group as a whole be put?

E. *Writing about Groups of Completed Events, Including Processes* [These
questions are in addition to questions about single completed events; such
questions are applicable to each event in the group. These questions also
apply to literary works, principally fiction and drama.]

What have the events in common?
If they have features in common, how do they differ?
How are the events related to each other (if they are not part of a chrono-
logical sequence)? What is revealed by the possibility of grouping them
in this way (these ways)?
What is revealed by the events when taken as a group?
How can the group be divided? On what bases?
What possible correlations can be found among the several sub-groups?
Into what class, if any, can the events taken as a group fit?
Does the group belong to any other structures than simply a larger group
of similar events? (Is it part of a more inclusive chronological sequence?

one more piece of evidence that may point toward a conclusion about history? and so on)

To what antecedents does the group of events look back? Where can they be found?

What implications, if any, does the group of events have? Does the group point to a need for some sort of action?

II. "Topics" with "Comments" Already Attached

A. *Writing about Propositions* (*statements set forth to be proved or disproved*)

What must be established for the reader before he will believe it?

Into what sub-propositions, if any, can it be broken down? (What smaller assertions does it contain?)

What are the meanings of key words in it?

To what line of reasoning is it apparently a conclusion?

How can we contrast it with other, similar, propositions? (How can we change it, if at all, and still have roughly the same proposition?)

To what class (or classes) of propositions does it belong?

How inclusive (or how limited) is it?

What is at issue, if one tries to prove the proposition?

How can it be illustrated?

How can it be proven (by what kinds of evidence)?

What will or can be said in opposition to it?

Is it true or false? How do we know? (direct observation, authority, deduction, statistics, other sources?)

Why might someone disbelieve it?

What does it assume? (What other propositions does it take for granted?)

What does it imply? (What follows from it?) Does it follow from the proposition that action of some sort must be taken?

What does it reveal (signify, if true)?

If it is a prediction, how probable is it? On what observations of past experience is it based?

If it is a call to action, what are the possibilities that action can be taken? (Is what is called for feasible?) What are the probabilities that the action, if taken, will do what it is supposed to do? (Will the action called for work?)

B. *Writing about Questions* (*interrogative sentences*)

Does the question refer to past, present, or future time?

What does the question assume (take for granted)?

In what data might answers be sought?

Why does the question arise?

What, fundamentally, is in doubt? How can it be tested? evaluated?

What propositions might be advanced in answer to it?

Is each proposition true?

If it is true:

What will happen in the future? What follows from it?

Which of these predictions are possible? probable?

What action should be taken (avoided) in consequence?

[Most of the other questions listed under "Propositions" also apply.]

The Five Key Terms of Dramatism

Kenneth Burke

What, one might ask, is contemporary about Kenneth Burke's Pentad —his five key terms of dramatism—for, after all, it has been around since 1945. My reason for including it in this book is simply that it is the most widely known and influential set of topics since Aristotle and Cicero, and yet I suspect that relatively few people have read Burke's own explanation of it. There are, of course, countless sets of topics, and only a very few of them appear in Contemporary Rhetoric, *but ending the section on invention with Burke gives the discussion a real finality, if not completeness.*

The Pentad—agent, agency, act, purpose, scene—is an elegantly simple little set of probes, leading to obvious questions: Who did it? By what means? What exactly was done? Why? Where (in time and place)? Complete answers to these questions will give anyone a fair survey of a work of drama, and also of any of the countless dramas of human history. Then, of course, there are ratios: agent–agency, act–scene, and so on. In effect, the Pentad can remain elementary, posing the five obvious questions, or it can become as complex a probe as the user desires. Burke explains all of this in the selection that follows, and he illustrates the use of the Pentad in A Grammar of Motives.

What is involved, when we say what people are doing and why they are doing it? An answer to that question is the subject of this book. The book is concerned with the basic forms of thought which, in accordance with the nature of the world as all men necessarily experience it, are exemplified in the attributing of motives. These forms of thought can be embodied profoundly or trivially, truthfully or falsely. They are equally present in systematically elaborated metaphysical structures, in legal judgments, in poetry and fiction, in political and scientific works, in news and in bits of gossip offered at random.

We shall use five terms as generating principle of our investigation. They are: Act, Scene, Agent, Agency, Purpose. In a rounded statement about motives, you must have some word that names the *act* (names what took place, in thought or deed), and another that names the *scene* (the background of the act, the situation in which it occurred); also, you must indicate what person or kind of person (*agent*) performed the act, what means or instruments he used (*agency*), and the *purpose*. Men may violently disagree about the purpose behind a given act, or about the character of the person who did it, or how he did it, or in what kind of situation he acted; or they may even insist upon totally different words to name the act itself. But be that as it may, any complete statement about motives will offer *some kind of* answers to these five questions: what was done (act), when or where it was done (scene), who did it (agent), how he did it (agency), and why (purpose).

If you ask why, with a whole world of terms to choose from, we select these rather than some others as basic, our book itself is offered as the answer. For, to explain our position, we shall show how it can be applied.

Act, Scene, Agent, Agency, Purpose. Although, over the centuries men have shown great enterprise and inventiveness in pondering matters of human motivation, one can simplify the subject by this pentad of key terms, which are understandable almost at a glance. They need never to be abandoned, since all statements that assign motives can be shown to arise out of them and to terminate in them. By examining them quizzically, we can range far; yet the terms are always there for us to reclaim, in their everyday simplicity, their almost miraculous easiness, thus enabling us constantly to begin afresh. When they might become difficult, when we can hardly see them, through having stared at them too intensely, we can of a sudden relax, to look at them as we always have, lightly, glancingly. And having reassured ourselves, we can start out again, once more daring to let them look strange and difficult for a time.

In an exhibit of photographic murals (*Road to Victory*) at the Museum of Modern Art, there was an aerial photograph of two launches, proceeding side by side on a tranquil sea. Their wakes crossed and recrossed each other in almost an infinity of lines. Yet despite the intricateness of this tracery, the picture gave an impression of great simplicity, because one could quickly perceive the generating principle of its design. Such, ideally, is the case with our pentad of terms, used as generating principle. It should provide us with a kind of simplicity that can be developed into considerable complexity, and yet can be discovered beneath its elaborations.

We want to inquire into the purely internal relationships which the five terms bear to one another, considering their possibilities of transformation, their range of permutations and combinations—and then to see how these various resources figure in actual statements about human motives. Strictly speaking, we mean by a Grammar of motives a concern with the terms alone, without reference to the ways in which their potentialities have been or can be utilized in actual statements about motives. Speaking broadly we could designate as "philosophies" any statements in which these grammatical resources are specifically utilized. Random or unsystematic statements about motives could be considered as fragments of a philosophy.

One could think of the Grammatical resources as *principles,* and of the various philosophies as *casuistries* which apply these principles to temporal situations. For instance, we may examine the term Scene simply as a blanket term for the concept of background or setting *in general,* a name for *any* situation in which acts or agents are placed. In our usage, this concern would be "grammatical." And we move into matters of "philosophy" when we note that one thinker uses "God" as his term for the ultimate ground or scene of human action, another uses "nature," a third uses "environment," or "history," or "means of production," etc. And whereas a statement about the grammatical principles of motivation might lay claim to a universal validity, or complete certainty, the choice of any one philosophic idiom embodying these principles is much more open to question. Even before we know what act is to be discussed, we can say with confidence that a rounded discussion of its motives must contain a reference to *some kind of* background. But since each philosophic idiom will characterize this background differently, there will remain the question as to which characterization is "right" or "more nearly right."

It is even likely that, whereas one philosophic idiom offers the best calculus for one case, another case answers best to a totally different calculus. However, we should not think of "cases" in too restricted a sense. Although, from the standpoint of the grammatical principles inherent in the internal relationships prevailing among our five terms, any given philosophy is to be considered as a casuistry, even a cultural situation extending over centuries is a "case," and would probably require a much different philosophic idiom as its temporizing calculus of motives than would be required in the case of other cultural situations.

In our original plans for this project, we had no notion of writing a "Grammar" at all. We began with a theory of comedy, applied to a treatise on human relations. Feeling that competitive ambition is a drastically overdeveloped motive in the modern world, we thought this motive might be transcended if men devoted themselves not so much to "excoriating" it as to "appreciating" it. Accordingly, we began taking notes on the foibles and antics of what we tended to think of as "the Human Barnyard."

We sought to formulate the basic stratagems which people employ, in endless variations, and consciously or unconsciously, for the outwitting or cajoling of one another. Since all these devices had a "you and me" quality about them, being "addressed" to some person or to some advantage, we classed them broadly under the heading of a Rhetoric. There were other notes, concerned with modes of expression and appeal in the fine arts, and with purely psychological or psychoanalytic matters. These we classed under the heading of Symbolic.

We had made still further observations, which we at first strove uneasily to class under one or the other of these two heads, but which we were eventually able to distinguish as the makings of a Grammar. For we found in the course of writing that our project needed a grounding in formal considerations logically prior to both the rhetorical and the psychological. And as we proceeded with this introductory groundwork, it kept extending its claims until it had spun itself from an intended few hundred words into nearly 200,000, of which the present book is revision and abridgement.

Theological, metaphysical, and juridical doctrines offer the best illustration of the concerns we place under the heading of Grammar; the forms and methods of art best illustrate the concerns of Symbolic; and the ideal material to reveal the nature of Rhetoric comprises observations on parliamentary and diplomatic devices, editorial bias, sales methods and incidents of social sparring. However, the three fields overlap considerably. And we shall note, in passing, how the Rhetoric and the Symbolic hover about the edges of our central theme, the Grammar.

A perfectionist might seek to evolve terms free of ambiguity and inconsistency (as with the terministic ideals of symbolic logic and logical positivism). But we have a different purpose in view, one that probably retains traces of its "comic" origin. We take it for granted that, insofar as men cannot themselves create the universe, there must remain something essentially enigmatic about the problem of motives, and that this underlying enigma will manifest itself in inevitable ambiguities and inconsistencies among the terms for motives. Accordingly, what we want is *not terms that avoid ambiguity, but terms that clearly reveal the strategic spots at which ambiguities necessarily arise.*

Occasionally, you will encounter a writer who seems to get great exaltation out of proving, with an air of much relentlessness, that some philosophic term or other has been used to cover a variety of meanings, and who would smash and abolish this idol. As a general rule, when a term is singled out for such harsh treatment, if you look closer you will find that it happens to be associated with some cultural or political trend from which the writer would dissociate himself; hence there is a certain notable ambiguity in this very charge of ambiguity, since he presumably feels purged and strengthened by bringing to bear upon this particular term a kind of attack that could, with as much justice, be brought to bear upon any other term (or "title") in philosophy, including of course the alternative term, or "title," that the writer would swear by. Since no two things or acts or situations are exactly alike, you cannot apply the same term to both of them without thereby introducing a certain margin of ambiguity, an ambiguity as great as the difference between the two subjects that are given the identical title. And all the more may you expect to find ambiguity in terms so "titular" as to become the marks of a philosophic school, or even several philosophic schools. Hence, instead of considering it our task to "dispose of" any ambiguity by merely disclosing the fact that it is an ambiguity, we rather consider it our task to study and clarify the *resources* of ambiguity. For in the course of this work, we shall deal with many kinds of *transformation*—and it is in the areas of ambiguity that transformations take place; in fact, without such areas, transformation would be impossible. Distinctions, we might say, arise out of a great central moltenness, where all is merged. They have been thrown from a liquid center to the surface, where they have congealed. Let one of these crusted distinctions return to its source, and in this alchemic center it may be remade, again becoming molten liquid, and may enter into new combinations, whereat it may be again thrown forth as a new crust, a different distinction. So that A may become non-A. But not merely by a leap from one state to the other. Rather, we must take A back into the ground of its existence, the logical substance that is its causal ancestor, and on to a point where it is consubstantial with non-A; then we may return, this time emerging with non-A instead.

And so with our five terms: certain formal interrelationships prevail among these terms, by reason of their role as attributes of a common ground or substance. Their participation in a common ground makes for transformability. At every point where the field covered by any one of these terms overlaps upon the field covered by any other, there is an alchemic opportunity, whereby we can put one philosophy or doctrine of motivation into the alembic, make the appropriate passes, and take out another. From the central moltenness, where all the elements are fused into one togetherness, there are thrown forth, in separate crusts, such distinctions as those between freedom and necessity, activity and passiveness, coöperation and competition, cause and effect, mechanism and teleology.

Our term, "Agent," for instance, is a general heading that might, in a given case, require further subdivision, as an agent might have his act modified (hence partly motivated) by friends (co-agents) or enemies (counter-agents). Again, under "Agent" one could place any personal properties that are assigned a motivational value, such as "ideas," "the will," "fear," "malice," "intuition," "the creative imagination." A portrait painter may treat the body as a property of the agent (an expression of personality), whereas materialistic medicine would treat it as "scenic," a purely "objective material"; and from another point of view it could be classed as an agency, a means by which one gets reports of the world at large. Machines are obviously instruments (that is, Agencies); yet in their vast accumulation they constitute the industrial scene, with its own peculiar set of motivational properties. War may be treated as an Agency, insofar as it is a means to an end; as a collective Act, subdivisible into many individual acts; as a Purpose, in schemes proclaiming a cult of war. For the man inducted into the army, war is a Scene, a situation that motivates the nature of his training; and in mythologies war is an Agent, or perhaps better a super-agent, in the figure of the war god. We may think of voting as an act, and of the voter as an agent; yet votes and voters both are hardly other than a politician's medium or agency; or from another point of view, they are a part of his scene. And insofar as a vote is cast without adequate knowledge of its consequences, one might even question whether it should be classed as an activity at all; one might rather call it passive, or perhaps sheer motion (what the behaviorists would call a Response to a Stimulus).

Or imagine that one were to manipulate the terms, for the imputing of motives, in such a case as this: The hero (agent) with the help of a friend (co-agent) outwits the villain (counter-agent) by using a file (agency) that enables him to break his bonds (act) in order to escape (purpose) from the room where he has been confined (scene). In selecting a casuistry here, we might locate the motive in the agent, as were we to credit his escape to some trait integral to his personality, such as "love of freedom." Or we might stress the motivational force of the scene, since nothing is surer to awaken thoughts of escape in a man than a condition of imprisonment. Or we might note the essential part played by the *co-agent,* in assisting our hero to escape—and, with such thoughts as our point of departure, we might conclude that the motivations of this act should be reduced to social origins.

Or if one were given to the brand of speculative enterprise exemplified by certain Christian heretics (for instance, those who worshipped Judas as a saint, on the grounds that his betrayal of Christ, in leading to the Crucifixion, so brought about the opportunity for mankind's redemption) one might locate the necessary motivational origin of the act in the *counter-agent.* For the hero would not have been prodded to escape if there had been no villain to imprison him. Inasmuch as the escape could be called a "good" act, we might find in such motivational reduction to the counter-agent a compensatory transformation whereby a bitter fountain may give forth sweet waters. In his *Anti-Dühring* Engels gives us a secular variant which no one could reasonably call outlandish or excessive:

> It was slavery that first made possible the division of labour between agriculture and industry on a considerable scale, and along with this, the flower of the ancient world, Hellenism. Without slavery, no Greek state, no Greek art and science; without slavery, no Roman Empire. But without Hellenism and the Roman Empire as a basis, also no modern Europe.
>
> We should never forget that our whole economic, political and intellectual development has as its presupposition a state of things in which slavery was as necessary as it was universally recognized. In this sense we are entitled to say: Without the slavery of antiquity, no modern socialism.

Pragmatists would probably have referred the motivation back to a source in *agency.* They would have noted that our hero escaped by using an *instrument,* the file by which he severed his bonds; then in this same line of thought, they would have observed that the hand holding the file was also an instrument; and by the same token the brain that guided the hand would be an instrument, and so likewise the educational system that taught the methods and shaped the values involved in the incident.

True, if you reduce the terms to any one of them, you will find them branching out again; for no one of them is enough. Thus, Mead called his pragmatism a philosophy of the *act.* And though Dewey stresses the value of "intelligence" as an instrument (agency, embodied in "scientific method"), the other key terms in his casuistry, "experience" and "nature," would be the equivalents of act and scene respectively. We must add, however, that Dewey is given to stressing the *overlap* of these two terms, rather than the respects in which they are distinct, as he proposes to "replace the traditional separation of nature and experience with the idea of continuity." (The quotation is from *Intelligence and the Modern World.*)

As we shall see later, it is by reason of the pliancy among our terms that philosophic systems can pull one way and another. The margins of overlap provide opportunities whereby a thinker can go without a leap from any one of the terms to any of its fellows. (We have also likened the terms to the fingers, which in their extremities are distinct from one another, but merge in the palm of the hand. If you would go from one finger to another without a leap, you need but trace the tendon down into the palm of the hand, and then trace a new course along another tendon.) Hence, no great dialectical enterprise is necessary if you would merge the terms, reducing them even to as few as one; and then, treating this as the "essential" term, the "causal ancestor" of the lot, you can proceed in the reverse direction across the margins of overlap, "deducing" the other terms from it as its logical descendants.

This is the method, explicitly and in the grand style, of metaphysics which brings its doctrines to a head in some over-all title, a word for being in general, or action in general, or motion in general, or development in general, or experience in general, etc., with all its other terms distributed about this titular term in positions leading up to it and away from it. There is also an implicit kind of metaphysics, that often goes by the name of No Metaphysics, and aims at reduction not to an over-all title but to some presumably underlying atomic constituent. Its vulgar variant is to be found in techniques of "unmasking," which would make for progress and emancipation by applying materialistic terms to immaterial subjects (the pattern here being, "X is nothing but Y," where X designates a higher value and Y a lower one, the higher value being thereby reduced to the lower one).

The titular word for our own method is "dramatism," since it invites one to consider the matter of motives in a perspective that, being developed from the analysis of drama, treats language and thought primarily as modes of action. The method is synoptic, though not in the historical sense. A purely historical survey would require no less than a universal history of human culture; for every judgment, exhortation, or admonition, every view of natural or supernatural reality, every intention or expectation involves assumptions about motive, or cause. Our work must be synoptic in a different sense: in the sense that it offers a system of placement, and should enable us, by the systematic manipulation of the terms, to "generate," or "anticipate" the various classes of motivational theory. And a treatment in these terms, we hope to show, reduces the subject synoptically while still permitting us to appreciate its scope and complexity.

It is not our purpose to import dialectical and metaphysical concerns into a subject that might otherwise be free of them. On the contrary, we hope to make clear the ways in which dialectical and metaphysical issues *necessarily* figure in the subject of motivation. Our speculations, as we interpret them, should show that the subject of motivation is a philosophic one, not ultimately to be solved in terms of empirical science.

Form

Translated into terms of the composition class, "form" becomes "organization" and brings with it overtones of outlining; orders of paragraph development; beginnings, middles, and endings—in short, the most dismal stuff that students and teachers must deal with.

And yet, the concept of form in discourse is utterly fascinating, for it concerns the way in which the mind perceives infinitely complex relationships. The way, indeed, in which the mind constructs discourse.

Some of the essays in the section on form are the most "theoretical" and least "practical" of any in this book, though finally some of the essays will "pay off" in the sense that they have immediate application in the composition class. In general, the movement in the section is from high-level theory toward more and more applicability, ending with Francis Christensen's eminently practical "A Generative Rhetoric of the Paragraph."

What is the nature of form? Susanne Langer tells us that

> There are certain aspects of the so-called "inner life"—physical or mental—which have formal properties similar to those of music—patterns of motion and rest, of tension and release, of agreement and disagreement, preparation, fulfillment, excitation, sudden change, etc.[1]

Then Miss Langer goes on to say that "Because the forms of human feelings are much more congruent with musical forms than with the forms of language, music can *reveal* the nature of feelings with a detail and truth that language cannot approach." [2] In a loose, analogical sense, music has a "grammar," but

This introduction incorporates a revised version of my essay "Dispositio: The Concept of Form in Discourse," *College Composition and Communication* 22 (February 1971), 39–45.

[1] *Philosophy in a New Key* (New York: New American Library, n.d.), p. 193.
[2] *Ibid.*, p. 199.

since it has no "lexicon," its effects must diverge from those of any art that depends on words. Music, that is, is pure form while a lyric poem is both form and meaning in the usual sense.

All of this, it seems to me, is clear enough. However, it is easy to overlook the fact that form and meaning are separable entities in discourse. Milton's grandeur and the splendor of Herman Melville both depend as much on their syntax (a formal matter) as on their sublime subjects. The reader—if he reads as he ought to—must be overwhelmed by the concatenation of almost miraculous sentences as he is by the attempt to justify the ways of God to men. Only the most boorish response to literature is totally unlike the response to music, and only the most boorish literature is incapable of eliciting a "musical" response.

One of the problems in grasping what Percy Lubbock calls the "shadowy and fantasmal form" of any discourse is the mere slipperiness of the word "form," a term with a variety of meanings that sometimes conflict with one another. In the first place, "form" and "genre" overlap and obscure one another's boundaries, even though to speak of the form "sonnet" and the form "lyric" are quite different things. Nor is the problem clarified by the semantic parallels between "organization" (Cicero and Quintilian called it *dispositio*) and "form." A bit of untangling is, then, in order.

No one, I take it, would contend that form in discourse has anything significant to do with the visual, with, for instance, the shapes of "Easter Wings" or "The Altar." The form that we perceive in discourse is nonvisual, conceptual—once again, musical. Chinese may have the virtue of combining the "significant sequaciousness" of events in real life "with the density and angularity of 'things,' the peculiar contribution of painting and sculpture," [3] but Chinese ideographs and the English alphabet are two disparate systems.

The sonnet—with its fourteen lines of iambic pentameter rhyming in any one of a limited variety of ways—and the drama—with its division into acts, its prologue and epilogue, its chorus and other such conventions—are forms, certainly, in one sense of the word. However, it is paradoxically quite possible to have a perfectly formless, perfectly formed sonnet, that is, a series of fourteen lines of iambic pentameter rhyming *ababcdcdefefgg* that nonetheless seems totally amorphous in most senses of the word. The game here is not merely semantics, and the stakes in criticism and pedagogy are high, high enough to warrant a bit of sifting out and definition.

Quite unlike the form "sonnet" is the form "classical oration," with its division into *exordium* to gain the audience's attention, *narratio* to state the speaker's case, *confirmatio* to prove that case, *reprehensio* to refute the opponent's case and *peroratio* to sum up.[4] While a perfectly formed sonnet can be

---

[3] Donald Davie, *Articulate Energy: An Inquiry into the Syntax of English Poetry* (London: Routledge & Kegan Paul, 1955), p. 34.

[4] Cicero, *De Partitione Oratorio,* Vol. II, *De Oratore,* trans. H. Rackham (2 vols.; Cambridge, Mass.: Harvard University, 1942), p. 27.

formless in most senses, a perfectly formed classical oration can never be formless. The reason for this apparent contradiction is that definition of the form sonnet is based on what I call *matrix,* the outward, mechanical features of that kind of poem. To define classical oration as a speech containing *exordium, narratio, confirmatio, reprehensio,* and *peroratio* is, however, quite a different sort of thing, for now the focus is not so much on matrix as on a construct, the parts of which become meaningful only in relation to each other and to two other entities which might be called the speaker's case and the opponent's case. That is, the definition of classical oration as a five-part entity implies an internal consistency of meaning and an "outside referent." Consider the sequence *narratio, confirmatio,* and *peroratio.* The concept *narratio* implies some kind of case involving judgment, choice or avoidance, praise or blame, and *confirmatio* implies exactly the same subject while *reprehensio* implies its obverse. In other words, there is an internal consistency, a "syntax" that is both unavoidable and apparent. In this sense, the definition of classical oration is generative. Applied again and again to different cases, the definitive schema for the classical oration will generate an infinity of classical orations. Of course, a definition of "sonnet" might be generative in roughly the same way:

> . . . it can be seen that the Italian sonnet will regularly divide between the eighth and ninth lines—between, that is, the octave and the sestet—while the Shakespearean sonnet, though there may be slight breaks after any one of the quatrains, will have a major break between the third quatrain and the final couplet. This means that the Italian sonnet tends to divide into two more or less coordinate considerations (whether complementary or opposed) of its topic, while the Shakespearean tends to arrive at a forceful, epigrammatic affirmation or denial, in the brief couplet, of the topic developed through the three quatrains.[5]

It is necessary, then, to differentiate between "form" and "form," between *matrix* and what I refer to when I speak of "form." Form might be defined as *the internal set of consistent relationships perceived in any stretch of discourse, whether poem, play, essay, oration, or whatever.* (As a corollary, it might be added that no discourse can be totally formless and still be discourse.)

Modern grammar leads me to believe that our perception of form in discourse comes about through the apprehension of an underlying set of relationships that, for each work, are invariable and basic, but that are "played off" against a variety of possible surface realizations. Grammar, of course, deals with the sentence, but it provides an analogy on which to build a theory of form for stretches of discourse beyond the sentence. The very notion *in medias res* implies that a work has an underlying configuration, a chronological dimension, that can achieve a variety of surface realizations. But

---

[5] Jerome Beaty and William H. Matchett, *Poetry, from Statement to Meaning* (New York: Oxford University Press, 1965), p. 326.

chronology is only one, and normally the most simple, of the sets of relation-ships that go to make up form.

Between the grammar of the sentence and a grammar of form there is undoubtedly a long leap, but perhaps an analogical bridge can be built. Chomsky has said,

> The principles that determine the form of grammar and that select a grammar of the appropriate form on the basis of certain data constitute a subject that might, following traditional usage, be termed "universal grammar." The study of universal grammar, so understood, is a study of the nature of human intel-lectual capacities.[6]

Sentence grammar indicates more and more forcefully that perception of meaning comes about through the interoperation of two concepts: deep struc-tures and grammatical transformations that bring about surface structures. To repeat, then: it is not unreasonable to posit that our perception of form is contingent upon recognition—intuitive or otherwise—of a set of relation-ships (i.e., a proposition) in the deep structure of units of discourse, relation-ships that can gain a variety of surface realizations. In this case, the form is not merely the surface structure—and certainly not the matrix—but the result of the interplay between (1) the invariable deep structure, (2) the surface structure that the author has chosen, and (3) the other alternatives made available by a finite system of "organizing" that the "proposition" itself makes possible. The classical oration can serve as a paradigm here. It is a classical oration because its segments are arranged *exordium, narratio, confirmatio, reprehensio,* and *peroratio,* but that is not the only arrangement possible. Obviously, *narratio* might come first, followed by *exordium,* and *reprehensio* can precede *confirmatio.* However, *peroratio* cannot precede *narratio* with-out causing formlessness. That is, the simple "proposition" of the classical oration has a variety of ways in which it can come into being, though only one of those ways will result in what can be termed "classical oration," which will be, in this sense, a matrix.

It is not to be assumed that the relationship between segments of discourse longer than the sentence are necessarily the same as those within the sentence: that is most definitely not the point. The point is, to reiterate, that an analo-gous situation must prevail whenever we can say that this poem or that essay has form or is well formed.

To explore another aspect of the sentence analogy: the language has built into it a tremendously complex system that dictates both syntax and the con-joining of semantic features.[7] We should expect then that forms beyond the sentence would have "semantic features" as well as "syntax." Lacking a syntax (as, supposedly, some modern poetry does), the poem would nonetheless be

[6] *Language and Mind* (New York: Harcourt Brace Jovanovich, Inc., 1968), p. 24.

[7] For an excellent introduction to the problem of semantics, see D. Terence Langen-doen, "The Nature of Semantics," *The Study of Syntax* (New York: Holt, Rinehart and Winston, 1969), pp. 34–51.

held together, would gain form, through a meaningful repetition of ideas, very much like what Donald Davie means when he says,

> The dislocated syntax of Ezra Pound in the *Cantos* may look like the dislocated syntax of William Carlos Williams, but in fact of course the *Cantos* are, or are meant to be, articulated most closely. They are articulated, however, by a syntax that is musical, not linguistic, by "the unifying, all-embracing artifice of rhythm," understood in its widest sense, to mean not only the rhythm that rides through tempo and metre in the verse-paragraph, but also the rhythmical recurrence of ideas hinted at in one canto, picked up in another much later, suspended for many more, and so on. . . .[8]

The recurrence of image, symbol, idea, or metaphor can serve as a kind of "semantic" device to outline form. An example that occurs to me is Robert Lowell's "Between the Porch and the Altar." It may be recalled that this work is a series of four loosely related poems which symbolically tell the story of a man's break with his maternal past and his subsequent entry into a sordid adulterous affair with "Katherine." "Mother and Son," the first poem, tells of the narrator's uncomfortable relationship with a domineering mother who "makes him lose ten years, / Or is it twenty?" every time he meets her. The poem ends with a pseudo-benediction from the mother's hand, "Dangling its watchchain on the Holy Book— / A little golden snake that mouths a hook." The second poem of the quartet, "Adam and Eve," tells, among other things, of the beginning of the affair with Katherine and how the narrator is torn between her and his wife and children: "I taste my wife / And children while I hold your hands. I knife / Their names into this elm." But later: "When we try to kiss, / Our eyes are slits and cringing, and we hiss; / Scales glitter on our bodies as we fall." The third poem, "Katherine's Dream," contains more of the reptilian imagery. However, the final poem, "At the Altar," is apocalyptic: both the narrator and Katherine know the enormity of what they have done. After a mad dash through the city at night, the pair end up in a church, where the priest "mumbles through his Mass." As day breaks, the narrator discovers that "Here the Lord / Is Lucifer in harness." The symbolic serpent of evil becomes the Evil One himself, and the poem ends. The recurrent imagery with its attendant ideas has created a "syntax" of sorts and has outlined, though vaguely, a kind of form—or has created one of the integuments whereby the reader perceives form.

There are other "semantic" elements that contribute to the sense of form versus formlessness—pronouns and their antecedents, for instance, and what tagmemicists call "equivalence classes" (i.e., words that have the same referent or that stand for the same thing in a stretch of coherent discourse).[9] And the list could be expanded greatly.

Strangely enough, however, the sense of form versus formlessness hovers

---

[8] *Articulate Energy*, pp. 19–20.

[9] A. L. Becker, "A Tagmemic Approach to Paragraph Analysis," *The Sentence and the Paragraph* (Champaign, Ill.: NCTE, 1966), pp. 33–38.

just slightly above the sense of meaning versus meaninglessness. It is quite possible to sense form without understanding meaning—at least in relatively short stretches of discourse. In fact, metaphor is an excellent example here, for that figure springs into being at the point where the cup of meaning runneth over, but formal requirements are ignored. Emily Dickinson, for instance:

> After great pain, a formal feeling comes—
> The Nerves sit ceremonious, like Tombs—
> The stiff Heart questions was it He, that bore,
> And Yesterday, or Centuries before?

The sequence of words in this stanza has its own internal formal requirements that prevail regardless of meanings in the real world or the world of the poet's imagination. The word "formal" (in the first line of the poem), like any other word in the language, functions according to a double set of meanings. There is first the referential, existential kind of meaning that a dictionary tries to capture and that might run something like this: pertaining to form; regular; ceremonial; done according to the rules.

But there is also a set of "meta-meanings" that are not referential in nature. The first metaphor in the poem comes to life when "formal" and "feeling" are coupled syntactically, because feelings are simply not formal in any literal sense. That is, the word "formal" has built into its total meaning certain restrictions that preclude it from functioning as an attributive adjective with "feeling," except in the metaphorical sense. The sequence "Nerves sit" is of exactly the same order.[10]

The most convenient unit of discourse to analyze for form and on which to test theories of form is the paragraph. The paragraph, of course, is not merely a collection of sentences, but a concatenation of transformational units.[11] Since this is the case, the first inquiry about the form ought to concern the way in which the sparks of coherence jump the gaps between T-units. In order to begin the investigation, I examined forty-seven paragraphs from expository prose written during the 1960s.[12] This investigation made it apparent that there

---

[10] I realize that my use of the term "formal" has been fast and loose in the foregoing, but not inadvertent. In two senses, lexical features are formal. In the first place, they are a regular set of rules and hence are formal in the same way that mathematical formulae are. In the second place, their formality often shows up in the forms that words take. Consider the following (for which I take dubious credit): "The glib runs through the mountains, / Over hill and dale. / Splashing in the fountains, / It guzzles beer and ale." Only with the appearance of the pronoun "it" with its feature *nonhuman* does the possibility of metaphor emerge, a sort of formal metaphor, the exact meaning of which can never be determined. All we can say is that "glib" must be nonhuman (or, just possibly, a baby) and that nonhuman subjects normally do not "guzzle" anything, let alone beer and ale.

[11] It will be remembered that a T-unit is the shortest stretch of discourse that can be set off legitimately with sentence punctuation. Thus, for instance, each of the coordinate clauses in a compound sentence is a T-unit.

[12] The paragraphs are from *The Sense of the 60's,* Edward Quinn and Paul J. Dolan, eds. (New York: The Free Press, 1968). This collection contains forty-eight essays. I examined the first paragraph in the first essay, the second paragraph in the second essay, and so on through the tenth; I examined the last paragraph in the eleventh essay,

must be two sorts of transitions between T-units: those that are marked and those that are not. In other words, we perceive the coherence of both of these utterances:

I would like to fly to Europe. I can't afford it.
I would like to fly to Europe. But I can't afford it.

The first transition is *implied;* the second is *expressed.* A survey of the forty-seven paragraphs revealed these totals for expressed transitions:

and	30	instead	1	repetition	1
and so	1	meantime	1	so	2
but	21	moreover	1	so that	3
for	6	of course	1	then	3
however	1	or	1	though	1
indeed	2	parentheses	2	thus	1
in other words	1	question	5	yet	3

Most of these transitions need no illustration or explanation, but three of them do. *Parentheses, questions,* and *repetitions* are special cases that warrant brief discussion. We are dealing here with "quantitative" transitions—transitions in which an "and" is really an "and" and a "so" is really a "so." In this sense, parentheses, questions, and repetitions are expressed transitions. For instance:

Parentheses. The disaster which Muller fears is a result of gene mutations. These are small structural changes in the genes (he calls them "submicroscopic accidents") which are usually harmful to the organism. Because Muller believes that mutations are accumulating, he concludes that the human race is beginning to decline. In the end, the whole world will become a hospital, "and even the best of us will only be ambulatory patients in it." [13]

Parentheses obviously serve to insert one T-unit within another *sans* transformations. They also serve to insert other material that has no grammatical link with the T-unit as well as material that does; for parentheses, quite arbitrarily, can substitute for commas. They are listed as expressed transitions because they do indeed bridge the gap between T-units.

Question. We are assured that more jobs will be created by new industry, that higher skills will be required, that economic stability will be guaranteed by automation. There are pitifully few facts available to support these euphoric hopes. More likely a vast trauma awaits us all, to use Irving Howe's phrase. Then why automate? The underlying motives were exposed with unaccustomed bluntness in one of the trade journals recently when an automation advocate wrote: "[Machines] don't call in sick; they don't talk back; they

and with the twelfth, I started the process over again. I skipped one author, Thomas Merton, because of the brevity of his essay. Among the authors whose paragraphs I did examine are Paul Goodman, Staughton Lynd, John F. Kennedy, Susan Sontag, Tom Wolfe, Jimmy Breslin, Martin Luther King, Jr., John Updike, Robert Lowell, Bruce Jay Friedman, John Barth, and Marshall McLuhan.

[13] Lucy Eisenberg, "Genetics and the Survival of the Unfit," *The Sense of the 60's,* p. 372.

work early and late and without overtime; they don't get tired; and last, but far from least, they don't line up at the cashier's window every week for a slice of the operating funds." [14]

The question tranformation is classed as an expressed transition because questions can be recognized on the basis of their form. And, simply, a question normally calls for an answer.

> *Repetition* . . . and when she told me about exploitation and economic forces I believed her. I believed her, but I was still afraid of Negroes.[15]

The mere fact of repetition creates form, as in the case of "Between the Porch and the Altar." When repetition occurs in adjacent T-units, the effect is to bridge the gap.

The other transitions are pretty much of the garden variety (on the surface, at least; investigation will reveal layers of complexity as, for instance, in the meanings of "and"). The data in my counts reveal clearly that modern prose relies heavily on "and" and "but" to get from T-unit to T-unit. The data also reveal that expressed transitions fall into four categories: (1) coordinating conjunctions; (2) moveable interrupters like "however," "then," "thus," and "in other words"; (3) parentheses (which may indeed not be transitions at all); and (4) sentence devices such as the question tranformation or repetition.

Much remains to be said about form or coherence in discourse. But this much is clear: discourse at all levels has as its "meanings" a "deep structure" that has the possibility of various surface realizations. Part of one's appreciation and understanding of any "message" should be cognizance, subconscious or not, that any given surface structure is only one among a variety of choices and that the actual utterance must be played off against the unchosen possibilities. Sometimes the transitions that bridge the gap between units of discourse longer than the T-unit are easily recognizable, for they appear in the surface structure, but just as often they do not appear and are merely implied. They are *particles* that may or may not come to the surface. But above all, in the discussion of form or coherence, it is well to keep in mind the grammar of the sentence as the most productive analogical model for exploration of "grammar" beyond the sentence.

Suggestions for Further Reading

Gleason, H. A., Jr. "Contrastive Analysis in Discourse Structure." *Georgetown University Monograph Series in Languages and Linguistics* 19 (1968), 39–63.

Hagen, Lyman B. "An Analysis of Transitional Devices in Student Writing." *Research in the Teaching of English* 5 (Fall 1971), 190–201.

Hanf, Marilyn Buckley. "A Study of Children's Thinking as Expressed Through Oral Discourse." *Research in the Teaching of English* 7 (Spring 1973), 13–29.

---

[14] Ben B. Seligman, "Man, Work, and the Automated Feast," *The Sense of the 60's,* p. 417.

[15] Norman Podhoretz, "My Negro Problem—and Ours," *The Sense of the 60's,* p. 242.

Hankiss, Elemér. "From Folk Song to Absurd Drama: On a Basic Structural Device of Literary Expression." *Language and Style* 4 (Fall 1971), 243–63.

Hart, Thomas Elwood. "Linguistic Patterns, Literary Structure, and the Genesis of C. F. Meyer's 'Der römische Brunnen.'" *Language and Style* 4 (Spring 1971), 83–115.

Hendricks, William O. "Folklore and the Structural Analysis of Literary Texts." *Language and Style* 3 (Spring 1970), 83–121.

Hollander, John. "The Poem in the Eye." *Shenandoah* 23 (Spring 1972), 3–32.

Joselyn, Sister M. "Aspects of Form in the Nun's Priest's Tale." *College English* 25 (May 1964), 566–71.

Klammer, Thomas P. "Multihierarchical Structure in a Middle English Breton Lay—A Tagmemic Analysis." *Language and Style* 4 (Winter 1971), 3–23.

Lohof, Bruce A. "Through a Shutter Brightly: Notes on the New Composition." *Centennial Review* 16 (1972), 180–91.

McCabe, Thomas H. "Rhythm as Form in Lawrence: 'The Horse Dealer's Daughter.'" *PMLA* 87 (January 1972), 64–68.

New Literary History 2 (Winter 1971).

Robertson, Duncan. "The Dichotomy of Form and Content." *College English* 28 (January 1967), 273–79.

Rosenthal, M. L. "Dynamics of Form and Motive in Some Representative Twentieth-Century Lyric Poems." *ELH* 37 (March 1970), 136–51.

Rousseau, G. S., ed. *Organic Form: The Life of an Idea.* London and Boston: Routledge & Kegan Paul, 1972.

Stevens, Walt. "A Proposal for Non-Linear Disposition." *Western Speech* 37 (Spring 1973), 118–28.

Sylvester, William. "The Existence of a Disjunctive Principle in Poetry." *College English* 28 (January 1967), 265–72.

In addition, the annual bibliography in *Style* contains a section on "Structures Beyond the Sentence."

Form, Authority, and the Critical Essay

Keith Fort

Fort's argument is twofold. First, and most important, he argues that available forms determine attitudes: "In general, we cannot have attitudes toward reality that cannot be expressed in available forms. If, for example, we can only express our relation to literature in the form of the standard critical essay, we can only have an attitude that would result in the proper form." Second, he argues that the critical essay has turned literature into a consumer product.

The composition class can be, and frequently is, ruled by formal tyranny. The tyranny of the expository essay is pervasive. If students must write expository essays, they are forced to respond to experience in given ways, the ways of cool rationality, objectivity, and clarity. There is, of course, nothing wrong with rationality, objectivity, and clarity, but they represent only a portion of the ways in which people experience the world. In the introduction to this book, I argued that the role of the composition teacher is to aid the student in expressing himself or herself, and that exposition is only one of a variety of modes of self-expression.

As far as literature is concerned, the critical expository essay has been disastrous for English classes. Responses to art are many and varied, and only the professional responds with a formal critical essay. Needless to say, the object of the English class is to produce sensitive, eager readers, not professional responders. To stress the critical or analytical essay as the only—or at least the most acceptable—way of responding to literature is to pervert reading and to alienate students from the experience that we have the most faith in.

Fort's article is extremely practical, then, since it argues against a destructive classroom practice.

His essay, however, is not totally negative, for it suggests an alternative to the critical essay: a form of writing that would enable the individual "to establish a meaningful relation between himself and art."

People in literary studies generally pride themselves on their liberality. Teachers give A's to diverse interpretations. Editors accept works with opposing conclusions. But while freedom is permitted in content, formal conformity is rigidly demanded. This contradiction is symbolized by the statement so often made to students: "Sure, almost any interpretation is okay if you prove it." In the implications of "prove" are found not only an insistence on logic but also a required attitude towards literature that results in papers with a prescribed structure.

The freedom to reach individual conclusions exists in part because literary studies are in a tradition that prizes initiative and that recognizes the evolution of ideas within movements of intellectual history. Until recently, however, little attention has been given to the history of forms. But forms do not exist in a vacuum any more than do ideas. Forms evolve to meet deep human needs that are in turn shaped by historical and personal situations. In the course of this paper I hope to examine the hypothesis that the form we have unconsciously assumed to be the best one (if not the only one) for expressing written ideas on literature both reflects and perpetuates attitudes that generate the structures in our society.

If teachers today were to insist that students reach only conclusions that were acceptable to our political establishment, violent protests would erupt. But when students are forced to use only one form, there is little rebellion although this formal tyranny may result in a more basic conformity than content tyranny.

Perhaps we regard the form of the essay only as a conventional tool that permits communication and believe that the tool is itself meaningless. But forms have their own kind of meaning. Twenty years ago a teacher who conducted a rigidly structured lecture class might well have said that his teaching method was "just a convention" that permitted learning. We know better than that now. The form in which a classroom is conducted is related to what is learned and has its own psychological implications in shaping a student's development. The form of the essay is no more a simple convention than is form in the classroom.

Like the literature in the class the form of the essay *conditions* thought patterns and, particularly, attitude towards authority. This conditioning might have an impact on the shaping of lives that would startle the English teacher who feels that the content of his work is "irrelevant." On the other hand, for many people the conditioning may have no lasting effect at all. Teachers complain that students leave writing courses and promptly forget everything they were taught (a particular form). Perhaps this happens because the form is so antithetical to the lives of some students that they refuse to make it a part of their minds.

Before beginning my discussion of the critical essay itself I need to give some explanation of the general theory of form on which my analysis is based. I can, however, do nothing more than sketch in the broad outlines of my ideas which are admittedly in a very incomplete state.

A speaker or writer has an attitude towards reality. By "attitude" I mean a set of expectations. In every encounter with reality the mind expects to find something. The attitude of one who wants to understand, for example, is to find meaning in the reality he perceives. The result of the encounter between attitude and object is an expression. "Form" as I will use the term comprises those elements in an expression that reflect the attitude of the speaker and that tend to control the audience's relation to the expression's subject matter and the speaker. Form is, then, the observable manifestation of attitude. Under this very broad concept the form of every human expression is unique since no two attitudes could ever be exactly alike. Only the limits of language make expressions seem similar.

To use Kenneth Burke's terminology, form is a "strategy" for establishing a relation to reality. A certain form is chosen (whether consciously or not) so that the self will exist in relation to reality and audience in a way that meets basic needs of the expresser. In broad terms, three factors determine an attitude: conception of self, conception of reality, and conception of audience. Form is the manifestation of all the devices available to a speaker or writer as he tries to establish a desirable relationship.

In most cases the form that we use is the result of our assessment of a situation, but because form and attitude are equal the control of the formal appearance of an expression will also tend to control attitude. In general, we cannot have attitudes towards reality that cannot be expressed in available forms. If, for example, we can only express our relation to literature in the form of the standard critical essay, we can only have an attitude that would result in the proper form.

Although every human expression is a reflection of personal uniqueness, broader formal patterns are common to groups. Both ideological and formal tyrannies create dogmas to control only those elements which, if violated, could do harm to political or psychological certainties. Under the Stalinist tyranny, for example, censorship of art was aimed at ideas that threatened the ideology that was the political basis of the state. In a formal tyranny censorship is also aimed at preventing expression in forms that would attack the prevailing structures of society. One need only look at what is forbidden in either to see what the controller fears.

Under either kind of tyranny a thinker has total freedom so long as these taboos are not violated. Hence every work will be different in its particulars although the elements that are crucial to maintaining the power of the group will be consistent.

To sum up this sketchy theory: imagine a student in a classroom. If he regards himself as truly inferior to a truth-possessing teacher, believes that the subject matter is difficult, but still wishes to relate himself to the subject and the teacher, he will express himself in the form of a question. The question is a strategy that the student has evolved that allows self expression without violation of the conception of himself (stupid), of reality (a difficult subject) and of the teacher (omniscient). Let us suppose next, however, that the student has no real conception of what he is when he comes into the course. If the teacher insists on the student's limiting himself to questions and gives rewards for the use of this form, the student will be conditioned to have the conception of himself implied by the form. And, as a third possibility, consider the student who thinks he is smart, the subject matter easy, and the professor incompetent. If he is forced to express himself through questions, his conception of self, situation, and audience will be violated and his anger is inevitable.

The teacher who would limit his students exclusively to the question form is obviously insisting on almost total conformity in the classroom—an uncommon rigidity in any age when most are conscious of the importance of form in teaching. But in the essay where form is less studied the insistence on formal conformity still exists.

Formal tyranny in essay writing, as in any other expression, is based on the need of those who are in control to make the appearance of the expression confirm a desired idea of which there is doubt. To reach some understanding of what causes the creation of this tyranny, the best approach is to consider the common element in the form that is most generally taken as a rule, for this common element is the one that binds the group together.

In the essay it would seem that this key rule is that there must be a thesis which the essay proves. The first question always asked about a prospective paper is whether the idea is "workable" or can be "handled." As I understand these terms, they mean "do you have a thesis that can be proved?" This formal requirement is a *sine qua non* for a paper. Meeting it does not necessarily mean that a paper will be successful (an A in the classroom or publication), but its absence guarantees failure.

This formal requirement permits an infinite number of individualized expressions, but like any formal limit, it obviously permits freedom only of a kind. And, furthermore, since a relation always exists between form and content, it also imposes broad restrictions on the kind of topics that may be chosen. Only those ideas are acceptable that can be proved. If a writer tries to force the "wrong" kind of idea into the right form failure will result. Teachers and editors look with dismay on "big" or very personal topics. Their abhorrence is reasonable so long as the form is fixed because these topics are not provable.

I do not wish to oversimplify here by creating a straw man—the modern essayist—whom I will triumphantly destroy. Nor do I wish to let myself be pulled over into what might be called new left paranoia by imputing with uncritical but appealing generalities a systematic tyranny to an "establishment." I would like to offer some qualifications. All college handbooks with which I am familiar insist on the form I am analyzing. I deduce from this that the form is dominant in undergraduate courses although I know of many teachers who are permitting greater formal freedom. From what I know about M.A. and Ph.D. requirements the insistence on this form is even more rigid. Among certain mature critics, however, a tradition of conversational, exploratory essays has continued. Even if this kind of criticism did not exist, however, I would not be justified in imputing systematic tyranny to an establishment if for no other reason than that the significance of form has not been given enough attention for any position to have been codified. Nor do I wish to suggest that liberal-minded men cannot write in the traditional form. Obviously they can, and the content of their writing will have great effect, but the unconscious effect of form will always partially override the ideas or at least set up tension between them.

As a point of reference for the analysis that follows, I will take the first part of Cleanth Brooks's essay, "Keats's Sylvan Historian: History without Footnotes." I think that this essay is representative of the dominant form used today:

> There is much in the poetry of Keats which suggests that he would have approved of Archibald MacLeish's dictum, "A poem should not mean / But be." There is even some warrant for thinking that the Grecian urn (real or imagined) which inspired the famous ode was, for Keats, just such a poem,

"palpable and mute," a poem in stone. Hence it is the more remarkable that the "Ode" itself differs from Keats's other odes by culminating in a statement —a statement even of some sentientiousness in which the urn itself is made to say that beauty is truth, and—more sentientious still—that this bit of wisdom sums up the whole of mortal knowledge.

This is "to mean" with a vengeance—to violate the doctrine of the objective correlative, not only by stating truths, but by defining the limits of truth. Small wonder that some critics have felt that the unravished bride of quietness protests too much.

The thesis of the Brooks essay is that the poem has dramatic unity. The statement of this thesis asserts a claim for the authority of the critic. The essay then proves the idea and the claim.

From the outset Brooks projects an image of authority. To cite several examples from the quoted sections: the MacLeish aphorism is presented in such a way that we are not to consider even the possibility that it is questionable. "Sentientiousness" suggests the authority of Brooks's taste. The statement that Keats has "violated" the doctrine of the objective correlative assumes another critical dogma.

But whether or not this overt authoritarianism were present, the very existence of a thesis is enough to stake a claim for the critic's being above and outside of the poem. The authority will be accepted if his thesis is validated. Thus, while readers are consciously learning about the poem, the form of the essay is eliciting a different kind of concern—whether or not the authority projected by the thesis and the dogmatic diction is going to be sustained. From the point of view of formal effect what is said later has meaning only in that it is part of an equation that adds up to the answer given in the thesis.

At the same time that this form reflects a critic's need to think of himself as an authority, it is also demanding a particular kind of relation between a reader and a work being studied. In broad terms the connection is between understander and thing-to-be-understood; more particularly it is between thesis hunter and source of thesis. In other words, if the only form in which a writer can express himself on literature is one that requires a thesis, then he has to look at literature as a source of theses.

If I am correct in saying that form establishes a relation between self, object, and audience that satisfies needs, the authoritarian nature of the form must have been created in response to a need in our collective psyches. Furthermore, the dogmatic way in which the form is generally taught and the absence of much discussion of why the form is "right" would suggest that the form itself that is being used to satisfy these needs is suspect to our own conscious minds.

This suspicion would seem to be justified because in an age of anxiety, when it is seemingly impossible to believe in authority of any kind, how can it be so readily accepted that a writer has transcended even so limited a problem as the meaning of a poem? The unconscious need to believe in the reality of a transcendent authority is, then, opposed to the conscious belief that such authority cannot exist. The form of the critical essay has, I think, evolved in large part as a strategy that will seem to solve this contradiction.

To allow for the satisfaction of the unconscious need to believe in a real authority, conscious censors have to be bypassed. It is for this purpose that most of the "rules" for essay writing have been established.

One of the most basic of the conscious doubts that prevents our being able to believe in real authority in life is an uncertainty about what is real.[1] The perception of reality as chaotic prevents the belief in anxiety relieving power, since authority, of the kind that is still hoped for unconsciously, rests as a meaningful apex at the top of a meaningful world. As with anyone aspiring to a position above reality, the critic must discover the order in the very reality over which he is to rule or else the understanding on which his claim rests is invalidated. In other words the basis of power has to be established before the power will be acknowledged. To cite an example from a different area: The person who claims power because of a religious position has first to convince others that the basis of reality is religious. The critic has a similar task. Before he can assert a claim to be an authority on the basis of his ability to draw conclusions about literature, he must first prove that the reality of art is that it produces conclusions. Most criticism today is concerned with *unity*—how the parts of a work function to support a central theme. In looking at a work with the expectation of finding this kind of unity, a critic necessarily interprets the poem; or, put in different terms, he redefines it because of his expectation. A new reality emerges, and only with this unified, ordered reality as subject-matter could the form of the essay establish that a critic has real authority. The reader is then immersed (to use the term Ortega applies to novel reading) in a new reality over which there is a meaningful authority.

(It may seem here that I have fallen into the trap that has, I think, ruined so many psychological critics. Having discovered that a writer has "suspect" motivations, they then totally discount the insights he has. In no way do I intend to suggest that unity is not actually present in art. Generally speaking I agree with Brooks's reading of the poem. However, unity is only one of a number of possible concerns a critic could have. I am trying to analyze why that is the concern picked from among others. The truth of what is said then obviously is valid only within the limits imposed by the intention.)

The limits to which a critic can go in establishing a new reality are held in check by what I would call the law of plausibility. A great many trivial and outlandish books are praised merely because they are formally correct (a thesis is validated), but there is probably a limit to such a success. All that plausibility means is that the new reality that is defined by the critic must not too openly violate our expectations of what reality should be. The interpretations in the Brooks essay, for example, are not ostensibly different in kind

---

[1] Ian Watt, Sartre and many others trace a great deal if not all of the problems of our times to this epistemological question.

from what I would normally expect to find if I analyzed a poem with my own standards for what a poem should be.

The more an essay seems to be reasonable, the more forceful the formal effect can be.

If, however, contemporary man lived in a state of total anxiety where he did not know at all what he could rely on as real, the plausibility law could never work because we would always see that the new reality was not exactly like the old. I have come to believe that we must still have a half-conscious belief in the ability of the scientific method to define reality, so that we are willing to accept authority if it seems to be based on impersonal scientific observation. The technique of "hidden omniscience" in both fiction and the essay allows for the creation of a new reality in which we can believe. It allows subjective interpretation to be presented in such a way that it does not appear to be dependent on the mind of a fallible human being. In the Brooks essay, for example, interpretation seems to be the result of a depersonalized mind:

> The poet is obviously stressing the fresh unwearied charm of a scene itself which can defy time and is deathless.

Nothing in that interpretation suggests anything other than that the conclusion has been reached with tools that are as precise as those of a scientist.

The insistence on a scientific appearance is, I think, responsible for a mistrust of anything but the third person in essays. The personal voice of the author has to be excluded from conscious view, for if it is heard, it is seen to be human and the authority is doubted.

While these few "rules" that I have been discussing are some of the elements in the strategy that has developed to permit formal effect, it is primarily in the organization of the essay that the actual effect is made. The key to proper organization is subordination. Every idea in a paper points towards and is under the thesis. If a careful outline of a well organized paper was made, with lines drawn to indicate interconnecting parts, it would have an astounding similarity to the organization chart of a military or governmental unit. Both organizations work to affirm the validity of the authority at the top. Both are hierarchical. Value orientation within such a structure is up. The military commander is rated by his own actions as a commander and by the way in which subordinate elements support him. The essay is similarly evaluated. Instead of marshalling men the critic marshals evidence.

To insist on the standard form of the essay is to condition students to think in terms of authority and hierarchy.

Form reflects an attitude and the formal patterning of the mind carries over from discipline to discipline in schools and among elements in society. In our society forms are interlocked and complementary. In the form of the critical essay is found the same manifestation of the "proper" attitude towards authority that would be found in almost any of the institutions of our society.

People in the apparently irrelevant corner of our society occupied by the business of literary studies and the teaching of composition may be doing as much as anyone to inculcate the attitude that generates the hierarchical and competitive society that is mocked by most of the literature that is the subject of these essays.[2]

As will always happen when the mind is patterned to think in terms of hierarchy, it will also have to be competitive. Most basically the critic is competing against his subject to establish his claim to mastery over it. And the form that has internal competition as its motive force will also generate extrinsic competition.

The claim to authority by an assertion of a thesis psychologically challenges the reader. Thus, while on the one hand the reader feels himself in the presence of a longed-for authority, another level of his being feels called upon to rebel against the critic's assertiveness. The rebellion may appear in a number of ways from outright competition by the production of another essay on the same subject to a passive adoption of authority by association in which the reader achieves a feeling of superiority by granting the critic the already claimed authority with a mental statement of agreement.

The competitive spirit implied by the form of the essay generates larger structures also. For the critic to bolster his own claim and to guard against the attack on his authority that he knows will come, he must take into account the existence of others who are pretenders in some degree to the same territory. Almost all critical essays, therefore, refer to other critics. In part these references may be merely informational for other scholars, but more importantly their inclusion is demanded as a way of showing that the critic is "master" of his subject. At the top of this heap we have vaguely acknowledged titles like "foremost authority in his field."

On an undergraduate level research is often not so important only because teachers feel that students are not ready for varsity competition. The same kind of protectiveness is evident in the topics to which many Ph.D. candidates are limited when they write their dissertations. What I am describing here is a market place of ideas where it is assumed that the best critic will "win" in open competition. The critic is a laborer who in a very real way must either play the game or withdraw from writing. As with any other worker, the end to which he is bound is the turning out of products. These products are theses

---

[2] Frequently during the writing of this essay (here was one such place) I have wondered whether I was justified in making a political or psychological case out of the critical essay even if my argument was plausible. At times I have felt like a politically-inclined, twentieth-century member of Swift's Grand Academy who was completely overlooking the common-sense aspects of the essay as an accepted means of communication. At one point I even considered turning this into a parody of new left writers who manage to find latent political attitudes in the simplest and most ordinary of human actions. But I always come back to the belief that Anglo-American common sense is not sacred and is often a disguise for the worst kind of bad faith. Revolutionary concerns are present in many areas of society including literary studies. Perhaps this argument is the wrong way to face this challenge, and adherence to slow evolution with an accompanying abhorrence of continental theorizing would be better. This latter attitude is reflected in those who ignore something like the New University Conference or treat it like a badly informed child who needs punishment rather than reason.

about literature. And in an age of intellectual affluence the critic must constantly create new markets in the form of magazines and publishing houses to sell his products to a world that is as surfeited with conclusions about literature as society is overfilled with automobiles.

This system, that is reflected in the structure of the simplest paper in freshman English, has worked according to its own terms. We have good interpretations of almost everything. So long as we don't look at the formal implications of this battle and concentrate on the products, we don't have to think either of the value of the shape of the minds formed by the competition or of the value of the relation to literature insisted upon by this form.

Although I don't know exactly what the aim of literary studies is, I do not think it has to be the production of conclusions.

My analogy between the form of the essay and the form of society (particularly the military) is an extreme one. I believe that the attitude needed for writing the standard essay always implies competition, but I also recognize that individual critics are engaged in this struggle to different degrees. Some of our best critics have stayed aloof as much as possible. For the most part, however, these are men of an older generation who have managed to maintain a somewhat detached position. Most critics probably share some part of this "gentleman of letters" attitude although it is increasingly difficult to maintain with the increasing professionalism of literary studies that leads to economic and psychological rewards for those who succeed. Given the pressure for grades, few students could be expected to have such disinterest even if they were familiar with a non-competitive view of criticism.

Furthermore, literature itself and the content of the conclusions about it are always working to check the implications of the form of the essay. I think that a certain amount of stress must exist in most who engage in literary studies as a result of the clash between the meanings of the form and the content of the work. The breaking of the authoritarian form in the classroom has in one way helped to alleviate this stress, but in another it has intensified the conflict because in our work it is still writing that counts for grades and promotions.

The form of the standard essay rests on a self-deceptive need for an authority whom we don't consciously believe can exist. Future students of the history of forms, however, may regard this strategy as a necessary part of a transition from a time of accepted values into some new kind of freedom. But, as has often happened before in the history of both forms and ideas, what was once a viable, necessary strategy has turned into a tyranny that is no longer capable of the flexibility needed to meet changing needs.

Perhaps it is even possible to say that the age of anxiety for which this form was, in a sense, created, is ending. The conclusions that were produced by this authority-oriented attitude have so changed our conceptions of reality that the form itself has been invalidated. For example, one of the major conclusions that has emerged from the humanities over the past few decades is that the world is "absurd." This conclusion may have permeated our unconscious enough so that the form used to reach the conclusion (based on a search for meaning with a scientific method) has to be discarded.

That needs are generally changing in our culture is evidenced by a formal revolution on a wide front. The demand for participatory democracy, experimental literature, the changing structures in classrooms, a theology that is rejecting the concept of a God who is above and outside of reality are all manifestations of a very basic change in attitude.

But the question has still to be answered as to whether a formal change could occur in the essay that could bring it into this formal revolution. The formal resources of the essay seem limited beside those of fiction, and if form becomes a primary concern in essay-writing, the genre might become fiction.[3] But I don't think this need happen. "They" said the novel was dead, but new forms have emerged in fiction that have revitalized this genre. And since the form of the standard essay has developed along similar lines to those of realistic fiction (and for similar causes) a look at a few of the many experiments in modern fiction might point some way to free the essay from the strictures that are as tight as those of the "prison of realism."

The role of the writer as God is being deliberately challenged by much new fiction. In older realistic fiction the novelist had a fairly static understanding that was "above" the action, and to some extent the book proves this theme as an essay proves its thesis. In some new fiction, however, the process of the writer's mind becomes the action of the work. Fiction unfolds. It is impossible to discover what the author means beyond what he says because his meaning develops in the course of his writing. Beckett, Robbe-Grillet, Bellow (in his last two novels) are all, in different ways, writing what might be called "process fiction." In these novels we sense that we are in the presence of fallible minds moving towards uncertain ends. The formal satisfaction that we obtain from reading such works comes close to being the pleasure of participating with another mind in exploration.

The change in the conception of the author's role has also led to an admission of uncertainty about what is real, so that we now read novels that openly admit that representations of reality are fictional. This admission blocks the anxiety-removing quality of most realistic fiction that permitted readers to immerse themselves in an orderly reality which they could believe was equivalent to the world in which they lived.

It might be possible for a similar attitude to be reflected in criticism. If the Brooks essay on Keats's poem, for example, had been written with the aim of eliciting participation in exploration rather than respect for authority, the thesis on the dramatic unity of the poem could have been a central concern of the essay itself. It would have been a frankly admitted hypothesis that could have been discarded or modified as the essay progressed instead of being

[3] In the attempt to find new strategies today old generic distinctions are obviously being broken down. It is quite possible that in time something like fictional criticism might emerge as a new genre more suited to present needs.

a static conclusion against which the poem was measured. Instead of *showing that* the thesis was correct the essay would have been concerned with whether it was correct.

To some extent process criticism would result in essays being about criticism (just as most experimental novels are about novel writing) since the critic would constantly be re-examining his assumptions during the course of the essay. But such a form would not mean the total substitution of theory of criticism for criticism. Just as fiction about fiction can have many other concerns, an experimental essay on Keats's ode would, similarly, still be about the poem.

A strategy that evokes participation with a critic would necessarily lead to a change in the nature of the relation established between self and literature. At present, as I have tried to suggest, the form of the essay tends to insist that the only possible relation of critic to work is that of thesis-hunter to source of thesis.

New forms of fiction are proposing new kinds of relations between man and reality. These forms are based, implicitly or explicitly, on far reaching social, political and even religious beliefs. One illustration of experimentation of this kind is found in the New Novelists in France. Robbe-Grillet, for example, proposes that man's relation to reality should change from understander/thing-understood to perceiver/thing-perceived.

Susan Sontag in *Against Interpretation* has tried to apply some of these ideas to criticism, but I think it is obvious that the broad relation of understander to thing-understood does not have to be destroyed merely to do away with the thesis-hunting attitude.

These not very fully developed suggestions of one or two possible ways in which the form of the essay could be broken are useful only as examples to bolster my contention that a new form in the essay is possible.

It might seem that by arguing against the present formal tyranny that I am suggesting a liberty that would result in the careless outpourings of free association. This is not the case. The development of a personal strategy that allowed an individual to establish a meaningful relation between himself and art would at once make writing more difficult and more exciting.

Nor would the overthrow of this tyranny negate the function of teachers in helping students learn the importance of precise language as a tool for expressing and creating self. Although a radically new form of criticism might propose non-analytic relations between self and literature, the experience of contemporary fiction should clearly indicate that open-ended (or process) essays could show the self thinking as well as feeling.

And I think it important to recognize that the breaking of the standard form of the essay does not mean replacing it with no form. All expression has form. A standard form with thesis and proof can be either polished or spontaneous. A new form could also. The choice is between forms, not between form and formlessness. And the choice of forms should be made with understanding of the implications and meaning of forms.

But there is no doubt that formal freedom, if permitted, would demand a major shift in attitude on the part of those who evaluate essays. The need for authority, the view of criticism as product, the competition for mastery over art would all have to be regarded not as *the* goals but only as one kind of goal. Conclusions, if they were reached, would be of secondary importance.

I don't know what would emerge if this freedom was granted. It might well be that many would choose the old form. I realize, for example, that this essay contains most of the formal qualities of the standard essay. In the course of writing down these ideas I experimented with many new forms and, for various reasons, discarded them. But there is a great deal of difference between choosing a form and using one under compulsion.

If formal freedom is not granted by those who have the power to give it, the freedom will be taken with all of the unhappiness that is attendant upon even so minor a revolution as one in literary studies. The control that form can exert over freedom is being understood, and, as has always seemed to happen, once man is made aware of a previously hidden tyranny, he rebels.

The Nature of Form

Kenneth Burke

One of the most arcane—and fascinating—rhetoricians of our age is Kenneth Burke. Paradoxically, one of the most practical discussions of form occurs in his Counter-Statement. *His definition of form as the "arousing and fulfillment of desires" is endlessly useful, for it makes the student ask: "Have I really honored all my promises to the reader?" It serves as the key to a check on the development of a paper.*

Burke's classification of kinds of form is also useful, for it illuminates the ways in which ideas can gain development in writing.

The Nature of Form

1. *Form* in literature is an arousing and fulfillment of desires. A work has form in so far as one part of it leads a reader to anticipate another part, to be gratified by the sequence. The five aspects of form may be discussed as

progressive form (subdivided into syllogistic and qualitative progression), repetitive form, conventional form, and minor or incidental forms.

2. *Syllogistic progression* is the form of a perfectly conducted argument, advancing step by step. It is the form of a mystery story, where everything falls together, as in a story of ratiocination by Poe. It is the form of a demonstration in Euclid. To go from *A* to *E* through stages *B, C,* and *D* is to obtain such form. We call it syllogistic because, given certain things, certain things must follow, the premises forcing the conclusion. In so far as the audience, from its acquaintance with the premises, feels the rightness of the conclusion, the work is formal. The arrows of our desires are turned in a certain direction, and the plot follows the direction of the arrows. The peripety, or reversal of the situation, discussed by Aristotle, is obviously one of the keenest manifestations of syllogistic progression. In the course of a single scene, the poet reverses the audience's expectations—as in the third act of *Julius Caesar,* where Brutus' speech before the mob prepares us for his exoneration, but the speech of Antony immediately after prepares us for his downfall.

3. *Qualitative progression,* the other aspect of progressive form, is subtler. Instead of one incident in the plot preparing us for some other possible incident of plot (as Macbeth's murder of Duncan prepares us for the dying of Macbeth), the presence of one quality prepares us for the introduction of another (the grotesque seriousness of the murder scene preparing us for the grotesque buffoonery of the porter scene). In T. S. Eliot's *The Waste Land,* the step from "Ta ta. Goonight. Goonight" to "Good night, ladies, good night, sweet ladies" is a qualitative progression. In Malcolm Cowley's sonnet *Mine No. 6* there is a similar kind of qualitative progression, as we turn from the octave's description of a dismal landscape ("the blackened stumps, the ulcerated hill") to the sestet's "Beauty, perfection, I have loved you fiercely." Such progressions are qualitative rather than syllogistic as they lack the pronounced anticipatory nature of the syllogistic progression. We are prepared less to demand a certain qualitative progression than to recognize its rightness after the event. We are put into a state of mind which another state of mind can appropriately follow.

4. *Repetitive form* is the consistent maintaining of a principle under new guises. It is restatement of the same thing in different ways. Thus, in so far as each detail of Gulliver's life among the Lilliputians is a new exemplification of the discrepancy in size between Gulliver and the Lilliputians, Swift is using repetitive form. A succession of images, each of them regiving the same lyric mood; a character repeating his identity, his "number," under changing situations; the sustaining of an attitude, as in satire; the rhythmic regularity of blank verse; the rhyme scheme of *terza rima*—these are all aspects of repetitive form. By a varying number of details, the reader is led to feel more or less consciously the principle underlying them—he then requires that this principle be observed in the giving of further details. Repetitive form, the

restatement of a theme by new details, is basic to any work of art, or to any other kind of orientation, for that matter. It is our only method of "talking on the subject."

5. *Conventional form* involves to some degree the appeal of form *as form*. Progressive, repetitive, and minor forms, may be effective even though the reader has no awareness of their formality. But when a form appeals as form, we designate it as conventional form. Any form can become conventional, and be sought for itself—whether it be as complex as the Greek tragedy or as compact as the sonnet. The invocation to the Muses; the theophany in a play of Euripedes; the processional and recessional of the Episcopalian choir; the ensemble before the front drop at the close of a burlesque show; the exordium in Greek-Roman oratory; the Sapphic ode; the triolet—these are all examples of conventional forms having varying degrees of validity today. Perhaps even the Jew-and-the-Irishman of the Broadway stage is an instance of repetitive form grown into conventional form. Poets who write beginnings *as beginnings* and endings *as endings* show the appeal of conventional form. Thus, in Milton's *Lycidas* we start distinctly with the sense of introduction ("Yet once more, O ye laurels, and once more . . .") and the poem is brought to its dextrous gliding close by the stanza, clearly an ending: "And now the sun had dropped behind the hills, And now had dropped into the western bay. . . ." But Mother Goose, throwing formal appeal into relief through "nonsense," offers us the clearest instance of conventional form, a "pure" beginning and "pure" end:

> "I'll tell you a story of Jack O'Norey
> And now my story's begun;
> I'll tell you another about his brother
> And now my story is done."

We might note, in conventional form, the element of "categorical expectancy." That is, whereas the anticipations and gratifications of progressive and repetitive form arise *during the process* of reading, the expectations of conventional form may be *anterior to* the reading. If one sets out to read a sonnet, regardless of what the sonnet is to say he makes certain formal demands to which the poem must acquiesce. And similarly, the final Beethoven rejoicing of a Beethoven finale becomes a "categorical expectation" of the symphony. The audience "awaits" it before the first bar of the music has been played. And one may, even before opening a novel, look forward to an opening passage which will proclaim itself an opening.

6. *Minor or incidental forms.* When analyzing a work of any length, we may find it bristling with minor or incidental forms—such as metaphor, paradox, disclosure, reversal, contraction, expansion, bathos, apostrophe, series, chiasmus—which can be discussed as formal events in themselves. Their effect partially depends upon their function in the whole, yet they manifest sufficient evidences of episodic distinctness to bear consideration

apart from their context. Thus a paradox, by carrying an argument one step forward, may have its use as progressive form; and by its continuation of a certain theme may have its use as repetitive form—yet it may be so formally complete in itself that the reader will memorize it as an event valid apart from its setting. A monologue by Shakespeare can be detached from its context and recited with enjoyment because, however integrally it contributes to the whole of which it is a part, it is also an independent curve of plot enclosed by its own beginning and end. The incident of Hamlet's offering the pipes to Guildenstern is a perfect instance of minor form. Euripides, when bringing a messenger upon the stage, would write him a speech which, in its obedience to the rhetorical laws of the times, was a separate miniature form. Edmund Burke sought to give each paragraph a structure as a paragraph, making it a growth, yet so confining it to one aspect of his subject that the closing sentence of the paragraph could serve as the logical complement to the opening one. Frequently, in the novel, an individual chapter is distinguished by its progress as a chapter, and not solely by its function in the whole. The Elizabethan drama generally has a profusion of minor forms.

7. *Interrelation of forms.* Progressive, repetitive, and conventional and minor forms necessarily overlap. A specific event in the plot will not be exclusively classifiable under one head—as it should not, since in so organic a thing as a work of art we could not expect to find any principle functioning in isolation from the others. Should we call the aphoristic couplet of the age of Pope repetitive form or conventional form? A closing scene may be syllogistic in that its particular events mark the dramatic conclusion of the dramatic premises; qualitative in that it exemplifies some mood made desirable by the preceding matter; repetitive in that the characters once again proclaim their identity; conventional in that it has about it something categorically terminal, as a farewell or death; and minor or incidental in that it contains a speech displaying a structural rise, development, and fall independently of its context. Perhaps the lines in *Othello,* beginning "Soft you, a word or two before you go," and ending "Seized by the throat the uncircumcised dog and smote him thus (*stabs himself*)" well exemplify the vigorous presence of all five aspects of form, as this suicide is the logical outcome of his predicament (syllogistic progression); it fits the general mood of gloomy forebodings which has fallen upon us (qualitative progression); the speech has about it that impetuosity and picturesqueness we have learned to associate with Othello (repetitive form); it is very decidedly a conclusion (conventional form), and in its development it is a tiny plot in itself (minor form). The close of the *Odyssey* strongly combines syllogistic and qualitative progression. Ulysses' vengeance upon the suitors is the logical outcome of their conduct during his absence—and by the time it occurs, the reader is so incensed with them that he exults vindictively in their destruction. In most cases, we can find some aspects of form predominant, with others tenuous to the point of imperceptibility. Keats's "Ode to a Nightingale" is a striking instance of

repetitive form; its successive stanzas take up various aspects of the mood, the *status evanescentiæ,* almost as schematically as a lawyer's brief; but of syllogistic form there is barely a trace. . . . As, in musical theory, one chord is capable of various analyses, so in literature the appeal of one event may be explained by various principles. The important thing is not to confine the explanation to *one* principle, but to formulate sufficient principles to make an explanation possible. However, though the five aspects of form can merge into one another, or can be present in varying degrees, no other terms should be required in an analysis of formal functionings.

8. *Conflict of forms.* If the various formal principles can intermingle, they can also conflict. An artist may create a character which, by the logic of the fiction, should be destroyed; but he may also have made this character so appealing that the audience wholly desires the character's salvation. Here would be a conflict between syllogistic and qualitative progression. Or he may depict a wicked character who, if the plot is to work correctly, must suddenly "reform," thereby violating repetitive form in the interests of syllogistic progression. To give a maximum sense of reality he may, like Stendhal, attempt to make sentences totally imperceptible as sentences, attempt to make the reader slip over them with no other feeling than their continuity (major progression here involving the atrophy of minor forms). Or conventional form may interfere with repetitive form (as when the drama, in developing from feudal to bourgeois subjects, chose "humbler" themes and characters, yet long retained the ceremonial diction of the earlier dignified period); and conversely, if we today were to attempt regaining some of these earlier ceremonial effects, by writing a play entirely in a ceremonial style, we should be using the appeal of repetitive form, but we should risk violating a contemporary canon of conventional form, since the non-ceremonial, the "domestic" dialogue, is now categorically expected.

9. *Rhythm, Rhyme.* Rhythm and rhyme being formal, their appeal is to be explained within the terms already given. Rhyme usually accentuates the repetitive principle of art (in so far as one rhyme determines our expectation of another, and in so far as the rhyme-scheme in one stanza determines our expectation of its continuance in another). Its appeal is the appeal of progressive form in so far as the poet gets his effects by first establishing, and then altering, a rhyme-scheme. In the ballade, triolet, etc., it can appeal as conventional form.

That verse rhythm can be largely explained as repetitive form is obvious, blank verse for instance being the constant recurrence of iambs with changing vowel and consonantal combinations (it is repetitive form in that it very distinctly sets up and gratifies a constancy of expectations; the reader "comes to rely" upon the rhythmic design after sufficient "coördinates of direction" have been received by him; the regularity of the design establishes conditions of response in the body, and the continuance of the design becomes an "obedience" to these same conditions). Rhythm appeals as conventional form in so far as specific awareness of the rhythmic pattern is involved in our enjoyment (as when the Sapphic meter is used in English, or when we turn from a pentameter sonnet in English to a hexameter sonnet in French). It can sometimes be said to appeal by qualitative progression, as when the poet, having established a pronounced rhythmic pattern, introduces a variant. Such a variant appeals as qualitative progression to the extent that it provides a "relief from the monotony" of its regular surroundings, to the extent that its appeal depends upon the previous establishment of the constant out of which it arises. Rhythm can also appeal as minor form; a peculiarity of the rhythm, for instance, may strikingly reinforce an incidental image (as with the use of spondees when the poet is speaking of something heavy).

In the matter of prose rhythms, the nature of the expectancy is much vaguer. In general the rhythmic unit is larger and more complex than the individual metric foot, often being the group of "scrambled" syllables between two cæsuras. Though the constants of prose rhythm permit a greater range of metric variation than verse rhythms (that is, though in prose much of the metric variability is felt as belonging to the *constant* rather than to the *variation*), a prose stylist does definitely restrict the rhythmic expectations of the reader, as anyone can readily observe by turning from a page of Sir Thomas Browne to a page of Carlyle. However, one must also recall Professor George Saintsbury's distinction: "As the essence of verse-meter is its identity (at least in equivalence) and recurrence, so the essence of prose-rhythm lies in variety and divergence," or again: "Variety of foot arrangement, without definite equivalence, appears to be as much the secret of prose rhythm as uniformity of value, with equivalence or without it, appears to be that of poetic meter." The only thing that seems lacking in this distinction between verse rhythms and prose rhythms is a statement of some principle by which the *variety* in prose rhythms is guided. Perhaps the principle is a principle of logic. An intellectual factor is more strongly involved in the appreciation of prose rhythm than of verse rhythm, as grammatical and ideational relationships figure prominently in the determination of prose balances (a prose balance being the rhythmic differentiation of units which have an intellectual correspondence, by parallelism or antithesis). Thus, to take from Sir Thomas Browne a typical "prose event" (we choose a very simple example from a writer who could afford us many complex ones): the series "pride, vain-glory, and madding vices" is made up of three units which are intellectually equivalent, but their ideational equality coexists with total syllabic asymmetry (the first a monosyllable, the second an amphibrach, the third dochmiac—or one, three, and five syllables, though it is true that in verse scansion the words "and madding vices" would not ordinarily be considered as constituting a single foot). It is also worth noting, as an example of the "intellectual" rhythms in prose, that the third noun is accompanied by an adjective, the second has an adjective engrafted upon it, and the first stands alone; also, the third differs from the other two in number. To consider a slightly more complex example: "Even Scylla, / that thought himself safe in his urn, / could not prevent revenging tongues, / and stones thrown at his monument." Here many complexities of asymmetric balance may be noted: contrast between long subject and short verb; contrast between short verb and long object; the two grammatical components of the subject (noun and clause) are unequal in value, whereas the two main grammatical components of the object ("tongues" and "stones") are equal in value; the modifier in the subject is a clause, whereas the modifiers of the object are participial adjectives; of these two participial adjectives, one ("revenging") is active, precedes its noun, and is of three syllables, but the other ("thrown") is passive, follows its noun, and is monosyllabic; and whereas "revenging" is an unmodified modifier, "thrown" is accompanied by the phrase "at his monument." We might further note that the interval from the beginning to the first cæsura ("Even Scylla") greatly contrasts in length with the interval between the first and second cæsura ("that thought himself safe in his urn"). In two notable respects the third and fourth intervals are surely inferior as prose to the first two. Their iambic quality is concealed with difficulty; there is more than a hint of homœoteleuton ("prevent"—"monument"), which is only suppressed by our placing the cæsura at "tongues" and rigorously avoiding the slightest pause after "prevent." The placing of the cæsura after "tongues," however, has the further advantage of putting "tongues" and "stones" in different intervals, thus once more giving us the asymmetrical by rhythmically separating the logically joined. [We do not imply that one consciously notes such a multitude of dissimilar balances, any more than one consciously notes the complexity of muscular tensions involved in walking—but as there is an undeniable complexity of muscular tensions involved in walking, so there is a multitude of dissimilar balances involved in expert prose. And we are trying to indicate that the rhythmic variations of prose are not haphazard, that their "planfulness" (conscious or unconscious) arises from the fact that the differentiations are based upon logical groupings. That is, by logically relating one part of a sentence to another part of the sentence, the prose writer is led to a formal differentiation of the two related parts (or sometimes, which is *au fond* the same thing, he is led to a pronounced parallelism in the treatment of the related parts). The logical grouping of one part with another serves as the guide to the formal treatment of both (as "planful" differentiation can arise only out of a sense of correspondence). The logical groupings upon which the rhythmic differentiations are based will differ with the individual, not only as to the ways in which he conceives a sentence's relationships, but also as to their number—and much of the "individuality" in a particular prose style could be traced to the number and nature of the author's logical groupings. Some writers, who seek "conversational" rather than "written" effects, apparently conceive of the sentence as a totality; they ignore its internal relationships almost entirely, preferring to make each sentence as homogeneous as a piece of string. By such avoidance of logical grouping they do undeniably obtain a simple fluency which, if one can delight in it sufficiently, makes every page of Johnson a mass of absurdities—but their sentences are, as sentences, uneventful.] The "written" effects of prose seem to stress the progressive rather than the repetitive principle of form, since one part of the sentence is differentiated on the basis of another part (the formal identity of one part awakens in us a response whereby we can be pleased by a formal alteration in another part). But "conversational" rhythm, which is generally experienced "in the lump," as a pervasive monotone rather than as a group of marked internal structures, is—like verse—more closely allied to the repetitive principle. The "conversational" is thus seen to fall halfway between verse-rhythm and prose-rhythm, sharing something of both but lacking the pronounced characteristics of either.

So much for prose rhythm regardless of its subject-matter. We must also recognize the "secondary" aspect of rhythms whereby they can often be explained "at one remove." Thus, a tumultuous character would constantly restate his identity by the use of tumultuous speech (repetitive form), and the rhythm, in so far as it became tumultuous out of sympathy with its subject, would share the repetitive form of the subject. Similarly, it may be discussed as conventional or minor form (as when the author marshals his more aggressive images to mark an ending, and parallels this with a kindred increase in the aggression of his rhythms). In a remote way, all such rhythmic effects may be described as a kind of "onomatopoetic parallelism," since their rhythmic identity would be explainable by the formal nature of the theme to which they are accommodated.

10. *"Significant form."* Though admitting the "onomatopoetic correspondence" between form and theme, we must question a quasi-mystical attempt to explain all formal quality as "onomatopoetic" (that is, as an adaptation of sound and rhythm to the peculiarities of the sense). In most cases we find formal designs or contrivances which impart emphasis regardless of their subject. Whatever the theme may be, they add saliency to this theme, the same design serving to make dismalness more dismal or gladness gladder. Thus, if a poet is writing in a quick meter, he may stress one point in his imagery as well as another by the use of spondees; or he may gain emphasis by injecting a burst of tonal saliency, as the aggressive repetition of a certain vowel, into an otherwise harmonious context. In either case the emphasis is gained though there be no discernible onomatopoetic correspondence between the form and the theme (the formal saliency being merely a kind of subtler italics, a mechanism for placing emphasis wherever one chooses, or such "absolute" stressing as comes of pounding the table with one's fist to emphasize either this remark or that). To realize that there is such absolute stressing, one has but to consider the great variety of emotions which can be intensified by climactic arrangement, such arrangement thus being a mere "coefficient of power" which can heighten the saliency of the emotion regardless of what emotion it may be.

As illustration, let us trace one formal contrivance through a set of diverse effects, as it is used in Wilde, Wordsworth, and Racine, and as it appeared by chance in actual life. Beginning with the last, we may recall a conversation between two children, a boy and a girl. The boy's mind was on one subject, the girl's turned to many subjects, with the result that the two of them were talking at cross-purposes. Pointing to a field beyond the road, the boy asked: "Whose field is that?" The girl answered: "That is Mr. Murdock's field"— and went on to tell where Mr. Murdock lived, how many children he had, when she had last seen these children, which of them she preferred, but the boy interrupted: "What does he do with the field?" He usually plants the field in rye, she explained; why, only the other day he drove up with a wagon carrying a plough, one of his sons was with him, they left the wagon at the gate, the two of them unloaded the plough, they hitched the—but the boy interrupted severely: "Does the field go all the way over to the brook?" The conversation continued in this vein, always at cross-purposes, and growing increasingly humorous to eavesdroppers as its formal principle was inexorably continued. Note in *Salome,* however, this mechanism serving to produce a very different effect:

SALOME: (*to Iokanaan*) . . . Suffer me to kiss thy mouth.
IOKANAAN: Never! daughter of Babylon! Daughter of Sodom! Never!
SALOME: I will kiss thy mouth, Iokanaan. . . .
THE YOUNG SYRIAN: . . . Look not at this man, look not at him. I cannot endure
      it. . . . Princess, do not speak these things.
SALOME: I will kiss thy mouth, Iokanaan.

And as the Young Syrian, in despair, slays himself and falls dead at her feet, she continues: "Suffer me to kiss thy mouth, Iokanaan."

Turning now to Wordsworth's "We Are Seven":

> " 'You say that two at Conway dwell,
>   And two are gone to sea,
>   Yet ye are seven. I pray you tell,
>   Sweet maid, how this may be.'

> "Then did the little Maid reply,
>   'Seven boys and girls are we;
>   Two of us in the churchyard lie,
>   Beneath the churchyard tree.' "

The poet argues with her: there were seven in all, two are now dead—so it follows that there are only five. But when he has made his point,

> " 'How many are you, then,' said I,
>   'If they two are in heaven?'
>   Quick was the little Maid's reply,
>   'O Master! we are seven.' "

Humor, *sournoiserie,* sentiment—we may now turn to Racine, where we find this talking at cross-purposes employed to produce a very poignant tragic irony. Agamemnon has secretly arranged to sacrifice his daughter, Iphigenia, on the altar; he is telling her so, but haltingly and cryptically, confessing and concealing at once; she does not grasp the meaning of his words but feels their ominousness. She has heard, she says, that Calchas is planning a sacrifice to appease the gods. Agamemnon exclaims: Would that he could turn these gods from their outrageous demands (his words referring to the oracle which requires her death, as the audience knows, but Iphigenia does not). Will the offering take place soon? she asks.—Sooner than Agamemnon wishes.—Will she be allowed to be present?—Alas! says Agamemnon.—You say no more, says Iphigenia.—"You will be there, my daughter"—the conflict in meanings being heightened by the fact that each of Agamemnon's non sequitur rejoinders rhymes with Iphigenia's question:

IPHIGÉNIE: Périsse le Troyen auteur de nos alarmes!
AGAMEMNON: Sa perte à ses vainqueurs coûtera bien des larmes.
IPHIGÉNIE: Les dieux deignent surtout prendre soin de vos jours!
AGAMEMNON: Les dieux depuis un temps me sont cruels et sourds.
IPHIGÉNIE: Calchas, dit-on, prépare un pompeux sacrifice?
AGAMEMNON: Puissé-je auparavant fléchir leur injustice!
IPHIGÉNIE: L'offrira-t-on bientôt?
AGAMEMNON: Plus tôt que je ne veux.
IPHIGÉNIE: Me sera-t-il permis de me joindre à vos veux?
              Verra-t-on à l'autel votre heureuse famille?
AGAMEMNON: Hélas!
IPHIGÉNIE: Vous vous taisez!
AGAMEMNON: Vous y serez, ma fille.

Perhaps the line, "Hurry up please, it's time," in the public house scene of *The Waste Land,* as it is repeated and unanswered, could illustrate the use of this formal contrivance for still another effect.

The Individuation of Forms

11. *Appeal of Forms.* Form, having to do with the creation and gratification of needs, is "correct" in so far as it gratifies the needs which it creates. The appeal of the form in this sense is obvious: form *is* the appeal. The appeal of progressive and repetitive forms as they figure in the major organization of a work, needs no further explanation. Conventional form is a shiftier topic, particularly since the conventional forms demanded by one age are as resolutely shunned by another. Often they owe their presence in art to a survival from a different situation (as the invocation to the Muses is the conventionalization of a prayer based upon an earlier belief in the divine inspiration of poetry; and the chorus in the religious rites of Dionysus survives in the secular drama that grew out of these rites). At other times a conventional form may arise from a definite functional purpose, as the ebb, flow, and close of a sonnet became a conventional form through repeated usage. Thereafter a reader will be disturbed at a sonnet of fifteen lines, even though it attains precisely the ebb, flow, and close that distinguishes the sonnet. The reader has certain categorical expectations which the poet must meet. As for

the formality of beginnings and endings—such procedures as the greeting of the New Year, the ceremony at laying a cornerstone, the "house-warming," the funeral, all indicate that the human mind is prone to feel beginnings and endings *as such*.

When we turn to minor form and carry examination down to the individual sentence, or the individual figure of speech, the relation between form and the gratification of desire becomes admittedly more tenuous. The formal appeal of the single sentence need not, it is true, be sought in the sentence alone—the sentence can also "gratify" us by its place in a context (it contributes to progressive form in so far as it contains a statement that advances the plot; and it contributes to repetitive form if, for instance, it corroborates our expectations with respect to a certain character). But, since the single sentence has form, we are forced by our thesis to consider the element of gratification in the sentence apart from its context. There are certain rudimentary kinds of balance in which the factor of desire is perceptible, as when a succession of monosyllables arouses the "need" of a polysyllabic word to break their monotony. And the same factor exists clearly enough in the periodic sentence, where the withholding of some important detail until the last drives us forward to the close. But is not every sentence a "periodic" sentence? If one, for instance, enters a room and says simply, "The man . . ." unless the auditor knows enough about the man to finish the sentence in his own thoughts, his spontaneous rejoinder will be, "The man what?" A naming must be completed by a doing, either explicit or implicit. The subject demands a predicate as resolutely as the antecedent of a musical phrase in Mozart calls for its consequent. Admittedly, when we carry the discussion to so small a particle (almost like discussing one brush stroke as a test of a definition of form in painting) the element of "gratification" will not usually be prominent. The formal satisfaction of completion will be clear only in cases where the process of completing is stressed, as in the periodic sentence. Otherwise it can be better revealed by our dissatisfaction with an uncompleted thought than by our satisfaction with a completed one.

The appeal of form as exemplified in rhythm enjoys a special advantage in that rhythm is more closely allied with "bodily" processes. Systole and diastole, alternation of the feet in walking, inhalation and exhalation, up and down, in and out, back and forth, such are the types of distinctly motor experiences "tapped" by rhythm. Rhythm is so natural to the organism that even a succession of uniform beats will be interpreted as a succession of accented and unaccented beats. The rhythm of a page, in setting up a corresponding rhythm in the body, creates marked degrees of expectancy, or acquiescence. A rhythm is a promise which the poet makes to the reader— and in proportion as the reader comes to rely upon this promise, he falls into a state of general surrender which makes him more likely to accept without resistance the rest of the poet's material. In becoming receptive to so much, he becomes receptive to still more. The varied rhythms of prose also have their "motor" analogies. A reader sensitive to prose rhythms is like a man hurrying through a crowd; at one time he must halt, at another time he can leap forward; he darts perilously between saunterers; he guards himself in turning sharp corners. We mean that in all rhythmic experiences one's "muscular imagination" is touched. Similarly with sounds, there is some analogy to actual movement, since sounds may rise and fall, and in a remote way one rises and falls with them.

12. *"Priority" of forms.* There are formal patterns which distinguish our experience. They apply in art, since they apply outside of art. The accelerated motion of a falling body, the cycle of a storm, the gradations of a sunrise, the stages of a cholera epidemic, the ripening of crops—in all such instances we find the material of progressive form. Repetitive form applies to all manner of orientation, for we can continue to discuss a subject only by taking up in turn various aspects of it. (Recalling the schoolmen's subdivisions of a topic: *quis, quid, ubi, quibus auxiliis, cur, quo modo, quando.* One talks about a thing by talking about something else.) We establish a direction by co-ordinates; we establish a curve by three points, and thereupon can so place other points that they will be intercepted by this curve. Thus, though forms need not be prior to experience, they are certainly prior to the work of art exemplifying them. Psychology and philosophy may decide whether they are innate or resultant; so far as the work of art is concerned they simply *are:* when one turns to the production or enjoyment of a work of art, a formal equipment is already present, and the effects of art are involved in its utilization. Such ultimate minor forms as contrast, comparison, metaphor, series, bathos, chiasmus, are based upon our modes of understanding anything; they are implicit in the process of abstraction and generalization by which we think. (When analyzed so closely, they manifest the principles of repetitive and progressive form so fraily that we might better speak of coexistent unity and diversity—"something" in relation to "something else"—which is probably the basic distinction of our earliest perceptions. The most rudimentary manifestation of such coexistent unity and diversity in art is perhaps observable in two rhyming monosyllables, room—doom, where diversity of sound in the initial consonants coexists with unity of sound in the vowels and final consonants, a relation describable either as repetitive or as progressive.)

Such basic forms may, for all that concerns us, be wholly conventional. The subject—predicate form of sentence, for instance, has sanction enough if we have learned to expect it. It may be "natural" only as a path worn across a field is natural. But if experience has worn a path, the path is there—and in using the path we are obeying the authority of a prior form.

An ability to function in a certain way implies gratification in so functioning. A capacity is not something which lies dormant until used—a capacity is a command to act in a certain way. Thus a pinioned bird, though it has learned that flight is impossible, must yet spread out its wings and go through the motions of flying: its muscles, being equipped for flight, require the process. Similarly, if a dog lacks a bone, he will gnaw at a block of wood;

not that he is hungry—for he may have his fill of meat—but his teeth, in their fitness to endure the strain of gnawing, feel the need of enduring that strain. So the formal aspects of art appeal in that they exercise formal potentialities of the reader. They enable the mind to follow processes amenable to it. Mother Goose is little more than an exerciser of simple mental functions. It is almost wholly formal, with processes of comparing, contrasting, and arranging. Though the jingles may, in some instances, have originated as political lampoons, etc., the ideas as adapted in the nursery serve purely as gymnastics in the fundamental processes of form.

The forms of art, to summarize, are not exclusively "æsthetic." They can be said to have a prior existence in the experiences of the person hearing or reading the work of art. They parallel processes which characterize his experiences outside of art.

13. *Individuation of forms.* Since there are no forms of art which are not forms of experience outside of art, we may—so far as form is concerned—discuss the single poem or drama as an individuation of formal principles. Each work re-embodies the formal principles in different subject-matter. A "metaphor" is a concept, an abstraction—but a specific metaphor, exemplified by specific images, is an "individuation." Its appeal as form resides in the fact that its particular subject-matter enables the mind to follow a metaphor-process. In this sense we would restore the Platonic relationship between form and matter. A form is a way of experiencing; and such a form is made available in art when, by the use of specific subject-matter, it enables us to experience in this way. The images of art change greatly with changes in the environment and the ethical systems out of which they arise; but the principles of art, as individuated in these changing images, will be found to recur in all art, where they are individuated in one subject-matter or another. Accordingly, the concept of the individuation of forms constitutes the bridge by which we move from a consideration of form to a consideration of subject-matter.

14. *Form and information.* The necessity of embodying form in subject-matter gives rise to certain "diseases" of form. The subject-matter tends to take on an intrinsic interest, to appeal independently of its functional uses. Thus, whereas realism originated to meet formal requirements (the introduction of life-like details to make outlandish plots plausible), it became an end in itself; whereas it arose in the attempt to make the unreal realistic, it ended by becoming a purpose in itself and making the real realistic. Similarly, description grows in assertiveness until novelists write descriptions, not for their use in the arousing and fulfilling of expectation, but because the novelists have something to describe which they consider interesting in itself (a volcano, a remarkable savage tribe, an unusual thicket). This tendency becomes frankly "scientific" in the thesis drama and the psychological novel, where the matter is offered for its value as the "exposure" of a burning issue. In the psychological novel, the reader may often follow the hero's mental processes as

noteworthy facts, just as he would follow them in a scientific treatise on the human mind, except that in the novel the facts are less schematically arranged from the standpoint of scientific presentation. In so far as the details in a work are offered, not for their bearing upon the business of molding and meeting the reader's expectations, but because these details are interesting in themselves, the appeal of form retreats behind the appeal of information. Atrophy of form follows hypertrophy of information.

There is, obviously, no "right" proportion of the two. A novelist, for instance, must give enough description for us to feel the conviction of his story's background. Description, to this extent, is necessary in the interests of form—and there is no clearly distinguishable point at which description for the purposes of the plot goes over into description for its own sake. Similarly, a certain amount of psychological data concerning the characters of a fiction helps the author to make the characters of moment to the reader, and thus has a formal function in the affecting of the reader's desires: yet the psychology can begin to make claims of its own, and at times the writer will analyze his hero not because analysis is formally needed at this point, but because the writer has some disclosures which he considers interesting in themselves.

The hypertrophy of information likewise tends to interfere with our enjoyment in the repetition of a work. For the presence of information as a factor in literature has enabled writers to rely greatly upon ignorance as a factor in appeal. Thus, they will relieve the reader's ignorance about a certain mountain of Tibet, but when they have done so they will have less to "tell" him at a second reading. Surprise and suspense are the major devices for the utilization of ignorance (the psychology of information), for when they are depended upon, the reader's interest in the work is based primarily upon his ignorance of its outcome. In the classic drama, where the psychology of form is emphasized, we have not surprise but disclosure (the surprise being a surprise not to the audience, but to the characters); and likewise suspense here is not based upon our ignorance of the forthcoming scenes. There is, perhaps, more formal suspense at a second reading than at a first in a scene such as Hamlet's giving of the pipes to Guildenstern. It is the suspense of certain forces gathering to produce a certain result. It is the suspense of a rubber band which we see being tautened. We know that it will be snapped— there is thus no ignorance of the outcome; our satisfaction arises from our participation in the process, from the fact that the beginnings of the dialogue lead us to feel the logic of its close.

Painting, architecture, music are probably more amenable to repetition without loss because the formal aspects are not so obscured by the subject-matter in which they are embodied. One can repeat with pleasure a jingle from Mother Goose, where the formality is obvious, yet one may have no interest whatsoever in memorizing a psychological analysis in a fiction. He may wish to remember the observations themselves, but his own words are as serviceable as the author's. And if he does choose to memorize the particular wording of the author, and recites it with pleasure, the passage will be found to have a formal, as well as an informational, validity.

15. *Form and Ideology*. The artist's manipulations of the reader's desires involve his use of what the reader considers desirable. If the reader believes in monogamistic marriage, and in the code of fidelity surrounding it, the poet can exploit this belief in writing an *Othello*. But the form of his drama is implicated in the reader's belief, and Othello's conduct would hardly seem "syllogistic" in polyandrous Tibet. Similarly, the conventional form which marks the close of Baudelaire's *Femmes Damnées,* as he turns from the dialogue of the two Lesbians to his eloquent apostrophe, *"Descendez, descendez, lamentables victimes,"* is an effect built out of precisely that intermingling of church morality and profanation which Baudelaire always relies upon for his deepest effects. He writes for neither pure believers nor pure infidels, but for infidels whose infidelity greatly involves the surviving vocabulary of belief. In war times, the playwright who would depict a villain has only to designate his man as a foreign spy—at other times he must be more inventive to find something so exploitable in the ideology of his audience. A slight change in ideology, in fact, can totally reverse our judgments as to the form which it embodies. Thus, Euripides was accused of misusing the *deus ex machina*. In his *Iphigenia at Aulis,* for instance, his syllogistic progression leads the heroine inexorably to the sacrificial altar—whereupon a god descends and snatches her unharmed from her father's knife. Approached from the ideology of an Aristotle, this would constitute a violation of form, since the dramatic causality leads to one end and the poet gives us another. But we can consider the matter differently: the drama was a survival of a religious rite; as such, the god certainly had a place in it; Euripides frankly attempted to regain some of the earlier dramatic forms which Æschylus and Sophocles had suppressed and which brought out more clearly its religious affiliations; could we not, accordingly, look upon the appearance of the god as a part of Euripides' program? Euripides would, that is, write a play in which the details of the plot led the heroine so inexorably towards destruction that nothing could save her but the intervention of the gods. By this ideology, the closing theophany is formally correct: it is not a way of avoiding a bad ending (the "syllogistically" required death of an Iphigenia who has won the audience's sympathies); it is a syllogistic preparation for the god's appearance. As another instance of how the correctness of the form depends upon the ideology, we may consider a piece of juvenile fiction for Catholic boys. The hero will be consistently a hero: he will show bravery, honesty, kindness to the oppressed, strength in sports, gentleness to women—in every way, by the tenets of repetitive form, he will repeat the fact that he is a hero. And among these repetitions will be his converting of Indians to Catholicism. To a Catholic boy, this will be one more repetition of his identity as an ideal hero; but to the Protestant boy, approaching the work from a slightly different ideology, repetitive form will be endangered at this point.

The shifts in ideology being continuous, not only from age to age but from person to person, the individuation of universal forms through specific subject-matter can bring the formal principles themselves into jeopardy.

16. *Re-individuation of forms.* The best proof that there is "individuation of forms" is the fact that there is "re-individuation of forms." The simplest instance is the literal translation, which fills the form with a complete change of matter (the words out of one social context are replaced by parallel words out of another social context). In free translation, the correspondences are conceived more broadly, the re-individuation often being effected not only by vocabulary, but also by adjustments to differences in ideology. Thus, a translator was bewildered by a chapter in German which spoke continually of the hero's spirit, or soul, or mind (*Geist*); the author told at great length what the hero's *Geist* was doing, wanting to do, and wanting not to do; but there seemed no natural equivalent for this in English until the translator discovered that, everywhere the German said "his soul desired such-and-such," the English could say quite simply "he desired such-and-such." In Germany the ideology behind the Hegelian vocabulary still flourishes in some quarters, thus making this survival of *Geist* in such a usage much less an oddity than it would be in America—wherefore the translator's "free re-individuation" took this slight difference of ideology into account. . . . It is with the adaptation of plays that the re-individuating process usually goes farthest in altering to fit differences of ideology. The "play doctors" think nothing of so re-individuating a German war play for American consumption that friend and foe of the original are reversed in the adaptation. Or one might, for contemporary theatrical uses, best "re-individuate" an ancient burlesque of political conditions in Athens by putting the Mayor of New York in place of Pericles. Playwrights are the arch-reindividuators. The writers of revues make a definite practice of adapting the vulgar story of the smoker, so re-individuating its underlying form by a more temperate situation and plot that the story becomes available for production on the stage, thus translating a story conceived by "private life" ideology into a story suited to "public life" ideology. (Since in Japan it is customary to smile on mentioning the death of a close friend, were we completely re-individuating a Japanese mention of smiling under such conditions, we might say, not "he smiled," but "his face fell," as the Western equivalent. We should thus be translating the accepted social usage of Japan into the corresponding accepted social usage of the West.)

Perhaps the most elaborate re-individuation in all history is James Joyce's *Ulysses.* But whereas in most instances the purpose of the new individuations is to make changes which reproduce under one set of conditions an effect originally obtained under another set of conditions, in the case of *Ulysses* each individuation is given a strictly "un-Homeric" equivalent. The new individuations intentionally alter the effect. The *Ulysses* is the Anti-Odyssey.

Suggestions for Further Reading

Burke's main works have appeared in a variety of editions, and the University of California Press is reissuing them.

Fogarty, Daniel John. *Roots for a New Rhetoric*. New York: Columbia University, 1959.

Holland, L. Virginia. *Counterpoint: Kenneth Burke and Aristotle's Theories of Rhetoric*. New York: Philosophical Library, 1959.

Knox, George. *Critical Moments: Kenneth Burke's Categories and Critiques*. Seattle: University of Washington, 1957.

Nichols, Marie Hochmuth. *Rhetoric and Criticism*. Baton Rouge: Louisiana State University, 1963.

Rueckert, William H. *Kenneth Burke and the Drama of Human Relations*. Minneapolis: University of Minnesota, 1963.

Turner, Linda M. "On First Reading Burke's 'A Rhetoric of Motives,'" *College Composition and Communication* 24 (February 1973), 22–30.

The Printed Word

Marshall McLuhan

McLuhan is now pretty old hat; he has seen his moment of glory as a pop savant flicker and fade away. However, I am inclined to think that McLuhan will have a lasting importance, particularly for rhetoricians. He is a man who had several sharp flashes of insight concerning the way in which discourse works, and he was dramatic enough as a personality to bring these insights to the attention of a large segment of the general public.

McLuhan claims that we are at the moment of "interface" between the print culture and the electronic culture—two contrasting, even conflicting, technologies; two disparate means of conveying information. In a very broad sense, the book and the television are forms; in an equally broad sense, the information they convey is differently formed. And in McLuhan's sense, the medium is the message. The book is an extension of the eye; the electronic media are extensions of the central nervous system.

The selection reprinted here raises questions, but provides no answers. What important questions are raised?

(1) Why are some of us panic-stricken concerning television? Why do some humanists, for instance, assign more value to a trashy detective story in a book than to a trashy detective story on TV?

(2) If the phonetic alphabet is the technology that created civilized man, what will happen (is happening) to civilization because of the electronic revolution?

(3) According to McLuhan, the phonetic alphabet, with its linearity, created Western logic. Will the electronic media take us back to a world of intuition, to the world of the all-at-onceness of myth?

(4) If the phonetic alphabet created autonomous man, will the electronic media recreate tribal man?

If McLuhan seems outrageous, that is beside the point. In claiming that the medium is the message, he puts the consideration of form in an interesting perspective.

"You may perceive, Madam," said Dr. Johnson with a pugilistic smile, "that I am well-bred to a degree of needless scrupulosity." Whatever the degree of conformity the Doctor had achieved with the new stress of his time on white-shirted tidiness, he was quite aware of the growing social demand for visual presentability.

Printing from movable types was the first mechanization of a complex handicraft, and became the archetype of all subsequent mechanization. From Rabelais and More to Mill and Morris, the typographic explosion extended the minds and voices of men to reconstitute the human dialogue on a world scale that has bridged the ages. For if seen merely as a store of information, or as a new means of speedy retrieval of knowledge, typography ended parochialism and tribalism, psychically and socially, both in space and in time. Indeed the first two centuries of printing from movable types were motivated much more by the desire to see ancient and medieval books than by the need to read and write new ones. Until 1700 much more than 50 per cent of all printed books were ancient or medieval. Not only antiquity but also the Middle Ages were given to the first reading public of the printed word. And the medieval texts were by far the most popular.

Like any other extension of man, typography had psychic and social consequences that suddenly shifted previous boundaries and patterns of culture. In bringing the ancient and medieval worlds into fusion—or, as some would say, confusion—the printed book created a third world, the modern world, which now encounters a new electric technology or a new extension of man. Electric means of moving of information are altering our typographic culture as sharply as print modified medieval manuscript and scholastic culture.

Beatrice Warde has recently described in *Alphabet* an electric display of letters painted by light. It was a Norman McLaren movie advertisement of which she asks

Do you wonder that I was late for the theatre that night, when I tell you that I saw two club-footed Egyptian A's . . . walking off arm-in-arm with the unmistakable swagger of a music-hall comedy-team? I saw base-serifs pulled together as if by ballet shoes, so that the letters tripped off literally *sur les pointes* . . . after forty centuries of the *necessarily static* Alphabet, I saw what its members could do in the fourth dimension of Time, "flux," movement. You may well say that I was electrified.

Nothing could be farther from typographic culture with its "place for everything and everything in its place."

Mrs. Warde has spent her life in the study of typography and she shows sure tact in her startled response to letters that are not printed by types but painted by light. It may be that the explosion that began with phonetic letters (the "dragon's teeth" sowed by King Cadmus) will reverse into "implosion" under the impulse of the instant speed of electricity. The alphabet (and its extension into typography) made possible the spread of the power that is knowledge, and shattered the bonds of tribal man, thus exploding him into agglomeration of individuals. Electric writing and speed pour upon him, instantaneously and continuously, the concerns of all other men. He becomes tribal once more. The human family becomes one tribe again.

Any student of the social history of the printed book is likely to be puzzled by the lack of understanding of the psychic and social effects of printing. In five centuries explicit comment and awareness of the effects of print on human sensibility are very scarce. But the same observation can be made about all the extensions of man, whether it be clothing or the computer. An extension appears to be an amplification of an organ, a sense or a function, that inspires the central nervous system to a self-protective gesture of numbing of the extended area, at least so far as direct inspection and awareness are concerned. Indirect comment on the effects of the printed book is available in abundance in the work of Rabelais, Cervantes, Montaigne, Swift, Pope, and Joyce. They used typography to create new art forms.

Psychically the printed book, an extension of the visual faculty, intensified perspective and the fixed point of view. Associated with the visual stress on point of view and the vanishing point that provides the illusion of perspective there comes another illusion that space is visual, uniform and continuous. The linearity, precision and uniformity of the arrangement of movable types are inseparable from these great cultural forms and innovations of Renaissance experience. The new intensity of visual stress and private point of view in the first century of printing were united to the means of self-expression made possible by the typographic extension of man.

Socially, the typographic extension of man brought in nationalism, industrialism, mass markets, and universal literacy and education. For print presented an image of repeatable precision that inspired totally new forms of extending social energies. Print released great psychic and social energies in the Renaissance, as today in Japan or Russia, by breaking the individual out of the traditional group while providing a model of how to add individual to individual in massive agglomeration of power. The same spirit of private enterprise that emboldened authors and artists to cultivate self-expression led other men to create giant corporations, both military and commercial.

Perhaps the most significant of the gifts of typography to man is that of detachment and noninvolvement—the power to act without reacting. Science since the Renaissance has exalted this gift which has become an embarrassment in the electric age, in which all people are involved in all others at all times. The very word "disinterested," expressing the loftiest detachment and ethical integrity of typographic man, has in the past decade been increasingly used to mean: "He couldn't care less." The same integrity indicated by the term "disinterested" as a mark of the scientific and scholarly temper of a literate and enlightened society is now increasingly repudiated as "specialization" and fragmentation of knowledge and sensibility. The fragmenting and analytic power of the printed word in our psychic lives gave us that "dissociation of sensibility" which in the arts and literature since Cézanne and since Baudelaire has been a top priority for elimination in every program of reform in taste and knowledge. In the "implosion" of the electric age the separation of thought and feeling has come to seem as strange as the departmentalization of knowledge in schools and universities. Yet it was precisely the power to separate thought and feeling, to be able to act without reacting, that split literate man out of the tribal world of close family bonds in private and social life.

Typography was no more an addition to the scribal art than the motorcar was an addition to the horse. Printing had its "horseless carriage" phase of being misconceived and misapplied during its first decades, when it was not uncommon for the purchaser of a printed book to take it to a scribe to have it copied and illustrated. Even in the early eighteenth century a "textbook" was still defined as a "Classick Author written very wide by the Students, to give room for an Interpretation dictated by the Master, &c., to be inserted in the Interlines" (O.E.D.). Before printing, much of the time in school and college classrooms was spent in making such texts. The classroom tended to be a *scriptorium* with a commentary. The student was an editor-publisher. By the same token the book market was a secondhand market of relatively scarce items. Printing changed learning and marketing processes alike. The book was the first teaching machine and also the first mass-produced commodity. In amplifying and extending the written word, typography revealed and greatly extended the structure of writing. Today, with the cinema and the electric speed-up of information movement, the formal structure of the printed word, as of mechanism in general, stands forth like a branch washed up on the beach. A new medium is never an addition to an old one, nor does it leave the old one in peace. It never ceases to oppress the older media until it finds new shapes and positions for them. Manuscript culture had sustained an oral procedure in education that was called "scholasticism" at its higher levels; but by putting the same text in front of any given number of students or readers print ended the scholastic regime of oral disputation very quickly. Print provided a vast new memory for past writings that made a personal memory inadequate.

Margaret Mead has reported that when she brought several copies of the same book to a Pacific island there was great excitement. The natives had seen books, but only one copy of each, which they had assumed to be unique. Their astonishment at the identical character of several books was a natural response to what is after all the most magical and potent aspect of print and mass production. It involves a principle of extension by homogenization that is the key to understanding Western power. The open society is open by virtue of a uniform typographic educational processing that permits indefinite expansion of any group by additive means. The printed book based on typographic uniformity and repeatability in the visual order was the first teaching machine, just as typography was the first mechanization of a handicraft. Yet in spite of the extreme fragmentation or specialization of human action necessary to achieve the printed word, the printed book represents a rich composite of previous cultural inventions. The total effort embodied in the illustrated book in print offers a striking example of the variety of separate acts of invention that are requisite to bring about a new technological result.

The psychic and social consequences of print included an extension of its fissile and uniform character to the gradual homogenization of diverse regions with the resulting amplification of power, energy, and aggression that we associate with new nationalisms. Psychically, the visual extension and amplification of the individual by print had many effects. Perhaps as striking as any other is the one mentioned by Mr. E. M. Forster, who, when discussing some Renaissance types, suggested that "the printing press, then only a century old, had been mistaken for an engine of immortality, and men had hastened to commit to it deeds and passions for the benefit of future ages." People began to act as though immortality were inherent in the magic repeatability and extensions of print.

Another significant aspect of the uniformity and repeatability of the printed page was the pressure it exerted toward "correct" spelling, syntax, and pronunciation. Even more notable were the effects of print in separating poetry from song, and prose from oratory, and popular from educated speech. In the matter of poetry it turned out that, as poetry could be read without being heard, musical instruments could also be played without accompanying any verses. Music veered from the spoken word, to converge again with Bartók and Schoenberg.

With typography the process of separation (or explosion) of functions went on swiftly at all levels and in all spheres; nowhere was this matter observed and commented on with more bitterness than in the plays of Shakespeare. Especially in *King Lear,* Shakespeare provided an image or model of the process of quantification and fragmentation as it entered the world of politics and of family life. Lear at the very opening of the play presents "our darker purpose" as a plan of delegation of powers and duties:

> Only we shall retain
> The name, and all th' addition to a King;
> The sway, revenue, execution of the rest,
> Beloved sons, be yours: which to confirm,
> This coronet part between you.

This act of fragmentation and delegation blasts Lear, his kingdom, and his family. Yet to divide and rule was the dominant new idea of the organization of power in the Renaissance. "Our darker purpose" refers to Machiavelli himself, who had developed an individualist and quantitative idea of power that struck more fear in that time than Marx in ours. Print, then, challenged the corporate patterns of medieval organization as much as electricity now challenges our fragmented individualism.

The uniformity and repeatability of print permeated the Renaissance with the idea of time and space as continuous measurable quantities. The immediate effect of this idea was to desacralize the world of nature and the world of power alike. The new technique of control of physical processes by segmentation and fragmentation separated God and Nature as much as Man and Nature, or man and man. Shock at this departure from traditional vision and inclusive awareness was often directed toward the figure of Machiavelli, who had merely spelled out the new quantitative and neutral or scientific ideas of force as applied to the manipulation of kingdoms.

Shakespeare's entire work is taken up with the themes of the new delimitations of power, both kingly and private. No greater horror could be imagined in his time than the spectacle of Richard II, the sacral king, undergoing the indignities of imprisonment and denudation of his sacred prerogatives. It is in *Troilus and Cressida,* however, that the new cults of fissile, irresponsible power, public and private, are paraded as a cynical charade of atomistic competition:

> Take the instant way;
> For honour travels in a strait so narrow
> Where one but goes abreast: keep, then, the path;
> For emulation hath a thousand sons
> That one by one pursue: if you give way,
> Or hedge aside from the direct forthright,
> Like to an enter'd tide they all rush by
> And leave you hindmost . . .
>
> (III, iii)

The image of society as segmented into a homogeneous mass of quantified appetites shadows Shakespeare's vision in the later plays.

Of the many unforeseen consequences of typography, the emergence of nationalism is, perhaps, the most familiar. Political unification of populations by means of vernacular and language groupings was unthinkable before printing turned each vernacular into an extensive mass medium. The tribe, an extended form of a family of blood relatives, is exploded by print, and is replaced by an association of men homogeneously trained to be individuals. Nationalism itself came as an intense new visual image of group destiny and status, and depended on a speed of information movement unknown before printing. Today nationalism as an image still depends on the press but has all the electric media against it. In business, as in politics, the effect of even jet-plane speeds is to render the older national groupings of social organization quite unworkable. In the Renaissance it was the speed of print and the ensuing market and commercial developments that made nationalism (which is continuity and competition in homogeneous space) as natural as it was new. By the same token, the heterogeneities and noncompetitive discontinuities of medieval guilds and family organization had become a great nuisance as speed-up of information by print called for more fragmentation and uniformity of function. The Benvenuto Cellinis, the goldsmith-cum-painter-cum-sculptor-cum-writer-cum-condottiere, became obsolete.

Once a new technology comes into a social milieu it cannot cease to permeate that milieu until every institution is saturated. Typography has permeated every phase of the arts and sciences in the past five hundred years. It would be easy to document the processes by which the principles of continuity, uniformity, and repeatability have become the basis of calculus and of marketing, as of industrial production, entertainment, and science. It will be enough to point out that repeatability conferred on the printed book the strangely novel character of a uniformly priced commodity opening the door to price systems. The printed book had in addition the quality of portability and accessibility that had been lacking in the manuscript.

Directly associated with these expansive qualities was the revolution in expression. Under manuscript conditions the role of being an author was a vague and uncertain one, like that of a minstrel. Hence, self-expression was of little interest. Typography, however, created a medium in which it was possible to speak out loud and bold to the world itself, just as it was possible to circumnavigate the world of books previously locked up in a pluralistic world of monastic cells. Boldness of type created boldness of expression.

Uniformity reached also into areas of speech and writing, leading to a single tone and attitude to reader and subject spread throughout an entire composition. The "man of letters" was born. Extended to the spoken word, this literate *equitone* enabled literate people to maintain a single "high tone" in discourse that was quite devastating, and enabled nineteenth-century prose writers to assume moral qualities that few would now care to simulate. Permeation of the colloquial language with literate uniform qualities has flattened out educated speech till it is a very reasonable acoustic facsimile of the uniform and continuous visual effects of typography. From this technological effect follows the further fact that the humor, slang, and dramatic vigor of American-English speech are monopolies of the semi-literate.

These typographical matters for many people are charged with controversial values. Yet in any approach to understanding print it is necessary to stand aside from the form in question if its typical pressure and life are to be observed. Those who panic now about the threat of the newer media and about the revolution we are forging, vaster in scope than that of Gutenberg, are obviously lacking in cool visual detachment and gratitude for that most potent gift bestowed on Western man by literacy and typography: his power to act without reaction or involvement. It is this kind of specialization by dissociation that has created Western power and efficiency. Without this dissociation of action from feeling and emotion people are hampered and hesitant. Print taught men to say, "Damn the torpedoes. Full steam ahead!"

Suggestions for Further Reading

Works by McLuhan that should interest rhetoricians are: *The Gutenberg Galaxy, The Medium is the Massage* (with Quentin Fiore), *Through the Vanishing Point: Space in Poetry and Painting* (with Harley Parker), *Understanding Media: The Extensions of Man* and *War and Peace in the Global Village* (with Quentin Fiore).

Mahony, Patrick. "McLuhan in the Light of Classical Rhetoric." *College Composition and Communication* 20 (February 1969), 12–17.
Murphy, James J. "The Metarhetorics of Plato, Augustine, and McLuhan: A Pointing Essay." *Philosophy and Rhetoric* 4 (Fall 1971), 201–14.
Stearn, Gerald Emanuel, ed. *McLuhan: Hot and Cool.* New York: New American Library, 1969.

Beyond Style

W. Ross Winterowd

This essay, I hope, speaks for itself. It is an exploration of the rhetorical consequences of form.

When I wrote the essay, I had no intention of applying the concepts in it to the teaching of writing, and yet I see now that the ideas behind it have shaped my own practice. For instance, if incoherence has value for T. S. Eliot, why should we insist that in every instance students must submit "well organized" essays? Furthermore, it becomes apparent to me that the best way to teach a sense of form is through a "formal" reading of a work, much like the reading of Rasselas *in this essay. What purely formal expectations does a work set up? And how does it pay off with completion?*

Finally, I have become interested in the notion of open forms, forms that might represent the mind in the process of its workings. Wallace Stevens wrote of "The poem of the mind in the act of finding / What will suffice." Why not "the theme of the mind in the act of finding what will suffice"?

It undoubtedly seems nugatory to remark that mind shapes discourse at the level of the sentence and beyond—and only slightly less so to say that, reciprocally, language shapes mind. That is, a given instrument, the brain, with its universals of "grammar" and its particularities of idiolect produces discourse, but only insofar as the system of language allows discourse to be produced, so that the process of discoursing involves the never-ending reciprocity of mind shaping message and language shaping both mind and message. Forms in discourse—forms *qua* forms, independent of meanings—must, then, have rhetorical consequences. It is not only words put together that persuade or move, but also the abstract structures themselves. For instance, in 1897, Adams Sherman Hill wrote in *The Foundation of Rhetoric:*

> To secure force in a sentence, it is necessary not only to choose the strongest words and to be as concise as is consistent with clearness, but also to arrange words, phrases, and clauses in the order which gives a commanding position to what is most important, and thus fixes the attention on the central idea.

This, of course, is precisely the reasoning that underlies the periodic sentence dogma. Namely, the "important" part of the sentence is the base, and its postposition ends the sentence with a bang, not a whimper.

Much can be said for and against such dogmas as that concerning the periodic sentence, but the point is that in even the most traditional discussions, it is generally conceded that form *qua* form has rhetorical value. Nonetheless, the tendency is for rhetorical treatises to neglect form; seldom are discussions of it more than rehashings of tired dicta: save the most important point for last, use periodic rather than loose sentences, do not introduce new topics in the conclusion.

And yet, anyone who has composed anything—from personal letters to arguments for a proposition to poems—must feel that the traditional notions concerning form (of sentences and units beyond, though this discussion will focus on units beyond) somehow belie the nature of the creative act, somehow make cut and dried a process that always, the nature of the human mind being what it is, will remain tantalizingly mysterious.

The one modern rhetorician who has made tremendous contributions to our understanding of form is, of course, Kenneth Burke. "Lexicon Rhetoricae" in *Counter-Statement* is surely one of the most significant essays on *"dispositio"* that has ever been published, and Burke's definition of form has been reverberating in my mind ever since I first encountered it: *"Form* in literature is an arousing and fulfillment of desires. A work has form in so far as one part of it leads a reader to anticipate another part, to be gratified by the sequence." [1] However, in his work on form in discourse, Burke is virtually unique among contemporary rhetoricians. No "department" of rhetoric has been more neglected than *dispositio.*

The discussion to follow will be a *speculative* inquiry into the rhetoric of forms (or dispositio). It is obviously a companion piece to other of my essays: "Style: A Matter of Manner"; [2] "The Grammar of Coherence"; [3] "Dispositio: The Theory of Form in Discourse." [4] The inquiry will use as points of departure a variety of works of literature.

The Value of Incoherence

It is paradoxical to start the body of an essay on the rhetoric of form by examining the power of formlessness, but such will be the *modus operandi* here.

The Waste Land is the first case in point, and that monumental poem, in the opinion of many responsible readers, is formless—a concept to which we will return.

Surely no poem of the twentieth century has been so widely influential as *The Waste Land;* its imagery has permeated the American and British consciousness; its message has become the message of our time—at least to many of those who do read poetry. In short, one can well say that *The Waste Land* is *the* poem of the twentieth century. Its impact is enormous.

Undoubtedly the importance of the poem is in large part thematic. As M. L. Rosenthal says,

> . . . one of the crucial symbols of modern poetry, in English at least, becomes Dante's pictured prisoners in the antechamber of Hell, 'wretches never born and never dead,' worthy of neither blame nor praise. These are the citizens of T. S. Eliot's Waste Land, who, lacking all moral perspective, mechanical in their motions, are trapped by their bodily selves and are incapable of meaningful commitment either to good or to evil. The modern city is their habitat. . . .[5]

In a sense, *The Waste Land* gives a symbolic summary of the preoccupations of modern man: faithlessness, a jejune society, sterile love, the loss of tradition, mere boredom, and a hundred other contemporary maladies sensed by the poet and his readers (for literary popularity comes about only when work and audience have a meeting of the minds or of the hearts, and as poetry goes, *The Waste Land* is unbelievably popular).

---

[1] "Lexicon Rhetoricae," *Counter-Statement* (Los Altos, Cal.: Hermes Publications, 1953), p. 124.
[2] *Quarterly Journal of Speech,* LVI (April 1970), 161–67.
[3] *College English,* XXXI (May 1970), 828–35.
[4] *College Composition and Communication,* XXII (February 1971), 39–45.
[5] *The Modern Poets* (New York: Oxford Univ. Press, 1960), p. 5.

However, themes are not our present concern, but rather how those themes emerge as a "coherent" totality in a poem entitled *The Waste Land*—one poem with five separate sections, a poem with "chapters," or perhaps a cycle of poems on one subject. In some way, *The Waste Land,* not simply because its pages are sequential in a black volume and not simply because five separate poems appear under one super-title, must represent for readers a coherent whole. Cleanth Brooks sees an over-all pattern in the poem, a pattern that in outline looks like this:

I   "The Burial of the Dead": *statement of theme.* "The first section of 'The Burial of the Dead' develops the theme of the attractiveness of death, or of the difficulty in rousing oneself from the death in life in which people of the waste land live." [6]

II   "A Game of Chess": *illustration supporting the theme.* "The easiest contrast in this section—and one which may easily blind the casual reader to a continued emphasis on the contrast between the two kinds of life, or the two kinds of death already commented on— is the contrast between life in a rich and magnificent setting, and life in the low and vulgar setting of a London pub. But both scenes, however antithetical they may appear superficially, are scenes taken from the contemporary waste land." [7]

III   "The Fire Sermon": *thematic restatement.* " 'The Fire Sermon' makes use of several of the symbols already developed." [8]

IV   "Death by Water": *contrast.* "The section forms a contrast with 'The Fire Sermon' which precedes it. . . ." [9]

V   "What the Thunder Said": *restatement of theme.* "The reference to the 'torchlight red on sweaty faces' and to the 'frosty silence in the gardens' obviously associates Christ in Gethsemane with the other hanged gods. The god has now died, and in referring to this, the basic theme finds another strong restatement. . . ." [10]

At one end of the spectrum Brooks sees in *The Waste Land* a coherent, unified poem, though not, perhaps, coherent or unified in the usual sense.

At the other extreme is Graham Hough, who says that *The Waste Land* and *Four Quartets* "will survive, not assisted by their structure, but in spite of it." [11] Hough tells us that "for a poem to exist as a unity more than merely bibliographical, we need the sense of one voice speaking, as in lyric or elegiac verse; or of several voices intelligibly related to each other, as in narrative

---

[6] *Modern Poetry and the Tradition* (Chapel Hill: Univ. of North Carolina Press, 1939), p. 138.

[7] *Ibid.,* p. 146.

[8] *Ibid.,* p. 151.

[9] *Ibid.,* pp. 157–58.

[10] *Ibid.,* p. 159.

[11] *Reflections on a Literary Revolution* (Washington, D.C.: The Catholic University of America Press, 1960), p. 38.

with dialogue or drama. . . ." [12] In short, Hough debunks what he considers to be the myth of unity in *The Waste Land*. The effect of the poem is "as though a painter were to employ pointilliste technique in one part of a picture and the glazes of the high renaissance in another." [13]

The interesting point here is not that Brooks views *The Waste Land* as a unified whole or that Hough views it as a series of disunified fragments. What interests us is that both of them might well be perfectly right! The poem might well be *both* a series of disunified fragments *and* a unified whole. If one looks at a schematization of Brooks' analysis of *The Waste Land,* here is what emerges: theme, illustration, restatement, contrast, restatement. While I am consciously oversimplifying Brooks' argument, in general the above five terms in sequence represent his view of the coherence of *The Waste Land*. It is interesting to note that these five terms might well describe the coherence of a paragraph, or even serve as the matrix in developing paragraphs of a certain kind. A model might look like this:

theme	Incoherence has a decided rhetorical value, for the incoherent utterance obliges the reader or listener to supply his own coherence.
illustration	It is clear, for instance, that each reader of *The Waste Land* must put the individual parts of the poem together in a way that is meaningful to him.
restatement	That is to say, where there is no "formal" coherence in discourse, the reader is quite likely to supply his own, and in the process to be engaged by the discourse that he is "putting together" or "interpreting." Thus it is that incoherence has rhetorical value, for it engages the reader or listener.
contrast	Totally coherent discourse, on the other hand, does not demand this particular kind of engagement and, therefore, paradoxically, lacks one of the many possible kinds of rhetorical force.
restatement	To state my main point in another, simpler way: there is a definite rhetorical value in the very nebulousness and fragmentation of some discourse (and much poetry), for lack of clear-cut connections (form) allows the reader or listener to participate as a "maker," conjecturally or intuitively supplying connections where none exist.

Whether or not the paragraph is a "good" one is beside the point. The fact is that the model which Brooks proposes for the coherence of *The Waste Land* is productive in generating more or less coherent stretches of discourse —and that *The Waste Land* is, for many readers, "incoherent." [14] What I am

---

[12] *Ibid.,* p. 34.
[13] *Ibid.,* p. 32.
[14] Whether or not *The Waste Land* is, in fact, coherent is beside the point. The important fact is this: many readers, I among them, see *The Waste Land* as incoherent,

suggesting is that in discourse, there are "twilight areas," where coherence is just tantalizingly out of reach and where the reader himself must "put the work together." Of such nature is *The Waste Land.*

It seems to me that fragmentation, disunification, in a word, incoherence, is one of the major rhetorical devices of modern poetry. It is, in fact, among the really significant features that allow us to speak of modern poetry as a genre. Time and again, poet captures reader by making reader "assemble the pieces" in a way that would have seemed downright perverse had that modern reader not been prepared by such works as *The Waste Land* and Pound's *Cantos.* (It must be remembered that Pound considered the *Cantos* a *whole* epic poem on the order of *The Divine Comedy* or *The Iliad.*) This ambiguity in structure is the eighth ambiguity, the one that often brings reader and poet together as co-conspirators in the making of the poem. (Note that reader and author cannot be co-conspirators in the making of a plot which has all segments of the outline filled in, but that, for instance, a lady-or-tiger ending immediately precipitates conspiracy.)

A great many modern poems are clusters of images, symbols, and metaphors (like *The Waste Land*) awaiting the receptive mind that will assemble them in a meaningful way. Modern poetry, then, often relies upon a participatory rhetoric for its effects. Examples of such poems are legion and, in a sense, characterize modern poetry: Leroi Jones' "A Poem for Willie Best"; Lowell's "Between the Porch and the Altar" and his *Notebook, 1967–68;* Stevens' "Thirteen Ways of Looking at a Blackbird"; "Hugh Selwyn Mauberley"; Ginsberg's "Journal Night Thoughts"; Crane's *The Bridge*—and the list could go on and on. The current undergraduate favorite, *Trout Fishing in America,* is a "novel" that employs the poetic technique of incoherence for its effect.

Formal Tension

Everyone knows that a kind of tension arises from the very nature of narrative. If one is interested, one asks, "And what happened next?" Insofar as the question arises and is momentarily unanswered, there is a tension in the story. In Kenneth Burke's terms, there is tension as long as the reader's appetite to know is unsatisfied. But there is another kind of tension, that which arises from the *form* of the work.

To explain what I intend here, I would like to discuss a novel that, it seems to me, deserves better than it has gotten from many critics. I mean Johnson's *Rasselas.* It is an exciting novel, the opinions of many to the contrary, but it is exciting in a particular way that is not characteristic of most fiction. Tension increases and slackens, but it is always present, even to the

that is, as a series of disunified fragments so far as the major sections are concerned. Equally important, the judgment that a poem or novel or whatever is incoherent is in itself an arhetorical, nonesthetic judgment. Coherence or incoherence can be effective for given audiences. I am only arguing that incoherence has the potentiality of being used for rhetorical effect.

last sentence and beyond, for the conclusion is, as Johnson might have said, an unended ending, an unresolved resolution. And the tension which impels the reader through the novel stems from the parallelism with which it is constructed. As parallelism wanes, so does tension; the parts which are the most perfectly parallel are the most vitally interesting.

The parallelism, of course, begins at the sentence level and pervades the whole structure of the book. Now one cannot dispute that balance in sentence structure is an inherently interesting thing; the reader is held in a state of suspense until the sentence achieves perfect balance, and then he is ready to go to the next and repeat the process. This sort of interest is, I grant, analogous to that which we give a tightrope walker; will he maintain balance from start to finish? If he does, we are relieved and normally would not want him to start the walk again. (Tension has been resolved.) And I think that we tend to admire the virtuosity of the writer's perfect equilibrium as much as we do that of the tightrope walker.

In his classic study of Johnson's prose style, Wimsatt defines the possibilities of parallelism. There can be parallelism or balance between like elements and between antithetical elements. Between like elements, there is normally a sequential relationship. "Suppose three clauses, the first of which tells the cause of an act, the second the act, and the third its consequences. These three meanings are parallel if the sequence is taken as a whole and if as a whole it is referred to a fourth meaning." [15] But this description of the parallelism at the sentence level is also a description of the parallelism of the novel as a whole. Take chapters nineteen through twenty-one as examples:

cause of act	[Rasselas] having heard of a hermit, that lived near the lowest cataract of the Nile, and filled the whole country with the fame of his sanctity, resolved to visit his retreat, and inquire whether that felicity which public life could not afford was to be found in solitude.[16]
act	[After the trip to the hermit's retreat, Imlac says] We have heard at Cairo of your wisdom, and came hither to implore your direction for this young man and maiden in the *choice of life.*[17]
consequence	[Rasselas concludes, after having visited the hermit, that] The life of a solitary man will be certainly miserable, but not certainly devout.[18]
fourth meaning	The problem of the novel.

Two observations should now be made. The excitement in *Rasselas* (as a novel) comes from basically the same principle that arouses excitement at the stylistic level, that is, the tension of the novel relies upon the perfect

---

[15] *The Prose Style of Samuel Johnson* (New Haven: Yale Univ. Press, 1941), p. 16.
[16] *Rasselas,* in *Shorter Novels of the Eighteenth Century,* ed. Philip Henderson (London: J. M. Dent & Sons, 1956), p. 38.
[17] *Ibid.,* p. 41.
[18] *Ibid.,* p. 42.

balance and antithesis with which Johnson constructs the larger part of his tale. Furthermore, as I have repeatedly contended, the individual sentences that an author characteristically uses are a good place to begin to search for devices that will constitute, in the round, that writer's technique. That is, if balance and parallelism are characteristic of the individual sentences, one would expect larger structures to have the same characteristics.

In the case of *Rasselas,* Wimsatt's outline of the four parts of the parallel structure of sentences provides a key to understanding the structure of the novel and an explanation of the strange sort of tension that one feels as he reads the novel. The reader sees the sequential relationship and is led, as in any good story, to ask, "Then what?" The relation of *cause of act* to *act* to *consequences* to *fourth meaning* provides the structural basis for a narrative which is apparently episodic. Herbert Read, as well as W. K. Wimsatt, recognizes the use of antithetical parallelism in Johnson's prose.[19] These antithetical parallels are another aspect of Johnson's virtuosity. They are a rhetorical adornment, but they also lie very near to the reason for tension in. *Rasselas.* The astronomer, speaking of his obsession, says, "Integrity without knowledge is weak and useless, and knowledge without integrity is dangerous and dreadful." [20] Here is a perfect antithetical balance, and it is a summation of the dilemma of the astronomer. He needed someone both knowledgeable and moral to receive the mystery of his delusion of power over the elements. He found such a person in Imlac. That the dilemma existed, however, is interesting; it had two parts that exactly balanced one another. But one should note that there are two elements here which are beyond mere virtuosity: the pause that one must make to ascertain the conditions of the formula (for such it is) and the recognition of the solution and the application of that solution. This balanced sentence is, then, a problem and a statement of a dilemma in a person. As soon as the reader grasps the dilemma, he is interested in the solution.

The plan of the novel is the turning again and again from hope to disillusionment. That which presages success in the search for happiness turns out immediately to demonstrate the folly of searching for contentment in any given pursuit. Such a scheme not only fosters parallelism, but demands it: on the one hand, hope of success; on the other, recognition of failure.

Earlier, I said that *Rasselas* is an exciting novel. Now I must qualify that statement. It is exciting if one is interested in the resolution of the problem. The particular answer that Johnson gives us demands that each hope be shattered, that each tentative answer be proved false. If the plot is to have tension, incident must be balanced against incident. However, one can see immediately that this particular necessity for balance must pair the incidents and isolate the pairs. Consequently, the story is episodic. For instance, Rasselas finds that every man in Cairo is apparently happy, but actually unhappy. The scales balance. The incident has its antithetical parallelism; it is self-

---

[19] *English Prose Style* (Boston: Beacon Press, 1955), p. 41.
[20] *Rasselas,* p. 78.

contained. Furthermore, the mechanics of transition from this episode to the next are rudimentary. "Rasselas rose next day, and resolved to begin his experiments upon life." [21] The mortar which joins these dual building blocks is not mechanics of plot; it is interest in the unsolved problem with which the novel begins: the futile search for perfect happiness.

The Decisive Moment

> While the money was in his hand the lock clicked. It had sprung! Did he do it? He grabbed at the knob and pulled vigorously. It had closed. Heavens! he was in for it now, sure enough.

The decisive moment in *Sister Carrie* occurs when Hurstwood, almost by inadvertence, by a stroke of malignant fate, becomes a thief. From this point on, the plot of the novel is, in general terms, predictable; the movement of the plot can be in only one direction.

This predictability can be rhetorically advantageous in much the same way that the unpredictability of "incoherent" works is. The rhetorical motive is to engage the reader, to woo or seduce or convince him to immerse himself totally in the work so that the universe of the work becomes his universe and so that he is willing to suspend disbelief or, if not disbelief, at least critical distrust. Because it gives plot a certain predictability, the decisive moment makes the reader and the author co-conspirators in constructing a work of art. (Often a "dishonest" ending is simply the result of the author's betraying the conspiracy between himself and his reader.)

There could not be a clearer example of the decisive moment than that found in *Troilus and Criseyde,* and I would like to examine that work to demonstrate in detail what happens to the reader once he is confronted with the decisive moment.

Statements such as the following are typical of commentaries on Criseyde: she is "less sentimental and more practical than either Pandarus or Troilus. . . ." [22] "The picture of the growth of her love is perfect, with a wonderful balance of feeling and good sense; a cool head and a warm heart are not inconsistent, and make a poised character." [23] I see no reason for not agreeing with the consensus that Troilus is essentially an attenuation of the courtly lover—to be sure, a courtly lover refined and made eminently human through Chaucer's artistry, but basically conventional nonetheless. Criseyde, I think, is just as conventional, but representative of another medieval tradition—Aristotelian logic.

Aristotle defines a dialectical problem as "an investigation leading either to choice and avoidance or to truth and knowledge, either by itself or as an aid to the solution of some other such problem." [24] Criseyde's whole problem

---

[21] *Ibid.,* p. 35.

[22] F. N. Robinson, *The Poetical Works of Chaucer* (Boston: Houghton Mifflin, 1933), p. 451.

[23] J. S. P. Tatlock, "The People in Chaucer's *Troilus,*" *PMLA,* LVI (1941), 98.

[24] *Topica,* trans. E. S. Forster (Cambridge, Mass.: Harvard Univ. Press, 1960), p. 299.

is one of "choice and avoidance" and that Chaucer would provide her with
Aristotelian means for ratiocination is, of course, entirely probable. Though
in his works Chaucer mentions Aristotle only nine times (as compared with
thirty times for Seneca),[25] medieval education took Aristotle as an entire
department of the trivium. In the medieval mind, Aristotle was semi-divine,
the very font and source of wisdom.

We see Criseyde the scholastic at many points in the tale, but never so
clearly as in Book III, at the decisive moment, when she rationalizes her
shock at Pandarus's lie concerning Troilus's jealousy over Horaste. The passage runs thus:

> "O brotel wele of mannes joie unstable!
> With what wight so thow be, or how thow pleye,
> Either he woot that thow, joie, art muable,
> Or woot it nought; it mot ben oon of tweye.
> Now if he woot it nought, how may he seye
> That he hath verray joie and selynesse,
> That is of ignoraunce ay in derknesse?

> "Now if he woot that joie is transitorie,
> As every joie of worldly thyng mot flee,
> Than every tyme he that hath in memorie,
> The drede of lesyng maketh hym that he
> May in no perfit selynesse be;
> And if to lese his joie he sette a myte,
> Than semeth it that joie is worth ful lite.

> "Wherfore I wol diffyne in this matere,
> That trewely, for aught I kan espie,
> Ther is no verray weele in this world heere." [26]

---

[25] George A. Plimpton, *The Education of Chaucer* (London: Oxford Univ. Press,
1935), pp. 167–68.

[26] The translation of George Philip Krapp (New York: Vintage Books, n.d.),
pp. 140–41, runs thus:

> O fickle fate! O worldly joy unstable!
> Of men thou makest but a sport and play!
> All know that they to hold their joy are able,
> Or know it not—there is no other way.
> Now if one knows it not, how may he say
> That he of perfect joy perceives the spark,
> If ignorance still leaves him in the dark–

> But if he knows that joy is transitory,
> Since joy in every worldly thing must flee,
> This troubling thought diminishes the glory
> Of earthly joy, and so in such degree,
> Imperfect must be his felicity;
> If loss of joy he fears a jot or tittle,
> This proves that earthly joy is worth but little.

> And so this problem I must thus decide,
> That verily, for aught that I can see,
> No perfect joy can in this world abide.

When Criseyde "diffynes" her argument, she propounds a phrase that indicates the essence of life, for a definition "is a phrase indicating the essence of something." [27] In the argument leading to the definition, Criseyde proceeds via Aristotle's either-or method, the theory of contrarieties: either man knows that joy is mutable, or he knows it not.[28] And her conclusion that "ther is no verray weele in this world heere" is not only logical; it is inevitable. The inevitable conclusion to the argument, it turns out, is a decisive moment that makes the rest of the plot largely predictable.

For instance, in Book V, desolate in the Trojan camp, Criseyde must resolve her situation, but since she has defined the essence of life as the impossibility of perfect felicity, the conclusion of her rationalization is predictable:

> The brighte Venus folwede and ay taughte
> The wey ther brode Phebus down alighte;
> And Cynthea hire char-hors overraughte
> To whirle out of the Leoun, if she myghte;
> And Signifer his candels sheweth brighte,
> Whan that Criseyde unto hire bedde wente
> Inwith hire fadres faire brighte tente.
>
> Retornyng in hire soule ay up and down
> The wordes of this sodeyn Diomede,
> His grete estat, and perel of the town,
> And that she was allone and hadde nede
> Of frendes help; and thus bygan to brede
> The cause whi, the sothe for to telle,
> That she took fully purpos for to dwelle.[29]

---

[27] *Topica*, p. 281.

[28] John Peter Anton, *Aristotle's Theory of Contrariety* (London: Routledge and Paul, 1957), pp. 95–96, explains, "The fundamental idea which seems to underlie Aristotle's conception of affirmation-negation opposition, especially its relation to contrariety, is that all statements are either *affirmations,* where a predicate is affirmed of a subject, or *negations,* where a predicate is denied of a subject. No third type is possible because of all four types of opposition the one of 'affirmation and negation' excludes intermediates."

[29] Krapp, p. 279:

> Bright Venus soon appeared to point the way
> Where Phoebus, wide and round, should down alight,
> And now her chariot horses Cynthia
> Whirls out of the Lion, driven by her might,
> And Signifer displays his candles bright;
> Then Cressida unto her night-rest went
> Within her father's fair and shining tent,
>
> Debating in her soul aye up and down
> The words of this impetuous Diomede,
> His high estate, the peril of the town,
> Her loneliness and all her pressing need
> Of friendly help, and thus began to breed
> The reasons why, the simple truth to tell,
> She thought it best among the Greeks to dwell.

This typically Senecan conclusion, arrived at by Aristotelian dialectic, leads Criseyde to the truism that one must accept the worst with the best and attempt to fashion some kind of happiness even in the most adverse circumstances. She is stoical rather than unfaithful, and we should expect Chaucer's audience to recognize immediately and to understand the wellsprings of her motivation.

All coherent works of art rely to some extent upon what I have called "participatory rhetoric"; the reader generally is more satisfied if he is able to say, "Ah! I told you so" than if he must say, "How strange!" Insofar as we are interested in motive rather than particular outcome, we are caught up in participatory rhetoric and proceed with the author in a deductive sequence from the critical moment.

Formal Control

The poet often feels himself caught up in the dilemma of creative cross-purposes, his sense of what he *wills* to say continually thrown off course by the demands of the form that he has chosen or that he has inadvertently let begin to develop in his poem. In his early compulsion to use rhyme in his poetry, James Dickey "felt continually carried past my subject, carried around it, sometimes close to it but never in it in the way I wished to be in it." [30] But in the same essay, Dickey tells of his development:

> I began to conceive of something I called—doubtless misleadingly—the 'open' poem: a poem which would have none of the neatness of most of those poems we call 'works of art' but would have the capacity to involve the reader in it, in all its imperfections and impurities, rather than offering him a (supposedly) perfected and perfect work for contemplation, judgment, and evaluation. . . . I experimented with short lines some more and, eventually, with putting several of these together on the same physical plane to make up what I called the 'split line,' in which spaces between word groups would take the place of punctuation. . . .
>
> Of late my interest has been mainly in the conclusionless poem, the open or ungeneralizing poem, the un-well-made poem. I hope in the future to get the reader more and more into the actions and happenings of the lines and require him less and less to stand off and draw either aesthetic or moral judgments. [31]

This is the same James Dickey who said of Allen Ginsberg that he "is the perfect inhabitant, if not the very founder of Babel, where conditions do not so much make tongues incomprehensible, but render their utterances, as poetry, meaningless." [32] And, at the risk of becoming too quotational, it was Ginsberg who said this (in a letter to John Hollander):

[30] "The Poet Turns on Himself," *Babel to Byzantium* (New York: Farrar, Strauss and Giroux, 1968), p. 283.

[31] *Ibid.,* pp. 290–91.

[32] *Babel to Byzantium,* p. 53.

Back to Howl: construction. After sick and tired of shortline free verse as not expressionistic enough, not swinging enough, can't develop a powerful enough rhythm. I simply turned aside, accidentally, to writing part I of Howl, in solitude, diddling around with the form, thinking it couldn't be published anyway (queer content my parents shouldn't see, etc.) also it was out of my shortline line. But what I did taught my theory, I changed my mind about "measure" while writing it. Part one uses repeated base who, as a sort of kithera BLANG, homeric (in my imagination) to mark off each statement, with rhythmic unit. So that's experiment with longer & shorter variations on a fixed base—the principle being, that each line has to be contained within the elastic of one breath—with suitable punctuatory expressions where the rhythm has built up enough so that I have to let off steam by building a longer climactic line in which there is a jazzy ride. *All the ear I've ever developed goes into the balancing of those lines.*[33]

This letter dates back to 1958, and whether or not Ginsberg would still defend his notion of the "elastic breath" line we have no way of knowing. (The concept pretty obviously shows considerable naïveté about both physiology and grammar.) The important point, though, is that a poet who writes "verse" that is formally indistinguishable from prose (except, of course, in typography) should so vehemently protest that he does, indeed, have formal control.

Each poet, in his own way, must reason or pray himself through to a concept of form that works for him in his poetry, and it is the rare poet who does not have a theory of form, who does not wrestle with the problem of what he wants to say versus the form in which he chooses to say it.

Mere typography has an obvious but magical effect. For instance, the following passage:

If God has been good enough to give you a poet then listen. But for God's sake let him alone until he is dead; no prizes, no ceremony, they kill the man. A poet is one who listens to nature and his own heart; and if the noise of the world grows up around him, and if he is tough enough, he can shake off his enemies but not his friends. That is what withered Wordsworth and muffled Tennyson, and would have killed Keats; that is what makes Hemingway play the fool and Faulkner forget his art.

It is, as a matter of fact, a poem by Robinson Jeffers—but a poem only by virtue of its typographic form.

If God has been good enough to give you a poet
Then listen to him. But for God's sake let him alone
    until he is dead; no prizes, no ceremony,
They kill the man. A poet is one who listens
To nature and his own heart; and if the noise of the
    world grows up around him, and if he is tough
    enough,
He can shake off his enemies but not his friends.

[33] Jane Kramer, *Allen Ginsberg in America* (New York: Vintage Books, 1970), p. 33. Italics mine.

> That is what withered Wordsworth and muffled
>   Tennyson, and would have killed Keats; that is what
>   makes
> Hemingway play the fool and Faulkner forget his art.[34]

Visual form, typographic form, then, has the strange and yet mundane effect of "raising" prose above itself, that is, form changes a reader's expectations and emotional sets and, in this respect, heightens the experience of reading. So much is almost truistic.

But what I would like to *speculate* about is the possibility that form also serves as a means whereby the poet makes that which is unendurable—for both himself and his reader—into a controlled, and hence endurable, experience.

A startling, agonized document in support of this possibility is "The Longing," the first poem in Theodore Roethke's *The Far Field*.[35] The first part of the poem is a lament concerning the poet in that Purgatory, the modern city of night, where

> The slag-heaps fume at the edge of the raw cities:
> The gulls wheel over their singular garbage;
> The great trees no longer shimmer;
> Not even the soot dances.
> And the spirit fails to move forward,
> But shrinks into a half-life, less than itself,
> Falls back, a slug, a loose worm
> Ready for any crevice,
> An eyeless starer.

The second section tells us, however, that "A wretch needs his wretchedness. Yes." As if there were no way out of the maddening personal dilemma—no way, that is, except the old escape that Roethke, who literally grew up in a greenhouse, nostalgically turns to time and time again:

> The rose exceeds, the rose exceeds us all.
> Who'd think the moon could pare itself so thin?
> A great flame rises from the sunless sea;
> The light cries out, and I am there to hear—
> I'd be beyond; I'd be beyond the moon,
> Bare as a bud, and naked as a worm.
>
> To this extent I'm a stalk.
>   —How free; how all alone.
> Out of these nothings
>   —All beginnings come.

The final section of the poem is contradictory, or at least ambivalent, for the poet longs for both the inhuman ("I would with the fish, the blackening salmon, and the mad lemmings") and the human ("The children dancing").

[34] "Let Them Alone," in *Selected Poems* (New York: Random House, Inc.).
[35] (New York: Doubleday and Co.)

The burden, however, is the yearning toward a pure simplicity, a world stripped of material complications, bone-bare, essential:

> In the summer heat, I can smell the dead buffalo,
> The stench of their damp fur drying in the sun,
> The buffalo chips drying.
>> Old men should be explorers?
>> I'll be an Indian.
>> Iroquois.

Thus the poem ends. The coda is perfect, for the Indian, romantically and actually, is the child of nature whose life is stripped bare of the hideous superfluities of civilization. However, the progress from the midsection of this poem to the resolution of the coda has been accomplished by a passage that bears some scrutiny—and that gets us to the point about formal control. It runs thus:

> I long for the imperishable quiet at the heart of form;
> I would be a stream, winding between great striated rocks
>> in late summer;
> A leaf, I would love the leaves, delighting in the redolent
>> disorder of this mortal life,
> This ambush, this silence,
> Where shadow can change into flame,
> And the dark be forgotten.

In this un-hip poet there are Zenist overtones, but I think that Roethke can be taken quite literally when he expresses his longing for "the imperishable quiet at the heart of form." If the poet can "form" experience to his own satisfaction, then he is able to be at rest in viewing "the redolent disorder of this mortal life." And, of course, it is the poet's task to achieve form so that both he and the reader can experience the quiet that poetry offers, a quiet that is, paradoxically, vibrant with life and sensation.

For another case in point, and there are countless, one might turn to Dylan Thomas, surely as compulsive a formalist as ever undertook the poetic task. In the "Author's Prologue" to his *Collected Poems,* he tells us,

> I hack
> This rumpus of shapes
> For you to know
> How I, a spinning man,
> Glory also this star, bird
> Roared, sea born, man torn, blood blest.[36]

And it is no accident that his imagery again and again echoes Genesis 2–6:

> And the earth was without form, and void; and darkness was upon the face
> of the deep. . . . And God said, Let there be light, and there was light.

[36] Dylan Thomas, *Collected Poems* (New York: New Directions Publishing Corp., 1952).

And God saw the light, that it was good: and God divided the light from the darkness. . . . And God said, Let there be a firmament in the midst of the waters.

John Ackerman has discussed Thomas' craftsmanship and has analyzed the intricate formal patterns of, for instance, "Fern Hill." [37] The syllable count of the poem is as follows:

Stanza	I	II	III	IV	V	VI
Line 1	14	14	14	14	14	14
2	14	14	14	14	14	14
3	9	9	9	9	9	9
4	6	6	6	6	6	6
5	9	9	9	9	9	9
6	15	14	14	14	14	14
7	14	14	14	14	14	15
8	7	7	8	8	8	7
9	9	9	6	6	6	9

Only a few comments on the intricacy of this pattern are necessary. Line 6 of Stanza I has fifteen syllables; therefore, almost inevitably one feels, Line 7 of Stanza VI has fifteen syllables. The sum total of syllables for all of the *eighth* lines in the six stanzas is forty-five, and that is also the total for all the syllables in the ninth lines.

This shaping of experience into controlled forms seems to have been an almost manic preoccupation with Thomas. J. M. Brinnin describes the poet's working methods. Regardless of how insignificant an addition or change might be, Thomas would recopy the whole poem, keeping the total form intact. "Fern Hill" went through more than two hundred revisions before Thomas was satisfied (if, indeed, he ever was satisfied).[38]

It seems to me that this ability—or need—to shape and control is one of Thomas' great successes, particularly when one compares Thomas with Ginsberg, whose failure is inability to give the raw data of experience the esthetic palliation that is the function of form in poetry.

In many ways the most original and intense of contemporary poets, Ginsberg, has made a methodological decision that will eternally preclude him from coming to terms with the experiences of his own scarifying existence and that, more disastrously, will tend to keep poetic interest at arm's length. It is precisely the lack of "imperishable quiet at the heart of form" that repels the reader from much of Ginsberg's poetry. The formal requirements of art enable the poet to divert his unnerving stare from the horrors of temporality to the eternity of pure configuration and hence provide the escape that art should be, for it is certainly true that art is, in part, an escape mechanism.

[37] *Dylan Thomas: His Life and Work* (London: Oxford Univ. Press, 1964), pp. 124–26.
[38] *Ibid.*, p. 124.

The theme of one of Ginsberg's most important poems, "THE CHANGE: Kyoto-Tokyo Express," [39] is that through learning to love oneself, one learns also to love the universe. What, after all, is more horrible than man's humanity?

> Shit! Intestines boiling in sand fire
>   creep yellow brain cold sweat
>   earth unbalanced vomit thru
>   tears, snot ganglia buzzing
>   the Electric Snake rising hypnotic
>   shuffling metal-eyed coils
>   whirling rings within wheel
>   from asshole up the spine
>   Acid in the throat the chest
>   a knot trembling Swallow back
>   the great furry ball of the great
> Fear

And, the poet asks, "How can I / be sent to Hell / with my skin and blood?" But the change comes when Ginsberg can ask yet another question:

> Who would deny his own shape's
>   loveliness in his
>   dream moment of bed
> Who sees his desire to be
>   horrible instead of Him

And the resolution is the poet's acceptance of his own corporeality.

Both Roethke and Ginsberg longed, but Roethke became a shaper of experience, Ginsberg a self-idolater. The craftsman is fashioning something outside himself, is arranging parts of the universe into meaningful and bearable wholes. The experience of poetic craftsmanship allows both a looking away from the impulse and a handling of that impulse. In his preoccupation with his own unique self, Ginsberg loses much of the control that makes for art. The reader, too, it seems to me, demands that healing salvation of a double vision, both the spontaneous cry of a hyperesthetic sensibility and the tough, rational shaping of experience.

I echo Yvor Winters when I say that no critic should deal with a poet for whom that critic does not have considerable affection, and I must confess that Ginsberg always intrigues me and often moves me (I think, in spite of his method, not because of it). In any case, in a loving spirit, I would like to look at the failure, not the success, of a poem that might well have been one of the most satisfying that I have encountered. I am thinking of "This Form of Life Needs Sex" from *Planet News*. It is one of those intensely honest poems that makes us feel certain that Ginsberg puts no barrier of reticence between himself and the reader:

[39] In *Planet News* (San Francisco: City Lights Books). Copyright 1968 by Allen Ginsberg.

> I will have to accept women
>   if I want to continue the race,
>   kiss breasts, accept
>   strange hairy lips behind
>   buttocks,
> Look in questioning womanly eyes
>   answer soft cheeks,
>   bury my loins in the hang of pearplum
>   fat tissue
>   I had abhorred. . . .

Now, such total honesty is a considerable virtue in itself, and the poem becomes even more brutal in its frankness:

> You can joy man to man but the Sperm
>   comes back in a trickle at dawn
> in a toilet on the 45th Floor—

What is missing here is the sense that the poet is dealing with experience. To repeat, there is this difference between art and experience: art has forms and configurations that the artist imposes. And that is why we turn to art. In a world that is essentially chaotic, we gain the illusion of order.

I realize that I stand the risk of backing myself into a logical corner, for there is no way to "prove" what I contend, though perhaps a fairly convincing demonstration can be made through comparison. It is not merely, I think, Ginsberg's subject matter, his total honesty, or his vocabulary that could well put sympathetic readers off. It is his essential formlessness.

Compare three stanzas from Anne Sexton's "The Ballad of the Lonely Masturbator" with the Ginsberg poem:

> The end of the affair is always death.
> She's my workshop. Slippery eye,
> out of the tribe of myself my breath
> finds you gone. I horrify
> those who stand by. I am fed.
> At night, alone, I marry the bed.
>
> Finger to finger, now she's mine.
> She's not too far. She's my encounter.
> I beat her like a bell. I recline
> in the bower where you used to mount her.
> You borrowed me on the flowered spread.
> At night, alone, I marry the bed.
>   .   .   .   .
> The boys and girls are one tonight.
> They unbutton blouses. They unzip flies.
> They take off shoes. They turn off the light.
> The glimmering creatures are full of lies.
> They are eating each other. They are overfed.
> At night, alone, I marry the bed.[40]

[40] In *Love Poems* (Boston: Houghton Mifflin Publishing Co.).

Granted: the subject matter of "The Ballad of the Lonely Masturbator" is probably a bit less shocking to the average sensibility than that of "This Form of Life Needs Sex," but, it seems to me, the reader inevitably will become involved with the Sexton poem because of its formal properties; the only involvement one might possibly have with the Ginsberg poem comes from the subject matter—and that is a good deal more likely to repel than to attract.

In the views of major critics, from Aristotle through Sidney to Kenneth Burke and I. A. Richards, the main function of art has been to heal (both the artist and the reader). I have suggested that the "what" of the salutary "message" is no more important than the "how." Perhaps the "what" gains significance only through the "how."

Conclusion

Studies of poetic form or structure as *abstract entities* are exceedingly rare and are somewhat primitive, especially in comparison with the number and sophistication of other critical approaches. Both Kenneth Burke and Yvor Winters have made significant contributions, but one is hard put to think of other modern critics who have thought much about form *qua* form.

Although my knowledge of folklore is minimal, it appears that significant theories of form have been developing in that discipline, and an excellent article by William O. Hendricks outlines current work.[41]

The present discussion in no sense purports to be a systematic handling of the problem of form in poetry. The intent of the essay, rather, has been to demonstrate how form, conceived as an abstract configuration of relationships, affects both the esthetics and the rhetoric of literature. Much of what was said is by its very nature speculative, particularly the matter of form making experience esthetically accessible to the reader.

Nonetheless, the theoretical underpinning of the discussion is valid, almost too obviously so: form has rhetorical consequences. The purpose of the essay has been to investigate some of the results that ensue from acceptance of the premise. And it bears repeating that far too little inquiry has been made into this crucial area where rhetoric and poetics overlap and become one.

Any such area is, of course, no man's land, the limbo of the faithless, for no self-respecting esthetician will vulgarize his subject by glancing, even momentarily, at rhetoric, and the rhetorician, though generally much more comprehensive in his viewpoint than the esthetician, is so busied with the "practical" discourses of history (both past and present) that he seldom has time to concern himself with poetry. It is perhaps in this neutral territory that the snobbish isolation of the esthetician and the busy practicality of the rhetorician will achieve "the imperishable quiet at the heart of form."

[41] "Folklore and the Structural Analysis of Literary Texts," *Language and Style,* III (Spring 1970), 83–121.

The Grammar of Coherence

W. Ross Winterowd

It has been disappointing to me that "The Grammar of Coherence" has been so little noticed by theoreticians and teachers, for I think it contains some valuable insights and that it hints at some useful classroom practices.

The piece argues, simply, that coherence has three levels: that of case relationships, that of syntax, and that of what I call transitions. Transitions, then, represent coherent relationships beyond the sentence, and these relationships, I think, are only six in number. (In the essay, I specify a seventh, sequential, but now it seems to me that the sequential relationship is only a special instance of what I call the coordinate relationship.)

If my argument is correct, then coherence in a paragraph, for instance, comes from various permutations of these six relationships. It is hardly surprising that the grammar has markers for the six relationships, namely, the coordinating conjunctions and, but, for, so, (n)or, *and the colon.*

It should be pointed out that the six constitute a little—but powerful—form-oriented set of topics. Once again we see, then, that the "departments" of rhetoric are not separate and discrete. From one point of view, all sets of topics belong to invention, but from another point of view, many of them belong either to style or to form. Conversely, any theory of form is, ipso facto, *a theory of invention.*

Just at the point where it could best serve rhetoric transformational generative grammar fails: it does not jump the double-cross mark (#) that signifies "sentence boundary" or, more accurately, "transformational unit boundary." The significance of this limitation is underscored by the inability of grammarians to write a rule for the simplest of all transformations: clause coordination.

Since the number of sentences that can be conjoined in this way is, theoretically at least, unlimited, it is not immediately obvious how to write a constituent-structure rule to permit the generation of compound sentences. . . . It is clearly unsatisfactory to have to postulate an infinity of rules. . . .[1]

As a result, transformational generative grammar has been tremendously useful in the study of style, but it has had little application (except metaphorically) to invention and organization. That is, it has cast only dim light on concepts of form and coherence.

The following discussion will argue that there is a grammar of *coherence* (or *form,* for in the following, the two terms are virtually synonymous). If one perceives form in discourse, he or she also perceives coherence, for form is the internal set of consistent relationships in any stretch of discourse, whether poem, play, essay, oration, or whatever. This set of relationships—like the relationships that rules of grammar describe—must be finite in number; otherwise: formlessness, for the very concepts of form and coherence imply a finite number of relationships that can be perceived. (A generative grammar implies a finite number of rules, some of which may be applied recursively.) Following the model of grammar, one might look for some sort of "constituent structure rules" that underlie coherent utterances beyond the sentence, and then for the equivalent of "lexical rules," and finally for something approximating "transformational rules." In a very rough, loosely analogous way, the following discussion concentrates only on the "phrase structure rules" of coherence and, as a result, excludes "lexical" data which is undoubtedly significant. For instance, one reason that a paragraph "hangs together" or is a convention is that chains of equivalent words run through it. A switch in equivalence chains signals: new paragraph.[2] The present discussion will ignore everything but the abstract configurations or sets of relationships that constitute coherence. (This, of course, is not to say that any one component of the whole body of discourse is unimportant.)

Modern grammar nicely describes the first two stadia in the hierarchy of discourse relationship sets that make up coherence. The first set of relationships is those that can develop from the application of rules to S and then to all constituents that develop from S. The result (after lexical rules have been applied) will be a sentence, divided into two parts: Modality and Proposition. As Charles J. Fillmore explains:

> In the basic structure of sentences . . . we find what might be called the 'proposition,' a tenseless set of relationships involving verbs and nouns (and embedded sentences, if there are any), separated from what might be called the 'modality' constituent. This latter will include such modalities on the sentence-as-a-whole as negation, tense, mood, and aspect.[3]

[1] D. Terence Langendoen, *The Study of Syntax* (New York: Holt, Rinehart and Winston, 1969), p. 31.

[2] A. L. Becker, "A Tagmemic Approach to Paragraph Analysis," *The Sentence and the Paragraph* (Champaign, Ill.: NCTE, 1966), pp. 33–38.

[3] "The Case for Case," *Universals in Linguistic Theory,* ed. Emmon Bach and Robert T. Harms (New York: Holt, Rinehart and Winston, 1968), p. 23.

Each noun in the proposition stands in a *case* relationship with the verb, thus:

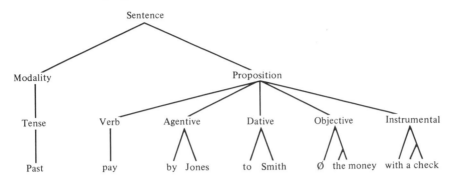

This *deep structure* can have the following surface manifestations, all of them synonymous:

(1) Jones paid Smith the money with a check.
(2) Jones paid the money to Smith with a check.
(3) The money was paid Smith by Jones with a check.
(4) The money was paid to Smith by Jones with a check.
(5) The money was paid by Jones to Smith with a check.
(6) Smith was paid the money by Jones with a check.

And with the cleft sentence transformation: *A check is what Jones paid Smith the money with.* It is worth pointing out that syntactic relationships in these sentences change, but case relationships ("who did what and with which and to whom") are invariable. Thus, in 1 and 2, "Jones" is the grammatical subject of the verb; in 3, 4, and 5, "the money" is the grammatical subject; in 6, "Smith" is the subject. But "Jones" is always in the agentive case, "the money" is always in the objective case, and "Smith" is always in the dative. That is, we never lose sight of the relationships among the noun phrases or of their relationships with the verb. It is also worth noting—in fact, crucial to this discussion—that certain "particles" which are represented in the deep structure diagram may or may not appear in the surface structure. Thus, the agentive "by" does not appear until after the passive transformation has been applied, and dative "to" disappears with application of the indirect object inversion transformation. These signals of case relationships may or may not be in the surface structure.

The first "layer" of relationships that make up coherence, then, is *cases*.

The second "layer" might well be called *syntax* (in a somewhat specialized and restricted use of the word). The relationships of syntax are described by those transformations that have to do with inserting sentences within other sentences by any means but coordination. Thus, the relationships characteristic of syntax (as I use the word) are, for instance,

complements:
> It is strange. He is here.
> It is strange that he is here.
> It is strange for him to be here.
> His being here is strange.

relatives:
> The banker owned the town. The banker was rich.
> The banker who was rich owned the town.
> The rich banker owned the town.

subordinates:
> He chews tobacco. He likes it.
> He chews tobacco because he likes it.

absolutes:
> The airport was fogged in. The plane circled for an hour.
> The airport being fogged in, the plane circled for an hour.

and so on.
> This is the cat. The cat chased the rat. The rat ate the malt. The malt lay in the house. Jack built the house.
> This is the cat that chased the rat that ate the malt that lay in the house that Jack built.

And this, of course, is just the point at which grammar ends—that very point at which *inventio* and *dispositio* really begin.

I argue that there is a set of relationships beyond case and syntax and that this set constitutes the relationships that make for coherence—among the transformational units in a paragraph, among the paragraphs in a chapter, among the chapters in a book. I call these relationships *transitions,* and I claim that beyond the sentence marker, the double-cross, we perceive coherence only as the consistent relationships among transitions. All of this, of course, is more easily illustrated than explained, and illustration is forthcoming. For the moment, however, I should like to underscore my claim that the relationships I am about to describe constitute the grammar of coherence for *all* units of discourse beyond the level of what I have called "syntax." [4]

In another place, I will detail the method whereby I arrived at the following conclusions. But for the time being, I will concentrate on results and their applications.

Analysis of thousands of transformational units in sequences reveals that there are seven relationships that prevail among T-units and, I would argue,

---

. [4] The reader who is familiar with modern logic will immediately perceive the similarity between what I am about to outline and the relationships among propositions listed in logic. They are *initial, additive* (and), *adversative* (but), *alternative* (or), *explanatory* (that is), *illustrative* (for example), *illative* (therefore), *causal* (for). I would urge the reader, however, to be more conscious of the differences between the two systems than of the similarities. What I call transitions are not merely an adaptation, but, it seems to me, are manifestations of some of the most basic properties of language.

in any stretch of discourse that is perceived as coherent. I have called these relationships (1) coordinate, (2) obversative, (3) causative, (4) conclusive, (5) alternative, (6) inclusive, and (7) sequential. These relationships can be either *expressed* or *implied.* They are expressed in a variety of ways: through coordinating conjunctions, transitional adverbs, and a variety of other moveable modifiers. Just how they are implied remains a mystery.[5] However, the relationships are easily demonstrated.

Coordination can always be expressed by *and.* (Synonyms: *furthermore, in addition, too, also, again,* etc.)

> Boswell was a Rousseau-ite, one of the first of the Romantics, an inveterate sentimentalist, *AND* nothing could be more complete than the contrast between his career and Gibbon's.   —*Lytton Strachey*

> They almost hid from us the front, but through the dust and the spaces between running legs we could see the soldiers in the trench leap their barricade like a breaking wave. *AND* then the impenetrable dust shut down *AND* the fierce stabbing needle of the machine guns sewed the mighty jumble of sounds together.   —*John Reed*

> . . . Marat is, in most of his speeches, tinsel, stage scenery, or an element in a great painting. *AGAIN,* the Brechtian songs are touching, but ironically and allusively touching; Charlotte Corday, the mad, beautiful country girl mouthing her lines, is *AGAIN* an element in a picture, an aesthetic contrivance.   —*Stuart Hampshire*

Obversativity can always be expressed by *but.* (Synonyms: *yet, however, on the other hand,* etc.)

> It has been ambitious and plucky of me to attempt to describe what is indescribable, and I have failed, as I knew I would. *BUT* I have discharged my duty to society. . . . .   —*E. B. White*

> And Johnson, as Kennedy has often acknowledged, was a man of force and decision to whom, in case anything happened, the government could responsibly be assigned.
> *ON THE OTHER HAND,* the designation of Johnson would outrage the liberal wing of the party.   —*Arthur Schlesinger, Jr.*

---

[5] When I first began working on these ideas, I communicated my ideas to Charles Fillmore. His comment on my tentative conclusions is revealing. I was talking strictly about the relationships in the paragraph, and he said, "Your ideas about paragraph structure are appealing, but it's hard to see, as you admit, how they can lead to any clarification of the problem of coherence on the paragraph level. The 'coherence' of clauses in a sentence is just as unsolved an issue as ever, but to the extent that your proposals are right you can at least claim to have demonstrated that what might have appeared to be two separate mysteries are reducible to one and the same mystery." The fact that coherence among clauses in a T-unit and coherence among T-units are reducible to the same mystery is, of course, the point here, not that coherence is mysterious. In general, I am indebted to Professor Fillmore for a great variety of insights.

Causativity can always be expressed by *for*. It is interesting to note that among the transitional adverbs commonly used (nevertheless, however, moreover, hence, consequently, nonetheless, accordingly, then, besides, likewise, indeed, therefore), none expresses the causative relationship.

> Now, on that morning, I stopped still in the middle of the block, *FOR* I'd caught out of the corner of my eye a tunnel-passage, an overgrown courtyard.
> —*Truman Capote*

Conclusivity can always be expressed by *so*. (Synonyms: *therefore, thus, for this reason,* etc.)

> She has a rattling Corsican accent, likes Edith Piaf records, and gives me extra shrimp bits in my shrimp salad. *SO* some things change. Last time I heard no Edith Piaf and earned no extra forkfuls of shrimp.—*Herbert Gold*

Alternativity can always be expressed by *or*.

> Now such an entity, even if it could be proved beyond dispute, would not be God: it would merely be a further piece of existence, that might conceivably not have been there—*OR* a demonstration would not have been required.
> —*John A. T. Robinson*

Inclusivity is often expressed with a *colon*.

> In the first century B.C., Lucretius wrote this description of the pageant of Cybele:
> Adorned with emblem and crown . . . she is carried in awe-inspiring state. . . .
> —*Harvey Cox*

The inclusive relationship is that of the example to the generality or the narration of the case to the statement of the case. Often, inclusivity is expressed by the transformational possibility of complementization:

> He realized that their discovery [Aristotle's discovery of the statues of Daedalus] would shatter his own "natural" law: Managers would no longer need subordinates, masters could dispense with slaves.—*Michael Harrington*

With the last two clauses complementized, the sentence reads like this:

> He realized that their discovery would shatter his own "natural" law, that managers would no longer need subordinates, and that masters could dispense with slaves.

The *sequential relationship* is expressed by such transitions as "first . . . second . . . third," "earlier . . . later," "on the bottom . . . in the middle . . . on top," and so on.

Three types of relationships, then, constitute coherence: cases, syntax, and transitions (with the transitions either expressed or implied). And it is, indeed, obvious that transitions can be implied, for it is common to find series of transformational units with no expressed transitions.

It is possible to love the theater and to revel in theatricality, to find the pretense and unreality of the stage wholly absorbing in its own right. It must be supposed that most actors and directors, if left to their own tastes and impulses, would strive after theatrical effects above all else. The satisfaction of any broader human interest might be quite secondary.—*Stuart Hampshire*

I read this as an "and . . . and" series, but another interpretation is possible: "and . . . for." That is, there can be ambiguity in transitions as well as in lexicon and syntax.

The interesting possibility, however, is that the seven relationships that prevail among T-units also prevail among larger elements of discourse. For instance, applied at the level of the T-unit, the seven constitute a series of topics that will automatically generate discourse, for the second T-unit must stand in one of the seven relationships to the first, and the third must stand in one of the seven relationships to the second, and so on. Therefore, transitions are topics for a generative rhetoric. But a rhetoric that will generate only paragraphs has limited usefulness. If, however, the seven topics isolate the relationships among any segments of discourse (except those related to one another by the grammar of the T-unit), then they might well be the basis for a true generative rhetoric.

Shakespeare's sonnets have proved to be useful models for my purposes, and they will serve here to demonstrate that the seven relationships prevail in "whole works," though, of course, one might argue that a sonnet is, after all, just another kind of paragraph. Expressed transitions in the following will be in capitals; implied transitions (according to my reading) will be in bracketed capitals.

Sonnet XVII

Who will believe my verse in time to come,
If it were fill'd with your most high deserts?
THOUGH YET, heaven knows, it is but as a tomb
Which hides your life and shows not half your parts.
[BUT] If I could write the beauty of your eyes
And in fresh numbers number all your graces,
The age to come would say 'This poet lies;
[FOR] Such heavenly touches ne'er touch'd earthly faces.'
SO should my papers, yellowed with their age,
Be scorn'd, like old men of less truth than tongue,
And your true rights be term'd a poet's rage
And stretched metre of an antique song:
    BUT were some child of yours alive that time,
    You should live twice, in it and in my rhyme.

In his cycle, Shakespeare upon occasion needs two sonnets rather than one to express his complete idea. In such cases, he supplies the proper transition. The relationship between V and VI is conclusive, expressed as *then*. (*So* is the minimal transition to express conclusivity.)

Sonnet V

Those hours that with gentle work did frame
The lovely gaze where every eye doth dwell,
Will play the tyrants to the very same
And that unfair which fairly doth excel:
FOR never-resting time leads summer on
To hideous winter and confounds him there;
Sap check'd with frost and lusty leaves quite gone,
Beauty o'ersnow'd and bareness every where:
THEN, were not summer's distillation left,
A liquid prisoner pent in walls of glass,
Beauty's effect with beauty were bereft,
Nor it, nor no remembrance what it was:
   BUT flowers distill'd, though they with winter meet,
   Leese but their show; [FOR] their substance still lives sweet.

Sonnet VI

THEN let not winter's ragged hand deface
In thee thy summer, ere thou be distill'd:
[BUT] Make sweet some vial; [AND] treasure thou some place
With beauty's treasure, ere it be self-kill'd.
[FOR] That use is not forbidden usury,
Which happies those that pay the willing loan;
[FOR] That's for thyself to breed another thee,
OR ten times happier, be it ten for one;
[FOR] Ten times thyself were happier than thou art,
If ten of thine ten times refigured thee:
THEN what could death do, if thou shouldst depart,
Leaving thee living in posterity?
   [SO] Be not self-will'd, FOR thou art much too fair
   To be death's conquest and make worms thine heir.

To apply this test to a series of paragraphs that make up an essay, for instance, is too cumbersome a job for the present discussion and is, in any case, unnecessary. The reader can make his own test. "What relationships prevail among the sections—paragraphs or other—of an extended piece of discourse?" is the question. If the seven outlined here are the answer, then the system has stood the test. (By the way, the question transformation might be viewed as a transition in itself. That is, it predicts some kind of answer.)

Finally, it is necessary to clarify the exact sense in which I take these seven relationships (they might be called "topics") to constitute a generative rhetoric. The term "generative" is of itself productive, for it exactly designates the process whereby discourse—at the sentence level and beyond—comes into being. An oversimplified explanation of the language process is to say that at any level of generality, one unit has the potential for generating other units and of combining these units in some meaningful way. Any set of topics is merely a way of triggering the process. Thus the student, say, who has difficulty with the invention of arguments, can use the seven-item list to tell him what might come next—not what content, to be sure, but what relation his next unit must take to the previous one. There are only seven possibilities.

Inability to write sentences stems not from the writer's lack of subject matter (everyone is the repository of an infinitude of subject matter), but from his not knowing how to get the subject matter into structures. The problem at levels beyond the sentence is, I think, exactly the same. The seven relation-oriented "topics" that I have outlined name the structures that can hold the writer's ideas.

A generative rhetoric, a heuristic model, even a grammar of form—whatever it might be called, the schema of these seven relationships ought to be easily applicable in the classroom. But equally important, they should have wide ranging theoretical possibilities, for instance, in explaining the disjunction of schizoid language, in identifying "the eighth ambiguity" (that which takes place between units larger than the sentence and results from the inability to perceive transitions) and in dealing with form in literature.

A Generative Rhetoric of the Paragraph

Francis Christensen

Francis Christensen, who was my friend and colleague, was not a rhetorician in any formal sense of the word. His career was largely devoted to teaching literature and to literary scholarship. But he had an uncanny ability to perceive how prose works, and his essays concerning the sentence and the paragraph have become classics in modern rhetoric.

His systems have two great advantages: they can be easily understood, and they work. That is, practice with free modifiers does improve students' prose, and work with Christensen's notions concerning the paragraph does enable students to write better paragraphs.

It was just a hundred years ago, in 1866, that Alexander Bain introduced the paragraph into rhetoric as a unit of discourse. Bain based his definition and his rhetoric of the paragraph on an analogy with the sentence. This analogy, a very loose one, has prevailed for a hundred years. I have continued it—but with a difference. Here there is a precise structural analogy, not with just any sentence, but with the cumulative sentence. The topic sentence of a paragraph is analogous to the base clause of such a sentence, and the supporting sentences of a paragraph are analogous to the added levels of the sentence. The validity of the analogy is proved by the fact that a mere change of punctuation will convert some sentences into paragraphs and some paragraphs into sentences.

There are two values in this way of looking at the paragraph that I have not mentioned in the essay itself. It is a natural way to help students feel their way through the paragraphs they are writing and give them the density of texture, the solidity of specification, so many of them woefully lack. And in reading what they have come up with, a quick structural analysis will tell exactly what they have done or left undone, done well or poorly. Without such analysis, one cannot very well make any relevant comments. And such analysis is implicit in any sort of reading. After all, it merely raises to the level of a conscious operation what every competent reader does automatically as his eyes scan the lines of the page and what, I suspect, the incompetent reader has not learned to do. One has to recognize the shifting direction of movement and the shifting levels of generality. Following a paragraph is more like following a dance than a dash. The topic sentence draws a circle, and the rest of the paragraph is a pirouette within that circle.

This article was followed in *CCC* by two others on the paragraph—by A. L. Becker, December 1965, and by Paul Rodgers, Jr., February 1966. The three authors joined with others in a Symposium on the Paragraph in the issue for May 1966. This symposium prompted the observations that I have transferred to a postscript.

In my article "A Generative Rhetoric of the Sentence," I said that the principles used there in analyzing the sentence were no less applicable to the paragraph. My purpose here is to make good that claim, to show that the paragraph has, or may have, a structure as definable and traceable as that of the sentence and that it can be analyzed in the same way. In fact, since writing that paper, I have come to see that the parallel between sentence and paragraph is much closer than I suspected, so close, indeed, that as Josephine Miles put it (in a letter) the paragraph seems to be only a macro-sentence or meta-sentence.

The chapters on the paragraph in our textbooks are so nearly alike in conception that one could almost say that, apart from the examples, the only striking difference is in the choice of *indention* or *indentation*. The prescription is always the same: the writer should work out a topic sentence and then choose one of the so-called methods of paragraph development to substantiate it. The topic sentence may appear at the beginning or at the end of the paragraph or anywhere in between, or it may be merely "implied," a sort of ectoplasmic ghost hovering over the paragraph. Besides this, some books speak of "paragraph movement"—chronological (as in narrative), spatial (as in description), logical (as in discursive writing). If the movement is logical, it may be inductive or deductive or a combination of the two, and some books offer diagrams, as systems analysts use flow charts, to picture the thought funneling down from the topic sentence or down to it.

This prescription for writers and the analysis it is based on are even more unworkable than the conventional treatment of the sentence as simple-compound-complex, with emphasis on the complex, or as loose-balanced-periodic, with emphasis on the periodic. I doubt that many of us write many paragraphs the way we require our charges to write them or that we could find many paragraphs that exemplify the methods of development or the patterns of movement.[1]

First, the methods of paragraph development. These methods are real, but they are simply methods of development—period. They are no more relevant to the paragraph than, on the short side, to the sentence or, on the long side, to a run of several paragraphs or to a paper as long as this or a chapter. They are the topics of classical rhetoric. They are the channels our minds naturally run in whether we are writing a sentence or a paragraph or planning a paper. There is no point in restricting a class (as for a whole semester in a freshman course I once taught) to a single method of development until the last week, when we reached what the textbook called a "combination of methods." It is almost impossible to write a paragraph without employing a combination of methods or to find paragraphs that do not.

In "A Lesson from Hemingway," I maintained that in representational (or narrative-descriptive) writing, where the aim is to *picture* actions and objects, there are only three methods of development, or description, as I called them, only three things one can do to present an image. These methods are to point to (1) a quality or attribute or to (2) a detail or (3) to make a comparison. A single sentence may exemplify all three: "The gypsy was walking out toward the bull again, walking heel-and-toe, insultingly, like a ballroom dancer, the red shafts of the banderillos twitching with his walk"—Hemingway. These methods are exactly parallel to the methods of development or support in discursive writing. The great difference is that in representational writing the methods are so few and in discursive writing so many. In either kind of writing the methods of description or development are hard to discern except in the light of what may be called a "structural analysis."

In the light of such a structural analysis, most paragraphs are like the sentences I called "cumulative." They exemplify the four principles proposed for the rhetoric of the sentence. Let us think of the topic sentence as parallel to the base clause of a sentence and the supporting sentences as parallel to the added sentence modifiers: clusters, absolutes, and nonrestrictive subordinate and relative clauses. (1) Then it is obvious that there could be no paragraphs without *addition*. (2) When a supporting sentence is added, both

---

[1] In this article I propose to deal only with the paragraphs of discursive writing and to exclude from these the short introductory and transitional and concluding paragraphs.

writer and reader must see the *direction of modification* or *direction of movement*. Discerning the direction is easier in the sentence because the sentence is self-contained and the elements added differ in form from the base clause. The direction of movement in the paragraph is explained below. The failure to see the relation of each upcoming sentence to what has gone before is probably one source of the difficulty many people have in reading. (3) When sentences are added to develop a topic or subtopic, they are usually at a lower *level of generality*—usually, but not always, because sometimes an added sentence is more general than the one it is added to. (4) Finally, the more sentences the writer adds, the denser the *texture*. The paragraphs our students write are likely to be as thin-textured as their sentences, and teachers can use this structural analysis of the paragraph to *generate* paragraphs of greater depth.

I have arranged the details of this approach to the paragraph under nine headings.

1 / The Paragraph May Be Defined As a Sequence of Structurally Related Sentences.

By a sequence of structurally related sentences I mean a group of sentences related to one another by coordination and subordination. If the first sentence of a paragraph is the topic sentence, the second is quite likely to be a comment on it, a development of it, and therefore subordinate to it. The third sentence may be coordinate with the second sentence (as in this paragraph) or subordinate to it. The fourth sentence may be coordinate with either the second or third (or with both if they themselves are coordinate, as in this paragraph) or subordinate to the third. And so on. A sentence that is not coordinate with any sentence above it or subordinate to the next above it, breaks the sequence. The paragraph has begun to drift from its moorings, or the writer has unwittingly begun a new paragraph.

2 / The Top Sentence of the Sequence Is the Topic Sentence.

The topic sentence is comparable to the base clause of a cumulative sentence. It is the sentence on which the others depend. It is the sentence whose assertion is supported or whose meaning is explicated or whose parts are detailed by the sentences added to it. In the examples that follow, it will always be marked 1, for the top level.

3 / The Topic Sentence Is Nearly Always the First Sentence of the Sequence.

The contrast between deductive and inductive, or between analytic and synthetic as it is sometimes put, seems to have led us to assume that the one kind of movement is as common as the other and that the topic sentence therefore is as likely to appear at the end as at the beginning. The many scores of paragraphs I have analyzed for this study do not bear out this assumption.

Except as noted in point 7 below, the topic sentence occurs almost invariably at the beginning. In fact, I do not have clear-cut examples of topic sentences in the other theoretically possible positions. Readers may check their own actual practice and mine in this piece.

In connected writing, the topic sentence varies greatly in how explicit it is in designating the thesis of the paragraph. Sometimes it is quite explicit; sometimes it is a mere sign pointing to the turn the new paragraph is going to take. Sometimes it is the shortest sentence of the paragraph; sometimes it is not even a grammatically complete sentence. Sometimes it is a question. It seems to me that these differences are irrelevant, provided only that the reader gets the signal and the writer remembers the signal he has called.

4 / Simple Sequences Are of Two Sorts— Coordinate and Subordinate.

Here the parallel between sentence and paragraph becomes fully evident. In analyzing the rhetoric of the sentence, I described what I called the two-level and the multilevel sentence. Here is an example of each and a paragraph exactly parallel in structure with each. The two sets of terms seem to me necessary to put the emphasis where it is needed in teaching and to avoid conflict with the use in grammar of *coordination* and *subordination*.

A. TWO-LEVEL SENTENCE

1 [Lincoln's] words still linger on the lips—
  2 eloquent and cunning, yes,
  2 vindictive and sarcastic in political debate,
  2 rippling and ribald in jokes,
  2 reverent in the half-formed utterance of prayer.

Alistair Cooke

A. COORDINATE SEQUENCE PARAGRAPH

1 This is the essence of the religious spirit—the sense of power, beauty, greatness, truth infinitely beyond one's own reach, but infinitely to be aspired to.
  2 It invests men with pride in a purpose and with humility in accomplishment.
  2 It is the source of all true tolerance, for in its light all men see other men as they see themselves, as being capable of being more than they are, and yet falling short, inevitably, of what they can imagine human opportunities to be.
  2 It is the supporter of human dignity and pride and the dissolver of vanity.
  2 And it is the very creator of the scientific spirit; for without the aspiration to understand and control the miracle of life, no man would have sweated in a laboratory or tortured his brain in the exquisite search after truth.

Dorothy Thompson

B. MULTILEVEL SENTENCE

1 A small Negro girl develops from the sheet of glarefrosted walk,
2   walking barefooted,
3   her brown legs striking and recoiling from the hot cement,
4   her feet curling in,
5   only the outer edges touching.

B. SUBORDINATE SEQUENCE PARAGRAPH

1 The process of learning is essential to our lives.
2   All higher animals seek it deliberately.
3   They are inquisitive and they experiment.
4   An experiment is a sort of harmless trial run of some action which we shall have to make in the real world; and this, whether it is made in the laboratory by scientists or by fox-cubs outside their earth.
5   The scientist experiments and the cub plays;
          both are learning to correct their errors of judgment in a setting in which errors are not fatal.
6   Perhaps this is what gives them both their air of happiness and freedom in these activities.

    J. Bronowski, *The Common Sense of Science* (Vintage), p. 111.

The analytical procedure for discovering the structure is really quite simple. There is no problem in locating the base clause of a sentence, and one can assume—provisionally (see 6 and 7 below)—that the first sentence of a paragraph is the topic sentence. Then, going sentence by sentence through the paragraph, one searches in the sentences above for likenesses—that is, for evidences of coordination. In both sets of two examples, the second element is *unlike* the first one; it is different and so it is set down as subordinate—that is, it is indented and numbered level 2. With the third element the two sets part company. In the examples marked A, the third element is *like* the second, it is parallel to the second, and so it is set down as coordinate. The clearest mark of coordination is identity of structure at the beginning of the sentence. The fourth element is like both the second and third; and the fifth is like the second, third, and fourth. All the elements marked 2 have the same relation to one another; they are siblings. And because of this, they all have the same immediate relation to level 1, the base clause or topic sentence; they are all children of the same mother. In the examples marked B, on the other hand, the third element is *unlike* the second, and of course unlike the first; the fourth is unlike the third or any other above it, and so on. Search as you may, you will find no signs of parallelism. So, instead of two generations, there are five in the sentence and six in the paragraph. No element after the second is related immediately to level 1; it is related to it only through all of the intermediate generations.[2]

---

[2] I use *generation* here metaphorically, in the biological sense, not in the sense of "levels generated."

The fact that there are two kinds of sequences makes all the difference in what we can say about the paragraph.

It should be evident how we must treat the methods of development or support. In the coordinate sequence, all the coordinate sentences employ the *same* method—in paragraph A they enumerate the *results* or *effects*. In the subordinate sequence, every added sentence may, and likely will, employ a *different* method. There is no theoretic limit to the number of levels, and the lists of methods in our textbooks are far from exhausting the whole range of what we may say in discursive writing to develop or support a topic.

It should be evident, also, that we need two separate sets of yardsticks for measuring such things as unity, coherence, and emphasis. Take coherence, for example. The repetition of structure in A is all that is necessary to join sentence to sentence at the same level. Any connectives other than the simple *and* for the last member would be an impertinence—*again, moreover, in the same vein, in addition* would be a hindrance rather than a help. But repetition of structure *is* necessary; like things in like ways is one of the imperatives of discursive writing. Any attempt to introduce variety in the sentence beginnings, by varying the pattern or by putting something before the subject, would be like trying to vary the columns of the Parthenon. In a subordinate sequence, just as clearly, repetition of structure must be avoided. Each added sentence, being different in the method of development, must be different in form. In a subordinate sequence, the problems of unity, coherence, and emphasis are altogether different—and more difficult.

Another paragraph will illustrate two other points. First, a writer sometimes intends a coordinate sequence but, like the dog that turns around once or twice before he settles down, takes, and sometimes wastes, a sentence or two before he begins his enumeration. (For other examples see paragraphs E and J.) Second, the coordinate sentences need not be identical in structure; they need only be like enough for the reader to place them. In this paragraph it is evident that all three sentences at level 3 present *examples*.

C. COORDINATE SEQUENCE

1 He [the native speaker] may, of course, speak a form of English that marks him as coming from a rural or an unread group.

2 But if he doesn't mind being so marked, there's no reason why he should change.

3 Samuel Johnson kept a Staffordshire burr in his speech all his life.

3 In Burns's mouth the despised lowland Scots dialect served just as well as the "correct" English spoken by ten million of his southern contemporaries.

3 Lincoln's vocabulary and his way of pronouncing certain words were sneered at by many better educated people at the time, but he seemed to be able to use the English language as effectively as his critics.

Bergen Evans, *Comfortable Words,* p. 6.

5 / The Two Sorts of Sequence Combine to Produce the Commonest Sort— the Mixed Sequence.

Simple sequences, especially coordinate ones, are not common. More often than not, subordinate sentences are added to add depth to coordinate sequences, and coordinate sentences are added to emphasize points made in subordinate sequences. The resulting mixed sequences reveal their origin as derived from either coordinate or subordinate sequences.

My justification for the term *generative* lies here. The teacher can, with perfect naturalness, suggest the addition of subordinate sentences to clarify and of coordinate sentences to emphasize or to enumerate. With these additions the writer is not padding; he is putting himself imaginatively in the reader's place and anticipating his questions and resistances. He is learning to treat his subject home.

D. MIXED SEQUENCE—BASED ON COORDINATE SEQUENCE

1 The other [mode of thought] is the scientific method.
  2 It subjects the conclusions of reason to the arbitrament of hard fact to build an increasing body of tested knowledge.
  2 It refuses to ask questions that cannot be answered, and rejects such answers as cannot be provided except by Revelation.
  2 It discovers the relatedness of all things in the universe—of the motion of the moon to the influence of the earth and sun, of the nature of the organism to its environment, of human civilization to the conditions under which it is made.
  2 It introduces history into everything.
    3 Stars and scenery have their history, alike with plant species or human institutions, and
    nothing is intelligible without some knowledge of its past.
      4 As Whitehead has said, each event is the reflection or effect of every other event, past as well as present.
  2 It rejects dualism.
    3 The supernatural is in part the region of the natural that has not yet been understood, in part an invention of human fantasy, in part the unknowable.
    3 Body and soul are not separate entities, but two aspects of one organization, and
    Man is that portion of the universal world-stuff that has evolved until it is capable of rational and purposeful values.
      4 His place in the universe is to continue that evolution and to realize those values.
      Julian Huxley, *Man in the Modern World* (Mentor), pp. 146–47.

This paragraph suggests careful calculation of what could be left to the reader and what must be made more explicit. Huxley took a chance on the first two items. What he added to the third made it a two-level sentence. The sentences he added to the last two made the paragraph a mixed one. He was under no obligation to expand all five items equally. The writer's guide is his own sense of what the reader must be told. In our classes we must work to develop this sense. The difference is often the difference between self-expression and communication.

E. MIXED SEQUENCE—BASED ON COORDINATE SEQUENCE

1 An obvious classification of meaning is that based on scope.
1 This is to say, meaning may be generalized (extended, widened) or it may be specialized (restricted, narrowed).
  2 When we increase the scope of a word, we reduce the elements of its contents.
    3 For instance *tail* (from OE *taegl*) in earlier times seems to have meant 'hairy caudal appendage, as of a horse.'
      4 When we eliminated the hairiness (or the horsiness) from the meaning, we increased its scope, so that in Modern English the word means simply 'caudal appendage.'
      4 The same thing has happened to Danish *hale,* earlier 'tail of a cow.'
        5 In course of time the cow was eliminated, and in present-day Danish the word means simply 'tail,' having undergone a semantic generalization precisely like that of the English word cited;

the closely related Icelandic *hali* still keeps the cow in the picture.
    3 Similarly, a *mill* was earlier a place for making things by the process of grinding, that is, for making meal.
      4 The words *meal* and *mill* are themselves related, as one might guess from their similarity.
        5 A mill is now simply a place for making things: the grinding has been eliminated, so that we may speak of a woolen mill, a steel mill, or even a gin mill.
    3 The word *corn* earlier meant 'grain' and is in fact related to the word *grain.*
      4 It is still used in this general sense in England, as in the "Corn Laws," but specifically it may mean either oats (for animals) or wheat (for human beings).
      4 In American usage *corn* denotes maize, which is of course not at all what Keats meant in his "Ode to a Nightingale" when he described Ruth as standing "in tears amid the alien corn."
    3 The building in which corn, regardless of its meaning, is stored is called a barn.
      4 *Barn* earlier denoted a storehouse for barley; the word is in fact a compound of two Old English words, *bere* 'barley' and *aern* 'house.'
        5 By elimination of a part of its earlier content, the scope of this word has been extended to mean a storehouse for any kind of grain.

> 5 American English has still further generalized by eliminating the grain, so that *barn* may mean also a place for housing livestock.
>
> Thomas Pyles, *The Origins and Development of the English Language,* pp. 306–07.

Here the development has proceeded so far that the four coordinate sentences (level 3) have become in effect subtopic sentences. The paragraph could be subdivided, making them the topic sentences of a series of paragraphs. The long paragraph looks well on a book page; the shorter paragraphs would look more palatable in narrow newspaper columns. Either way, the effect would not be essentially different.

The problem of a reader tackling a long paragraph like this is to identify the coordinate sentences. He reads one 3rd-level sentence and then some sentences explaining it as an example of semantic generalization. He must be aware when he has come to the end of that explanation and must then shift his attention back to level 3. He must recognize the direction of movement. The first three 3rd-level sentences are easy to spot because like things have been put in like ways: the italicized words chosen as examples have been made the grammatical subject or apposed to the subject. But the opportunity to make a deft transition led the author to vary the pattern for the fourth. I have seen readers stumble at this point, and I have seen some make Danish *hale* parallel to the four English words.

F. MIXED SEQUENCE—BASED ON COORDINATE SEQUENCE

1 This is a point so frequently not understood that it needs some dwelling on.
  2 Consider how difficult it is to find a tenable argument that *thrown,* say, is intrinsically better than *throwed.*
    3 We can hardly say that the simple sound is better.
      4 For if it were, we would presumably also prefer *rown* to *rowed, hown* to *hoed, strown* to *strode,* and
      we don't.
    3 Nor can we argue convincingly that *throwed* should be avoided because it did not occur in earlier English.
      4 Many forms which occurred in earlier English cannot now be used.
        5 As we mentioned earlier, *holp* used to be the past tense form of *help; helped* was incorrect.
        5 But we could not now say "He holp me a good deal."
  2 As for "me and Jim," the statement that *I* should be used in the subject position begs the question.
    3 One can ask why *I* should be the subject form, and
    to this there is no answer.
      4 As a matter of fact, *you* was at one time the object form of the second personal plural, *ye* being the subject form.
      4 But no one objects now to a sentence like "You were there."

Paul Roberts

I have included this paragraph to illustrate further the kind of clues that mark coordination: at the first level 3, *we can hardly say: nor can we argue;* at level 5, *used to be: now;* at the second level 4, *was at one time: now.* At level 2 there are no verbal clues; the reader just has to recognize that "me and Jim" is another example like "throwed" to illustrate the point that needs dwelling on.

G. MIXED SEQUENCE—BASED ON SUBORDINATE SEQUENCE

1 The purpose of science is to describe the world in an orderly scheme or language which will help us to look ahead.
  2 We want to forecast what we can of the future behavior of the world; particularly we want to forecast how it would behave under several alternative actions of our own between which we are usually trying to choose.
  3 This is a very limited purpose.
    4 It has nothing whatever to do with bold generalizations about the universal workings of cause and effect.
    4 It has nothing to do with cause and effect at all, or with any other special mechanism.
    4 Nothing in this purpose, which is to order the world as an aid to decision and action, implies that the order must be of one kind rather than another.
      5 The order is what we find to work, conveniently and instructively.
      5 It is not something we stipulate; it is not something we can dogmatise about.
      5 It is what we find; it is what we find useful.
           J. Bronowski, *The Common Sense of Science,* pp. 70–71.

This would be a simple five-level sequence but for the repetition at levels 4 and 5. It is a fair guess that the desire for rhetorical emphasis generated these additions. With five statements there could be five 5th-level sentences, but the author has chosen to put them in three groups. This is a matter of paragraph punctuation (see 9 below).

H. MIXED SEQUENCE—BASED ON SUBORDINATE SEQUENCE

1 Science as we know it indeed is a creation of the last three hundred years.
  2 It has been made in and by the world that took its settled shape about 1660, when Europe at last shook off the long nightmare of religious wars and settled into a life of inquisitive trade and industry.
  3 Science is embodied in those new societies; it has been made by them and has helped to make them.
    4 The medieval world was passive and symbolic; it saw in the forms of nature the signatures of the Creator.
    4 From the first stirrings of science among the Italian merchant adventurers of the Renaissance, the modern world has been an active machine.

5 That world became the everyday world of trade in the seventeenth century, and
the interests were appropriately astronomy and the instruments
of voyage, among them the magnet.

5 A hundred years later, at the Industrial Revolution, the interest
shifted to the creation and use of power.

6 This drive to extend the strength of man and what he can do
in a day's work has remained our interest since.

7 In the last century it moved from steam to electricity.

7 Then in 1905, in that wonderful year when . . . he published papers which made outstanding advances in three
different branches of physics, Einstein first wrote down the
the equations which suggested that matter and energy are
interchangeable states.

7 Fifty years later, we command a reservoir of power in matter
almost as large as the sun, which we now realize manu-
factures its heat for us in just this way, by the annihilation
of its matter.

J. Bronowski, *The Common Sense of Science,* pp. 97–98.

Conventionally, the "movement" of this paragraph might be called chronological; but it is only roughly so—it leaps, and at levels 4, 5, and 7 it lingers.
Note the marks of coordination: level 4, *the medieval . . . passive: the
modern . . . active;* level 5, *the seventeenth century: a hundred years later;*
level 7, depending on *since* at level 6, *in the last century: then in 1905: fifty
years later.*

The first sentence at level 4 ("The medieval world . . .") is interesting
because the topic sentence limits the time to "the last three hundred years."
One could easily read through levels 1–5 skipping "The medieval world . . ."
The sentence has been inserted—extralogically and extra-chronologically—
in order to set up a contrast. Such inserted sentences are fairly common and
were at first very puzzling to me. Occasionally, also, one encounters and is
puzzled by a parenthetic sentence. Such sentences should be set off by parentheses, but all sentences so set off are not extrasequential.

6 / Some Paragraphs Have No
Top, No Topic, Sentence.

I. PARAGRAPH WITHOUT TOPIC SENTENCE

2 In Spain, where I saw him last, he looked profoundly Spanish.

3 He might have passed for one of those confidential street dealers who
earn their living selling spurious Parker pens in the cafés of Málaga
or Valencia.

4 Like them, he wore a faded chalk-striped shirt, a coat slung over his
shoulders, a trim, dark moustache, and a sleazy, fat-cat smile.

 4 His walk, like theirs, was a raffish saunter, and
   everything about him seemed slept in, especially his hair, a nest of
   small, wet serpents.
 3 Had he been in Seville and his clothes been more formal, he could have
   been mistaken for a pampered elder son idling away a legacy in dribs
   and on drabs, the sort you see in windows along the Sierpes, apparently stuffed.
2 In Italy he looks Italian; in Greece, Greek:
 wherever he travels on the Mediterranean coast, Tennessee Williams takes
   on a protective colouring which melts him into his background, like a
   lizard on a rock.
2 In New York or London he seems out of place, and is best explained away
   as a retired bandit.
 3 Or a beach comber: shave the beard off any of the self-portraits Gauguin
   painted in Tahiti, soften the features a little, and you have a sleepy
   outcast face that might well be Tennessee's.

                                    Kenneth Tynan, *Curtains*, p. 266.

The three sentences marked level 2 are clearly coordinate. But there is no
superordinate sentence to umbrella them; that is, there is no level 1, no topic
sentence. With paragraphs such as this the topic can usually be inferred from
the preceding paragraph. But sometimes the topic sentence is actually part
of the preceding paragraph, arbitrarily and illogically separated. Or, as in J,
the preceding paragraph *is* the topic sentence; the two paragraphs of J constitute a single sequence. The basic pattern here is like that of C; but with
the series of three examples disjoined, they stand alone in a paragraph that
has no topic sentence. Paragraphs without topic sentences are always coordinate sequences, either simple or mixed.

J. TOPIC SENTENCE IN PRECEDING PARAGRAPH

1 The mystical artist always sees patterns.
 2 The symbol, never quite real, tends to be expressed less and less realisti-
   cally, and as the reality becomes abstracted the pattern comes forward.
  ¶3 The wings on Blake's angels do not look like real wings,
    nor are they there because wings belong to angels.
   4 They have been flattened, stylized, to provide a curving pointed
     frame, the setting required by the pattern of the composition.
  3 In Hindoo art and its branches, stylization reaches its height.
   4 Human figures are stylized far beyond the point of becoming a type;
     they too are made into patterns, schematic designs of the human
     body, an abstraction of humanity.
  3 In the case of an Eastern rug all desire to express any semblance of
    reality has gone.
   4 Such a work of art is pure decoration.
    5 It is the expression of the artist's final withdrawal from the visible
      world, essentially his denial of the intellect.

                           Edith Hamilton, *The Greek Way* (Mentor), p. 33.

7 / Some Paragraphs Have Sentences
at the Beginning or at the End
That Do Not Belong to the Sequence.

Occasionally a paragraph has one or more introductory (I) or transitional (T) sentences before the sequence begins. And occasionally one has a sentence or more added after the sequence has run its course; that is, the first of such sentences is not coordinate with any sentence above it or subordinate to the one next above it. They are related to the sequence, but are not a part of it; they form a conclusion or coda (C) or provide a transition (T) to what follows. To save space, I have quoted only enough to establish that the sentences so marked are extrasequential.

K. PARAGRAPH WITH INTRODUCTION

I1 If you are at the beach, and you take an old, dull, brown penny and rub it hard for a minute or two with handfuls of wet sand (dry sand is no good), the penny will come out a bright gold color, looking as clean and new as the day it was minted.
1 Now poetry has the same effect on words as wet sand on pennies.
  2 In what seems an almost miraculous way, it brightens up words that looked dull and ordinary.
    3 Thus, poetry is perpetually 're-creating languages.'
      4 It does this in several ways.
        5 . . . .

C. Day Lewis, *Poetry for You,* pp. 8–9.

Most of the examples of what I would call introductory sentences are like this in offering a comparison. The comparison is not carried through the paragraph, but is used only as a starter.

L. PARAGRAPH WITH TRANSITION

T1 So far I've been talking about some of the world-shapes out of which poetry is built.
  T2 But images, metaphors, and similes are not the only things which may go to make the pattern of a poem.
1 There are meter and rhyme.
  2 You may be surprised that I have not put meter first, after talking so much about rhythm in the last chapter.
    3 Well, the fact is that poetry can be made without meter or rhyme. . . .

C. Day Lewis, *Poetry for You,* p. 33.

Transitions from paragraph to paragraph are ordinarily embedded in the topic sentence, as a single word or a phrase, a subordinate clause, or the first part of a compound sentence. But sometimes, as here, they take a full sentence or more.

The first sentence of a paragraph may even be a major transition. It may be the topic sentence of a series of paragraphs or even the thesis sentence of an article.

M. PARAGRAPH WITH CONCLUSION

1 When we follow the growth of science, we come to understand how that movement has been probing for these unifying concepts.

  2 Look at the movement of biology since the days of Ray and Linnaeus: . . . .

  2 Look at chemistry, from Dalton's law. . . .

  2 Look at the march of physics to unity: . . .

    3 We have seen this lead to the creation of energy from matter; to a picture of space as closed but possibly expanding; and now . . . .

C1 Science is a process of creating new concepts which unify our understanding of the world, and

  the process is today bolder and more far-reaching, more triumphant even than at the great threshold of the Scientific Revolution.

            J. Bronowski, *The Common Sense of Science*, pp. 132–33.

Concluding sentences are rather rare, and some of them, like this one, round off a sequence of paragraphs rather than the one they are joined to. Such concluding sentences are ordinarily at a higher level of generalization than the sentences they follow, and those who take the most general sentence to be the topic sentence may take them for topic sentences. They may say that the paragraph has two topic sentences, fore and aft. The practice of professional writers gives no support to the classroom notion that the paragraph should end with a "clincher."

8 / Some Paragraphing Is Illogical.

N.

1 Rhymes, as you know, generally come at the end of lines.

  2 They are put there because it helps to create and make clear the musical pattern of the stanza:

  the ear learns to expect a rhyme, just as it expects a beat, at certain definite intervals, and

  it's pleased when it finds one there.

1 But you may get a rhyme in the middle of a line, too: and

  some poets are extremely skillful in making assonances and other sound-echoes all over a poem.

  2 This is often done by the use of alliteration.

    3 For example,

        I hear lake water lapping with low sounds by the shore.

    ¶4 Those three 'l's' make a pleasant liquid sound:

    the sound here, in fact, corresponds with the sense.

    4 So it does in

        Dry clashed his armour in the icy caves,

    where the hard 'c' of 'clashed' and 'caves' seems to dry one's mouth up when one speaks the line aloud.

            C. Day Lewis, *Poetry for You*, pp. 35–36.

The two sentences marked 1 are clearly coordinate. One has to say, then, that the paragraph is compound (a reasonable solution; there are such paragraphs), or that the first two sentences are introductory or transitional, or that the paragraphing is simply illogical, breaking up a short sequence.

Paragraphing at level 4 is even more illogical. It breaks up a sequence at the most unexpected point. Perhaps the tired teacher will sigh "If gold rusts. . . ."

On the other hand, many a run of four or five paragraphs totaling 500–600 words can be analyzed as a single sequence, with the paragraph divisions coming logically at the subtopic sentences. This is the consummation we should work for.

9 / *Punctuation Should Be by the Paragraph, Not by the Sentence.*

O.

 1 This brings me to the third failing of eighteenth century science, which I
    find most interesting.
    2 A science which orders its thought too early is stifled.
        3 For example, the ideas of the Epicureans about atoms two thousand
           years ago were quite reasonable; but
           they did only harm to a physics which could not measure temperature
           and pressure and learn the simpler laws which relate them.
        3 Or again, the hope of the medieval alchemists that the elements might
           be changed was not as fanciful as we once thought.
           4 But it was merely damaging to a chemistry which did not yet under-
             stand the composition of water and common salt.
                  J. Bronowski, *The Common Sense of Science*, p. 47.

This is a minor example of punctuating without an eye to the paragraph as a whole. The two sets at level 3 are the same in intent and, except for the punctuation, the same in form. Likes have been put in unlike ways.

Paragraph punctuation usually involves the choice of whether to make compound sentences or not. In paragraph G the same author wisely grouped five coordinate statements into three sentences, sorting them out on the basis of content. Paragraph E does not really have two topic sentences, and a semi-colon would avoid that appearance. I have taken it as a rule that a sentence that merely restates another is on the same level with it. If this is a bad rule, then all the numbers for level should be raised one. In paragraph P the effects of repetition and balance would be obscured if the sentences were not punctuated as compound.

P.

 1 Nowhere, at no time, have there been five and a half years so alternately
    wondrous, compelling, swift and cruel.
    2 As the Sixties began, our aspirant astronauts had yet to enter space;
    now, they practice giant steps to the moon.

2   Then, jet travel was a conversation piece;
     now, we change the flight if we've seen the movie.
2   Then, we were about to be swamped by a recessionary wave;
     now, riding history's highest flood of prosperity, we are revising our
        assumptions about the inevitability of ebbs in our economic life.
2   Then, our Negroes were still marshaling their forces;
     now, they have marshaled the conscience of mankind.
2   Then, we were arguing over the fitness of a Roman Catholic to be Presi-
        dent;
     now, we subdue the nightmare of his murder.
2   Then, a Southerner in the White House seemed politically unthinkable;
     now, a Southerner builds with the most emphatic mandate we have ever
        bestowed.
2   Then, John Birch was an unknown soldier, actresses still wore clothes at
        work, and dancing was something a man and woman did together.

Leonard Gross, *Look*, 6/29/65.

Postscript

In defining the paragraph, we encounter some of the same difficulties as in defining the word and the sentence. The natural impulse is to take as a word whatever lies between the white spaces in lines of print or script, as a sentence whatever lies between a capitalized word and a mark of end punctuation, and as a paragraph whatever lies between two indented sentences. But these typographic criteria are inadequate. Linguists have had to resort to what they call the phonologic word, and Mr. Kellog Hunt, in his study of the language growth of children, had to disregard their capitals and periods and take as a sentence what he called a T-unit, another definition based on phonologic criteria. Tagmemic grammarians are attempting a phonologic definition of the paragraph.

I have defined the paragraph as a sequence of structurally related sentences. Here structure is a matter of coordination and subordination. Coordination is often, and perhaps always ought to be, marked by identity or similarity of grammatical structure. Subordination is marked, but only vaguely, by difference. The difference is definite and clear within the sentence, where coordination and subordination are readily distinguishable. In the paragraph, as I have tried to demonstrate with paragraph F, we have to refer to the content to determine what goes with what.

My definition is useful as a description of the internal structure of any given paragraph, but it does not delimit the paragraph. Many a run of several paragraphs proves on analysis to be a single sequence. And this is as it should be; the 500-word theme may well be such a sequence. But a discourse of some length necessarily has introductory, transitional, and concluding material that does not strictly belong to any of the paragraphs that carry the burden of the discourse. These could, and perhaps should, be paragraphed separately, the frame separated from the framed. But we have come to expect the paragraphs of a piece to be of about the same length. So we run the frame into the framed, the way decorators paint the walls and trim the same color. This procedure accounts for the anomalies I have treated briefly in sections 7–8. Here is a summary, from the Symposium, of the analysis of a 600-word, 25-sentence, 5-paragraph summary of a dissertation.

> The first sentence of each of the first two paragraphs might be taken as a topic sentence, but the first was the thesis sentence of the entire summary and the second the thesis sentence of the second of its two parts. If these structural sentences had been paragraphed separately, as would have been logical, what was left of each would have been a coordinate sequence without a topic sentence. The five subtopics of the second part were portioned out to three paragraphs—3, 1, 1. The controlling consideration here must have been physical; the paragraphs came out about of a length. The last paragraph was a conclusion.

Another observation concerns the topic sentence, a subject of much unwarranted abuse. A better term might be *lead sentence* or *thesis sentence*. I have used *topic* so that I could call it the *top* sentence of the sequence and describe it as the one the other sentences depend from, the one they develop or amplify, the one they are a comment on. This, I submit, is a better key to the structure of the paragraph than the common notion that the topic sentence is the most general or the most abstract sentence of the paragraph. It is difficult to gauge the relative generality or abstractness of the sentences of a paragraph, and the attempt to do so has led to finding topic sentences all up and down the paragraph—at beginning or end or between or at both ends. Many of these sentences are the extrasequential transitions or conclusions that I have described. But some are not; they are part of the sequence. In saying this, I have to give up the notion implicit in the principle of levels of generality that *each* sentence in a paragraph is less general or abstract than the one it is added to. The trend of the added sentences is toward the concrete and specific. In a coordinate sequence, the coordinate sentences are at the same level of generality, and the set is at a lower level than the topic sentence. But in a subordinate sequence one simply cannot maintain that each is at a lower level of generality than the one above it. This is another way of saying that the common notion of paragraph movement as deductive (most general sentence at the beginning) or inductive (most general sentence at the end) or a combination of the two (most general sentence at both ends or in the middle) is not fruitful, except of confusion.

Suggestions for Further Reading

In addition to *Notes Toward a New Rhetoric,* the reader should be aware of the following works by Christensen:
The Christensen Rhetoric Program. New York: Harper & Row, 1968.
"The Problem of Defining a Mature Style." *The English Journal* 57 (April 1968).

A considerable literature concerning Christensen's work has developed:

Bond, Charles A. "A New Approach to Freshman Composition: A Trial of the Christensen Method." *College English* 33 (March 1972), 623–27.

Christensen, Bonniejean. "Francis Christensen, a Personal View—Teacher, Scholar, Friend, Master-Student of the Language." *California English Journal* 8 (April 1972), 30–37.

————. "Strictures on Mrs. Johnson's Strictures." *College English* 31 (May 1970), 878–81.

Grady, Michael. "A Conceptual Rhetoric of the Composition." *College Composition and Communication* 22 (December 1971), 348–54.

Johnson, Sabina Thorne. "Some Tentative Strictures on Generative Rhetoric." *College English* 31 (November 1969), 155–65.

Palmer, William S. "What Yolly, Willy, and Harriet Learned to Do—The Free Modifier: A Fresh Mode of Teaching Composition." *California English Journal* 7 (December 1971), 17–28.

Shearer, Ned A. "Alexander Bain and the Genesis of Paragraph Theory." *Quarterly Journal of Speech* 58 (December 1972), 408–17.

Tibbetts, A. M. "On the Practical Uses of a Grammatical System: A Note on Christensen and Johnson." *College English* 31 (May 1970), 870–78.

Walker, Robert L. "The Common Writer: A Case for Parallel Structure." *College Composition and Communication* 21 (December 1970), 373–79.

Walshe, R. D. "Report on a Pilot Course on the Christensen Rhetoric Program." *College English* 32 (April 1971), 783–89.

Style

For the purposes of this discussion, stylistics (the study of style) will be divided into two categories that will be handy, though not necessarily mutually exclusive nor even logically defensible. *Pedagogical stylistics,* as the term implies, deals with teaching students to develop style, and *theoretical stylistics* is concerned with definitions, the place of style in literary studies, and so on.

Pedagogical Stylistics

For the moment, let's assume that there is something called style and that we know in a fairly precise way what it is. This being the case, we can divide style into two parts: structure and editing. Structure concerns, primarily, the surface syntax of sentences and, particularly, the ways whereby propositions are embedded. Editing concerns such surface features as spelling, punctuation, verb agreement, and so on. Structure is obviously more fundamental and more interesting than editing. Even though a badly edited text may fail in its purpose (whatever that might be), nonetheless, the "cleaning up" of editing (or teaching a student to punctuate and spell) is not so basic a matter as dealing with the structures of sentences is. Paradoxically, however, it might be an easier matter to teach structure than editing.

If modern linguistic theory is correct—and there is plenty of evidence that it is, on the following point at least—then a high-school or college student who is a native speaker enters his composition class with virtually a total knowledge of his language. That is to say, his competence is total even though his performance may be "substandard." It would seem, then, that the job of the composition teacher is not to "teach" structure, but to activate competence so that it spills over into the area of performance.

How does the teacher go about activating? In the first place, we now have extremely valuable theories and materials that are ready to be applied to this problem. In this connection, one thinks of the work of Francis Christensen,[1] John Mellon,[2] and Frank O'Hare.[3] As discussions that appear in this section indicate, we now have a useful and productive "technology" for teaching sentence structure. (Is the following account unfair? The teaching of structure *in the typical composition class* involves the teacher's noting—in red— on the margins of themes "Your prose is choppy" or "Vary your sentence structure" or "Your sentences are too long" or "Awkward," leaving students to figure out as best they can what steps they will take to remedy the fault.) The question is not "Should we use the technology?" for that is merely a fatuous query, but "How should we use this technology?"

The question boils down to this: Should we or should we not program? Should we or should we not run students through a series of exercises designed to activate their competence? In answering this question, it is well to remember that no sentence—no language use—is "good" or "bad" out of the context of purpose, audience, time, and place. Therefore, in the absolute sense, a syntactically mature sentence is no better and no worse than one that is immature.

I am most reluctant to criticize the really productive work done by Christensen, Mellon, and O'Hare (and others), but their weakness does lie in having taken the business of activating syntactic competence out of the rhetorical situation, hermetically sealing it in a series of exercises that have only a tangential relationship to the real use of language. Perhaps it was necessary for their purposes that they achieve this isolation, but the teacher who uses their work should consider the consequences of isolating syntax from purpose and audience.

It seems to me that the skilled teacher can use modern theories and techniques within the rhetorical situation, by working with the sentences that students produce in their own writings—writings that attempt (we should hope) to convey ideas to an audience for a purpose—and by analyzing the structures that other writers use and relating these structures to the effects that those writers achieve. Thus the business of "teaching" sentence structure will have all of the glorious and productive *lack of system* that characterizes most real language learning tasks.

Perhaps I am merely succumbing to my own prejudices here, but I do feel that systematic exercises have no place in the composition class.

Theoretical Stylistics

To survey the various definitions of style that have accrued throughout the centuries is beyond the purpose of the present discussion. However, most

[1] *Notes Toward a New Rhetoric* (New York: Harper & Row, 1967).

[2] *Transformational Sentence-Combining* (Champaign, Ill.: NCTE, 1969).

[3] *Sentence Combining: Improving Student Writing without Formal Grammar Instruction* (Urbana, Ill.: NCTE, 1973).

current definitions fall into one of two categories: (a) style as choice among alternative expressions and (b) style as deviation from a norm. The first notion is expressed by Rulon Wells:

> So far as the writer of English has a choice, what he writes is *his* diction and *his* style; so far as he has none, it is the English language.[4]

And the second is expressed by Charles E. Osgood:

> . . . Style is defined as an individual's deviations from norms for the situations in which he is encoding, these deviations being in the statistical properties of those structural features for which there exists some degree of choice in his code.[5]

Particularly common in the past decade, the view that style consists in the options that language offers its users has serious flaws that make it less than useful for both the theoretician and the teacher. If, for instance, we take the deep structure of a sentence, as diagramed below,

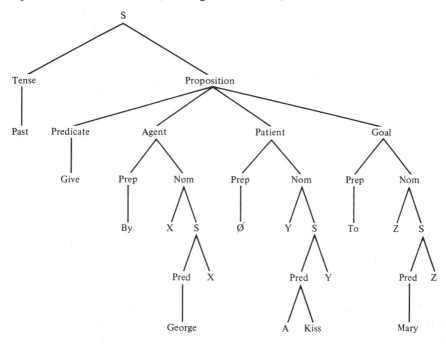

we can ask, "Where does choice end, and where do the inflexible laws of the language begin?" These are telling questions. For instance, which of the two statements on the following page more nearly represents the "norm" that might develop from the deep structure that is diagramed?

[4] Thomas A. Sebeok, ed., "Nominal and Verbal Style," *Style in Language* (New York: John Wiley and Sons, 1960), p. 215.
[5] "Some Effects of Motivation on the Style of Encoding," *Style in Language,* p. 293.

(1) George gave a kiss to Mary.
(2) George gave Mary a kiss.

Is the active or the passive the more "normal," and, in any case, which of the following passives is more "normal" than the others?

(3) A kiss was given to Mary by George.
(4) Mary was given a kiss by George.

Or even:

(5) What Mary was given was a kiss by George.

In other words, the problem of separating the "normal" from the extranormal becomes extremely complex—and finally not worthwhile!

A slightly different angle on the subject could possibly clear up some of the problems of deciding where choice is exercised. "Classical" transformational generative grammar divides rules into two sorts, those that are obligatory and those that are not. From this point of view, the indirect object inversion transformation is clearly not obligatory, and it and others like it might be called "stylistic transformations." But even here significant problems arise.

If one accepts Charles Fillmore's premise that deep structures are basically a group of cases or roles related to a predicate and to a sentence "modality," [6] then the concept of obligatory versus nonobligatory rules becomes meaningless. For instance, the diagram on page 255 is an abbreviated deep structure diagram for a variety of synonymous sentences, as, for example, the five sentences listed above. These various surface structures eventuate from the application of rules of subjectivization, objectivization, and so on. Thus, if from the deep structure in the diagram I choose to subjectivize Mary, a passive is automatically triggered, but one cannot say that the passive transformation is nonobligatory. From the point of view of case grammar, all transformations are obligatory. (It is important to note that the diagram on page 255 does not imply a syntactic linearity in the deep structure. The rule underlying deep structures as represented in case grammar—S → Modality + Proposition—has quite different consequences from the rule underlying deep structures as represented by the "classical" Chomskian grammar, namely, S → NP + Aux + VP.)

Thus, if one takes the model of case grammar for the analysis of style, the notion of choice becomes somewhat vacuous. One merely surveys the transformations that appear.

There are telling arguments, also, against the notion of style as deviation from a norm. The most obvious objection is the difficulty of first defining and then describing the norm. Though I would assume that the following three sentences have the same deep structure (and hence the same meaning), I would hesitate to say that one is the norm or that there is a norm that comes about from some kind of obligatory transformation:

[6] Emmon Bach and Robert T. Harms, eds., "The Case for Case," *Universals in Linguistic Theory* (New York: Holt, Rinehart and Winston, 1968).

(1) That he wears gloves is funny.
(2) For him to wear gloves is funny.
(3) His wearing gloves is funny.

In regard to style as deviation, Rosengren points out that "the main effect . . . is gained by violation of rules of some underlying system. This type of style can be recognized without any comparison among texts. The norm must consist of the grammatical system, syntactic and semantic rules . . . or any other system in relation to which the deviation is recognized." [7]

It is worthwhile, however, to examine the consequences of accepting the notion that style lies in the occurrences of deviations from some norm, whether that norm be a system of grammar or a body of texts that have been surveyed to determine a statistical norm. Namely, the concept of style as deviation leads us to the conclusion that some texts have more style than others or that some texts have no style whatsoever, and such a viewpoint is valid only in the metaphorical sense, as when Pope speaks of "character":

> Nothing so true as what you once let fall,
> "Most women have no character at all."
> Matter too soft a lasting mark to bear,
> And best distinguished by black, brown, or fair.

That is, every text is describable; therefore, insofar as style and describability coincide, every text has style.

But with the introduction of the concept "describability," another significant problem arises; namely, what is it we are to describe when we describe style?

This question, at first glance, might seem vacuous, for we can answer that we will describe the word usages and structures of a text, of an author's whole corpus, of a period, or whatever. But, of course, we can reduce style even further, and say that it is nothing but black squiggles on a white background or patterned excitations of air molecules. Style does not become style until it is perceived, just as meaning is not immanent, but is constructed by a reader or hearer.

Speech act theory provides a way of understanding—if not unravelling—the complexities of what we mean when we say that a stretch of language has style. (Every stretch of language must have style in the sense that it will have features that you can "point at.")

According to John Searle, a fully consummated speech act will have the following elements: an *utterance act,* the mere uttering of words or morphemes or strings of them; a *propositional act,* which consists of referring and predicating; an *illocutionary act,* which has to do with intention (such as promising, threatening, stating, etc.); and a *perlocutionary act,* which has to do with effect on a hearer (convincing, frightening, deterring, etc.).[8] To take a simple example, if I say to my wife, "You are beautiful," I have performed the utterance act of saying the words *you are beautiful;* I have performed the

---

[7] Inger Rosengren, "Style as Choice and Deviation," *Style* 6 (Winter 1972), 13–18.
[8] *Speech Acts* (Cambridge, England: Cambridge University Press, 1969).

propositional act of predicating *beauty* of the referring expression *you;* I have performed the illocutionary act of *stating;* I have (perhaps) performed the perlocutionary act of *convincing*. Notice, however, that my illocutionary intention of *stating* might be misinterpreted. For instance, my wife might think I am being ironic, in which case, the perlocutionary act will not be *convincing*, but might well be *insulting*.

Speech act theory, like most linguistic theory, has to do with single sentences, not what might be called discourses. Therefore, to apply the theory strictly to units of discourse beyond the sentence does a certain violence to the theory—blurs the fairly sharp edges that have been worked out by Searle and others. But if we view the theory as a heuristic or a method of generating knowledge concerning style and do not make excessive claims for an "extended" theory, we can gain some valuable insights.

Suppose, for instance, keeping sharply in mind what we are doing, we view Andrew Marvell's poem "To His Coy Mistress" as a speech act (which it is) and apply speech act theory to it (which we can do only in a loose way).

Viewed as an utterance act, the poem is, first, a series of marks on paper (for an utterance need not have meaning; I can perform an utterance act without meaning anything and without my utterance having the potential for meaning). It is, furthermore, a systematic collocation of morphemes, words, immediate constituents, clauses, sentences, and stanzas—all of which can be reliably "pointed to" (named, classified, counted, etc.).

The propositional act is what the poem is "about"; in this case, the poem is about the brevity of life and the consequent necessity to enjoy sensual pleasures while one can. If the proposition of the poem is reduced to the appropriate cliché, something of the nature of poetry as a conveyor of meaning is revealed. The appropriate cliché is, of course, "let's make hay while the sun shines." In what sense is this a proposition? To what does it refer, and what does it predicate? The main clause predicates, to be sure, with "make," but in what sense can "hay" be called a referring term? One of the axioms for reference is the following:

> A necessary condition for the successful performance of a definite reference in the utterance of an expression is that either the utterance of that expression must communicate to the hearer a description true of, or a fact about, one and only one object, or if the utterance does not communicate such a fact the speaker must be able to substitute an expression, the utterance of which does.[9]

Notice how neatly an expression can be substituted for "hay": "use of every moment of our lives." (Let's make use of every moment of our lives.) It is precisely this sort of substitution that constitutes our knowledge about the meaning of any work of literature, as when we answer the question "What is the work about?" For instance, *Heart of Darkness* is only at the most superficial level "about" Marlow's adventures; more profoundly, it is about colo-

[9] Ibid., p. 80.

nialism; even more profoundly, it is about the darkness of the human heart; and so on.

The existential poem as an illocutionary act is, of course, a terribly interesting subject, one that could take us into dimly lit corridors of the maze of interpretation, and also into the perilous territory of the intentional fallacy. We will not ask the question "What did the poet intend?" Rather we will consider two simple (but not simple-minded) examples.

> Murphy first encounters the poem in a collection of writings that is entitled *The Techniques of Courtship and Marriage.*
> Murgatroyd first encounters the poem in an anthology entitled *Great Love Poems of the Western World.*

Now note the following paradox carefully. After reading the poem, Murphy mutters to himself, "Marvell didn't know much about courtship and marriage, but he certainly created an exquisite work of art." Murgatroyd, however, says, "Hell, with that stupid line, Marvell could never make out."

In other words, it is almost—or even quite—impossible not to approach a literary work as if it were an illocutionary act of a given kind, and it is totally impossible that a literary work not have perlocutionary force.

In summary, the work itself is nothing but black marks (utterance act) that have the potential to be meaningful (propositional act); the reader himself will ascribe an intention to the work (illocutionary act) and will in some way be affected by the work (perlocutionary act). This is, basically, a useful oversimplification, since the ascribed intention is usually many-faceted and response is always very complex. Is *Heart of Darkness* an adventure story, a psychological thriller, a moral tale, a political commentary? From my point of view, it is all four.

Of course, what we must do here is separate "reading act" from "speech act." In the speech act, the speaker (as writer) ascribes or predicts effect on the basis of his intention. In the reading act, the reader ascribes intention on the basis of his attitude toward the text (as sociology, fiction, history, polemic, etc.) and on the basis of the effect that he derives from the text. (In other words, if the reader comes to the poem as a treatment of psychosexual hang-ups, he will view the poem as a treatment of such, and, after he has read the poem, he will form conclusions such as: "The poet obviously wasn't up on his Freud"; "The poet did a good job of capturing the way in which the sexual urge overcomes reason"; "The poet is a lousy psychologist, but he did a good job of making me feelingly aware of the brevity of life.")

Of course, we are not here interested in exploring the ramifications of speech act theory, except insofar as it raises the question "What is style?" Clearly style is not merely propositional acts, since all of the following, as Searle points out, have the same propositional content:

(1) Sam smokes habitually.
(2) Does Sam smoke habitually?

(3) Sam, smoke habitually!

(4) Would that Sam smoked habitually.

The reference in all four sentences is "Sam," and the predication is "smoke."

Nor can we say that style is merely the illocutionary act, for we can never be certain of intention. And surely if we say that style is the perlocutionary act, we have involved ourselves in a solipsistic reduction.

We can all agree that "style is what we perceive in discourse," but that definition leaves us exactly where we began. What, indeed, do we perceive in discourse?

Well, for one thing, we can all agree that before we speak of style there must be a discourse, produced in a language that we understand. We must further agree that there must be—at a minimum—features that we can "point to." (It is perfectly conceivable that there could be an imaginary discourse which was never uttered or written and that we could, quite rightly, feel that its style was excellent. Yet, if we wanted to discuss the style of the discourse, we would be compelled to make it manifest by either uttering or writing it so that someone else could *see* or *hear* it. In other words, we would need to render it in such a way that it could be pointed to.) For style to exist there must be at least the propositional act: a sentence or a series of sentences.

The discussion will now progress to a systematic taxonomy of the features of style. What, in style, can we point at, and how should we go about pointing? For teachers of writing, the value of "pointing at" should be obvious. The teacher is able to point at features of the student's own writing and at features of the writing that the student is "imitating."

For the purposes of our discussion, we will say that the utterance act and the propositional act constitute the locutionary act. The locutionary act is merely a sentence or a string of sentences, however long. There is a strangeness to this procedure, for it is saying that real discourse can be without purpose or effect, which is on the face of it an absurdity. It is viewing discourse as an artifact, and thus falsifying it. Suppose that an archeologist were to uncover some strange object, apparently the product of human beings but totally without "meaning" to the discoverer. In his notes he could only describe it: its dimensions, coloration, composition, and so on. In our terms, the locutionary act is just such an artifact.

To be maximally useful, an analytical schema must meet certain criteria. It must be (1) simple enough that the complexity of its operation does not obscure the purpose of that operation; (2) comprehensive enough to reveal all aspects of its subject; (3) transparent enough that it does not mask any of its subject's features; and (4) theoretically defensible. The schema that is developed in this discussion meets these four criteria.

If the schema herein developed applies only to the locutionary act, one must ask, nonetheless, what the components of the locutionary act are. And all aspects of the locutionary act can be subsumed under *transformations, lexicon,* and *figures of thought* (that is, such figures as metaphor, irony, and litotes, as opposed to such figures as chiasmus, asyndeton, or alliteration) that make up the sentences of the act. It will be noted that such features of style as transcend the sentence are excluded from the schema and would, presumably, be handled at another level of analysis—for it is *not* claimed that the schema herein outlined will generate all of the data that one might desire concerning style.

In outline, the schema looks like this:

Transformations	*Lexicon*	*Figures of Thought*
Intersentence	Parts of speech	
Embedding	Structure words	
Subordinating		
Conjunction		
Intrasentence		

Ideally, transformations are the devices whereby sentences are generated. In practice, we can say that they are the "rules" whereby we can explain the evolution of a sentence from a theoretical deep structure to the surface structure. It is not necessary to argue in behalf of transformational generative grammar, for the purpose of stylistic analysis is to discover a significant number of differentiae so that the style of *A* can be contrasted with the style of *B* and described in exact terms. No one, I think, would argue that traditional or structural grammar offers the possibility of finding more differentiae in a given passage than does transformational generative grammar. On this subject, Louis Milic says:

> In his syntax, the writer is expressing himself more fully than in his vocabulary. Can it be because he does not realize that he is doing so, blinded as he is by the overwhelming semantic luster of the words? It is no mere accident that *style* has always had *diction* as a synonym. However interesting the study of vocabulary may be for other uses, in eliciting the personal, unconscious style, it must be set aside in favor of grammar.[10]

And to this, I would subjoin the notion that the most important devices of grammar, the most fundamental to style, are the ones whereby sentences are conjoined by embedding, subordination, and conjunction.

In order that there be no misunderstanding, I would like to explain and illustrate my somewhat specialized uses of the terms "embedding," "subordination," and "conjunction."

By embedding, I mean all sentence-combining devices *except* those that create adverb clauses and those that coordinate independent clauses. Typical devices of embedding are the following:

> *Clause, gerund, and infinitive complementization:*
>   (1) It is tragic *that George guzzles gin.*
>   (2) *That George guzzles gin* is tragic.

[10] *A Quantitative Approach to the Style of Jonathan Swift* (The Hague: Mouton & Co., 1967), p. 79.

(3) It's tragic, *George's guzzling of gin.*

(4) *George's guzzling of gin* is tragic.

(5) It's tragic *for George to guzzle gin.*

(6) *For George to guzzle gin* is tragic.

Relativization and the constructions that develop from it:

(7) The team *that is winning the game* is jubilant.

(8) The team *winning the game* is jubilant.

(9) The riffle *which is just out of reach* contains the biggest trout.

(10) The riffle *just out of reach* contains the biggest trout.

Noun phrase complements:

(11) I know (that) *my Redeemer liveth.*

(12) *Whoever comes late* misses supper.

A diagram of a sentence with a two-level embedding looks like this:

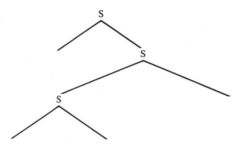

Since under subordination I include only those operations that create adverb clauses, diagramatically the sentences so combined might be represented thus:

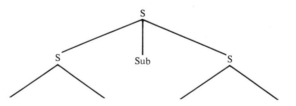

And, of course, clause coordination looks like this:

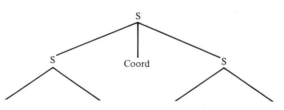

There is, however, one problem with this system of classification; namely, what to do with "reduced" coordinations. For instance,

(13) Paul likes to fish.

and

(14) Paul doesn't like to drink.

can be coordinated:

(15) Paul likes to fish, but he doesn't like to drink.

There is another alternative, however:

(16) Paul likes to fish, but doesn't like to drink.

and yet another:

(17) Paul likes to fish, but not to drink.

Does a sentence such as (17) fit the diagram in Figure 3 or that in Figure 5? At one point in its development, it clearly fits Figure 5, but it metamorphoses itself, with coordinate reduction transformations, so that in an intermediate structure it fits Figure 3. That is, conjunction reduction transformations are embedding transformations. Though I hesitate to enter the quagmire of speculation about coordination, it is clear enough that there is a basic structural difference between coordinated clauses and the reduction of those clauses:

(18) The Montana furry trout eats worms, and it thrives in cold water.
(19) The Montana furry trout eats worms. And it thrives in cold water.
(20) The Montana furry trout eats worms and thrives in cold water.[11]

There are, of course, a great variety of intrasentence transformations, including such common ones as the *passive,*

(21) Worms are eaten by the Montana furry trout.

and the *cleft sentence,*

(22) What are eaten by the Montana furry trout are worms.

It is not the purpose of this discussion to catalogue the intrasentence and intersentence transformations. They exist in great variety and belong, properly, not to a discussion of an analytical schema but to a treatment of the grammar of English.

However, it is worthwhile to call attention to the auxiliary, and it is useful to refer back to "primitive" transformational generative theory in relation to AUX. The old, rule-centered grammar presented a composite and accurate system for classifying such functions on the sentence-as-a-whole as tense, aspect, and modal. In fact, an extremely simple list of rules allows handy classification of all the stylistic features that develop from AUX. Those rules, it will be remembered, are:

[11] In effect, clause coordination is of a different order than reduced coordination, for clause coordination joins transformational units. Rephrased in "natural" language, all of this turns out to be much less complicated than its jargonistic expression would indicate. Basically, the point is that coordinate clauses can be punctuated as independent sentences, but when those clauses are reduced they cannot be separated by sentence punctuation. Thus: Herman smokes, and he drinks. / Herman smokes. And he drinks. / Herman smokes and drinks. But not: Herman smokes. And drinks.

$$\text{Aux}\rightarrow\text{Tense (Modal) (Aspect)}$$

$$\text{Tense}\rightarrow\left\{\begin{array}{l}\text{Present}\\\text{Past}\end{array}\right\}$$

Modal→Can, May, Must, Shall, Will

Aspect→(Have + Past Part) (Be + Pres Part)

This brief and simple rubric allows for the systematic analysis of everything that develops from the auxiliary, and if anyone doubts the importance of the AUX in stylistic analysis, it is necessary only to mention historical present to indicate that AUX is, indeed, crucial in style.

It should be noted that surveys of transformations in a text will automatically generate data, for the surveys will be based upon a more or less complete set of rules that will be catalogued. The completeness of the transformational phase of the stylistic analysis depends, of course, upon the completeness of the syntactic component of the grammar.

There is little that the present discussion can add to the general understanding of lexicon. To be sure, the student of style should keep in mind Charles C. Fries's distinction between parts of speech and function words,[12] and just as surely the subcategorized semantic features of nouns will be important. Milic says that vocabulary is a relatively unstable aspect of the writer's prose.

> For one thing, the vocabulary is strongly affected by the type and subject matter of a piece of writing. Two sermons by different writers may have more words in common than a sermon and a romance by the same writer. It follows that the study of a writer's vocabulary, though it may be informative about his reading (for instance), is likely to be useless as a criterion of identification.[13]

We sense almost intuitively, however, that a writer's use of function words is more likely to be consistent and probably reveals more about his characteristic style than does his choice of parts of speech. For instance, the following sentence by James Baldwin is almost palpably prepositional:

(23) I read about it in the paper in the subway on my way to work.

Compare the Baldwin sentence with one by James Joyce:

(24) The raisins and almonds and figs and apples and oranges and chocolates and sweets were now passed about the table, and Aunt Julia invited all the guests to have either port or sherry.

Joyce's sentence can be characterized as "conjunctional."

It will be recalled that Fries lists fifteen categories of function words. Whether or not Fries's catalogue is accurate need not concern us here. The point is that the analyst must separate the open classes from the closed classes in the lexicon. (Is there not even the possibility that the lexicon should

---

[12] *The Structure of English* (New York: Harcourt Brace Jovanovich, 1952).
[13] *A Quantitative Approach to the Style of Jonathan Swift,* p. 138.

consist only of the four parts of speech? For instance, prepositions are only case markers that occur in the deep structure of propositions with nouns. Are not conjunctions, both coordinating and subordinating, relation markers that somehow surface with various transformations?)

At any rate, the point at which one begins to analyze function words is obviously where transformations and lexicon overlap, for a preposition occurs only in a prepositional phrase, and conjunctions occur only when clauses are conjoined, though, of course, the conjoined clauses can be reduced.

As has been said earlier, in the analytical schema, only figures of thought will be considered, for figures of grammar will come under analysis as transformations.

There are some obvious problems with this formulation, however. A variety of figures—both of grammar and of thought—extend beyond the sentence (and, more important, beyond the transformational unit). For instance, *anadiplosis* (repetition of an important word contained in one clause in a succeeding clause) can work either between clauses or between sentences, depending entirely upon punctuation.

> Fight to be *free,* but be *free* of fear.

> For I have loved long, I crave reward
> Reward me not unkindly: think on kindness,
> Kindness becommeth those of high regard
> Regard with clemency a poor man's blindness. . . .[14]

Another problem of the same sort is where metaphor ends and allegory begins. Or, how irony and allegory relate:

> . . . Irony and allegory ought to bear some relation, since irony is clearly a particular, 180–degree reversed, instance of allegory's double meaning. That is, the ironist depends on an allegorical habit of mind in his reader, a habit that will juxtapose surface and real meanings.[15]

One less than satisfactory solution is to decide arbitrarily that figures in style—as opposed to figures in metastyle—occur only within the bounds of T-units. The other, and more unsatisfactory solution, is to set no boundaries, to rely upon the intuition and sensitivity of the analyst.

No other alternatives presenting themselves, we opt for the first and state arbitrarily that figures in style do not extend beyond the T-unit—whether those figures are structurally recognizable or not, that is, whether they are figures of grammar or figures of thought. And, since figures of grammar within the T-unit are analyzed under transformations, we are left with figures of thought within the T-units as the only stylistic figures.

A word about metaphor, certainly the most important of the figures, is in order. One of the most useful discussions of that figure that I have encountered

---

[14] Bartholomew Griffin, *Fidessa,* XVI, quoted in Richard A. Lanham, *A Handlist of Rhetorical Terms* (Berkeley and Los Angeles: University of California Press, 1968), p. 7.
[15] Ibid., pp. 61–62.

is by Rosemarie Gläser.[16] What she points out is that each noun has built into it certain semantic features. For instance, "boy" has the feature +human, as does "man." If, then, we say "A boy is a young man," we have no sense of metaphor, because metaphor comes about when semantic features are disjunctive. "Homer is a lion in battle" is metaphorical because "Homer" has the feature +human, and "lion" has the feature −human. The strangeness and appeal of "Happiness is a warm blanket" must come about because "happiness" has the feature −concrete and "blanket" has the feature +concrete.

Finally, I would like to say a word about the usefulness of this schema. That it does serve as a useful procedural basis for analysis seems to me to be beyond doubt. Traditional approaches to style were based either on some variation of the modes of discourse or on categories of grammar and rhetoric. For instance, here is the table of contents of Bonamy Dobrée's *Modern Prose Style:* [17]

> *Part I. Descriptive Prose:* 1. Description of Action (Narrative). 2. Description of People. 3. Description of Things.
> *Part II. Explanatory Prose:* 1. Science. 2. Law. 3. Philosophy. 4. Morals. 5. Theology. 6. Political Science. 7. History. 8. Criticism.
> *Part III. Emotive Prose:* Rousing the Emotions.
> *Part IV. Modern Prose Style:* 1. The New Way of Writing. 2. Experiments.

Herbert Read's *English Prose Style* [18] is divided into two sections, Composition (Words, Epithets, Metaphor and Other Figures of Speech, The Sentence, The Paragraph, Arrangement) and Rhetoric (Exposition, Narrative, Fantasy, Imagination or Invention, Impressionism, Eloquence, Unity).

Louis T. Milic points out that vocabulary, a relatively superficial aspect of style, is connected with discourse at what might be termed the rhetorical level, while syntax, in which "the writer is expressing himself more fully than in his vocabulary," is at the expressive level.[19] The implication seems to be that analysis of style should deal with vocabulary and syntax.

These three examples of schemata pretty well exhaust the general kinds of frameworks that have been used for stylistic analysis—except, perhaps, the "impressionistic," in which one attempts to characterize one's reaction to the style rather than the style itself.[20]

---

[16] "The Application of Transformational Generative Grammar to the Analysis of Similes and Metaphors in Modern English," *Style* 5 (Fall 1971), 265–83.

[17] 2nd ed. (Oxford: The Clarendon Press, 1964).

[18] (Boston: Beacon Press, 1955.)

[19] *A Quantitative Approach to the Style of Jonathan Swift.*

[20] In *Grammar as Style* (New York: Holt, Rinehart and Winston, 1971), my friend and colleague Virginia Tufte says (pp. 2–3), "In the summer of 1966, I conducted an experiment at the NDEA Institute at the University of California, Los Angeles, asking forty-four college and high school English teachers to jot down a half-dozen words or phrases they would use to describe the style and tone of thirty sentences, the opening of Truman Capote's *In Cold Blood*. Their lists included 222 different adjectives, and there was only one adjective that was used by as many as twelve of the teachers. These are some of the words they used: *plain, elaborate, formal, informal, detailed, general, specific, objective, matter-of-fact, stylized, literary, poetic. . . ."

Each of these theoretical stances has weaknesses that are worth brief mention. An analytical schema based on the modes is more classificatory than analytical. It also fails to meet some of the criteria for usefulness. In the first place, it is not comprehensive enough to reveal all aspects of its subject, for there is in practice almost no such thing as "pure" narrative, exposition, and so on. As his first example of narrative (he calls it "description of action"), Dobrée quotes from Herbert Read's *The Sense of Glory:*

> I've forgotten that walk: it was only about two miles, but our utter dejection induced a kind of unconsciousness in us. It would be between ten and eleven o'clock when we got to Roye. I reported to a staff officer, who sent me off to the town major to get billets. The town major I found distracted, unable to say where I should find a billet. Apparently the town was packed with stragglers. We peered into two great gloomy marquees, floored densely with recumbent men. Meanwhile two other officers joined me with their men, and together we went off to search on our own. We found a magnificent house, quite empty, and here we lodged the men. Some kind of rations had been found. They soon had blazing wood fires going, and seemed happy in a way.[21]

One might say that if one is looking for the characteristic feature of narrative style, a good deal in the example passage must be ignored, for quite typically intermingled with the implied "then . . . and then . . . and then" of narrative is both description and exposition.

In the second place, a schema based on the modes is theoretically indefensible, for it does not address the question of style versus subject matter, of form versus content. In fact, the schema seems to lead to something like this: "Ah, it seems that I can classify this piece as narrative. I shall now proceed to look for narrative features in it." Though I am not attempting to set up a straw man, and though I think Dobrée's work has great virtue in its own way, the general tone of *Modern Prose Style* can, I think, be fairly characterized by the following quotation:

> But then prose can only be plain when it deals with plain things, as normally with Defoe; if, for instance, the story to be told has to do with very complicated emotional and intellectual states, the prose is bound to be complicated; the classic instance might be Marcel Proust's great work. . . .[22]

The method in *Modern Prose Style,* then, is to start from highly general assumptions about how prose should work and to make a series of somewhat haphazard and fairly generalized remarks about various passages that fit the modal category.

Paradoxically, though Herbert Read's *English Prose Style* is inferior to Dobrée's *Modern Prose Style,* Read's schema is theoretically sounder than Dobrée's. Analysis of words, epithets (i.e., adjectivals), metaphor and other figures of speech, the sentence, the paragraph, and arrangement is likely to

[21] Dobrée, pp. 17–18.
[22] Ibid., p. 16.

yield valuable data. But, nonetheless, this schema, similar to countless others, leaves much to be desired. It tends to mask some aspects of style. For instance, it is clear that metaphor is of a different order from some other figures of speech, such as chiasmus, in that chiasmus can be analyzed structurally, whereas metaphor cannot. Read's schema is not comprehensive enough to reveal all aspects of its subject; for instance, it does not take into account the crucial intricacies of the auxiliary.

Of course, negative criticism is easy, but the intent here has not been vandalistic. I have attempted to show certain weaknesses in typical analytical approaches to style. I do not mean to use Read, Dobrée, and Milic as straw men, but they are exemplary of both the theoretical and practical need for a rigorously defined analytical schema.

The schema that I have outlined does, as a matter of fact, automatically generate the empirically verifiable, crucial data concerning locutionary style. Using transformational generative grammar as its model, it traces the development of each sentence from a hypothetical deep structure to a surface structure, and in so doing catalogues the transformations that the process involves. Furthermore, the schema deals with vocabulary and figurative language. And it is worth mentioning that the schema would be tremendously useful in computer assisted studies, for it would generate quantitative data with which the computer could work. Of course, the schema makes relatively modest claims and ignores a very great deal of what every reader conceives of and experiences as style.

Since the schema does systematically cover all of the territory claimed for it, it serves as an extremely useful pedagogical device. Everyone who has attempted to discuss style with either undergraduates or graduate students must have been impressed with the haphazard way in which most people approach the subject, and certainly the most perceptive students have been frustrated by their inability to get their hands on anything definite when they began to discuss style. The result, in my experience, has been that style is usually discussed casually and impressionistically, almost as an afterthought when the "substance" of the text has been exhausted. The schema outlined in this paper will serve as a heuristic for students who are interested in style, so that they can systematically explore a text and assemble concrete data concerning their sense of its style.

It is worth repeating that this discussion has not attempted to advance theory in stylistic studies. But it is also worth noting that, while arcane speculation goes on, some less heady concerns have been neglected. The whole intent of the discussion just completed has been, really, in the nature of pointing out the obvious, for if one thinks carefully about transformational generative grammar, one sees that it *does* suggest perhaps the best framework for the analysis of style.

As for the organization of this section of *Contemporary Rhetoric,* the first two selections (by Milic and Ohmann) briefly introduce some of the important theoretical considerations in the study of style. The next two selections (by Gläser and Perrine) discuss figurative language (specifically metaphor). Taken together, these four selections might be considered as explorations of theoretical stylistics.

The final three selections are, in effect, introductions to the exciting work that is now being done in practical or pedagogical stylistics. In the first piece, Christensen outlines his concept of the cumulative sentence and free modifiers. This is followed by Sabina Thorne Johnson's critique of Christensen's work. The final piece, by John Mellon, constitutes an overview of the problem of syntactic fluency and the bearing that transformational sentence-combining has on that problem.

Suggestions for Further Reading

THEORETICAL STYLISTICS

Bridgman, Richard. *The Colloquial Style in America*. New York: Oxford University Press, 1966.

Chatman, Seymour, and Samuel R. Levin, eds. *Essays on the Language of Literature*. Boston: Houghton Mifflin, 1967.

Chatman, Seymour, ed. *Literary Style: A Symposium*. New York: Oxford University Press, 1971.

Fish, Stanley E. "What Is Stylistics and Why Are They Saying Such Terrible Things About It?" *Approaches to Poetics*. Seymour Chatman, ed. New York: Columbia University Press, 1973.

Milic, Louis T. "Metaphysics in the Criticism of Style." *College Composition and Communication* 17 (October 1966), 124–29.

————. *Style and Stylistics*. New York: The Free Press, 1967. [bibliography]

————. *Stylists on Style*. New York: Charles Scribner's Sons, 1969. [collection]

Poirier, Richard. *A World Elsewhere: The Place of Style in American Literature*. New York: Oxford University Press, 1966.

Rosengren, Inger. "Style as Choice and Deviation." *Style* 6 (Winter 1972), 3–18.

Sebeok, Thomas A., ed. *Style in Language*. New York: MIT Press and John Wiley and Sons, 1960.

Sontag, Susan. "Style." *Against Interpretation*. New York: Dell, 1967.

PEDAGOGICAL STYLISTICS

Bateman, Donald, and Frank Zidonis. *The Effect of a Study of Transformational Grammar on the Writing of Ninth and Tenth Graders*. Champaign, Ill.: National Council of Teachers of English, 1966.

Bond, Charles A. "A New Approach to Freshman Composition: A Trial of the Christensen Method." *College English* 33 (March 1972), 623–27.

Christensen, Bonniejean McGuire. "Strictures on Mrs. Johnson's Strictures." *College English* 31 (May 1970), 878–81.

Christensen, Francis. *The Christensen Rhetoric Program*. New York: Harper & Row, 1968.

————. *Notes Toward a New Rhetoric*. New York: Harper & Row, 1967.

————. "The Problem of Defining a Mature Style." *The English Journal* 57 (April 1968).

Cooper, Charles R. "An Outline for Writing Sentence-Combining Problems." *The English Journal* 62 (January 1973), 96–102; 108.

D'Angelo, Frank J. "Imitation and Style." *College Composition and Communication* 24 (October 1973), 283–90.

Endicott, Anthony L. "A Proposed Scale for Syntactic Complexity." *Research in the Teaching of English* 7 (Spring 1973), 5–12.

Johnson, Sabina Thorne. "A Reply to Mrs. Christensen." *College English* 31 (May 1970), 881–83.

Mellon, John C. *Transformational Sentence-Combining.* Champaign, Ill.: National Council of Teachers of English, 1969.

O'Hare, Frank. *Sentence Combining: Improving Student Writing without Formal Grammar Instruction.* Urbana, Ill.: National Council of Teachers of English, 1973.

The Sentence and the Paragraph. Champaign, Ill.: National Council of Teachers of English, 1966.

FIGURATIVE LANGUAGE

Darian, Steven G. "Similes and the Creative Process." *Language and Style* 6 (Winter 1973), 48–57.

Emig, Janet. "Children and Metaphor." *Research in the Teaching of English* 6 (Fall 1972), 163–75.

Hastings, Arthur. "Metaphor in Rhetoric." *Western Speech* 34 (Summer 1970).

Jordan, William J. "A Reinforcement Model of Metaphor." *Speech Monographs* 39 (August 1972), 223–26.

Loewenberg, Ina. "Truth and Consequences of Metaphors." *Philosophy and Rhetoric* 6 (Winter 1973), 1–29.

Miriam Joseph, Sister. *Shakespeare's Use of the Arts of Language.* New York: Columbia University, 1947.

Paul, Anthony M. "Figurative Language." *Philosophy and Rhetoric* 3 (Fall 1970), 225–48.

————. "Metaphor and the Bounds of Expression." *Philosophy and Rhetoric* 5 (Summer 1972), 143–58.

Pry, Elmer R., Jr. "That 'Grand, Ungodly, God-Like Man': Ahab's Metaphoric Character." *Style* 6 (Spring 1972), 159–78.

Shibles, Warren. *Metaphor: An Annotated Bibliography and History.* Whitewater, Wisc.: The Language Press, 1971.

Wheeless, Lawrence R. "A Functional Theory of Metaphor." *Language and Style* 4 (Fall 1971), 273–78.

The Problem of Style

Louis Tonko Milic

This discussion of the problem of style is obviously not the last word, for it was published in 1967 and stylistic studies have continued with increasing fury since then. However, the piece does have a great many virtues. It is synoptic, but not unduly superficial. It gives one a historical perspective on the study of style, and it introduces the main issues.

Of course, the overwhelmingly central issue in the study of style is the matter-versus-manner controversy, which boils down to the question of whether or not there is such an entity as style. If, as the "unitarians" claim, each separate collocation of words represents not a different style but a different thought, then what might be called stylistic studies are really the study of the various forms in which ideas are manifested. From this point of view, the sentence (1) Dog is bitten by man *is not a stylistic variant of (2)* Man bites dog, *but is a different thought, a different meaning. It is undeniable that (1) and (2) have different emphases—must have different emphases, for in the first, we have ZYX, and in the second we have XYZ. In both, however, we have the same predication and the same reference, or, to put it another way, the same proposition, that is, the predicate* bite *functioning with two roles, which might be called "agent" and "patient." Thus the proposition in both (1) and (2) is give: Agent (man) Patient (dog). Furthermore, (1) and (2) can both be taken as the same kind of speech act, a statement, which it is unlikely that the following could be, even though they contain the same proposition:*

> *(3) Does man bite dog?*
> *(4) Man doesn't bite dog.*
> *(5) Man, bite dog!*

In other words—without worrying the point to death—common sense tells us that two different sentences can share the same meaning. Therefore, it must be possible to talk of both style and meaning.

The matter-manner controversy, of course, has great importance in pedagogy. If there is no such thing as style, then the teacher can concentrate exclusively on improving the student's ability to think, on the assumption that clear thinking will result in clear writing. On the other hand, if style is a kind of ornamentation for thought, then certainly style can, in theory at least, be taught. But who would bother?

One other way of looking at the matter is perhaps the most rational. Namely, language is structure permeated with meaning, or, to put it another way, the languaging process involves permeating structures with meanings. From this point of view, the job of the teacher is to give the student syntactic competence so that he or she will have command of structures that can be permeated with meanings.

When the author of the recent book, *The Style of Don Juan,*[1] explains his purpose and choice of title, he first makes reference to the classical theory of styles, which he considers important for an understanding of *Don Juan.* But he quickly passes on to the candid admission that he needed a title which did not promise a new or complete interpretation of the poem. He therefore settled on *style,* a term which, aside from its rhetorical connotations, implies an interest in an author's ways of shaping experience, in his vision.[2] In other words, he wanted a title which would not bind him to a precise task but which had the proper semantic aura. The choice he made illustrates one of the problems of style today.

There is much evidence to indicate that the word has become fashionable. A preoccupation with "the origins of the acutely pragmatic national style" [3] is the basis of another book, *The American Style.* In expatiating on this theme, one of the contributors to this work tries to define the matter he is supposed to be investigating: "How men cope with . . . problems as they go about their business reflects what is here called a national style." [4] There is no doubt that the contributors to this volume are indeed studying something. It is possible to guess that they chose to call it *style* because of the vagueness and expressiveness of the word rather than its exact meaning.

If we may judge by the twenty-nine subdivisions of meaning given in the latest edition of Webster's unabridged dictionary,[5] compared with the twenty of the previous edition,[6] it is obvious that the word is not losing its popularity. This apparent increase of nearly fifty per cent does not signify that many new meanings have arisen. Rather, a variety of new applications for existent meanings have developed,[7] as for example to describe the carriage of an ani-

---

[1] George M. Ridenour, *The Style of Don Juan* (New Haven, 1960).

[2] *Ibid.,* pp. x–xii.

[3] Ed. Elting Morison (New York, 1958), p. viii.

[4] W. W. Rostow, "The National Style," *ibid.,* p. 247.

[5] *Webster's Third New International Dictionary* (Springfield, 1961), s.v. *style.*

[6] *Webster's New International Dictionary of the English Language,* Second Edition (Springfield, 1954); this edition was originally published in 1934.

[7] It may also show a greater precision on the part of the new editors in discriminating among closely-related meanings.

mal, the combination of shape and ornament in certain artifacts, or a manner of dancing.[8] The meaning previously cited under "style of life" and labelled *"Psychol."* is now simply listed as one of the senses of style.[9] Some innovation is noticeable under the verb entry ("to style a manuscript") and under the gerund *styling,* in the sense of adding a stylish quality to something.

All this suggests that the modern user of English at least dimly senses the complex and sophisticated notion summarized by the term *style* and its derivatives. Perhaps it appeals to his sense that the mysterious totality which constitutes any real or synthetic organism can only be invoked as a whole, as if it were a tutelary deity. There is in fact more than a hint of reverence for word-magic in the popular use of this term and the notion it represents. But there is scarcely any sense of the relation between matter and manner which is a prerequisite to any mature treatment of the subject.

Surely style needs to be discussed from a more analytical point of view and for this a critical vocabulary is required. Although a number of disciplines are cooperating to this end, a proper vocabulary does not yet exist, at least in English. A good beginning for such an undertaking would be a definition of the term itself.

The material object which gave rise to the complex modern term was the pointed stake, employed in military operations and agriculture, that the Romans called *stilus.*[10] The name also was applied to the pointed tool used to scratch on wax tablets. The use of the same term for two different, though similarly-shaped objects, required no great play of the imagination, but when it was applied to the scratches themselves—to the writing—a metonymic leap of considerable implication had been made. After that, it was an easy step to the whole composition, the assembly of scratches on the wax tablets. But Classical Latin did not progress to the modern sense of the term.[11] That was a development which began in Late Latin and emerged fully only in the modern European languages.[12]

In English, the history of the derivative *style* has followed a similar but more extensive path. The twenty-six items given by the *Oxford English Dictionary* may be divided into three major classes of meaning which arose in order: writing tool, writing or manner of writing, manner or fashion in general. The second of these classes contains the conflicting senses of the word.

The literary meanings of *style* are basically three, with subdivisions. The earliest meaning, which dates from the fourteenth century, is "characteristic

[8] Senses 6a(3), 6b(2), and 4d in *Webster's Third,* s.v. "style," n.

[9] Sense 4c(2).

[10] *Stilus* was later misspelled *stylus* by confusion with the Greek for column.

[11] Charlton T. Lewis and Charles Short, *A New Latin Dictionary* (New York, 1907), s.v. "stilus." This work gives the Classical Latin equivalents as *sermo, oratio, dictio, dicendi, modus, ars, forma.*

[12] Alexander Souter, ed., *A Glossary of Later Latin* (Oxford, 1949), s.v. "stilus," gives the sense "language" and indicates it must not be sought before the third century. Incidentally, *style* is closely related to *stigma, stick, stimulus,* all of which look back to the primary meaning.

manner of expression . . . considered in regard to clearness, effectiveness, beauty and the like," [13] as in "Therefore Petrak writeth / This storie which with heigh stile he enditeth." [14] Manner of composition, in this sense, is equally applicable to a group or literary school, a genre, a nation, a period or an individual, as "Euphuistic style," "Italian style," "ancient style," "Miltonic style." The remaining two senses developed during the Renaissance. First, the word was refined to specify the formal rather than the substantive aspects of literary composition.[15] Then, by a regular process of melioration, it came to mean *good style,* as *poetry* is frequently used to mean *good poetry.*

These three meanings (expression, form of expression, good form) tend in practice to merge and overlap. How much they do may be realized by considering the range of terms used as synonyms for *style: manner, mode, expression, way, language, fashion, diction,* among others. The interaction between these terms and the notion of style is vaguely reciprocal. The trajectory of meaning from pointed stick to modern style, in all its variety, though it may be traced, cannot be accounted for, except in the sketchiest way (metonymy, specialization, melioration). The influences acting upon the users of a language which lead them to adopt this or that variation of meaning at a given time are extremely mysterious. There can be no positive method for reaching the minds of those who have left us no record of their thought. But, by examining the root-metaphors of these synonyms, we may be able to gain some insight into the minds of the modern users of the term. It may be possible, that is, to find the limits of the extension of a term by making a collection of the primitive notions which surround it.

Language and *manner* are very closely related to the physical body of the user of language, one through his tongue (*lingua*) and the other through his hand (*manus*). Both of these buried figures of speech have a continuing life in the consciousness of the modern reader and writer in such expressions as "slip of the tongue," "the hand of the writer," or even, at a slight remove, "the voice of the writer." The writer may also be visualized as taking part in a process. As a maker, he is prefigured in the origin of *poet.* In the process of making (*fashioning*), he is presented as a producer of words, an artisan. *Expression* implies a more laborious process of "squeezing out," recalling a wine-press. *Diction* symbolizes the gap between wordless and verbal statement, its ultimate derivation being from *showing,* presumably by pointing.

More elaborate concepts are concealed in *way* and *mode.* In *way* there is the suggestion of a choice of routes to be travelled from the same origin. The quantitative aspect of *mode* (from *modus,* a measure) reflects a willingness to believe that a man's words are a measure of something about him. All together, these words seems to stress the individual nature of the concept of style, in its origins and its current uses. They may be easily distinguished

---

[13] OED, s.v., "style," n., sense 13.

[14] Chaucer's "Clerk's Tale," 11. 1147-8.

[15] This is what *Webster's Third* describes as "aspects of literary composition as distinguished from content or message" in sense 2a(2), s.v. "style," n.

from two words of related meaning: *system* and *method*. That they are related is emphasized by the presence of the idea of *way* in the word *method*.[16] A method is an investigation after the event. *System,* however, derives from a collection of objects placed together, thus an arrangement of principles. Both of these terms imply a procedure leading to a goal, a notion absent from *style* which is concerned with the way itself. The distinction in exactness is quite evident in the difference between *systematic* and *methodical,* on the one hand, and *stylish,* on the other.

In comparison with such precise terms as *system* and *method, style* has no clear-cut nucleus but rather an outline of amorphous dimensions which tends to collect meanings within itself. In mentalistic phrase, it is a word trying to express the inexpressible. How this situation came about has been documented with etymological data stemming from the ancients. But, as has been seen, they did not use the protean modern term,[17] though they were much concerned with the thing itself. Most of the theories which still govern the thinking of those who worry about style had their origin in Greece and Rome.

The ancient theory of style (Style as ornate form) is probably older than Plato.[18] Of the two modern theories (Style as a reflection of the individual and Style as meaning), the first has its roots in the ancient past and the second is modern. "The theory of ornate form" as Croce has named it,[19] requires a fundamental separation between content and form. Aristotle held this view and, in urging the student of rhetoric to learn not only what to say but also how to say it, clearly implies the independence of thought from its linguistic clothing.[20]

The analogy between applied rhetorical ornament and clothing appropriate to the occasion becomes most evident in the classification of styles practised by the Roman theorists.[21] The author of *Rhetorica ad Herennium,* for example, was supposedly the first to classify styles into the Grand, the Middle,

---

[16] The components of *method* are Greek: *meta,* after; and *hodos,* way.

[17] Its ubiquity is illustrated by the fact that some form of the same word is used in most European languages, e.g.: French *style,* Italian *stile,* Dutch *stijl,* Spanish and Portuguese *estilo,* German and Danish *Stil,* Czech and Polish *styl,* and Norwegian, Swedish, Romanian, Irish, Serbo-Croation, Bulgarian and Russian *stil* (with suitable transliteration).

[18] It may have originated with Plato's teacher, Gorgias, who was born half a century earlier (in 483 B.C.) and who doubtless inherited some ideas from his own predecessors.

[19] Benedetto Croce, *Aesthetic,* tr. D. Ainslie (New York, 1958 [1909]), p. 422.

[20] *Art of Rhetoric,* tr. J. H. Freese, Loeb Classical Library (London, 1926), Bk. III, Ch. 1, p. 345. Aristotle elsewhere shows a belief in the organic unity of the work of art, but his commitment to the ancient view is surely reflected in such a statement as "written speeches owe their effect not so much to the sense as to the style" (p. 349). In this passage, the translator renders *lexis* as *style.*

[21] This view was popular in the eighteenth century: Chesterfield says "Style is the dress of thoughts," *Letters to his Son, Philip Stanhope, Esq.,* 11th ed. (London, 1800), II, 303, in the letter dated November 24, 1749 O.S. William Melmoth cites an unidentified passage from Addison: " 'there is as much difference between comprehending a thought cloathed in Cicero's language and that of an ordinary writer, as between seeing an object by the light of a taper or the light of the sun,' " *Letters on Several Subjects by the Late Sir Thomas Fitzosborne, Bart.* (London, 1748), p. 162.

and the Simple, which are distinguished mainly by diction.[22] Quintilian's extensive and detailed treatise represents the culmination of the rhetorical view of style, with lists of figures of speech and figures of thought.[23] The system espoused by these rhetoricians was based on a belief in ideas unrelated to their form, on a hierarchy of occasions (linked to the hierarchy of styles), on teachability of style from models to the virtual exclusion of individuality, and on the dominance of diction as an expressive feature of style. This system, refined and subtilized, was carried over into the Middle Ages without much change.[24] In fact, this tradition concerning style has had adherents until the nineteenth century, reflected especially in handbooks of rhetoric used in schools.[25]

However influential this theory may have been, exceptions to it existed in the ancient world, and they may have furnished if not the basis at least the sanction for one of the modern theories, style as a reflection of character. Even with uniform education and similar outlook individuals think differently, and this difference is reflected in their mode of expression. Naturally enough, the modern development of this view may be found in the writings of Montaigne, to whose assertion on behalf of the individual we continue to be indebted: "Comme à faire, à dire aussi je suy tout simplement ma forme naturelle . . ."[26] "Est-ce pas ainsi que je parle par tout? me représente-je pas vivement? suffit! J'ay faict ce que j'ay voulu: tout le monde me reconnoit en mon livre, et mon livre en moy."[27] When this is compared with Plato's notion, the distant original of Montaigne's opinion, that virtue will express itself in eloquence (as in graceful dancing),[28] the basic difference between the ancient and modern viewpoints can be detected. The belief has persisted, however, that a thoroughly bad man could not write a good book.[29] Plato's argument seems built out of a belief in the equality of ideals. Thus goodness in the abstract leads to excellence in specialized performance. There is clearly no room for the individual in this system.

What seems at first glance to be a more modern collection of views can

---

[22] *Rhetorica ad Herennium,* tr. Harry Caplan, Loeb Classical Library (London, 1954), Bk. IV, Ch. 8, p. 253.

[23] *Institutio Oratoria,* Bk. IX, passim.

[24] See Charles Sears Baldwin, *Medieval Rhetoric and Poetic* (New York, 1928), pp. 304–5, where a list of figures drawn from the *Rhetorica ad Herennium* is reproduced.

[25] E.g., Richard Whately, *The Elements of Rhetoric* (London, 1828); Alexander Bain, *English Composition and Rhetoric* (London, 1866).

[26] *Essais,* ed. A. Thibaudet (Paris, 1946), Bk. II, Essai 17, p. 625. ["That is to say, also I am quite simply my natural form."]

[27] *Ibid.,* Bk. III, Essai 5, p. 848. ["Is it not thus that I speak elsewhere? Do I not represent myself in a lively manner? Enough! I have done what I wanted to: everyone recognizes me in my book and my book in me."]

[28] *Republic,* tr. Paul Shorey, Loeb Classical Library (London, 1953), Bk. III, Ch. 11, p. 255.

[29] George Orwell addresses himself to an aspect of this question relating to Swift in "Politics *vs.* Literature," in *Selected Essays* (Harmondsworth, 1957), pp. 138 ff. The history of this belief is touched on by M. H. Abrams, *The Mirror and the Lamp* (New York, 1958), p. 229.

be found in Cicero and Seneca. Cicero rejects the theory of set styles in favor of a range arising out of varied subject matter and personal preference.[30] Seneca connects the degeneracy of morals with the corruptions of style (an idea borrowed later by Swift) and even finds the defective character of Maecenas reflected in his faulty style, full of inversions and "surprising thoughts." [31] He seems modern in not only rejecting fixed styles but insisting that style is dominated by usage and changes constantly. After coming as close to a respect for individuality as to admit that errors may not be the result of a debased mind but rather the reflection of a peculiar temperament, Seneca concludes that the soul must be guarded from contamination because it emits expression. A sound soul will produce a vigorous and manly style. This is obviously not very divergent from Plato's conception of the *vir bonus*.[32]

The individualist view has grown steadily since Montaigne, as an increasing number of maxims demonstrates. Pascal's "Quand on voit le style naturel, on est tout étonné et ravi, car on s'attendait de voir un auteur, et on trouve un homme," [33] is less well known, though more pungent, than Buffon's famous dictum. Not "le style est l'homme même," but "le style n'est que l'ordre et le mouvement qu'on met dans ses pensées" [34] represents Buffon's contribution to the growth of the individualist theory. The number of statements of this view after Buffon is large.[35] But the view has become so well established in this century that it has achieved the status of an unconscious (or unspoken) assumption and as a result is no longer stated in axiomatic form. As diluted into the misapplied "Style is the man," it is the predominant popular view, though it coexists at times with the theory of ornate form.[36] No inconsistency seems to be felt by those who hold those essentially inimical opinions, perhaps by reason of the minor importance usually attached to theories of style, since any compromise offering pragmatic satisfaction makes theoretical consistency unnecessary.

The latest modern theory of style, however, involves no compromise what-

---

[30] *Brutus*, tr. G. L. Hendrickson, Ch. XXI, p. 77; *Orator*, tr. H. M. Hubbell, Ch. XVI, p. 345; Loeb Classical Library (London, 1952).

[31] *Epistulae Morales*, tr. Richard M. Gummere, Loeb Classical Library (London, 1953), Epistle CXIV, III, 303–5. The translator renders "hoc sensus miri" as "surprising thoughts" (304).

[32] In this context the earlier statement of *Demetrius on Style:* "everybody reveals his soul in his letters. In every form of composition, it is possible to discern the writer's character, but in none so clearly as in the epistolary," may, in spite of its seeming modernity, be disregarded as atypical or ambiguous. The citation is the translation of W. Rhys Roberts, Loeb Classical Library (London, 1960), p. 441.

[33] *L'Œuvre de Pascal*, ed. Jacques Chevalier (Paris, 1941), p. 831. Cf. "L'éloquence est une peinture de la pensée" (p. 834). ["When one sees the natural style, one is quite astonished and charmed, for one expected to see an author, and one finds a man." "Eloquence is a portrait of the thought."]

[34] "Discours sur le style," in *Œuvres Philosophiques de Buffon,* ed. Jean Piveteau (Paris, 1954), pp. 500, 503. ["Style is nothing but the order and the movement that one gives his thoughts."]

[35] For English examples, see Abrams, pp. 226–35.

[36] A compromise of all three theories can be found in Sumner Ives, *A New Handbook for Writers* (New York, 1960), pp. 274–319.

ever. It postulates that there can be no segmentation between the thought (or "intuition") and its form or expression. Croce, the most important advocate of this theory, states it thus:

> Every true intuition or representation is also *expression*. That which does not objectify itself in expression is not intuition or representation, but sensation and mere natural fact. The spirit only intuites in making, forming, expressing. He who separates intuition from expression never succeeds in reuniting them.[37]

The implications of this aesthetic theory are far-reaching for the theory of style. Obviously it follows that no intuition has any reality until it has achieved expression. In turn this denies the possibility of a choice among means of expression for a given intuition. The intuition is unique with the individual and is so to speak identical with the expression, which is thus also a delineation of the will of the particular individual. Here then is the coalescence of the two modern views of style, as meaning and as a reflection of the individual.[38] In the progress from the early rhetorical to the modern organic view, it seems as if style itself has disappeared. If style is acknowledged as distinct from content, each may be examined separately. But if style and content are so interfused that every change in the one affects the other, there is no style or there is no meaning, at least as analyzable entities. Thus, according to the modern theory, every possible arrangement of the same set of words represents a different meaning. To take an illustration, does each of the following statements have a different sense?

> Only the miserable confess the power of fortune.
> Only by the miserable is the power of fortune confessed.
> The power of fortune: only the miserable will confess it.
> The power of fortune is confessed only by the miserable.[39]

[37] *Aesthetic*, p. 8. I. A. Richards, *Principles of Literary Criticism* (New York, n.d.), in a chapter entitled "Truth and Revelation Theories," mentions what he considers to be Croce's "confusion between value and communicative efficacy" (p. 255). He also cites with approval the comment of Giovanni Papini, in *Four and Twenty Minds:* "If you disregard critical trivialities and didactic accessories, the entire aesthetic system of Croce amounts merely to a hunt for pseudonyms of the word 'art,' and may indeed be stated briefly and accurately in this formula: art = intuition = expression = feeling = imagination = fancy = lyricism = beauty. And you must be careful not to take these words with the shadings and distinctions which they have in ordinary or scientific language. Not a bit of it. Every word is merely a different series of syllables signifying absolutely and completely the same thing" (*ibid.*, fn. 4).

[38] An interesting corroboration of this theory is furnished by a non-theoretician, Ernest Hemingway: "In stating as fully as I could how things really were, it was often very difficult and I wrote awkwardly and the awkwardness is what they called my style." A. E. Hotchner, "Hemingway Talks to American Youth," *This Week,* Oct. 18, 1959, p. 11.

[39] Only one of the four was written by Swift. The others are restatements of the original. The implication is that, if the version composed by a great literary artist is difficult to distinguish from casual variations of it, then the unitary theory is to some extent weakened. See "Thoughts on Various Subjects," *Works,* I, 245.

The changes involve word-order and the adjustment of function words and inflections to syntactic necessity. In the Crocean view, these are not alternative phrasings but substantive changes: because they are different expressions, they convey different meanings.[40]

There is no question that this is an attractive view logically. It seems to accord with present-day psychological emphases on minute and unconscious significances. Moreover, it is to some extent congruent with the experience of writers and speakers, who have found that there are no real synonyms, no two ways of saying exactly the same thing. But this Crocean theory entails some difficulties, partly because it dispenses with the necessity of style, term and notion, and because, logic apart, *some* alternatives seem to be equivalent. [41] If style and meaning are in fact identical, a student of style must study meaning or be merely working with phlogiston. If he studies meaning, he is no longer mainly or even at all concerted with those details of the literary text which are usually called "stylistic," but is planted helplessly before the entire work without a method of approach.

Further, there are unexpected implications in the organic view. If any external aspect of the text is alive with meaning, then any change, not only of the words themselves, affects the meaning. The text is embedded in a context which includes the size and shape of the letters, the margins on the page, the paper and binding of the book, the reader and attendant circumstances of reading, his state of mind, the time of day and a host of other variables over which the author can have no control. Ultimately, no literary statement can have the same meaning twice and any comment about it is likely to be true only for the commentator and perhaps not even for him on a subsequent occasion. Thus, the implications of this organic view reduce all criticism, including that of meaning, to futility. In order to salvage something usable for the study of style, it becomes necessary to return to the modern theory and see whether it may not permit an accommodation.

The perplexity engendered by the logic of the Crocean position has produced not a little ingenuity in the finding of solutions. The problem clearly is how to go on studying style (words, metaphor, arrangement) without seeming to overturn the essential identity of form and content.[42] The solution to the problem seems to lie in an appropriate re-definition of meaning, according to some modern students of the problem.

John Middleton Murry, who seems to be a thorough-going Crocean dismisses the whole question with "style is not an isolable quality of writing; it

[40] A brilliant demonstration tending to support the Crocean theory may be found in Raymond Queneau, *Exercises de Style* (Paris, Gallimard, 1947), in which the same trivial incident is told in one hundred different ways, only some of them stylistic.

[41] What, for example, is the substantive difference between "the prose of Swift" and "Swift's prose"? Such alternative phrasings are regularly considered equivalent in composition in order to avoid repetition or alliteration or too long a sequence of prepositional phrases.

[42] The problem is reminiscent of the dilemma faced by seventeenth-century Englishmen, who were at once admirers of Shakespeare and adherents to French Aristotelianism.

is writing itself." [43] But he is not actually ready to dismiss it; he wants to examine it from the viewpoint not of the reader (who is style-oriented) but that of the writer, who is most conscious of effects. He therefore presents Stendhal's maxim as the best thing on the subject, provided some qualification may be made of a key term: "Le style est ceci: Ajouter à une pensée donnée toutes les circonstances propres à produire tout l'effet que doit produire cette pensée." [44] But *pensée* is not to be taken literally: "it is a general term to cover intuitions, convictions, perceptions, and their accompanying emotions before they have undergone the process of artistic expression or ejection." [45] That this is only a version of the Crocean view is evident. That it is not a satisfactory resolution of the problem is suggested by the content of Murry's book, which seems devoted more to literary criticism than to what is usually associated with discussions of style. [46]

No such objection can be lodged against the work of W. K. Wimsatt, whose book about Johnson's style [47] is exclusively devoted to what the term usually suggests. His awareness of the Crocean dilemma is sharpened by Croce's explicit rejection of rhetorical categories, something that Wimsatt cannot spare, for his examination of Johnson's style proceeds along rhetorical lines (Parallelism, Antithesis, Inversion, even Chiasmus). He finds a solution in the tendency of works to mean something, at all times, whether the writer has expressed what he intended or not. Thus bad style is a deviation, not of words from meaning but of the meaning conveyed from the meaning intended. Even when the fault of style is "awkwardness," the meaning is conveyed completely. The awkwardness is a missing part of the meaning or a contrary or irrelevant meaning which is unnecessarily present, but which is disregarded because the writer's intention can be inferred. [48] The real difficulty is in deciding what the author ought to have said: "It is the only difficulty, for it is the only question, and it is one we implicitly answer every time we judge style." [49] It is done, he contends, by a constant reference of the detail to the "central and presiding purpose." [50] Faults of style can be classed and presumably so can merits, though Wimsatt concedes that useful classification can also be done by those who continue to keep style and meaning separate. He concludes: "That which has for centuries been called style differs from the rest of writing only in that it is one plane or level of the organization of mean-

[43] *The Problem of Style* (Oxford, 1922), p. 77.

[44] From *Racine et Shakespeare,* as quoted by Murry, p. 79. ["Style is this: to give a thought all the circumstances necessary to produce the effect that this thought must produce."]

[45] *Ibid.*

[46] His dependence on the notion of perfection suggests a contamination by Platonic ideas. See, for example, pp. 34, 36, 45, 67, 84, 88, 99, etc. . . .

[47] *The Prose Style of Samuel Johnson* (New Haven, Conn., 1941).

[48] *Ibid.,* p. 10. Cf. the remarkably similar comment of Hemingway, p. 278, fn. 38, above.

[49] *Ibid.*

[50] Cf. Leo Spitzer's circular procedure, p. 290, below.

ing . . . it is the furthest elaboration of the one concept that is the center." [51] It is difficult to conclude that this definition is anything but a pretext designed to permit the critic to get on with his job of analyzing Johnson's style. The furthest elaboration of meaning still requires the critic to have an impossibly accurate knowledge of the author's intention.

Much less subjectivity marks the work of a recent scholar who has attacked this problem. Richard M. Ohmann [52] tries to provide a justification for the study of style as a main concern of literary critics, by means of a philosophical argument, in a volume devoted to the "concept of style as a writer's conscious or subconscious choice among alternatives offered by a language for the expression of thought or feeling." [53] Ohmann criticizes the compromise which considers style as a part of meaning because in his opinion it is difficult to establish the limits of meaning as style, as opposed to meaning as "not-style." [54] He begins with the notion of experience as an infinite set of possible relations between events and the person experiencing them, relations which differ between any two people. Because of the infiniteness of experience, then, no available categories of thought can be made to fit any given person's response to events. "What nature does offer to experience, however, and experience to language, is a constant *formlessness*." [55] In the search for order, each person selects the "perceptual forms" most useful to him, "though most often the choice is unconscious and inevitable." [56] These primitive choices which underlie a writer's prose represent the basis of his epistemology, his particular sorting of perceptions, although of course this task has already been performed in part by the writer's native language.[57] The "epistemic" bias of his language limits a writer's linguistic choices while it encourages his originality, which can help him to overcome the deficiency of his language by the creation of words, and metaphors, by changing syntax. Even short of this possible extreme, his choices remain considerable and meaningful. That a writer may be given to abstraction, a peculiar use of the present tense, or an avoidance of causal words, signifies a habit of meaning, that is, a particular

[51] Wimsatt, p. 11. An interesting variant of Wimsatt's formulation is expressed by George Steiner, in a review of John Updike's *The Centaur:* "It is both fashionable and logically cogent to deny the hoary distinction between form and content, to proclaim that they are indivisible. But . . . they are indivisible only where we are dealing with literature in the most serious, fully realized sense; only where the writer's medium strikes us as inevitable because it is controlled, from within, by pressure of adequate vision. Where such a vision is in default, form and content can and will drift apart. Style, the manipulation of image or verbal sound, will make its independent claims," "Half Man, Half Beast," *Reporter,* XXVIII (March 14, 1963), 52.

[52] "Prolegomena to the Analysis of Prose Style," in *Style in Prose Fiction,* ed. Harold C. Martin, English Institute Essays, 1958 (New York, 1959), pp. 1–24.

[53] In the words of the editor, p. xi.

[54] *Ibid.,* p. 3. He pretends (p. 14) to exonerate Wimsatt and Murry from having resorted to compromise, but it is clear that he cannot be sure.

[55] *Ibid.,* p. 8.

[56] *Ibid.,* p. 9.

[57] *Ibid.,* pp. 10–11.

way of classifying experience.[58] Thus, the problem is resolved: by preserving for the writer a kind of choice (an inevitable prerequisite for the study of style), the choice among the components of the world-stuff by means of his particular mental predisposition to classify this way or that. Unfortunately, this kind of choice seems to be no more a choice than the alternatives it was designed to supplant. As Ohmann admits, the decision may be unconscious and pre-verbal. By the time the writer comes to this "choice," the intellectual machinery governing his outlook upon the world has already been determined and it is no more a true choice than the selection of reading matter by a person who can read only English.

The difficulty with any organic theory is that it precludes the dissection into parts which is both a convenience and a necessity for the successful study of detailed organization. The same problem exists in medicine, wherein the student of human ailments is required to reject the convenient division of disease into psychic and somatic or in the study of psychology, in which the customary division into thought and feeling must be exorcised for a genuine understanding of the mind. But any organic theory is a corrective, rather than a method. By overstating the unity of aspects often ruthlessly dichotomized, such a theory brings into closer contact what ought to be considered parts of the same thing. It does not, however, furnish a procedure for dealing with the reconstituted unity. The only possible result, if analysis is to proceed at all, is to acquire a respect for the whole and a consciousness of the totality, even while separating what seems to be inseparable. If "theoretical paralysis" is to be avoided, Austin Warren and René Wellek observe, "process and work, form and content, expression and style, must be kept apart, provisionally and in precarious suspense, till the final unity." [59]

If, then, the process of writing is considered as a continuum leading from thought to expression, it may be possible to formulate a practical solution to the dilemma posed by the organic view. If the influence of thought or conceptualization is strongest at the origin and diminishes as expression is approached and the influence of expression or form grows as the former diminishes, the two being co-extensive, it can be seen that the two processes are kept together and yet separate for the process of anaylsis. They are, it may be said, like two wedges which, fitted together, make a perfect quadrilateral. A vertical section of the figure, at whatever point, intersects both areas. But if the section is made near the end belonging to expression, only a small part of thought is involved. In non-metaphoric terms, the consideration of style can never exclude the simultaneous consideration of meaning, but if the style is examined at the level of literal expression the influence of the component of meaning can be reduced to negligible size for the purpose of the examination.[60] The totality remains intact in spirit, as the study remains

[58] *Ibid.*, pp. 13–14.
[59] *Theory of Literature* (New York, 1949), p. 188.
[60] Cf. "Here the word style will be used as a convenient designation of the linguistic structure which underlies and indeed constitutes a work of literature." R. A. Sayce, *Style in French Prose* (Oxford, 1953), p. 1.

in constant tension between the poles of thought and expression, but the tendency is constant toward the verbal and literal side, which is to say the the study of style rather than of thought (meaning).

That style can be studied, regardless of the theoretical justification for it,[61] can be verified by a glance at the more than two thousand items listed in a recent bibliography of work in Romance stylistics alone.[62] That the problems of style have been attracting increasing interest in recent years is evidenced by a number of books containing the proceedings of groups met for the purpose of discussing problems of style and form. The English Institute in 1958,[63] the International Federation for Modern Languages and Literatures in its Seventh Congress at Heidelberg in 1957,[64] the Conference on Style at Bloomington, Indiana, in 1958,[65] all brought together large numbers of people interested in the study of style. Significantly, the difficulty of the problem was recognized by the variety of approaches represented at two of the meetings.

The International Congress contributed to this task by confronting students of style working with traditional approaches in a dozen or more languages [66] and compelling them to consider the possible virtues of alternative methods. The Conference was frankly interdisciplinary and at the risk of speaking to uncomprehending audiences, linguists, poets, critics, philosophers, psychologists, folklorists, anthropologists and statisticians presented papers attacking the subject from many sides. There was in all this activity nothing new except the simultaneity, for style like anything elusive and fascinating, has been long studied in various ways.

However variegated the particular methods, they all have much in common, for studies of style can have but few aims. They can hope to teach how to write or how to understand writing; they can try to understand or identify an author or group of authors; they can contribute illumination to another subject, such as linguistics, psychology, statistics, anthropology, or the history of ideas.

The use of illustrious models as incentives and exemplars in the study of composition was one of the foundations of rhetoric. Though no longer basic, this procedure is still considered valuable.[67] The categories devised by the rhetoricians are still useful in literary study, but they serve more as convenient

[61] Students of style have something in common with the bumblebee that did not know it lacked adequate wing surface to fly, according to the findings of aerodynamics engineers. It therefore continued to fly. In a sense they are also like psychologists who know that their intelligence tests measure something which they cannot define and are reduced to defining intelligence as that which intelligence tests measure. A similar problem of definition is discussed in Raymond B. Cattell, "The Nature and Measurement of Anxiety," *Scientific American,* CCVIII (March 1963), 96–104.

[62] Helmut Hatzfeld, *A Critical Bibliography of the New Stylistics* (Chapel Hill, 1953).

[63] Martin, see p. 281, above.

[64] Paul Böckmann, ed. *Stil- und Formprobleme in der Literatur* (Heidelberg, 1959).

[65] *Style in Language,* ed. Thomas A. Sebeok (New York, 1960).

[66] The book itself contains articles written in German, English, French and Italian.

[67] Nearly all college composition courses are based on sets of "readings," some of which are undoubtedly proposed as models for emulation, if not imitation.

labels than as fundamental constituents of the style process. Although not much is known about the relation of thought to language, it is considered unlikely that the simplified psychology underlying the rhetorical figures can be anywhere near the mark.[68] But the study of styles as an aid to developing skill in writing is clearly incidental to the study of an author's style as a prelude, or as part of the attempt, to understand him or his methods of composition. Most of the work to be considered has resulted from a concern with the author, his psychology, his creativity, his mind and his personality.[69]

The most common approach to styles of authors by literary critics and historians has been the subjective or intuitive, sometimes called "impressionistic." It is an eclectic procedure in which the critic refers to passages which have struck him in terms of categories drawn from grammar, rhetoric, aesthetics and whatever other fields he may be acquainted with. Or he may simply describe adjectivally the impression which the writer has made upon him. Such criticism is readily found in older critical studies, in which it occupies some pages toward the end of the book, sometimes (if the subject is a notable "stylist") a whole chapter, but it is not lacking in more recent work.[70] It seems almost to be an afterthought, added after everything of importance has been settled, or an unpleasant necessity, fulfilled because of tradition. The vocabulary of these studies is unstable, and the terms used seldom bear any precise application. Burke's style, for example, is "noble, earnest, deep-flowing." [71] Sterne, however, has no style, but "it is a perfectly clear vehicle for the conveyance of thought." [72] On the other hand, Sir Thomas Browne has only style (no substance), but he clothes this non-existent substance in splendors, "turning the rough yarn of statement into heavy cloth of gold." [73] The two styles of Joseph Conrad have, respectively, "murky splendour" and "elastic suavity." [74] Fanny Burney's sentence-structure is occasionally "natural." [75] These figures of speech reveal most of all the helplessness of the writers to deal with the question, a weakness of which they seem

---

[68] "The study of language is an integral part of the study of thinking. Unfortunately psychologists have little to offer . . . so far their studies have been exploratory." Robert Thomson, *The Psychology of Thinking* (Harmondsworth, 1959), p. 181. This suggests, as Thomson says passim, that thought involving reasoning of a complex kind cannot be carried on without language.

[69] Here belong, presumably, such sophisticated rhetorical treatments as those of Wimsatt on Johnson, and that of Martin Price, *Swift's Rhetorical Art* (New Haven, 1953). Although these studies make use of rhetorical categories, they are in some part historical studies, dealing with the meaning and function of these categories during the periods considered.

[70] John Morley, *Burke* (New York, 1879), Ch. X, "Burke's Literary Character"; H. D. Traill, *Sterne* (London, 1882), Ch. X, "Style and General Characteristics"; Edmund Gosse, *Sir Thomas Browne* (New York, 1905), Ch. VII, "Language and Influence"; Richard Curle, *Joseph Conrad: A Study* (London, 1914), Ch. IX, "Conrad's Prose"; Eugene White, *Fanny Burney, Novelist* (Hamden, Conn., 1960), Ch. V, "Style."

[71] Morley, p. 210.

[72] Traill, pp. 142, 143.

[73] Gosse, pp. 190, 192.

[74] Curle, p. 181.

[75] White, p. 55.

vaguely aware. But the usefulness of such treatment cannot be easily estimated. It is doubtful whether it provides more than merely a generalized approval.[76] A number of modern studies operate more responsibly within the same impressionistic tradition, making their subjective points by means of a substantial number of examples or the juxtaposition of an author's views on composition to appropriate instances of his practice.[77]

The limitations of such a procedure must have become apparent earlier than is commonly supposed. The nineteenth-century faith in the power of science to solve every problem yielded a number of results in the realm of stylistic study. The turn of the century was the great age of laboriously-compiled concordances.[78] A concordance, even though painfully compiled by human hands, implies scientific objectivity, doubtless the result of its dependence on quantitative evidence. In any case, the labor that goes into such an index always has a potential usefulness. Not all quantitative work can claim so much.

Enumerative methods applied to literary work have, at least, the advantage of a very ancient tradition. The standardization of the Homeric text was accomplished by Alexandrian scholars, who compiled lists of words appearing in the text (and nowhere else) and of *hapax legomena* (words appearing only once).[79] Similarly, the Masoretic text of the Bible was safeguarded by devoted scholars, who counted the verses and words of each book and determined its middle word and middle letter.[80] Their modern descendants derived their stimulus from observing the success of scientific methods in all fields of human endeavor. Professor Lucius A. Sherman of the University of Nebraska, having noted the improvement in chemistry classes after the students were permitted to perform experiments themselves (instead of merely watching the instructor's demonstration), found that similar successes attended his introduction of objective laboratory methods into the study of English Literature. The usual lecture method was profitable, he had discovered, to only a few of the best students, and, in any case, it failed to exploit the literary or linguistic elements common to both Chaucer and Shakespeare.[81]

[76] As was inferred by the student who wrote at the top of the page containing Traill's speculations about Sterne's style: "Style good."

[77] For the first type, see H. L. Bond, *The Literary Art of Edward Gibbon* (Oxford, 1960), Ch. VII, "Language"; for the second, Mary Lascelles, *Jane Austen and Her Art* (Oxford, 1939), Ch. III, "Style."

[78] Biblical, 1894, 1897, 1900, etc.; Shakespeare, 1895; Milton, 1894.

[79] G. U. Yule, *The Statistical Study of Literary Vocabulary* (Cambridge, 1944), pp. 7–8. Cf. J. E. Sandys, *A History of Classical Scholarship* (New York, 1958): "The scholars of Alexandria were . . . concerned with the verbal criticism of the Greek poets, primarily with that of Homer. . . . They were the earliest examples of the professional scholar and they deserve the gratitude of the modern world. . . ." The study of *hapax legomena* has a place in modern "stylo-statistics." See Gustave Herdan, *Type-Token Mathematics* ('s-Gravenhage, 1960), pp. 66–8.

[80] The Numerical Masorah is treated in *The Jewish Encyclopedia* (New York, 1901–6), s.v. "Masorah."

[81] The chemical analogy may be found in the preface to his *Analytics of Literature* (Boston, 1893).

The actual research upon which his objective method was based arose from an interest in the genealogy of the English sentence. In a series of articles by Sherman and two of his students, a number of conclusions were reached about English sentence-structure.[82] Sherman found that, despite a gradual decrease in sentence-length (measured in number of words) between Thomas More and Macaulay, a remarkable consistency existed in any single writer's average sentence-length. For example, Thomas More's *Richard III* averages 53 words per sentence; by De Quincey's time, the average is down to 32. But Macaulay's average of 23-plus is entirely his own peculiarity. Sherman counted the words of all the sentences in Macaulay's *Essays* and his *History of England* and found a constant average of a little over 23 words per sentence in any sample larger than 500 periods. This he ascribed to the author's sentence-sense, the ability to cast a "mind-full" into an independent syntactic unit. The writer seems subject to "some conception or ideal of form which, if it could have its will, would reduce all sentences to procrustean regularity . . . ."[83] The study of a variety of other authors, at various stages of their writing lives, convinced Sherman that he had discovered a constant characteristic in sentence-length and that, therefore, other constants must exist:

> If it were true that each author writes always in a consistent numerical sentence average, it would follow that he must be constant in other peculiarities, as proportions of verbs, substitutes for verbs, conjunctions etc. . . . if a sufficiently large sample were taken as the basis.[84]

Some of the peculiarities were sought for by a student of Sherman's (Gerwig), who observed that modern writers used fewer than the half-dozen verbs in each sentence affected by their literary ancestors. The modern tendency was to suppress the superfluity of finite verbs by such means as apposition and verbals and to write more simple sentences.[85] Gerwig devised a percentage-of-clauses-saved index as a measure of modernity of style and tirelessly examined a great range of authors in considerable detail. Unfortunately industry is not proof against error, and a least some of Gerwig's and Sherman's work was invalidated by their ignorance of statistics and experimental design.

The consistency of the sentence-length averages for Macaulay was shown by Moritz to be the result of the uniformity of the material tested: history and essays.[86] A similar bias, he showed, had infected all of Sherman's selec-

---

[82] Lucius A. Sherman, "Some Observations upon the Sentence-Lengths in English Prose," and "On Certain Facts and Principles in the Development of Form in Literature," *University of Nebraska Studies,* I (Oct. 1888), 119–30 and I (July 1892), 337–66; George W. Gerwig, "On the Decrease of Predication and of Sentence-Weight in English Prose," *University of Nebraska Studies,* II (July 1894), 17–44; Carson Hildreth, "The Bacon-Shakespeare Controversy," *University of Nebraska Studies,* II (Jan. 1897), 147–62.

[83] "On Certain Facts . . ." p. 353.

[84] *Ibid.,* p. 350.

[85] Gerwig, p. 18.

[86] Robert E. Moritz, "On the Variation and Functional Relation of Certain Sentence-Constants in Standard Literature," *University of Nebraska Studies,* III (July 1903), 229–53.

tions. He was easily able to demonstrate very wide ranges of sentence-length in individual authors both German and English by examining works in different genres. Further, he pointed out, the decreases of predication-average and increases of simple-sentence average were not merely parallel, as Gerwig had thought, but were functionally related.[87] Although this discussion did not invalidate all of what Sherman and his students had done, it apparently showed the danger of venturing into the territory of science unarmed, for little work of this type appeared during the two decades following Moritz's article.[88]

In the same tradition of numerical tabulation but more carefully qualified in both procedure and conclusions are some articles by Robert R. Aurner.[89] It is the apparatus of clause diagrams, bar-graphs and the like, which is interesting, as it seems to represent a continuing expression of the yearning of a segment of the literary community to reach a level of precision with the sciences.

The next full-scale manifesto of the scientific approach to literature came from the hand of Edith Rickert,[90] who had been impressed by the power of code and cipher analysts to bring sense out of meaningless symbols during the First World War. The book was an attempt "to substitute for the impressionistic, hit-or-miss, every-man-for-himself, method of approaching literature"[91] some "graphical and statistical methods" through which the several strands of style "may be understood with a definiteness and certainty impossible through reading alone."[92] She was aware that her methods were neither rigorously scientific nor really original. As far as it is possible to tell, her suggestions have had very little influence.[93] The defect of these methods (from Sherman to Edith Rickert) is that they seem to represent a mere emulation of the outward aspect of the sciences. The mathematical and statistical aspects were only half-understood and the results were negligible and always seemed suspect to more traditional scholars. For that reason, the historical study of style has been far more influential.

The historical approach is well-established in literary studies and, though

[87] As one went down, the other was bound to go up: as the use of finite verbs per sentence decreased and sentences became shorter, the percentage of simple sentences naturally rose. Moritz even presented a formula by means of which either could be computed if the other was known: $P\sqrt{S} = C$, where P is the predication-average, S the simple-sentence percentage, and C a constant (13.57). *Ibid.*, p. 250.

[88] Interest continued, however, in the study of the Saxon-Romance components of the vocabulary.

[89] "Caxton and the English Sentence," *Wisconsin Studies in Language and Literature,* XVIII (1923), 23–59, and "The History of Certain Aspects of the Structure of the English Sentence," *Philological Quarterly,* II (1923), 187–208.

[90] *New Methods for the Study of Literature* (Chicago, 1927).

[91] *Ibid.*, p. 6.

[92] *Ibid.*, p. 7.

[93] One derivative result is Howard L. Runion's "An Objective Study of the Speech Style of Woodrow Wilson," *Speech Monographs,* III (Oct. 1936). It is interesting to compare this dispassionate and colorless study with the highly subjective, hostile and vigorous book of William Bayard Hale, *The Story of a Style* (New York, 1920), which seems to have been inspired by political motives.

it has its detractors, it so permeates the thinking of literary scholars that they do not even think of it as a method. Historicism is the invisible outward limit which guides overt methods. Sherman, for example, and Aurner later, cast their researches into the form of studies of the prose sentence beginning with Caxton and ending with some near-contemporary. Their *method,* however, was not historical but enumerative. But there are also students of prose form who have openly adopted the historical approach and have made comments about the progress of English prose style and the forces that have directed it by examining writers as representatives of their time rather than as individuals speaking in their own unique voices.

Within the historical approach itself, the dominant problem in dealing with style is identifying the styles of particular periods and accounting for the changes which seem to have taken place. A standard history such as Krapp's [94] presents an examination of samples and a discussion of characteristics in terms of some generally-useful categories (form of the sentence, diction) without being primarily concerned with the motive power behind the changes.[95] The Classical influence, for instance, can be detected in every genre and form up to about 1850 by anyone intent on pursuing that pervasive element.[96] A more pointed attribution of causes and results, however, concerns itself with such matters as the Ciceronian and Senecan styles.[97] Another side of the matter, the influence of the Royal Society, was suggested long ago by Joel E. Spingarn [98] and extensively developed and elaborated by R. F. Jones, with whose name it is now usually connected.[99] Jones acknowledges the difficulty of analyzing style and limits himself to "pointing out those more obvious influences that are combined and reflected in speech and writing . . . ignoring other factors that may escape detection." [100] No quarrel can be picked with the conclusions of R. F. Jones or George Williamson [101] except that they do not seem to account for the very important individual element, and in fact, deliberately exclude it. It is obvious that in any period a variety of writing patterns can be found. Of necessity, the historian pressing a point is con-

[94] George Philip Krapp, *The Rise of English Literary Prose* (New York, 1915).

[95] "The main point . . . has been to trace the growth of a temper and attitude of mind towards the use of speech, to show the development of taste and feeling for prose expression . . . ," *op. cit.,* p. xiii. The emphasis is on the panorama not on factors influencing changes in the landscape. A more limited conspectus is George Saintsbury's *A History of English Prose Rhythm* (London, 1912).

[96] E.g. J. A. K. Thomson, *Classical Influences on English Prose* (London, 1956).

[97] See the well-known work of Morris Croll and also George Williamson, *The Senecan Amble* (London, 1951).

[98] Introduction, *Critical Essays of the Seventeenth Century* (Oxford, 1908), I, xivii.

[99] "Science and English Prose Style in the Third Quarter of the Seventeenth Century" [1930] and "The Attack on Pulpit Eloquence in the Restoration" [1931], both reprinted in *The Seventeenth Century* (Stanford, 1951).

[100] "Science and English Prose Style . . . ," p. 75.

[101] As explanations for the undoubted change which took place in the last quarter of the seventeenth century, they are rejected by James R. Sutherland, *On English Prose* (Toronto, 1957), pp. 56, 66–7. He favors the influence of aristocratic conversation.

strained to select representative illustrations. Even when he is aware of contradictory tendencies, he is bound to underrate the likelihood that within a highly mannered style, such as the Ciceronian, there were important individual variations, differences so great that they obscured the significance of the common pattern. The brilliant demonstration offered by Jones,[102] contrasting two versions of Glanvill's *Vanity of Dogmatizing,* one earlier and one later than his exposure to the Royal Society's program of prose reform, is not wholly convincing because it does not consider the possible tendency of a "late" style to diverge from an early one, often in the direction of "simplicity." Whatever the undeniable truths uncovered by the historical study of style,[103] it affords no more than a negative value to the student of an individual author's style. Historical influences are abstractions of a high order and their effect, even their existence and applicability, are impossible to measure. A more concrete method, whatever its theoretical justification, implies a more successful resolution of the style-problem. Everyone interested has heard of and superficially pays homage to the Ciceronian-Senecan squabble and the influence of the Royal Society, but he does not feel reliably armed with the information because the terms involved (Ciceronian . . .) disguise the inconstancy of the phenomena they refer to. An approach which begins with the stylistic phenomena and carries them back to some historical sequence at least suggests a firmly-grounded empiricism and to that extent it is persuasive. Such a procedure is the study of modern "Stylistics," mainly concerned with the Romance languages, especially French.[104]

Stylistics is related to linguistics and consequently is much concerned with structures definable in grammatical or philological terms.[105] The stylistic device is considered a conscious deviation from the linguistic norm of a writer's period.[106] In fact, to the stylistician only that which is beyond the neutral common denominator qualifies as style. Where there is an alternative available, the possibility of a stylistic choice exists. For example, the French adjective may be placed before or after the noun it modifies, subject to a complicated list of exclusions. The consistent or even the occasional use of the unexpected word-order represents a stylistic device. Obviously such a method depends on a close familiarity with the grammar and the linguistic norms of the period studied.

Though its origins are in linguistics, stylistics proceeds independently and has amassed a diverse body of doctrine also including elements of psychology,

[102] *Ibid.,* pp. 91 ff.

[103] It is useful in isolating the ideas of prose style which govern certain periods and exert an influence on criticism, if not on practice.

[104] Hatzfeld, p. 15.

[105] Synoptic accounts of stylistics may be found in Stephen Ullmann, *Style in the French Novel* (Cambridge, 1957), pp. 1–39; and Pierre Guiraud, "Stylistiques," *Neophilologus,* XXXVIII (1954), 1–12.

[106] A fresh emphasis is given to the idea of the stylistic device, in a procedure based on context and predictability, by M. Riffaterre, "Criteria for Style Analysis," *Word,* XV (1959), 154–74 and "Stylistic Context," *Word,* XVI (1960), 207–18.

statistics, rhetoric, and even information theory. Most followers of stylistics, however, would agree with Ullmann's summary:

> At the risk of oversimplification, one might say that everything which, in language, transcends pure communication belongs to the province of style. Whether the choice, and the effects it produces, are conscious or not is fundamentally irrelevant to a purely stylistic inquiry, and it is also most difficult to determine.[107]

The concern, it is clear, is with effects on the reader, not the sources in the writer, and with the particularity of the device itself, its variant forms, its diffusion. Such studies have been highly productive (at least in numbers), although they have tended to the mechanical application to an author of a predetermined schedule of devices.[108] Following the grammars of style provided for the French language by Marcel Cressot [109] and others, some critics have produced treatises examining French prose,[110] individual authors, the use of particular devices in various authors.[111] In such careful scholars as Sayce and Ullmann, this procedure turns up a good many significant insights. It is to be noticed, however, that in a language like French, which has far stricter standards of grammatical propriety than English, the norm is clearer and deviations more readily perceptible. But the insistence on the consciousness of the whole artistic process minimizes, when it does not totally ignore, the considerable component of literary composition which is not subject to consciousness, but represents the unconscious expression of personal tendencies. Besides, despite their disciplined and traditional procedure, some followers of Romance stylistics continue to be bound to something of the impressionism which has been a constant handicap to the criticism of style.[112]

Implicitly connected with this approach is a scholar whose work requires particular mention because of its influence. Leo Spitzer's own "philological circle," with which he tries to bridge linguistics and literary history, parallels Romance stylistics in its notion of the deviation from the linguistic norm and its emphasis on linguistic features of style, but it is also dependent on the

---

[107] *Op. cit.*, p. 6. But cf. Guiraud, p. 2, who is concerned to distinguish conscious from unconscious choice.

[108] Ullmann (p. 35) mentions a number of Sorbonne theses on the 'language and style' of a given author as offenders in this direction. A better-than-average example in this vein is Joseph-Barthélemy Fort, *Samuel Butler l'Écrivain: Etude d'un Style* (Bordeaux, 1935). The inherent defects are visible in the contents of some chapters: Butler's ideas about style, his diction, his imagery, his "styles."

[109] *Le Style et ses Techniques* (Paris, 1947).

[110] R. A. Sayce, *Style in French Prose* (Oxford, 1953).

[111] See bibliographies in Ullmann and Sayce; also P. Guiraud, *La Stylistique* (Paris, 1954), pp. 81–86 and Hatzfeld, *Critical Bibliography*.

[112] Here might be mentioned also the hybrid works (part *modus dicendi*, part style-history, part study of stylistic ideals and devices) represented by such works as Read, *English Prose Style*, and Lucas, *Style*, the first of which is full of judicious criticism and keen historical observations and the second a hotbed of such concepts as 'urbanity,' 'sincerity,' 'gaiety.'

idealist position of Croce.[113] Spitzer's technique, however, does not conveniently fit into any classification, partly because it draws on so extensive a set of disciplines and partly because its success is in large part dependent on the method's being applied by Spitzer himself, according to his detractors, who point to its highly subjective aspects, those derived from psychoanalysis.

Not all application of psychology to the study of style need be wholly subjective, however. Psychologists have studied language for some three decades, most recently with the objective means provided by statistics. The aim of the psychologists is not to study style as a literary phenomenon but rather to use the information supplied by literary style in the study of personality.[114] Experimental psychology has produced results in the form of numerical data, which could be treated statistically. Unfortunately most experiments depend on unstable definitions or classifications, with the consequence that one experimenter's results cannot be compared with another's and some doubt is cast on the validity of the conclusion, though workers in this field have not been forward to claim too much for their discoveries. One experiment, for instance, required the matching of sets of nine anonymous themes written by a class of students in composition. The three experimenters had very good success in grouping the themes written by individual students, but they were powerless to explain how they did it. They were unable to point to the clues they had used and concluded that they had done so intuitively (that is, they had recognized clues they were not aware of).[115] The verb-adjective ratio devised by Busemann connects emotional stability in children with the use of a low number of verbs for each adjective.[116] The extension of this method to adult literary work (Emerson) revealed wild fluctuations in the writings of the same author, depending on the type of literary work examined. The most obvious variable in such an experiment is the concept of emotional stability, the estimate of which is bound to be vague.[117] A sufficient number of experiments have been made to indicate that results from this approach will eventually be useful to literary students, but to date the yield has been low.

The statistical approach to the study of language and literature, unlike the merely enumerative, is perhaps the furthest removed from the usual activities and the kind of thinking practiced by literary students. In fact, for some time the two have not too happily mixed. The literary workers seem resentful of

[113] For Spitzer's own explanation, see *Linguistics and Literary History* (Princeton, 1948), Ch. I and passim; for the accounts of favorably-disposed scholars, Ullmann, pp. 25–28 and Guiraud, *Stylistique*, pp. 71–77; for a negative view, J. Hytier, "La Méthode de M. L. Spitzer," *Romanic Review*, XLI (1950), 42–59.

[114] Summaries of work done in this field may be found in Fillmore H. Sanford, "Speech and Personality," *Psychological Bulletin*, XXXIX (Dec. 1942), 811–45 and George A. Miller, *Language and Communication* (New York, 1951), especially Ch. VI, "Individual Differences," pp. 119–39.

[115] Allport, Walker and Lathers, recounted in Miller, pp. 119–20.

[116] Miller, pp. 127–28.

[117] The divergence between works in different literary genres, here as in Sherman's earlier work, seems to constitute a significant stumbling-block. Any theory of consistent style must give an account of this divergence.

having their domains invaded by the uncouth practitioners of an obscure ritual, whom they often rightly accuse of fundamental ignorance. The statisticians are either apologetic, attempting to disarm criticism by admitting that they are not entirely qualified for their venture, or aggressively assertive of the possible advantages of a scientific approach to the problems of literary study.[118] It may be asked what the appropriateness might be of an approach to literature which seems equally suited to the charting of beer-drinkers' preferences or the distribution of shirt sizes. Literature is a matter of the spirit to be understood and appreciated by nothing less than the subtlest intellectual effort of trained and sensitive minds. Statisticians concede this point but argue that an opportunity for their science still remains because language is a mass phenomenon (involves a great many small units in various distributions) and statistics is a method for treating masses of any units with a verifiable amount of accuracy. Although an individual work is a unique creation, it is part of the greater enveloping mass of the language, among whose users the author is only one: "What before were regarded as quite unique events, the products of wilful creation, appear now when studied quantitatively as mere variants of typical expenditure of linguistic material. . . ."[119] This is not to be taken as rejecting the scope of the individual contribution in composition but as merely narrowing it in some phases. For example, whatever might be the divergence—artistic, ideological—between Dickens and James Joyce, it seems likely that the frequency with which they use the letters, phonemes, and word-sizes in letters and syllables of the English language will be very similar and quite predictable within certain limits.[120] Of course, to say this is only to say that the English language has some features which bind all its users to a certain kind of uniformity. But it also means that on some levels, a writer may be powerless to escape the effect of chance. It is almost as if he were picking words blindly from a bag. Obviously the deterministic threat posed by this view is mitigated by the realization that such uniformity operates at the fundamental level of language and that there is a considerable sphere in which the individual talent may exert itself.

It was to this fundamental level that the founder of statistical linguistics addressed himself. George Kingsley Zipf discovered in language the vast number of units in which statistics is most at home and the high repetitiveness which makes categorizing convenient. In investigating "the relationship which exists between the form of the various speech elements and their behavior, in so far as this relationship is revealed statistically," he sought to prepare the way to "the formulation into tentative laws of the underlying forces which impel and direct linguistic expression." [121]

[118] See, for example, G. Herdan, *Language as Choice and Chance* (Groningen, 1956), p. 1; Yule, *Statistical Study*, pp. 1–2.
[119] Herdan, *Language*, p. 2.
[120] *Ibid.*, p. 66.
[121] G. K. Zipf, *The Psycho-Biology of Language* (Boston, 1935), p. 3.

Examining words according to their size in syllables,[122] Zipf found that in German, one-syllable words were used half the time, two-syllable under a third and so on to one lone fifteen-syllable word.[123] To verify the tentative conclusion that short words are more common than long ones, Zipf demonstrated that Chinese [sic], English and Latin accord very closely to the same proposition, whether the measurement be based on morphemes, syllables or phonemes.[124] From this evidence, he formulated a "Principle of Least Effort," which supposedly governs word-length and tends to preserve equilibrium among the various components of language.[125] Statistical linguistics has developed since Zipf's time.[126]

The application of statistics, rather than mere enumeration, to literary problems, specifically problems of style, or "individual differences" (in the phrase of the psychologists), has moved more slowly. The reason may be sought in the characteristics of statistics itself, which is a means of dealing with masses of units, grouped in discrete quantitative categories. A natural language supplies inexhaustible materials for a count of letters, syllables and phonemes. But the application of this method to the study of an author introduces two difficulties. First, the size of the material (the sample) is vastly reduced. Secondly, the categories applied to the material tend to be less simple and larger in size, shrinking the size of the sample still further. Whereas the number of words available for study in a language has no practical limit and the number of units, therefore, of whatever size, is similarly unlimited,[127] the size of any author's word-hoard is rather modest by comparison, and it becomes smaller as the units into which it is divided become larger.[128] The tendency of analysts of style to design cumbrous and ambiguous categories and to study no more than a fraction of the available units goes far to explain the skepticism with which such attempts are greeted.[129] However, there does

[122] He used the count of ten million words of German prose made in 1897–8 by F. W. Kaeding.

[123] Zipf, p. 23. Another investigator's results, based on samples of a book length (c. 100,000 words), were very close to Kaeding's, one-syllable words ranging between 48.6 and 52.91 per cent for five prose works of four German authors, with excellent uniformity for two- to six-syllable words, except that one philosophical writer (Jaspers) used fewer two- and more three-, four-, and five-syllable words. The aggregate average for the five, if it could be computed, would probably come very close to Kaeding, the variations being accounted for by individual differences. See William Fucks, "On Mathematical Analysis of Style," *Biometrika*, XXXIX (1952), 125, Table 1.

[124] Zipf, pp. 24–28.

[125] *Human Behavior and the Principle of Least Effort* (Cambridge, Mass., 1949).

[126] He lived long enough to be a member of the "Committee on Quantitative Linguistics" established by the Sixth International Congress of Linguistics, Paris, 1948. For a review of work in this field, see John B. Carroll, *The Study of Language* (Cambridge, 1959), pp. 61–65 and Miller, *Language and Communication*, pp. 80–98 and consult Herdan, *Language*, passim.

[127] It is not infinite, obviously, but unlimited within the ability of any person to deal with it, especially since it can be generated faster than it can be examined.

[128] A canon of 100,000 words contains fewer than 20,000 units if searched for prepositional phrases, and perhaps no more than 4,000 if sentences are the units.

[129] By Wimsatt, for example, p. 24.

not seem to be much doubt that substantial findings in the matter of individual differences between authors can be made by careful workers who are not tempted to claim more than the evidence will allow.[130] The attribution problems involved in the *Imitatio Christi,* which Yule [131] attempted to settle by a study of the nouns it contained as compared with those in the works of two possible authors, may not be considered solved, but they have been taken a certain distance toward that goal. Yule suggests, near the end of his study [132] that a safe minimum in statistical stylistics might be a sample of 10,000 words. But since this may not always be available, as in disputed short tracts, the shortage could be made up for by considering other sections of the vocabulary, excluding only the function words, which might have uniform distribution in any author and thus tend to blur differences.

Just this dearth of sample handicapped the students of the *Equatorie of the Planetis,*[133] tentatively attributed to Chaucer on the basis of a minute study of the percentage of native vs. Romance words (as well as other items). The superiority of the modern treatment of the linguistic evidence lies in its ability to deal with the problem raised by the fluctuation of the native-Romance word ratio with the size of the work.[134] Not many studies of the same type have been conducted, perhaps because attribution-problems of importance are not common. However, various studies have dealt statistically with one stylistic feature or another. Both Elderton [135] and Fucks [136] rely on syllable-counts as tests of authorship with stable properties, Elderton specifying samples of 10,000 to 20,000 words for likely stability.[137] The authors each has examined do not coincide, except for Shakespeare. Elderton counted the prose and the verse of *Henry IV, Part I,* whereas Fucks counted the words in *Othello.* The percentages for each word-length correspond very closely and the average

[130] Problems of attribution by internal evidence are well illustrated in a series of articles ("The Case for Internal Evidence") which ran in the *Bulletin of the New York Public Library* in 1957, 1958, and 1959. Part of this material, which rehearsed arguments presented before a Symposium of the English Institute in 1958, combines claims for the value of internal evidence with the most unreliable demonstration of its use for attribution (verbal parallels, areas of interest, peculiarities of spelling). See Arthur Sherbo, "Can *Mother Midnight's Comical Pocket Book* be attributed to Christopher Smart?", *ibid.,* LXI (Aug. 1957), 373–82 and George F. Lord, "Two New Poems by Marvell?", *ibid.,* LXII (Nov. 1958), 551–70. The latter explicitly states that though no single piece of evidence is conclusive, the lot amounts "to a strong probability" (p. 564). Some useful cautions may be found in Ephim G. Fogel, "Salmons in Both, or some Caveats for Canonical Scholars," *ibid.,* LXIII (May 1959), 223–36 and LXIII (June 1959), 292–308.

[131] *Statistical Study,* passim.

[132] P. 281.

[133] Ed. Derek J. Price (Cambridge, 1955).

[134] G. Herdan, "Chaucer's Authorship of the *Equatorie of the Planetis,*" *Language,* XXXII (1956), 254–9. But see the adverse review of his procedure by C. Douglas Chretien, "A New Statistical Approach to the Study of Language," *Romance Philology,* XVI (Feb. 1963), 299–301.

[135] W. P. Elderton, "A Few Statistics on the Length of English Words," *Journal of the Royal Statistical Society* (Series A), CXII (1949), 436–43.

[136] See fn. 123, above.

[137] P. 443.

number of syllables per word agrees to two decimal places.[138] Such agreement depends on large enough samples, adequately selected, on the careful definition of categories (even in the case of syllables), and of course on accurate counting. That this approach will likely have a place in certain types of literary work seems inescapable, especially in view of the ease with which very large counts may now be made with the aid of electronic data-processing equipment.[139] Manuals of technique and bibliographies of past work have been published [140] and concordances been produced with the aid of this newest of all research tools.[141] Projects of even greater scope have been announced: Samuel Johnson's works, the *Iliad* and the *Odyssey,* St. Paul, Junius, the authors of the *Federalist* have all been subjected to quantitative analysis.[142] It is understandable that the introduction of such a technological advance as the electronic computer into literary study should stir some opposition.[143] Even the printed book and the typewriter were not unopposed at their introduction, and Swift himself may be numbered among those taking a short view of the quantification of literature.[144] Nonetheless, the advantages of such equipment seem too great to discard. If it is remembered that electronic machines are merely clerks who can count and sort at very high speed and only under human instruction, it may be realized that objections to their use are not entirely rational. It is obviously not the tool but the wielder of it who is the responsible party. Statistics is a means of processing data and of evaluating their predictive accuracy, and electronic-data processing equipment is a means of doing this more rapidly than the unaided mind and pencil can do it. The quarrel must be with the assumptions, and the definitions according to which the study is undertaken. It is when these are not plainly stated that untrustworthy results are produced. Therefore, as the first step toward introducing rigor into this study of style, let the major assumptions be stated along with the basis on which they rest and the consequences which are expected to follow.

[138] Elderton (Verse): 1-syllable, 78.4; 2, 16.5; 3, 4.1; 4-5, 1.0. Average word-length in syllables: 1.28 (p. 441). Fucks: 1, 78.81; 2, 15.11; 3, 4.95; 4, 1.16. Average: 1.287 (p. 125).

[139] See Andrew D. Booth, L. Brandwood and J. P. Cleave, *Mechanical Resolution of Linguistic Problems* (London, 1958).

[140] Pierre Guiraud, *Les Caractères Statistiques du Vocabulaire* (Paris, 1953), *Problèmes et Méthodes de la Statistique Linguistique* (Dordrecht, 1959), and *Bibliographie Critique de la Statistique Linguistique* (Utrecht, 1954), 2500 titles; also G. Herdan, *Language as Choice and Chance,* and *Type-Token Mathematics.*

[141] E.g., Dryden and Matthew Arnold.

[142] A Johnson project has been under way at Michigan State University for some time. The Homer study of James T. McDonough, Jr., is described in "Classics and Computers," *Graduate Faculties News-Letter* (March 1962), 4-5. For Junius and the *Federalist,* see Appendices G and D. News of a project designed to distinguish the genuine Epistles of St. Paul from the spurious (by means of a test based on the frequency and patterning of *kai*) is contained in *Time,* LXXXI (March 15, 1963), 56.

[143] And yet the London *Times Literary Supplement* published a series of articles and a correspondence about the advantages for humane studies of technological aids (March–June 1962). These have been collected into a pamphlet entitled "Freeing the Mind."

[144] *Works,* XI, 168.

Literature as Sentences

Richard Ohmann

Ohmann's essay is certainly one of the most widely reprinted modern discussions of style. It is included in this volume, not because of its bearing on literary theory particularly, but because it is so penetrating a commentary on what John Mellon calls "syntactic fluency," i.e., the ability to embed one proposition within another, which is one of the crucial language skills.

What Ohmann demonstrates clearly is that the meaning of a sentence is a great deal more than the sum of the meanings of its words. From the strictly practical viewpoint, the essay shows how syntactic fluency can work to carry meaning, and thus it is (though Ohmann certainly didn't intend it to be) an argument in favor of the sort of pedagogical stylistics that are defended in Contemporary Rhetoric.

Critics permit themselves, for this or that purpose, to identify literature with great books, with imaginative writing, with expressiveness in writing, with the non-referential and non-pragmatic, with beauty in language, with order, with myth, with structured and formed discourse—the list of definitions is nearly endless—with verbal play, with uses of language that stress the medium itself, with the expression of an age, with dogma, with the *cri de coeur,* with neurosis. Now of course literature is itself and not another thing, to paraphrase Bishop Butler; yet analogies and classifications have merit. For a short space let us think of literature as sentences.

To do so will not tax the imagination, because the work of literature indubitably *is* composed of sentences, most of them well-ordered, many of them deviant (no pejorative meant), some of them incomplete. But since much the same holds for dust-jacket copy, the Congressional Record, and transcripts of board meetings, the small effort required to think of literature as sentences may be repaid by a correspondingly small insight into literature as such. Although I do not believe this to be so, for the moment I shall hold the question in abeyance, and stay mainly within the territory held in common by all forms of discourse. In other words, I am not asking what is special about the sentences *of literature,* but what is special about *sentences* that they should interest the student of literature. Although I employ the framework of generative grammar and scraps of its terminology,[1] what I have to say should not ring in the traditionally educated grammatical ear with outlandish discord.

First, then, the sentence is the primary unit of understanding. Linguists have so trenchantly discredited the old definition—"a sentence is a complete thought"—that the truth therein has fallen into neglect. To be sure, we delimit the class of sentences by formal criteria, but each of the structures that qualifies will express a semantic unity not characteristic of greater or lesser structures. The meanings borne by morphemes, phrases, and clauses hook together to express a meaning that can stand more or less by itself. This point, far from denying the structuralist's definition of a sentence as a single free utterance, or *form,* seems the inevitable corollary of such definitions: forms carry meanings, and it is natural that an independent form should carry an independent meaning. Or, to come at the thing another way, consider that one task of a grammar is to supply structural descriptions, and that the sentence is the unit so described. A structural description specifies the way each part of a sentence is tied to each other part, and the semantic rules of a grammar use the structural description as starting point in interpreting the whole. A reader or hearer does something analogous when he resolves the structures and meanings of sentences, and thereby understands them. Still another way to approach the primacy of the sentence is to notice that the initial symbol for all derivations in a generative grammar is "S" for sentence: the sentence is the domain of grammatical structure—rather like the equation in algebra—and hence the domain of meaning.

These remarks, which will seem truisms to some and heresy to others, cannot be elaborated here. Instead, I want to register an obvious comment on their relevance to literary theory and literary criticism. Criticism, whatever else it does, must interpret works of literature. Theory concerns itself in part with the question, "what things legitimately bear on critical interpretation?" But beyond a doubt, interpretation begins with sentences. Whatever complex apprehension the critic develops of the whole work, that understanding arrives mundanely, sentence by sentence. For this reason, and because the form of a sentence dictates a rudimentary mode of understanding, sentences have a good deal to do with the subliminal meaning (and form) of a literary work. They prepare and direct the reader's attention in particular ways.

My second point about sentences should dispel some of the abstractness of the first. Most sentences directly and obliquely put more linguistic apparatus into operation than is readily apparent, and call on more of the reader's linguistic competence. Typically, a surface structure overlays a deep structure which it may resemble but little, and which determines the "content" of the

[1] I draw especially on Noam Chomsky, *Aspects of the Theory of Syntax* (Cambridge, Mass., 1965) and Jerrold J. Katz and Paul Postal, *An Integrated Theory of Linguistic Descriptions* (Cambridge, Mass., 1964).

sentence. For concreteness, take this rather ordinary example, an independent clause from Joyce's "Araby": "Gazing up into the darkness I saw myself as a creature driven and derided by vanity." The surface structure may be represented as follows, using the convention of labeled brackets: [2]

$$^S[^{Adv}[V + Part\ ^{PP}\ [P\ ^{NP}\ [D + N]]]\ ^{Nuc}\ [N\ ^{VP}\ [V +$$
$$N\ ^{PP}\ [P\ ^{NP}\ [D + N\ ^{Adj}\ [V + and + V\ ^{PP}\ [P + N]]]]]]]$$

The nucleus has a transitive verb with a direct object. In the deep structure, by contrast, the matrix sentence is of the form $^S[NP\ ^{VP}[V + $ Complement $+$ NP]]: "I $+$ saw $+$ as a creature $+$ me." It has embedded in it one sentence with an intransitive verb and an adverb of location—"I gazed up into the darkness"—and two additional sentences with transitive verbs and direct objects—"Vanity drove the creature," and "Vanity derided the creature." Since "darkness" and "vanity" are derived nouns, the embedded sentences must in turn contain embeddings, of, say "(Something) is dark" and "(Someone) is vain." Thus the word "vanity," object of a preposition in the surface structure, is subject of two verbs in the deep, and its root is a predicate adjective. The word "creature," object of a preposition in the surface structure, also has a triple function in the deep structure: verbal complement, direct object of "drive," and direct object of "deride." Several transformations (including the passive) deform the six basic sentences, and several others relate them to each other. The complexity goes much farther, but this is enough to suggest that a number of grammatical processes are required to generate the initial sentence and that its structure is moderately involved. Moreover, a reader will not understand the sentence unless he grasps the relations marked in the deep structure. As it draws on a variety of syntactic resources, the sentence also activates a variety of semantic processes and modes of comprehension, yet in brief compass and in a surface *form* that radically permutes *content*.

I choose these terms wilfully: that there are interesting grounds here for a form-content division seems to me quite certain. Joyce might have written, "I gazed up into the darkness. I saw myself as a creature. The creature was driven by vanity. The creature was derided by vanity." Or, "Vanity drove and derided the creature I saw myself as, gazer up, gazer into the darkness." Content remains roughly the same, for the basic sentences are unchanged. But the style is different. And each revision structures and screens the content differently. The original sentence acquires part of its meaning and part of its unique character by resonating against these unwritten alternatives. It is at the level of sentences, I would argue, that the distinction between form and content comes clear, and that the intuition of style has its formal equivalent.[3]

Sentences play on structure in still another way, more shadowy, but of

---

[2] Each set of brackets encloses the constituent indicated by its superscript label. The notation is equivalent to a tree diagram. Symbols: S = Sentence, Adv = Adverbial, V = Verb, Part = Participle, PP = Prepositional Phrase, P = Preposition, NP = Noun Phrase, D = Determiner, N = Noun, Nuc = Nucleus, VP = Verb Phrase, Adj = Adjectival.

[3] I have argued the point at length in "Generative Grammars and the Concept of Literary Style," *Word* 20 (Dec. 1964), 423–39.

considerable interest for criticism. It is a commonplace that not every noun can serve as object of every verb, that a given noun can be modified only by adjectives of certain classes, and so on. For instance, a well-defined group of verbs, including "exasperate," "delight," "please," and "astound," require animate objects; another group, including "exert," "behave," and "pride," need reflexive objects. Such interdependencies abound in a grammar, which must account for them by subcategorizing nouns, adjectives, and the other major classes.[4] The importance of categorical restrictions is clearest in sentences that disregard them—deviant sentences. It happens that the example from Joyce is slightly deviant in this way: in one of the underlying sentences —"Vanity derided the creature"—a verb that requires a human subject in fact has as its subject the abstract noun "vanity." The dislocation forces the reader to use a supplementary method of interpretation: here, presumably he aligns "vanity" (the word) with the class of human nouns and sees vanity (the thing) as a distinct, active power in the narrator's psyche. Such deviance is so common in metaphor and elsewhere that one scarcely notices it, yet it helps to specify the way things happen in the writer's special world, and the modes of thought appropriate to that world.

I have meant to suggest that sentences normally comprise intricacies of form and meaning whose effects are not the less substantial for their subtlety. From this point, what sorts of critical description follow? Perhaps I can direct attention toward a few tentative answers, out of the many that warrant study, and come finally to a word on critical theory. Two samples must carry the discussion; one is the final sentence of "The Secret Sharer":

> Walking to the taffrail, I was in time to make out, on the very edge of a darkness thrown by a towering black mass like the very gateway of Erebus— yes, I was in time to catch an evanescent glimpse of my white hat left behind to mark the spot where the secret sharer of my cabin and of my thoughts, as though he were my second self, had lowered himself into the water to take his punishment: a free man, a proud swimmer striking out for a new destiny.

I hope others will agree that the sentence justly represents its author: that it portrays a mind energetically stretching to subdue a dazzling experience *outside* the self, in a way that has innumerable counterparts elsewhere in Conrad. How does scrutiny of the deep structure support this intuition? First, notice a matter of emphasis, of rhetoric. The matrix sentence, which lends a surface form to the whole, is "# S # I was in time # S #" (repeated twice). The embedded sentences that complete it are "I walked to the taffrail," "I made out + NP," and "I caught + NP." The point of departure, then, is the narrator himself: where he was, what he did, what he saw. But a glance at the deep structure will explain why one feels a quite different emphasis in the sentence as a whole: seven of the embedded sentences have "sharer" as grammatical subject; in another three the subject is a noun linked to "sharer" by the copula; in two "sharer" is direct object; and in two more "share" is the

---

[4] Chomsky discusses ways of doing this in *Aspects of the Theory of Syntax,* Chapter 2.

verb. Thus thirteen sentences go to the semantic development of "sharer," as follows:

1) The secret sharer had lowered the secret sharer into the water.
2) The secret sharer took his punishment.
3) The secret sharer swam.
4) The secret sharer was a swimmer.
5) The swimmer was proud.
6) The swimmer struck out for a new destiny.
7) The secret sharer was a man.
8) The man was free.
9) The secret sharer was my second self.
10) The secret sharer had (it).
11) (Someone) punished the secret sharer.
12) (Someone) shared my cabin.
13) (Someone) shared my thoughts.

In a fundamental way, the sentence is mainly *about* Leggatt, although the surface structure indicates otherwise.

Yet the surface structure does not simply throw a false scent, and the way the sentence comes to focus on the secret sharer is also instructive. It begins with the narrator, as we have seen, and "I" is the subject of five basic sentences early on. Then "hat" takes over as the syntactic focus, receiving development in seven base sentences. Finally, the sentence arrives at "sharer." This progression in the deep structure rather precisely mirrors both the rhetorical movement of the sentence from the narrator to Leggatt via the hat that links them, and the thematic effect of the sentence, which is to transfer Leggatt's experience to the narrator via the narrator's vicarious and actual participation in it. Here I shall leave this abbreviated rhetorical analysis, with a cautionary word: I do not mean to suggest that only an examination of deep structure reveals Conrad's skillful emphasis—on the contrary, such an examination supports and in a sense explains what any careful reader of the story notices.

A second critical point adjoins the first. The morpheme "share" appears once in the sentence, but it performs at least twelve separate functions, as the deep structure shows. "I," "hat," and "mass" also play complex roles. Thus at certain points the sentence has extraordinary "density," as I shall call it. Since a reader must register these multiple functions in order to understand the sentence, it is reasonable to suppose that the very process of understanding concentrates his attention on centers of density. Syntactic density, I am suggesting, exercises an important influence on literary comprehension.

Third, by tuning in on deep structures, the critic may often apprehend more fully the build of a literary work. I have already mentioned how the syntax of Conrad's final sentence develops his theme. Consider two related points. First, "The Secret Sharer" is an initiation story in which the hero, through moral and mental effort, locates himself vis à vis society and the natural world, and thus passes into full manhood. The syntax of the last sentence schematizes the relationships he has achieved, in identifying with Leggatt's heroic defection, and in fixing on a point of reference—the hat—that connects him to the darker powers of nature. Second, the syntax and meaning of the last sentence bring to completion the pattern initiated by the syntax and meaning of the first few sentences, which present human beings and natural objects in thought-bewildering disarray. I can do no more than mention these structural connections here, but I am convinced that they supplement and help explain an ordinary critical reading of the story.

Another kind of critical point concerns habits of meaning revealed by sentence structure. One example must suffice. We have already marked how the sentence shifts its focus from "I" to "hat" to "sharer." A similar process goes on in the first part of the sentence: "I" is the initial subject, with "hat" as object. "Hat" is subject of another base sentence that ends with "edge," the object of a preposition in a locative phrase. "Edge" in turn becomes object of a sentence that has "darkness" as subject. "Darkness" is object in one with "mass" as subject, and in much the same way the emphasis passes to "gateway" and "Erebus." The syntax executes a chaining effect here which cuts across various kinds of construction. Chaining is far from the only type of syntactic expansion, but it is one Conrad favors. I would suggest this hypothesis: that syntactically and in other ways Conrad draws heavily on operations that link one thing with another associatively. This may be untrue, or if true it may be unrevealing; certainly it needs clearer expression. But I think it comes close to something that we all notice in Conrad, and in any case the general critical point exemplified here deserves exploration: that each writer tends to exploit deep linguistic resources in characteristic ways—that his style, in other words, rests on syntactic options within sentences (see fn. 3)— and that these syntactic preferences correlate with habits of meaning that tell us something about his mode of conceiving experience.

My other sample passage is the first sentence of Dylan Thomas' "A Winter's Tale":

> It is a winter's tale
> That the snow blind twilight ferries over the lakes
> And floating fields from the farm in the cup of the vales,
> Gliding windless through the hand folded flakes,
> The pale breath of cattle at the stealthy sail,
>
> And the stars falling cold,
> And the smell of hay in the snow, and the far owl
> Warning among the folds, and the frozen hold
> Flocked with the sheep white smoke of the farm house cowl
> In the river wended vales where the tale was told.

Some of the language here raises a large and familiar critical question, that of unorthodox grammar in modern poetry, which has traditionally received a somewhat facile answer. We say that loss of confidence in order and reason leads to dislocation of syntax, as if errant grammar were an appeal to the irrational. A cursory examination of deep structure in verse like Thomas', or even in wildly deviant verse like some of Cummings', will show the matter to be more complex than that.

How can deviance be most penetratingly analyzed? Normally, I think, in terms of the base sentences that lie beneath ungrammatical constructions. Surface structure alone does not show "the river wended vales" (line 10) to be deviant, since we have many well-formed constructions of the same word-class sequence: "machine made toys," "sun dried earth," and so on. The particular deviance of "the river wended vales" becomes apparent when we try to refer it to an appropriate underlying structure. A natural one to consider is "the river wends the vales" (cf. "the sun dries the earth"), but of course this makes "wend" a transitive verb, which it is not, except in the idiomatic "wend its way." So does another possibility, "NP + wends the vales with rivers" (cf. "NP + makes the toys by machine"). This reading adds still other kinds of deviance, in that the Noun Phrase will have to be animate, and in that rivers are too cumbersome to be used instrumentally in the way implied. Let us assume that the reader rejects the more flagrant deviance in favor of the less, and we are back to "the river wends the vales." Suppose now that "the vales" is not after all a direct object, but a locative construction, as in "the wolf prowls the forest"; this preserves the intransitivity of "wend," and thereby avoids a serious form of deviance. But notice that there is *no* transformation in English that converts "the wolf prowls the forest" into "the wolf prowled forest," and so this path is blocked as well. Assume, finally, that given a choice between shifting a word like "wend" from one subclass to another and adding a transformational rule to the grammar, a reader will choose the former course; hence he selects the first interpretation mentioned: "the river wends the vales."

If so, how does he understand the anomalous transitive use of "wend"? Perhaps by assimilating the verb to a certain class that may be either transitive or intransitive: "paint," "rub," and the like. Then he will take "wend" to mean something like "make a mark on the surface of, by traversing"; in fact, this is roughly how I read Thomas' phrase. But I may be wrong, and in any case my goal is not to solve the riddle. Rather, I have been leading up to the point that every syntactically deviant construction has more than one possible interpretation, and that readers resolve the conflict by a process that involves deep and intricately motivated decisions and thus puts to work considerable linguistic knowledge, syntactic as well as semantic.[5] The decisions nearly always go on implicitly, but aside from that I see no reason to think that deviance of this sort is an appeal to, or an expression of, irrationality.

[5] See Jerrold J. Katz, "Semi-sentences," in Jerry A. Fodor and Jerrold J. Katz, eds., *The Structure of Language* (1964), pp. 400–16. The same volume includes two other relevant papers, Chomsky, "Degrees of Grammaticalness," pp. 384–89, and Paul Ziff, "On Understanding 'Understanding Utterances,'" pp. 390–99. Samuel R. Levin has briefly discussed ungrammatical poetry within a similar framework in *Linguistic Structures in Poetry* (The Hague, 1962), Chapters 2 and 3.

Moreover, when a poet deviates from normal syntax he is not doing what comes most habitually, but is making a special sort of choice. And since there are innumerable kinds of deviance, we should expect that the ones elected by a poem or poet spring from particular semantic impulses, particular ways of looking at experience. For instance, I think such a tendency displays itself in Thomas' lines. The construction just noted conceives the passing of rivers through vales as an agent acting upon an object. Likewise, "flocked" in line 9 becomes a transitive verb, and the spatial connection Thomas refers to— flocks in a hold—is reshaped into an action—flocking—performed by an unnamed agent upon the hold. There are many other examples in the poem of deviance that projects unaccustomed activity and process upon nature. Next, notice that beneath line 2 is the sentence "the twilight is blind," in which an inanimate noun takes an animate adjective, and that in line 5 "sail" takes the animate adjective "stealthy." This type of deviance also runs throughout the poem: Thomas sees nature as personal. Again, "twilight" is subject of "fer-ries," and should thus be a concrete noun, as should the object, "tale." Here and elsewhere in the poem the division between substance and abstraction tends to disappear. Again and again syntactic deviance breaks down categori-cal boundaries and converts juxtaposition into action, inanimate into human, abstract into physical, static into active. Now, much of Thomas' poetry dis-plays the world as process, as interacting forces and repeating cycles, in which human beings and human thought are indifferently caught up.[6] I suggest that Thomas' syntactical irregularities often serve this vision of things. To say so, of course, is only to extend the natural critical premise that a good poet sets linguistic forms to work for him in the cause of artistic and thematic form. And if he strays from grammatical patterns he does not thereby leave language or reason behind: if anything, he draws the more deeply on linguistic structure and on the processes of human understanding that are implicit in our use of well-formed sentences.

Most of what I have said falls short of adequate precision, and much of the detail rests on conjecture about English grammar, which at this point is by no means fully understood. But I hope that in loosely stringing together several hypotheses about the fundamental role of the sentence I have indicated some areas where a rich exchange between linguistics and critical theory might eventually take place. To wit, the elusive intuition we have of *form* and *content* may turn out to be anchored in a distinction between the surface structures and the deep structures of sentences. If so, syntactic theory will also feed into the theory of *style*. Still more evidently, the proper *analysis* of styles waits on a satisfactory analysis of sentences. Matters of *rhetoric,* such as emphasis and order, also promise to come clearer as we better understand internal relations in sentences. More generally, we may be able to enlarge and deepen our concept of literary *structure* as we are increasingly able to make it subsume linguistic structure—including especially the structure of

[6] Ralph Maud's fine study, *Entrances to Dylan Thomas' Poetry* (Pittsburgh, 1963), describes the phenomenon well in a chapter called "Process Poems."

deviant sentences. And most important, since critical understanding follows and builds on understanding of sentences, generative grammar should eventually be a reliable assistant in the effort of seeing just how a given literary work sifts through a reader's mind, what cognitive and emotional processes it sets in motion, and what organization of experience it encourages. In so far as critical theory concerns itself with meaning, it cannot afford to bypass the complex and elegant structures that lie at the inception of all verbal meaning.

The Application of Transformational Generative Grammar to the Analysis of Similes and Metaphors in Modern English

Rosemarie Gläser

Often style in language is equated with figures of speech, so that literal, straightforward language has no style, but as it becomes more metaphorical, as more figures of grammar and of thought accrue to it, it gains style. In other words, this view rests on the notion that figurative language is decoration and that decoration is style.

The case that metaphor is basic to language hardly needs to be reargued, however. And literal, nonfigurative language might be able to say so many things in almost an equal number of words, but, nonetheless, language would hardly be able to sustain the loss of figurativeness. So much seems clear.

In her essay, Gläser uses semantic theories that developed from transformational generative grammar to explain the nature of metaphor. Briefly, her argument is that a noun such as "man" has the semantic feature [+human], and a noun such as "lion" has the semantic feature [−human]; when these two nouns are collocated in a proposition such as "That man is a lion," the disjunction of semantic features creates a metaphor.

Gläser does not deal with another sort of metaphor that can be explained, at least partially, by transformational generative semantics, and it is worth noting.

All verbs, obviously, have characteristics that have to do with the subjects, objects, and so on, that they can appear with. Thus, the verb "think" can only appear, in normal usage, with a subject that is "humanoid" ("man," "child," "dog," "dolphin" . . .), that is, a subject that we can conceive as having the typical human ability to think rationally. We can express this idea thus: think: [+*humanoid*____]. *Now then, watch how the following series slides from literalness to metaphor to surrealism:*

> *The boy thinks the torpedo is a dolphin.*
> *The dolphin thinks the torpedo is a shark.*
> *The gopher thinks the dog is a coyote.*
> *The earthworm thinks it's raining when I water the lawn.*
> *The carrot thinks Vigoro is steer manure.*
> *The rock thinks the pebble is a midget.*

As Aristotle said in the Rhetoric, *". . . midway between the unintelligible and the commonplace, it is a metaphor which most produces knowledge."*

Or consider a sentence such as the following: "Melvin drew the line." On the face of it, it is not metaphorical. Its semantics (greatly oversimplified) look like this:

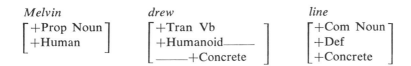

In other words, "Melvin" is a human proper noun; *"drew" is a* transitive verb *that must have a* humanoid subject *and a* concrete object; *"line" is a* definite concrete common noun. *But suppose we put the sentence into a context like this:*

> *Melvin would steal bubble gum. Melvin would fib to his teacher. But he wouldn't peddle grass. Melvin drew the line.*

In this case, "line" has the feature [−*concrete*], *i.e., abstract, for "the line" here is a moral limit. The metaphorical effect arises from the interaction between the verb "draw," which normally takes a concrete object* ([____+*concrete*]) *and the feature* [−*concrete*] *which has been imposed upon "line" by the context.*

One more example. The first of the following sentences is literal, and the second is metaphorical:

> *Geoffrey gulped beer.*
> *Geoffrey gulped knowledge.*

The difference between the literal and the metaphorical uses of the verb "gulp" can be economically explained in the following way:

gulp
$$\begin{bmatrix} +\text{Trans Vb} \\ +\text{Humanoid}\underline{} \\ \underline{}+\text{Liquid} \end{bmatrix}$$

beer
$$\begin{bmatrix} +\text{Com Noun} \\ +\text{Liquid} \end{bmatrix}$$

knowledge
$$\begin{bmatrix} +\text{Com Noun} \\ -\text{Concrete} \end{bmatrix}$$

In other words, "gulp" is a transitive verb which takes an object that is a liquid, and "beer" is a liquid, but "knowledge" is abstract ([−Concrete]), and, therefore, is neither liquid, solid, nor gas.

Gläser quite rightly points to disjunction of semantic features as the source for metaphor. If her illuminating discussion has any single weakness it is that, as we have pointed out, she does not go far enough in her probing.

One further comment needs to be made. Any sort of grammatical description is merely an attempt to make explicit that which we know intuitively. Gläser's discussion does lucidly and economically move toward an explicit account of our implicit understanding of metaphor.

At the outset, the topic under discussion may raise the general question as to what extent Chomsky's generative model is applicable to the field of stylistics. In the recent development of transformational generative grammar, Chomsky's so-called Standard Theory, as suggested in *Aspects of the Theory of Syntax* [1] has undergone a number of modifications even touching such basic presuppositions as the nature of deep and surface structure. In the light of criticism levelled by such transformationalists as Ross, Lakoff, Fillmore and McCawley against the Standard Theory there might be some doubt whether it is still legitimate to deal with linguistic facts in terms of Chomsky's *Aspects*. And yet, only a few systematic attempts have been made so far to test Chomsky's concept of deep structure rules on the material of a living language. As I see it, sufficient evidence for what parts of Chomsky's model will be of lasting importance can only be provided by new data of practical linguistic analysis. Chomsky's generative grammar has been conceived as an explanation of the native speaker's competence which is defined as his ability to make infinite use of a finite number of elements, to form and understand sentences and to decide whether a sentence is well-formed or deviant. With these general theoretical aims, Chomsky's model is intended as a contribution to a universal grammar of meta-linguistic character and of high explanatory power.

If we consider the generative model in this abstract lay-out, there seems to be little or no place for style. Stylistic phenomena can only be incorporated in Chomsky's model if we correlate linguistic competence with linguistic performance, the actual speech event. It is true that Chomsky only wants to deal with the notion of competence, but in fact there is no competence as an end in itself. When the native speaker forms and evaluates actual sentences, per-

[1] The M.I.T. Press, 1967, 4th ed.

formance comes into play, since sentences are results of performance. Sentences, moreover, are isolated parts of discourse, and an immanent feature of discourse is style. In this way, style enters the description of performance as an ingredient of any speech act. Although Chomsky has emphasized that the terms *competence* and *performance* should not be identified with the Saussurean dichotomy of *langue* and *parole,* the wide range of competence is well suited to cover stylistic features that are traditionally attributed to *parole.* It is in current usage that deviant structures or particular arrangements of units of speech occur, having different stylistic functions.

So far, Chomsky has regarded studies on performance as "by-products" of the description of competence. Such "by-products," as he puts it, are "deviations from rules, as a stylistic device." [2] As regards stylistic features in performance, I think, we are justified in applying the set of rules provided by the speaker's linguistic competence.

Undoubtedly, one of the lasting achievements of transformational generative grammar is the idea of the *gradation of grammaticalness.* As studies on both German [3] and English [4] texts have proved, this concept can be applied to the analysis of style, especially to poetic diction and tropes. In these explorations, the linguistic unit under research is, however, the sentence, and not the whole text. The micro-linguistic core of the widely accepted gradation of grammaticalness is Chomsky's sub-division of the base-component into context-free and context-sensitive sub-categorization rules. These rules allow a more delicate description than the former binary distinction between right and wrong. The descriptive mechanism of grammaticalness, however, cannot contribute to the *stylistic interpretation* of deviant structures, nor can it account for their stylistic effect.

Violations of the phonological norm (phonological rules of the surface structure respectively) will be easily discovered in such sentences as these from Arnold Wesker's *Roots:*

> *Watcha* Jimmy Beales, how you *doin', bor?* (watcha = what you, expressing a greeting, "hallo"; doin' = doing; bor = neighbour).

Context-free sub-categorization rules, e.g., morphological rules of well-formedness, are violated in the following case:

> His wife *driv* him up in the ole Armstrong. (drive = drove)
> Mother *reckon* some people get indigestion *so bad* that *go* right through

[2] *Aspects,* pp. 11, 15.

[3] Manfred Bierwisch, "Poetik und Linguistik," *Sprache im technischen Zeitalter* (1965), pp. 1258–1273. Anita Steube, *Gradation der Grammatikalität und stilistische Adäquatheit* (diss. Leipzig 1966).

[4] Richard Ohmann, "Generative Grammars and the Concept of Literary Style," *Word,* XX (December 1964), pp. 423–39. James Peter Thorne, "Stylistics and Generative Grammars," *Journal of Linguistics* (1965), pp. 49–59. Cf. also, *Style in Language,* ed. Thomas A. Sebeok (The M.I.T. Press, 1964). Rosemarie Gläser, *Linguistische Kriterien der Stilbeschreibung (dargestellt an einigen Tropen des modernen Englischen)* (professorial thesis, Leipzig, 1969).

their stomach to the back. (reckon = reckons; so bad = so badly; go = it goes)

Such deviations from grammaticalness in terms of a received standard may have an artistic function. Sub-standard forms may be an indicator of a *regional dialect* (in the quoted example of Norfolk dialect) and at the same time of a *sociolect* (here working class background), a powerful method of character drawing, in stylistics known as the *linguistic portrait*. We should take into consideration that dialects proper form a sub-system of the national standard language and may be described as the linguistic competence of the dialect speaker. Hence, dialect forms should be distinguished from such morphological errors occurring in the usage of small children or foreigners, based on wrong analogy; e.g., the oxes drawed the cart.

Other deviations from context-free sub-categorization rules are demonstrated by the following examples:

John Heath-Stubbs, *Selected Poems:*

> I invoke the ambiguous veiled *Venuses*
> In their avatars

(Venus has the syntactic marker [−plural] as a proper noun.)

Dylan Thomas:

> *Myselves*
> The grievers
> Grieve

(Myself shares the feature [−plural].)

Virginia Woolf, *To the Lighthouse:*

> That was the view, she said, stooping, growing *greyer-eyed*, that her husband loved.

(syntactic marker [−comparable].)

Deviations from context-sensitive sub-categorization rules may concern strict sub-categorization rules and selectional rules. A strict sub-categorization rule is violated when verbs are used in new syntactic functions, as does Dylan Thomas:

> There could I *marvel* my birthday *away*

(*Marvel* has the syntactic marker [−transitive], *marvel away* may be understood as a nonce formation of a phrasal verb or rather a contamination between "marvel at" and "twaddle away.")

Deviations from selectional rules are in fact the source of many figures of speech such as metaphors, synaesthesia, personification, simile, metonymy and oxymoron.

Dylan Thomas begins a poem:

> *A grief ago*
> She who was who I hold, the fats and flower . . .

Figures like these are based on structural incompatibility or incongruence, since *ago* presupposes a noun with the semantic marker [+temporal]. This particular figure not only occurs in elevated poetry but may also be found in advertising texts where surprise effects are intended. Leech quotes an advertising slogan used by an English firm.[5]

> Only two *Alka-Seltzers ago*
> You were feeling down-hearted and low
> Who would ever know you were under the weather
> Only *two Alka-Seltzers ago!*

More examples from literary texts:
Virginia Woolf, *The Waves:*

> I let *silence* fall, *drop by drop*
> (*Silence* has the semantic marker [−liquid.])

William Golding, *Lord of the Flies:*

> . . . the *trees* in the forest *sighed* . . .
> (*Sighed* is restricted to a human agent, since it is linked with emotions.)

Naturally, not all deviant structures bring about a stylistic effect, but some of them can immediately be identified as stylistic devices. On the other hand, it would be absurd to reduce phenomena of style to linguistic deviations only. A macro-linguistic model of communication which according to Roman Jakobson implies addresser, addressee, context, message, contact and code[6] calls for other than micro-linguistic categories. Functional varieties of speech and registers which are linked with various spheres of activity are determined by selectional rules of a special kind, e.g., settings for casual or non-casual speech, cf. Martin Joos, "The Five Clocks."[7] A functional classification of discourse therefore cannot be based on deviations from grammaticalness, but rather on an adequate description of speech situations. With these general restrictions, we can say that Chomsky's gradation of grammaticalness can only form a *micro-linguistic* core for style analysis.

Another aspect of Chomsky's theory which may be extended to the matter of style is the native speaker's *linguistic competence.* From this competence he derives the ability to understand and even produce poetic structures such as those found in imagery, poetic diction, tropes, and prose fiction. To some extent figures of speech are predictable in poetic discourse. They represent what is generally called "poetic license" or "individual creations." Tropes immediately come to mind when we speak of stylistic features or devices. The effect of such structures and their acceptability in a poetic context, however,

---

[5] Geoffrey N. Leech, *English in Advertising,* English Language Series (London, 1966), p. 177.

[6] Roman Jakobson, cf. *Style in Language* (Note 4), p. 353.

[7] Martin Joos, "The Five Clocks," *International Journal of American Linguistics,* XXVIII (Number 2, April 1962), pp. 9–62.

cannot be the subject of the native speaker's linguistic competence in Chomsky's terms, but rather an additional faculty of it. It is the speaker's *poetic competence* that evaluates sentences for their poetic, emotional, or aesthetic value. The term "poetische Kompetenz" was coined by Manfred Bierwisch; the same phenomenon was described by Richard Ohmann as the speaker's "stylistic intuition." The poetic competence is defined as a special function of the linguistic competence which enables the native speaker to produce and understand poetic structures and to interpret their effect in literary texts. In this respect, the poetic competence is interrelated with an *aesthetic competence* that accounts for aesthetic values in other semiotic systems (music, art) as well. Such considerations lead us to the field of pragmatics, and far beyond Chomsky's micro-linguistic model.

With regard to style analysis (as style is an ingredient part of every speech act), we may even introduce the term *situational* or *pragmatic competence*. In daily usage the speaker follows certain patterns of style imposed by functional varieties in various fields of activity. As a matter of experience, he knows how to choose the proper formulas of address for finishing a letter or where to choose a casual register. Deviations from situationally motivated linguistic norms are easily recognized and often the source of humour and mockery. The speaker's situational or *sociolinguistic competence* thus determines the acceptability of an utterance.

(An illustrative example was quoted by Nils Erik Enkvist:

> Your Majesty, My Lords—It is my painful duty to impart to you the momentous and doleful tidings that this morning Lord X peacefully kicked the bucket.) [8]

Finally, in connection with the native speaker's linguistic competence we could assume an *empirical* or *cognitive competence* on which the logical validity, or the "truth conditions" (cf. Paul Ziff [9]) of an utterance are examined. Paradoxical statements are frequently found in poetry and may cause a strong effect of estrangement; e.g., Lawrence Durrell, *Justine:*

> Clouds of dried blood walk the streets like prophesies, the sand is settling into the sea like powder in the curls of a stale wig.

In fact, this competence is closely connected with the semantic component of the speaker's linguistic competence (which accounts for the semantic compatibility of lexicon entries).

With these extensions of Chomsky's model of competence we have obtained a broader basis for the application of the generative model to the complex phenomenon of style. The various competences discussed so far will serve as an evaluation procedure in *style analysis;* in a model of stylistics, where style is *generated* they may even form a contextual blocking device or

---

[8] Nils Erik Enkvist, "Topic, Focus and Linkage. Notes Towards Inter-sentence Linguistics," *AFTIL 1* (Abo, 1967), p. 1.

[9] Paul Ziff, *Semantic Analysis* (New York, 1961, 2nd ed.).

corrective in order to exclude sentences which are ill-suited to the given situation. Such extensions of the generative model actually presuppose an explicit description of patterns of style in various situations, such as registers or functional varieties.

If we re-examine the micro-linguistic requirements for such a comprehensive model of stylistics, we may come to the conclusion that much spade-work is still to be done. The transformational description of modern English syntax undertaken by Paul Roberts [10] and supported by individual contributions from Lees, Fillmore and other M.I.T. transformationalists is far from being satisfactory. For the purpose of style analysis of such structures as figures of speech in the sense of ancient rhetoric we need a fairly wide inventory of semantic markers in order to be able to describe semantic transfers. In other words, the deviations from selectional rules which are, for example, the source of metaphors, call for a developed semantic component of the transformational system.

For the following practical analysis of figures of speech we need a subtle and suitable inventory of semantic markers of nouns, verbs and adjectives. Unfortunately, the segmentation ("atomizing") of meaning, which has been attempted by several people (e.g., Katz-Postal, Chomsky, Weinreich, Greimas, Pottier) [11] has not yet led to a satisfactory number of ultimate semantic constituents with regard to the English language, let alone to semantic universals. In a similar way, the combinatory process of semantic markers has only been described in rough outlines so far. For the present stylistic analysis of tropes and small segments of discourse, we have modified and considerably extended the tree diagram of the semantic sub-classification of the noun which Chomsky has suggested as a binary scheme, thus dividing nouns into common and proper. With a view to actual speech, we have projected the two branches of his draft on one, due to the fact that proper nouns tend to take an article and a plural ending (there are three *Bills* in our team, *Hoovers* sell well, Malan was regarded as a *South African Hitler*). Besides, the necessary cross classification (animate, non-animate, individual, collective) would have led to a cumbersome repetition and redundancy. In contrast to Chomsky we have discarded the node "count"/"non-count," since there is a syntactic and a semantic notion of countability which can hardly be united in one tree diagram (e.g., semantic countability is absent in such collective nouns as herd, flock, staff, government; whereas syntactically seen, such nouns as snow, deer, trout are non-count).

The tree diagram of the semantic markers of the noun has the following shape:

[10] Paul Roberts, *English Syntax. A Book of Programed Lessons: An Introduction to Transformational Grammar* (New York, 1964).

[11] Jerrold J. Katz and Paul M. Postal, *An Integrated Theory of Linguistic Descriptions* (The M.I.T. Press, 1965, 2nd ed.); Uriel Weinreich, "Explorations in Semantic Theory," *Current Trends in Linguistics,* III (1965); A. J. Greimas, *Sémantique Structurale* (Paris, 1966).

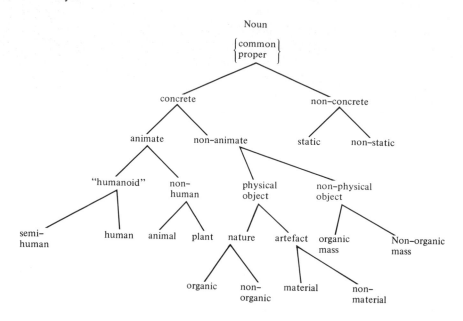

(As an auxiliary node, the marker "humanoid" had to be included because in poetic diction there occurs the vocabulary of mythology, such as proper names of ancient gods; in everyday usage we find figures from fairytales and allusions to them quite often in advertising texts.)

Comment on the tree diagram:

> [*Non-human*] comprises the markers [*animal*] and [*plant*]
> [Nature] covers [organic] and [non-organic] matter:
>> organic: parts of body, parts of a plant, e.g., trunk, finger, root, organs, secretions, e.g., tear.
>> non-organic: ores, topographic formations such as mountain, hill, river, island; elementary forces like rain, thunderstorm, etc.
> [Artefact] is understood as the result of intentional production of man, the result of work:
>> physical objects: table, bread, fibre, book;
>> non-material: song, poem, word.
> [Organic mass]: substance not having contours: blood, sweat; organic substance and mixtures: flour, dough.
> [Non-organic mass]: metals, gravel, sand, lava, raw material like Orlon.
> [Non-concrete] (= abstract)
>> static: moods like happiness, frustration, system;
>> non-static (= dynamic): revolution, war, upheaval, development.

(The classificatory scheme touches a general problem: it is extremely difficult to classify the whole material and immaterial world on a logical basis and even more so on a linguistic principle. A number of dictionaries compiled as a thesaurus have demonstrated the problem of finding logical categories that cover linguistic homonymy and polysemy and do not disturb semantic relations.)

The present tree diagram of semantic markers of the noun may provide the basis for a sub-classification of verbs and adjectives. These parts of speech have to a lesser degree inherent (context-free) semantic features; their syntactic and semantic compatibility with other parts of the sentence greatly depends on the semantic markers of the noun (e.g. selectional restrictions of subject and object). Inherent features of the verb are, e.g., such markers as surface contact—hit, break, touch—(cf. Fillmore),[12] motion, and state. The inherent semantic features of the verb, on the other hand, dominate the selection of an adverbial.

In the following part of my paper, which is to illustrate the application of transformational grammar to stylistic devices, I focus attention on some figures of speech which have in common the "violation" of selectional rules of the base. These figures are the simile, various sub-groups of metaphors such as personification (anthropomorphism), and animal metaphor.

As a figure of speech the *simile,* or *stylistic comparison,* shares the structural pattern of the grammatical comparison: both are based on an embedding transformation and form a semantic and syntactic parallelism. The peculiarity of the stylistic comparison, however, is that it has a semantic tension between the noun comparing (*le comparant*) and the noun compared (*le comparé*). As a rule, in the grammatical comparison the missing link, traditionally called *tertium comparationis (le trait commun),* which is the expression of equality or inequality, is represented in the surface structure, whereas in the simile it is not. The deletion of the *tertium comparationis* in the surface structure makes a simile more subtle: only from the context of the sentence in the surface structure can we reconstruct the missing link, by comparing the semantic markers of the correlated lexical items and by attributing to them associative features derived from the whole sentence. In terms of transformational syntax the comparison may be understood as an intensifier.

   i. John works as hard as a miner vs. John works extremely hard.
  ii. John works like a horse.
 iii. John works like a machine.

Sentence ii. compares John [+human] to an animal. As both nouns belong to the category *animate,* their semantic tension is not so strong as in iii., where the semantic distance between human (John) and *artefact* (machine) is greater. The common element in ii. and iii. results from the semantics of the sentence, which is the interrelation of a bundle of semantic features which we empirically attribute to horse and machine:

> horse: animal, quadruped, mammal, . . . domestic animal, working
> hard, obediently, incessantly . . .

[12] Charles F. Fillmore, "The Grammar of 'hit' and 'break' " (unpublished manuscript, 1968/1969).

machine: physical object, artefact material, labour device . . . labour-
and time-saving, effective, powerful . . .

For the purpose of stylistic interpretation, the categories *human, animal,* and
artefact are obviously insufficient; the comparison proper is established on
grounds of more delicate semantic features from which the *tertium comparationis* (=T.C.) is derived.

Which semantic element is fitted in as the missing link is a matter of experience and of individual interpretation and association. At any rate, the
relevant features are not so much the categorical markers as the non-hierarchical features (in terms of Fodor-Katz "distinguishers"). Therefore in the simile
under discussion such categorical features as animal, mammal, artefact, labour device are of minor importance for the understanding and interpretation.
The relevant features which account for the effect of a simile can be understood as a non-hierarchical list, being correlated in the way of a logical conjunction. As a very illustrative example I quote an advertising slogan from
The Observer (5.3. 1967, p. 29):

> **An Exciting Advance in Skin Care**
> **MOISTURA by Cyclax Acts Like Magic on Tired Skin.**

This simile is rather complicated because of its different embeddings. The
T.C. is not represented in the surface structure. It can only be inserted hypothetically in the deep structure, as a dummy symbol in the base phrase
marker, functioning as an adverbial of manner which we derive from the
associative features of the lexical item Magic (unbelievable, wonderful, irre-
sistible . . .). The tree diagram illustrates the various levels of embedding
and the transformation mechanism. The semantic tension is based on the distance of the two lexical items in the tree diagram (MOISTURA [artefact
material] magic [non-concrete/static]).

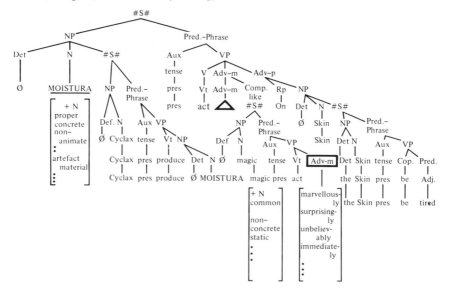

There are various types of similes where the T.C. is either represented or deleted, fulfilling the function of an adverbial of manner or a noun modifier. The semantic tension depends on the proximity or remoteness of the prevailing semantic markers of the nouns concerned, according to our suggested tree diagram.

G. Durrell, *My Family and Other Animals:*

> Our *rivers* were wide, and *blue* as *forget-me-nots,* freckled with canoes and crocodiles.

D. H. Lawrence, *Lady Chatterley's Lover:*

> My *heart* is *numb* as a *potato.*

Journalism: Alan Warner, *A Short Guide to English Style:*

> In the long run I think that *prose,* like *peace,* is *indivisible.*

W. Golding, *Lord of the Flies:*

> A *tree exploded* in the fire like a *bomb.*

(In this example the T.C. can only be derived from the verb.)

L. Durrell, *Justine:*

> The house was perpetually alive to the fern-like pattern of a quartet, or to the foundering plunge of *saxophones crying* to the night like *cockolds.*

Newspaper text: *The Listener:*

> Economists study statistics, not human beings. For the sociologist, *men* in houses are like *rats* in mazes.

A. Sillitoe, *Key to the Door:*

> *Sweat,* helped by the high up blistering sun, poured out of him like a *refugee soul.*

The semantic proximity between the nouns compared is greater in the relation men/rats than in saxophones/cuckolds where there is in fact no natural similarity, unless we restore the missing link from the context of the verb; the T.C. thus serves as an adverbial of manner (cry shrilly, hysterically, whiningly . . .). Intuitively, we feel that the similes comparing MOISTURA and magic, sweat and refugee soul, prose and peace are rather arbitrary, far-fetched and even incompatible. Our empirical competence tells us that there is no natural link between saxophones and cuckolds, sweat and refugee soul, but that there may be common features between men and rats, blue rivers and forget-me-nots, a numb heart and a potato. The principle of semantic proximity and remoteness which we tried to derive from the above-mentioned cases has not yet been formulated, although it was approached in previous studies. What R. A. Sayce has remarked about the semantic relations in a metaphor has also some bearing on the simile. In his book, *Style in French*

Prose (1961, p. 45) he writes that the " 'angle' of the metaphor (angle of the image)" should be wide enough to attract the reader's attention. Too much similarity between two nouns forming a metaphor or a simile would be trite and boring. In terms of generative transformational grammar, the opinion held by Sayce and backed by Stephen Ullmann means that the stylistic effect of a simile or a metaphor increases with the semantic remoteness of the nouns compared. The stemma of the semantic classification of nouns thus seems to provide an objective criterion for this relation and for the subsequent stylistic interpretation.

The tree diagram, furthermore, helps us in the analysis of other figures of speech, especially various kinds of metaphors such as personification (anthropomorphism) and animal metaphor ("animalification"). In nominal metaphors the identity between two correlated nouns is expressed in the surface structure by such verbs as to be, become, turn, grow, remain, etc.; the T.C. is always absent. The semantic proximity or remoteness results from the categorical markers plus the additional associative, idiosyncratic features of the nouns. Metaphors are generated in the deep structure.

W. Golding, *Lord of the Flies:*

> *Ralph* was a *shock of hair* and *Piggy* a *bag of fat.*

L. Durrell:

> His real *life* became a buried *stream.*

Relations of remoteness like these may occur in transforms with post-nominal modifiers as for instance,

> He was a *dead fish* of a *gentleman.*

Animal metaphors and anthropomorphisms are generally based on verbs. These are characterized by the selectional restrictions (human or animal agent). Apart from their context-sensitive semantic markers, these verbs may be classified in subgroups according to subordinate inherent semantic features.

Anthropomorphisms or *personifications* are based on verbs with the categorical contextual feature [human]. Morton M. Bloomfield has emphasized [13] that personifications are formed by verbs rather than nouns. In poetic texts and in prose writing we find recurrent patterns of semantic transfer which may be relevant in, and characteristic of, a future poetic glossary; i.e., selectional rules in a special register or functional variety. Verbs of human vocal utterance and communication (such as to whisper, murmur, shout) occur with human agents, even with such nouns which are characterized by the absence of sound production.

---

[13] Morton M. Bloomfield, "Generative Grammars and the Theory of Literature," *Résumés des Communications.* Xème Congrès International des Linguistes (Bucarest 28 août—2 septembre 1967). Morton M. Bloomfield, "A Grammatical Approach to Personification Allegory," *Modern Philology,* LX (Febr. 1963), p. 161 ff.

cicada
waters
Whisper [+human] is collocated with wind
waltz
heart

The semantic remoteness between heart and whisper is much greater than between waters, wind + whisper. We are inclined to accept these examples as empirically correct, since in our empirical competence they fulfil a truth condition: the soft noise of the wind and waters may be identified as, or associated with, a whispering sound, which we cannot attribute to heart, and probably not to waltz.

Sean O'Casey, *Red Roses For Me:*

> 1st Man: . . . . Regal and proud She was, an' wondrous, so that me eyes failed; me knees thrembled an' bent low, an' me *heart whispered* a silent prayer to itself as th' vision passed me by . . . .

John Heath-Stubbs, "The Don Juan Triptych," *Selected Poems:*

> And he can remember that night when he stood on the terrace
> Sunning himself in the black beams of vicarious sin,
> While the *waltz whispered* within . . . .

The collocations of wind, waters and whisper are a violation of selectional rules in terms of generative grammar; they are, however, acceptable on a deep structure underlying that of the base. We may describe this deeper layer as the empirical or cognitive deep structure, a model of the native speaker's empirical or cognitive competence. On this level, such metaphors which Ernst Leisi has aptly called "indirekte Metaphern" (e.g., *die Steine schweigen*) [14] can be interpreted.

A similar anthropomorphic transfer occurs in a group of verbs describing emotions (to cry, weep, rage, sigh, etc.). Collocations with sigh are manifold:

waters
trees
fields   + sigh
trousers

The first three examples show a semantic proximity in the sense of an indirect metaphor, whereas the selection of trousers + sigh strikes us as far-fetched.

W. Golding, *Lord of the Flies:*

> Maurice's *trousers* gave way with a *sigh* and he abandoned them as a wreck . . .

(Sigh is represented in a nominalization transformation; the semantic remoteness remains the same.)

[14] Ernst Leisi, *Der Wortinhalt. Seine Struktur im Englischen und im Deutschen* (Heidelberg, 1961, 2nd ed.).

Incompatible are such combinations as "Comets weep" (T. S. Eliot), "my blood cries" (J. Heath-Stubbs), and "the moon rages" (Dylan Thomas).

Animal metaphors are also based on deviations from selectional rules in that way. Verbs and adjectives with the restriction to a noun with the semantic marker [+animal] are transferred to lifeless objects. In handbooks on style, this figure of speech is hardly ever mentioned. Only Jerome Beaty and William H. Matchett (*Poetry—From Statement to Meaning,* OUP, 1965) point out that there is a gap in terminology: "We have no word like 'animalification' to describe the comparable (if not identical) process by which a lifeless object is given the attributes of a beast" (p. 233). Verbs of animal movements are for instance combined with nouns not having the semantic marker [animal] (to crawl, gallop).

V. Woolf, *The Waves:*

> Words and words and *words,* how they *gallop*—how they lash their long manes and tails . . . .

John Wain, *Hurry On Down:*

> . . . the *phrases* that insistently *barked* inside his brain.

In the case of verbs of animal voices, when to roar is combined with tram, bus, wind, one can recognize a semantic proximity; whereas the sentences "the *blood roared* in Ralph's ears" (W. Golding, *Lord of the Flies*) and "Now hot towels envelop me, and their roughness, as I rub my back, makes my *blood purr*" (V. Woolf, *The Waves*), seem to be semantically incompatible.

What strikes us most is the recurrence of a number of such figures in literary texts, as clichés of poetic licence. "Waves" and "water," collocated with verbs such as "to hobble" and "to leap" are nearly predictable. Selectional rules of the micro-linguistic model of the base as presented in the Standard Theory could obviously be completed by sub-rules of poetic usage, operating on a different level of grammaticalness.

Conclusion

In conclusion we can state that the concept of deep and surface structure can help us, as a sort of discovery procedure, to find out regularities of semantic transfer which underlie various figures of speech. It is important to note that not all deviations from selectional rules create a metaphor or a simile. Random selections of lexical items are not yet a metaphorical string. Apart from the semantic proximity or remoteness of the categorical semantic markers, there must be a minimum of semantic correspondence between the idiosyncratic semantic features of the lexical items compared. Besides inherent (categorical) features we need associative, contextual features for stylistic interpretation. These are derived from our empirical competence.

The poetic transfers discussed in this article give rise to the assumption that we can set up a *lexicon of poetic collocations* which occur either in similes or metaphors. The material for such a corpus could be drawn from an analysis of various kinds of texts, ranging from poetry and prose fiction to scientific prose. In literary texts semantic transfers may be predictable to a certain extent. By means of close reading a number of recurrent patterns of poetic transfers can be easily distinguished. When some basic types of poetic collocations are evident, they can be illustrated by new material. In certain poetic texts they may have a high degree of probability. A future lexicon of poetic collocations could be arranged either alphabetically or as a thesaurus. At any rate, the spadework needed for such a project would contribute to the endeavours of the lexicographer who has to list transferred usages.

Undoubtedly the concept of transformational generative grammar has provided new methods for style analysis. Much basic work remains to be done to demonstrate the explanatory power of the Standard Theory in the field of text analysis, let alone text generation. The application of this theory to the description of tropes is one more evidence for its heuristic value.

Four Forms of Metaphor

Laurence Perrine

In The Philosophy of Rhetoric (*1936*), *I. A. Richards proposed that every metaphor has two parts, the* tenor, *which is the whole meaning in context, and the* vehicle, *which is the device. In the essay reprinted here, Laurence Perrine develops a useful taxonomy of tenor and vehicle, thus making a logical extension to Richards's influential work.*

Richards collected a number of memorable quotations concerning metaphor, and they are worth reproducing here:

> *As to metaphorical expression, that is a great excellence in style, when it is used with propriety, for it gives you two ideas for one.—Dr. Johnson*

> *Language is vitally metaphorical; that is, it marks the before unapprehended relations of things and perpetuates their apprehension, until words, which represent them, become, through time, signs for portions or classes of thought instead of pictures of integral thoughts: and then, if no new poets should arise to create afresh the associations which have been thus disorganized, language will be dead to all the nobler purposes of human intercourse.—Shelley*

The greatest thing by far is to have a command of metaphor. . . . This alone cannot be imparted to another: it is the mark of genius, for to make good metaphors implies an eye for resemblances.—Aristotle

To compare two objects, as remote from one another in character as possible, or by any other method put them together in a sudden and striking fashion, this remains the highest task to which poetry can aspire.—André Breton

Finally, I. A. Richards says, "If we cannot distinguish tenor from vehicle then we may provisionally take the word to be literal; if we can distinguish at least two cooperating uses, then we have metaphor." *

1

For the poet, declared Aristotle, "the greatest thing by far is to have command of metaphor." For the poetry reader, I would add, the ability to interpret metaphor is equally important. Indeed, the shores of poetry explication are littered with the bones of ships commanded by captains, both amateur and professional, who could not distinguish literal statement from metaphorical, or who, if they could, could not tell what was being compared to what, or why. In this essay I wish to propose, not a guaranteed remedy against disaster, but a new way of looking at and classifying metaphors, which I think may be pedagogically useful.

A metaphor, as I define it, consists of a comparison between essentially unlike things. There are two components in every metaphor: the concept being actually discussed, and the thing to which it is compared. I shall refer to these, ordinarily, as the literal term and the figurative term. The two terms together compose the metaphor.

The established method of classifying metaphors, I take it, is through grammatical analysis, which begins by identifying the part of speech of the figurative term. According to this system, there are noun metaphors of various kinds; there are also verb metaphors, adjective metaphors, and occasionally adverb and even preposition metaphors. My own analysis will take a different approach. Based on the underlying assumption that both the literal and figurative terms of a metaphor are expressible as substantives, it will classify metaphors according to whether these terms are respectively stated or implied.

Consider, for example, the following passage from *The Life of Samuel Johnson:*

When I called upon Dr. Johnson next morning, I found him highly satisfied with his colloquial prowess the preceding evening. "Well, (said he,) we had good talk." *Boswell.* "Yes, Sir, you tossed and gored several persons."

A grammatical analysis would classify Boswell's remark as a verb metaphor. The figurative term is "tossed and gored." The literal meaning is something

* *The Philosophy of Rhetoric,* p. 119.

like "humiliated by besting in argument." But actually the literal term of this metaphor is hard to express by this method without using other figurative expressions ("put down," "injured," "treated roughly"). In addition, this analysis omits to mention the image which jumps immediately into the reader's head. Boswell's metaphor is more easily and naturally described as one in which the literal term (stated) is Dr. Johnson, and the figurative term (implied) is a bull.

Under the assumption that in all metaphors the concepts likened to each other are expressible as substantives, there are four possible forms of metaphor. In the first, both the literal and figurative terms are named; in the second, only the literal term is named; in the third, only the figurative term is named; in the fourth, neither the literal nor the figurative term is named.

2

In Form 1 metaphors both the literal and figurative terms are named. The most familiar type is a simple statement of identity following the formula "A is B":

> All the world's a stage,
> And all the men and women merely players.
> Shakespeare: *As You Like It*

So frequently, in fact, do textbooks use the "A is B" metaphor as an example that beginning students may be left thinking that all metaphors are of this type. Actually, even Form 1 metaphors exhibit much greater variety. In a very common type, the figurative and literal terms are linked through a genitive construction:

> The Bird of Time has but a little way
> To flutter—and the Bird is on the Wing.
> FitzGerald: *The Rubaiyat*

They may also be linked by apposition:

> Come into the garden, Maud,
> For the black bat, night, has flown.
> Tennyson: *Maud*

Or through the vocative:

> O wild West Wind, thou breath of Autumn's being.
> Shelley: *Ode to the West Wind*

Or by means of a demonstrative adjective:

> Be watchful of your beauty, Lady dear!
> How much hangs on that lamp, you cannot tell.
> Meredith: *Modern Love*

A transitive verb may be used to "transform" the literal term into the figurative:

> Too long a sacrifice
> Can make a stone of the heart.
> Yeats: *Easter 1916*

Occasionally the connection may be indicated merely by parallel construction:

> Fools change in England, and new fools
>   arise;
> For, though the immortal species never
>   dies,
> Yet every year new maggots make new
>   flies.
> Dryden: *Epilogue to*
> *"The Husband his own Cuckold"*

The identification can be made through context alone:

> They called me to the Window, for
> " 'Twas Sunset"—Some one said—
> I only saw a Sapphire Farm—
> And just a Single Herd—
>
> Of Opal Cattle—feeding far
> Upon so vain a Hill—
> As even while I looked—dissolved . . .
> Emily Dickinson

These examples only partially suggest the considerable variety of shapes that Form 1 metaphors may take.[1]

3

In Form 2 metaphors, only the literal term is named, the figurative term must be inferred. Like Form 1 metaphors, they may take a variety of grammatical shapes. Frequently the metaphorical agent is a verb:

> Tom showed such . . . open-mouthed interest in his narrations, that the old guard rubbed up his memory, and launched out into a graphic history of all the performances of the boys on the roads for the last twenty years.
> Thomas Hughes: *Tom Brown's Schooldays*

In this example the verb "rubbed up" transforms memory into a graven brass plate, tarnished, but capable of being shined.

> Sheathe thy impatience; throw cold water on thy choler.
> Shakespeare: *Merry Wives of Windsor*

---

[1] A thorough grammatical study of metaphor is made by Christine Brooke-Rose in *A Grammar of Metaphor* (London: Secker, 1958). I am partially indebted to her in this analysis.

In the first of these two metaphors, the verb "sheathe" makes impatience into a sword; in the second, the verb plus its object—"throws cold water"—makes choler into a fire. In all three of these examples, the action of the verb is forward, affecting later elements in the sentence. In the example cited from Boswell, the action is backwards: the verbs "tossed and gored" work upon their subject, changing Dr. Johnson into a bull. The action may go in both directions: insofar as "launched" in the Hughes example is not a dead metaphor, it transforms the old guard into a ship and graphic history into a sea.

Though verbs are the most frequent metaphorical agents in Form 2 metaphors, the work can also be done by other parts of speech. In Homer's famous "rosy-fingered dawn" an adjective transforms the dawn into a person. In the following example, two adjectives turn light into an animal, probably a horse:

> Pride, like that of the morn,
> When the headlong light is loose.
> Yeats: *The Tower*

Occasionally the work will be done by an adverb:

> Ye quenchless stars! so eloquently bright.
> Robert Montgomery:
> *The Starry Heavens*

Here "eloquently" makes the stars into persons. In the next example a noun does the principal work, assisted by the verb:

> For we are old, and in our quick'st de-
> grees
> The inaudible and noiseless foot of Time
> Steals ere we can effect them.
> Shakespeare:
> *All's Well That Ends Well*

At first glance this metaphor has the appearance of the Form 1 example from *The Rubaiyat* about the "Bird of Time"; actually it is quite different. The noun "foot," though figurative, not literal, is not the figurative term of the metaphor; rather, it is the agent which serves to personify Time. It has no literal equivalent.

Most frequently, in Form 2 metaphors, the work is done by a combination of grammatical elements:

> The tawny-hided desert crouches watch-
> ing her.
> Francis Thompson: *Sister Songs*

In this example the adjective "tawny-hided" and the verb "crouches," plus the participle "watching," make the desert a lion. Neither verb nor adjective by itself would turn the trick. "Crouches" by itself might point to a tiger; "tawny-hided" by itself could point to a camel.

As may have become apparent, personifications are normally Form 2 metaphors:

> Grim-visaged war hath smoothed his
> wrinkled front.
> Shakespeare: *Richard III*

4

In Form 3 metaphors, only the figurative term is named, the literal term must be inferred. At first thought, the interpretive problem with Form 3 metaphors might seem similar to that with Form 2: one half of the comparison is given, the other half must be guessed. Form 3 metaphors, however, frequently introduce an additional problem: they can easily be mistaken for literal statements.

> Night's candles are burnt out.
> Shakespeare:
> *Romeo and Juliet*

A Form 2 version of this comparison might read "The stars had burnt down to their smoky wicks and flickered out." Here a discrepancy between the logical meanings of the subject and the predicate of the sentence signals the presence of metaphor. In Shakespeare's line, however, the subject and predicate belong to the same area of discourse, and there is no internal clue that Romeo is not talking about real candles—candles that have been burning all night and now, with the approach of morning, have burnt out. We must depend upon a larger context for the clues that indicate a metaphorical reading. When we restore the statement to the speech in which it occurs, we see that Romeo is looking at the sky:

> Look love, what envious streaks
> Do lace the severing clouds in yonder
> East—
> Night's candles are burnt out and jocund
> Day
> Stands tiptoe on the misty mountain tops.

Because in Form 3 metaphors the writer's real subject of discourse is suppressed, riddles often take this form:

> In Spring I look gay
> Decked in comely array,
> In Summer more clothing I wear;
> When colder it grows,
> I fling off my clothes,
> And in Winter quite naked appear.
> *Nursery Rhyme*

Unless presented in a context which makes us understand we are to guess the answer, this little rhyme might be taken as a perfectly literal bit of nonsense verse. Though the speaker's behavior is eccentric, it is no more so than that of many persons in Edward Lear's limericks. Ordinarily, however, a poem like this one will be printed on a page labeled "Riddles" or followed by the question "Who am I?"

Many proverbs and familiar sayings also are Form 3 metaphors: "You can lead a horse to water, but you can't make him drink," "Don't put the cart before the horse," "Make hay while the sun shines," "There's lots of good fish in the sea," "A rolling stone gathers no moss," "A bird in the hand is worth two in the bush." All these examples show the ambiguous nature of Form 3 metaphors, for all would be literal statements in the appropriate context. A sea captain, taking refuge from a hurricane in the harbor of an unfriendly city, would be speaking literally if he exclaimed, "Any port in a storm!" A respectable lady, seeking shelter from a heavy rain in a low tavern, would be speaking partly metaphorically and partly literally if she made the same exclamation. If she went into the tavern to avoid meeting her ex-husband, she would be speaking pure metaphor.

Allegories also often belong to this class, though often too, as in *Pilgrim's Progress* and *Everyman,* the literal meanings are provided in the names of characters or places. When the meanings are provided, the allegory is an extended Form 1 metaphor. When they are not, it belongs to Form 3. Some allegories go back and forth between the two forms, labeling some characters and places with their intended meanings, but not others.

Extended Form 3 metaphors are not necessarily riddles and allegories, however, and some of the most interesting examples are those in which this kind of metaphor is sustained throughout a poem. A few examples are Frost's "A Hillside Thaw," Dickinson's "She sweeps with many-colored brooms," Melville's "The Night-March" and "The Swamp Angel," Joyce's "I hear an army charging upon the land." I shall return later in this essay to the problems of interpretation offered by such poems. For the present let the following short example stand as representative of the class:

> The largest Fire ever known
> Occurs each Afternoon—
> Discovered is without surprise
> Proceeds without concern—
> Consumes and no report to men
> An Occidental town,
> Rebuilt another morning
> To be burned down again.
> Emily Dickinson

5

In Form 4 metaphors, neither the literal nor the figurative term is named; both must be inferred. I shall not pretend that I have a long list of examples. There are, however, at least four circumstances in which a Form 4 metaphor may occur.

First, both the literal and figurative terms may be represented by parts of speech other than substantives:

> Let us eat and drink, for tomorrow we shall die.
>
> Isaiah 22:13

The literal element in this metaphor is expressed by the verb "shall die" and the figurative element by the adverb "tomorrow." The suppressed literal term is a lifetime and its figurative equivalent is one day. The general meaning is that life is very short.

Second, the apparent subject of the metaphor may be actually the figurative term in some other figure of speech:

> Now all the truth is out,
> Be secret and take defeat
> From any brazen throat.
>
> Yeats:
> *To a Friend Whose Work
> Has Come to Nothing*

The apparent subject in these lines is "throat," but "throat" is a synecdoche for a person. The literal meaning, therefore, is a person or an enemy. The figurative term is an object made of brass, probably a bell or a cannon, for both of these are connected with victory, either by announcing it or aiding in its achievement, and both have "throats."

Third, an extended series of subsidiary metaphors may imply a controlling metaphor of which they all are part:

> All the world's a stage,
> And all the men and women merely players.
> They have their exits and their entrances,
> And one man in his time plays many parts,
> His acts being seven ages. . . .

Jaques' famous speech is a series of related Form 1 and Form 3 metaphors. The world is a stage, men and women are actors, births are entrances, deaths are exits, the different phases of a man's personality development and interest are parts, and the seven ages into which his life may be divided are acts. But these separate metaphors add up, like any column of figures, and imply a total. Their sum is a Form 4 metaphor in which the literal term is Life and the figurative term a play.

Fourth, the literal term may be expressed by a pronoun of which the antecedent is left unspecified:

> I like to see it lap the miles,
> And lick the valleys up,
> And stop to feed itself at tanks;
> And then, prodigious, step

Around a pile of mountains,
And, supercilious, peer
In shanties by the sides of roads;
And then a quarry pare

To fit its sides, and crawl between,
Complaining all the while
In horrid, hooting stanza;
Then chase itself down hill

And neigh like Boanerges;
Then, punctual as a star,
Stop—docile and omnipotent—
At its own stable door.

Emily Dickinson's poem compares a train to a horse. Neither train nor horse is named. The literal term is represented by an unidentified "it."

6

For the most part I have so far used fairly simple examples, in order to isolate the features I have been discussing. Metaphorical language, however, is often far from simple. Poets typically weave together literal and metaphorical language, the different forms of metaphor, metaphor and other figures of speech. I would like to examine some of these more complicated examples, but first I must introduce two technical terms.

The *extension* of a metaphor may be measured in either of two ways: (a) by the number of words or lines required for its completion, (b) by the number of subsidiary metaphors evolved in its development. By the first of these criteria, Herrick's "To Dianeme" might be called an extended metaphor, but not by the second:

Give me one kiss,
    And no more;
If so be, this
    Makes you poor,
To enrich you
    I'll restore
For that one, two
    Thousand score.

On the other hand, the following line from Noyes's "The Highwayman" is an extended metaphor by the second of these criteria but not by the first:

The moon was a ghostly galleon tossed
    upon cloudy seas.

Herrick's poem extends for eight lines a simple Form 2 metaphor in which a kiss is likened to money. The single line from Noyes involves two related metaphors, one in which the moon is compared to a galleon, and a second in which the clouds are compared to seas. In the rest of this discussion I shall use the term *extended metaphor* to refer to examples of this latter type.

A *complex metaphor* is one in which the literal meaning is expressed through more than one figurative term and the figurative terms belong to different figurative contexts. The line just quoted from Noyes is a complex metaphor as well as an extended metaphor, because, in addition to the two metaphors cited, it contains a third metaphor in which the moon, already compared to a galleon, is simultaneously compared to a ghost, and the ghost image belongs to a different figurative context than the galleon-seas image.

A complex metaphor is not to be confused with a series of simple metaphors in which the literal term is named only once. In the familiar "sleep" passage in *Macbeth* (II, ii), for instance, or in the following lines from George Walter Thorbury's "The Jester's Sermon," each metaphorical comparison is completed before the next one is begun:

> Man's life is but a jest,
> A dream, a shadow, bubble, air, a vapor
> at the best.

In this example the phrase "man's life is but" may be understood as preceding each noun in the list. In a complex metaphor the disparate figurative terms are all part of one image, not of a series of images. For instance, in Browning's "Meeting at Night" the speaker, as he rows to shore, sees

> the startled little waves that leap
> In fiery ringlets from their sleep.

Here the literal term—"waves"—is expressed through three figurative terms. The words "startled," "leap," and "sleep" compare the waves, unobtrusively, to a person. The word "ringlets" compares them to hair. The adjective "fiery" compares them (as they catch the light of the moon) to flames. The three figurative terms are all part of one metaphor, and they work together to make one image.

A complex metaphor might be called a mixed metaphor except that the term "mixed metaphor" suggests something bad. The truth is that a poet may mix his metaphors as much as he pleases so long as he can get away with it. A "mixed metaphor" is simply an unsuccessful complex metaphor, one in which the figurative terms clash rather than harmonize. I do not know of a logical test by which successful and unsuccessful complex metaphors may be separated. The only test is the imagination of a sensitive reader. I do know that a complex metaphor may be one of the most meaningful devices of poetry. For example, in Robert Frost's "The Tuft of Flowers" the speaker is turning over the grass in a field which has been mowed by a different worker earlier in the morning. The speaker is *alone*—"as all must be," he tells himself, "whether they work together or apart." He then discovers a tuft of flowers which the earlier worker had spared while mowing everything around it:

A leaping tongue of bloom the scythe had
   spared
Beside a reedy brook the scythe had
   bared.

The literal term is "tuft of flowers" or "bloom," and the figurative term—suggested by the noun "tongue," the participle "leaping," and the sound structure of "bloom"—is a flame. At this point the metaphor is perceived as a simple one, for the figurative implications of "tongue" remain dormant: a "tongue of flame" is a dead metaphor, like the "leg of a table" or the "arm of a chair." Six lines further on, however, when the speaker says that in the tuft of flowers he has lit upon a "message from the dawn," the dead metaphor leaps to life: the "tongue of bloom" has spoken, and it enables the speaker, in fancy, to hold "brotherly speech" with the earlier worker. The tongue and the flame are now seen to be separately figurative, and the metaphor to be a complex one. Structurally, this complex metaphor provides the turning point of the poem, for the "message" of the tuft of flowers changes the attitude of the speaker, who concludes that men work *together,* "whether they work together or apart."

It should by now be apparent that figurative language has a Protean quality: it shifts shapes with lightning-like rapidity. In the rest of this section I wish to discuss some of these shape-shiftings.

First, in metaphors that are even slightly extended, there may be among the subsidiary metaphors more than one of the four forms:

The welkin had full niggardly inclosed
In coffer of dim clouds his silver groats.
                  Sidney: *Arcadia*

The controlling image in these two lines is a Form 2 metaphor in which the sky is compared to a miser. It is supported, however, by a Form 1 metaphor in which the clouds are represented as a coffer, and by a Form 3 metaphor in which the stars become silver coins. Even a simple, non-extended, metaphor may involve more than one of the four forms.

Ye quenchless stars! so eloquently bright.

Earlier in the essay I over-simply presented this line as a Form 2 metaphor in which the adverb "eloquently" personifies the stars. Upon reflection, however, it becomes apparent that even more important here is a Form 4 metaphor in which shining is compared to speech. The literal term is presented in the adjective "bright," the figurative term in the adverb "eloquently." Neither the literal nor the figurative term in this comparison is named.

Just as a single image may combine more than one form of metaphor, so it may combine more than one figure of speech:

I am soft sift
In an hour glass.
            Hopkins: *The Wreck of the Deutschland*

In Hopkins' lines "sift" is a metonymy for sand, which in turn is the figurative term of a metaphor of which the literal term is "I."

> The tower said, "One!"
> And then a steeple.
> They spoke to themselves . . .
>
> Frost: *I Will Sing You One-O*

In this example "tower" and "steeple" are both personified; at the same time both are metonymies for a clock.

> No, it took all the snows that clung
> To the low roof over his bed,
> Beginning when he was young,
> To induce the one snow on his head.
>
> Frost: *They Were Welcome to Their Belief*

In this passage "snows" and "snow" are both figurative terms, but they have different referents, and are different figures. "Snows" is a metonymy for winters, which in turn is a metonymy for years, or time; "snow" is the figurative term of a Form 3 metaphor whose literal term is white hair. And so it goes. A passage may be at once ironical and metaphorical. The resolution of a paradox may depend on seeing that one of its contradictory terms is a metaphor. Metaphor and simile are constantly sliding into each other:

> O thou art fairer than the evening air
> Clad in the beauty of a thousand stars!
>
> Marlowe: *Dr. Faustus*

The comparison of a woman to the evening air is simile, but the evening air is immediately personified because it is "clad," and the stars are the literal term of a Form 2 metaphor in which the figurative term is a garment.

Even figurative and literal language may exist side by side in strange ways:

> The hand that signed the paper felled a
>   city;
> Five sovereign fingers taxed the breath,
> Doubled the globe of dead and halved a
>   country;
> These five kings did a king to death.
>
> Dylan Thomas: *The hand that signed the paper*

In this passage the "five kings" are metaphorical, whereas "king" three words later is literal. The sudden shift from figurative to literal is what gives the line its "play," its vitality.

Let me conclude this section by examining a whole poem:

> There is a garden in her face,
> Where roses and white lilies grow;
>   A heavenly paradise is that place,
> Wherein all pleasant fruits do flow.

There cherries grow which none may buy
Till cherry-ripe themselves do cry.

Those cherries fairly do enclose
Of orient pearl a double row,
    Which when her lovely laughter shows,
They look like rosebuds filled with snow.
    Yet them nor peer nor prince can buy,
    Till cherry-ripe themselves do cry.

Her eyes like angels watch them still;
Her brows like bended bows do stand,
    Threat'ning with piercing frowns to kill
All that attempt with eye or hand
    Those sacred cherries to come nigh,
    Till cherry-ripe themselves do cry.
                              Thomas Campion

The controlling image in the poem is a Form 1 metaphor in which the lady's face is compared to a garden. This is developed in the first stanza through a series of subsidiary Form 3 metaphors. Within the garden are roses and white lilies (the colors of her complexion), pleasant fruits (matured and appealing features), and cherries (her lips).

In the second stanza the garden metaphor is made complex by the introduction of another Form 3 metaphor, in which the lady's teeth are compared to pearls. Through similes the lady's teeth are also compared to snow and her lips to rosebuds, images which return the poem to the garden metaphor. (It should be noticed, however, that neither lips nor teeth are mentioned in the poem: the literal terms of the simile are represented by the figurative terms of the metaphor, so we have here what might be called a Form 3 simile, if that is possible.)

In the third stanza we find that the garden is inhabited. The lady's eyes are compared to angels through simile, and her brows to bended bows. At the same time that the brows are compared to bows, however, they are also personified (since they "threaten") through a Form 2 metaphor. In the development of this simile, another Form 2 metaphor is evolved, in which "piercing frowns" are compared to arrows.

The most remarkable metaphorical development of this poem, however, is in its refrain. The plain sense of these lines, as I read them, is that no one may kiss the lady's lips until she herself issues the invitation or at least gives her consent. This plain sense is rendered through three Form 4 metaphors. Kisses are compared to the purchase of cherries. An invitation or consent to a kiss is compared to calling out "Cherry-ripe." And the lips that call out "Cherry-ripe" are not only cherries to be sold but the cherry-vendor who sells them. Campion's poem thus involves all four forms of metaphor as well as simile. Its basic metaphor is both extended and complex. The poem as a whole is a combination of logically inconsistent but poetically consistent ideas which results in something altogether charming.

7

It might be supposed that the series of figures beginning with simile and ascending through metaphors of Forms 1, 2, 3, and 4 offer a progressively greater difficulty for the reader, but this is only partially true. Actually, there is a much greater variance among examples in a single class than there is among representative examples of the different classes. It is probable, for instance, that the simile which opens Eliot's "Love Song of J. Alfred Prufrock"—

> Let us go then, you and I,
> When the evening is spread out against
>   the sky
> Like a patient etherized upon a table—

has troubled many readers who have not had a moment's difficulty with Emily Dickinson's extended Form 4 metaphor "I like to see it lap the miles." The reason is that the difficulty of a figure of speech depends upon a number of considerations.

Considering problems of interpretation from the viewpoint of metaphorical analysis only, there are four basic questions that must be answered:

1. Is the passage metaphorical or literal?
2. What two things are being compared?
3. Which is the literal and which the figurative term?
4. What are the grounds of the comparison?

The first of these questions is the most hazardous, for the danger is that it may not get asked. Unless a reader recognizes a passage as metaphorical, he will have no reason to ask the other questions in this list. The difficulty arises with Form 3 and Form 4 metaphors, which may often be mistaken for literal statements. Many students, confronted with Emily Dickinson's poem for the first time, read it simply as being about a horse. Form 3 and Form 4 metaphors vary considerably in the number and subtlety of clues presented that they are non-literal.

The second and third of these questions arise with metaphors of Forms 2, 3, and 4. Obviously, if only the literal term is stated, the figurative term must be inferred; if only the figurative term is stated, the literal term must be inferred; if neither is stated, both must be inferred. And, again, there is much variation in the number and subtlety of the clues to the identity of the suppressed terms. Metaphors in which the literal term is suppressed will be more hazardous than those in which the figurative term is suppressed, for the literal term is more important to a passage's plain sense. Occasionally, even when he has identified the two things being compared, a reader will fail to recognize which is the literal term and which the figurative.

The fourth of these questions arises with all similes and metaphors. The two things being compared may be obviously alike or obscurely alike. This is why Eliot's simile in "Prufrock" may be more difficult than Dickinson's Form 4 metaphor. Once the literal and figurative terms have been identified, Emily Dickinson's poem offers little difficulty. The literal and figurative terms of Eliot's simile are obvious, but the likenesses between them may baffle a reader coming to Eliot's poetry for the first time.

In the rest of this section I should like to illustrate the problems raised by the first three questions. Since problems raised by the fourth question are unrelated to the form of metaphor used, I shall not address myself to them specifically.

The problem of recognizing a passage as metaphorical has already been discussed in connection with a line from *Romeo and Juliet*. There the issue was resolved by reference to the context. The problem becomes more acute when metaphors of this type are extended throughout a poem, for then there is no surrounding context to refer to, and understanding of the whole poem depends upon recognition of the metaphor. A reader who missed the metaphor in "Night's candles are burnt out" would suffer very little in his understanding of *Romeo and Juliet*. Quite otherwise would be the case of a reader who missed the metaphor in the following poem:

The Night-March

With banners furled, and clarions mute,
    An army passes in the night;
And beaming spears and helms salute
    The dark with bright.

In silence deep the legions stream,
    With open ranks, in order true;
Over boundless plains they stream and
        gleam—
    No chief in view!

Afar, in twinkling distance lost,
    (So legends tell) he lonely wends
And back through all that shining host
    His mandate sends.
              Herman Melville

Elsewhere I have discussed a classroom experience with this poem, in which no one in an Honors class of freshmen identified the metaphor.[2] Most read the poem literally as a description of an army marching at night. The poem, in fact, is an extended Form 3 metaphor. The "army" is figurative; its literal term (like that of Romeo's "candles") is stars. The clues are (1) the close repetition of such words as "beaming," "bright," "gleam," "twinkling," and "shining"; (2) the night setting; (3) the emphasis on the deep silence

[2] "The Nature of Proof in the Interpretation of Poetry," *English Journal* 51 (1962), 393–98.

of the procession; (4) the emphasis on infinite space—"boundless plains," "twinkling distance"; (5) the fixed yet open formation of the marchers; (6) the absence of a commander.

Another example is offered by one of Emily Dickinson's poems:

> The Snow that never drifts—
> The transient, fragrant snow
> That comes a single time a Year
> Is softly driving now—
>
> So thorough in the Tree
> At night beneath the star
> That it was February's self
> Experience would swear—
>
> Like Winter as a Face
> We stern and former knew
> Repaired of all but Loneliness
> By Nature's Alibi—
>
> Were every storm so spice
> The Value could not be—
> We buy with contrast—Pang is good
> As near as memory—

The poet's editors, when they included this poem in *Bolts of Melody,* interpreted the snow as literal and classified the poem as a late winter poem. Actually it is not about snow at all, but about a fall of white blossoms in late spring.[3] Again, the poem is an extended Form 3 metaphor.

Even when it is suspected that a passage may be metaphorical, it can be difficult, with a Form 3 metaphor, to determine whether or not it is actually so. The problem is illustrated vividly by a controversy waged in the pages of *The Explicator* a number of years ago over the proper reading of Housman's "Loveliest of trees." The poem begins:

> Loveliest of trees, the cherry now
> Is hung with bloom along the bough
> And stands about the woodland ride,
> Wearing white for Eastertide.

It ends:

> And since to look at things in bloom
> Fifty springs are little room,
> About the woodlands I will go
> To see the cherry hung with snow.

The snow in this poem is a Form 3 metaphor like that in Emily Dickinson's poem: its literal meaning is white blossoms. But some five scholars and critics

---

[3] See Ralph Marcellino, *Explicator* 13 (1955), item 36, who corrects the misreading. Another and similar misreading of Form 3 metaphors as literal appeared some years ago in an interpretation of Elinor Wylie's "Velvet Shoes" published in *College English*. For my own correction of the error, see *Explicator* 13 (1954), item 17.

in *The Explicator,* recognizing the possibility of this interpretation, argued seriously that this snow is literal.[4]

Once a passage has been diagnosed as metaphorical, there still remains the problem of determining what two things are being compared. A Form 4 metaphor offers two opportunities for going wrong. Emily Dickinson's poem about the train has caused disagreement as to both its literal and figurative terms. Any teacher who presents this poem for analysis to a class of college freshmen will find, among students who have not encountered it before, considerable bafflement as to what the poem is about. In addition to those who read the poem literally as about a horse, I have had students tell me that it is about a river, a road, poetry, and death. Scholars, on the other hand, have had little difficulty with what the poem is about, but have differed about the figurative element. The usual interpretation is that the image throughout is, as Charles R. Anderson puts it, of "a fabulous horse." Some critics, however, have suggested that the figurative term is a monstrous dragon; that it is a mythological beast at first catlike and later horselike; that it is a "zoological exhibit of cat, dragon, *and* horse"; or that it changes progressively from cat to hunting dog to colt to horse as the train approaches the viewer.[5] Although I agree with the first of these interpretations, my purpose here is not to argue a case but simply to illustrate the difficulties.

When literal and figurative terms have been correctly identified, there still remains the problem of determining which is which. This problem rarely causes difficulty, but occasionally it does. The point was forcefully brought to my attention recently in a graduate seminar discussion of A. D. Hope's poem "The Brides."[6] The poem begins as follows:

> Down the assembly line they roll and pass
> Complete at last, a miracle of design;
> Their chromium fenders, the unbreakable glass,
> The fashionable curve, the air-flow line.

The whole poem, which continues for five more stanzas, is in fact an extended Form 2 metaphor in which brides are compared to new automobiles. At the end of the poem one of them is driven off by her purchaser. My students had no difficulty at all in identifying the two things being compared, and in seeing that the poem is satirical; but they divided as to whether the poem is a satire against society's preparing girls for marriage as if they were automobiles for

---

[4] See *Explicator* 1 (1943), item 57; 1 (1943), item 69; 5 (1946), item 4. W. L. Werner in this exchange convincingly maintains the case for a metaphorical reading, and at least four of the literalists—the editors of *The Explicator*—now concede the victory to him. If his arguments fail to convince any reader of this essay, I stand ready to offer confirmation.

[5] See Charles R. Anderson, *Emily Dickinson's Poetry: Stairway of Surprise* (New York: Holt, 1960), p. 16; I.O.N. in *Explicator* 2 (1944), item Q31; Austin Warren in *Sewanee Review* 65 (1957), 581; and James McNally in *CEA Critic* 26 (Nov. 1963), 9–10.

[6] A. D. Hope, *Collected Poems, 1930–1965* (New York: Viking, 1966), p. 82.

purchase, or against men's falling in love with automobiles and treating them as if they were brides.

8

What advantages has my system of classifying metaphors?

First, I think, it has advantages of simplicity and naturalness. I have discussed these points briefly in my remarks on a metaphor from Boswell. They are illustrated even better by the example from Francis Thompson:

> The tawny-hided desert crouches watching her.

This line contains three figurative expressions—"tawny-hided," "crouches," and "watching." By a grammatical analysis we should have to consider them as three separate metaphors. The adjective is the easiest. "Tawny-hided" means "having a dull yellowish surface" or "sandy." The verb is somewhat more difficult. "Crouches," implying a readiness to spring, means here "extends around her full of menace." For the participle—"watching"—it is almost impossible to find a literal equivalent. We can say easily enough what is meant: that the girl is in danger, that if she makes the slightest slip she will be overcome by heat prostration, thirst, or savage attack. But it seems impossible to translate "watching" satisfactorily into a literal equivalent. And surely this analysis avoids the key image. Is it not simpler and more natural to see this image in terms of one metaphor rather than three? What two things are being compared? we ask. Answer: the desert and a lion. Then we ask, In what ways is the desert like a lion? Answer: Both are dullish yellow in color; both are treacherous; both may cause terrible death. In answering this second question we have brought out, but more naturally and easily, all the equivalences we struggled for so laboriously through a grammatical analysis.

The example cited from *All's Well That Ends Well* further shows the difficulties of grammatical analysis:

> For we are old, and in our quick'st degrees
> The inaudible and noiseless foot of Time
> Steals ere we can effect them.

In this passage there are two figurative expressions: "foot" and "steals." "Steals" may be translated as "passes unobtrusively or unnoticed." But what do we do with "foot"? As remarked earlier, it is figurative, yet it has no literal equivalent. The metaphor in this passage likens Time to a person, and "foot" is an elaboration of its figurative term, not a figurative term in itself. It *belongs* to a metaphor without *being* a metaphor. Elaboration of the figurative term is seen most markedly in Homeric simile, but it is a phenomenon of metaphor in all ages.

A second advantage of the proposed scheme is that it gives us a much clearer conceptual framework for comparing simile and metaphor. Critics have long been given to making sweeping generalizations about the differences between simile and metaphor, both as to their effects and their effectiveness.

But they have not always been clear about what they were comparing. Simile is in fact closely comparable only to Form 1 metaphor. In each of them both literal and figurative terms are named, and the only significant difference is the use in simile of some word such as *like* or *as* which makes the comparison overt. Simile indeed might be logically classed as a subspecies of Form 1 metaphor, for the likenesses are more important than the difference. Certainly, however, in comparisons between simile and other forms of metaphor, the use of *like* or *as* in simile is the least important difference. It is not true, as textbooks may sometimes lead one to believe, that any metaphor can be converted to a simile simply by the introduction of *like* or *as.*

Third, the scheme presents a simple conceptual framework for teaching metaphor and for clarifying the ways in which metaphor works. Though no conceivable method of teaching metaphor will prevent the kinds of misinterpretation illustrated in the previous section of this essay, yet possession of this conceptual scheme may cut down on a few misreadings. Its advantage is that it gives the student a notion of what to expect. If he knows what he may expect, he is better prepared to deal with what he finds. The explorer of the realms of gold, like any other explorer, is less likely to suffer shipwreck if he sails forth provided with compass and sextant.

A Generative Rhetoric of the Sentence

Francis Christensen

In the disquietingly uncertain world of the composition class, the teacher should eagerly welcome the few certainties that are available. One of those certainties is that we can help students with the problem of invention. That is, we can give them ways whereby they can generate ideas concerning a subject, whatever that may be. The introduction to Contemporary Rhetoric *and the section on invention attempted to make that point.*

One more certainty is that we have the means whereby we can help students increase their syntactic fluency. *And anyone who thinks about it will realize that a high degree of syntactic fluency is an accomplishment hardly to be overestimated. Whether or not there can be ideas without language, ideas cannot be expressed—adequately, at least—unless the writer has the ability to embody those ideas in appropriate structures. Syntactic fluency is the ability to use the syntactic resources of the language in order to express ideas.*

We associate two terms with the concept of syntactic fluency: free modifiers *and* embedding. *The term* free modifiers *comes from Francis Christensen, and* embedding *will be explained in the piece by John Mellon that appears later in this section.*

There is no need to summarize here what Christensen is getting at, for his essay is admirably clear and apposite. But the concept that he outlines does imply a major problem that writing teachers must address.

Programs—series of exercises—can be developed to activate in students the ability to use free modifiers in their sentence-building. No rational person, I think, would argue that the ability to use these modifiers is not a worthwhile accomplishment, but from many points of view, including my own, programed exercises are at best dubious means of pedagogy in writing. No doubt, anyone who pays attention to Christensen's essay can devise a systematic series of exercises that will probably give the student the ability to use the free modifiers—that is, anyone can have students write x number of sentences containing adjective clusters and then x number containing noun clusters, and so on.

Such exercises, however, take sentences out of the living context of the rhetorical situation and make them into largely meaningless dry runs. In writing classes, the great effort should be to avoid dry runs, not to create more of them than necessarily exist already.

There is no reason, it seems to me, why students cannot learn to use free modifiers—or, as I choose to call them, cumulative *modifiers—within the living context of a piece of writing that has a purpose and an audience.*

Insofar, then, as Christensen's outline of the free modifiers tends to move us backward toward writing classes that are based largely or in part on exercises, it is destructive. But, used with living prose by intelligent, sensitive teachers, it can be a tremendous step forward—simply because free modifiers do, in fact, represent something organic and basic to the way real writers write, to the way in which modern prose functions, and also because as a "system" they are easily grasped by the teacher and easily made a part of the repertory of devices for student writing.

Let me be very specific about the use of the concept "free modifiers" as a pedagogical device in the classroom. Students write or begin to write something with a purpose and for an audience. Their problem—every writer's problem—is a lack of strategies for conveying meaning effectively. One set of strategies is the free modifiers, and the teacher can explain the free modifiers by helping students use them in their actual writing. That is, the teacher should show *students how they can put their ideas into sentence bases that are modified by noun clusters, verb clusters, absolutes, and so on. Furthermore, the teacher can point out the free modifiers that the class encounters in its reading.*

Thus, the student will see that free modifiers can make things happen or that they have made things happen in writing. This kind of knowledge is a great deal more fundamental than the kind that exercises will bring about.

For a bibliography of writings by Christensen and about Christensen's work, see "A Generative Rhetoric of the Paragraph."

We do not have time in our classes to teach everything about the rhetoric of the sentence. I believe in "island hopping," concentrating on topics where we can produce results and leaving the rest, including the "comma splice" and the "run-on sentence," to die on the vine. The balanced sentence deserves some attention in discursive writing, and the enormous range of coordinate structures deserves a bit more. The rhythm of good modern prose comes about equally from the multiple-tracking of coordinate constructions and the down-shifting and backtracking of free modifiers. But the first comes naturally; the other needs coaxing along.

This coaxing is the clue to the meaning of *generative* in my title. (It is not derived from generative grammar; I used it before I ever heard of Chomsky.) The teacher can use the idea of levels of structure to urge the student to add further levels to what he has already produced, so that the structure itself becomes an aid to discovery.

This system of analysis by levels is essentially an application of immediate constituent analysis. IC analysis reveals what goes with what. In such analysis the free modifiers are cut off first. The order in which initial, medial, and final elements are cut off is immaterial, but one might as well start at the beginning. Thus, in sentence 2, the first cut would take off the whole set of initial modifiers. Then the members of a coordinate set are separated and, if the dissection is to be carried out to the ultimate constituents, analyzed one by one in order. In sentence 1, the first cut would come at the end of the base clause, taking off levels 2, 3, and 4 together since they are dependent on one another. Another cut would come at the end of level 2, taking off levels 3 and 4 together since 4 is a modifier of 3. Medial modifiers have to be cut *out* rather than *off*.

If the new grammar is to be brought to bear on composition, it must be brought to bear on the rhetoric of the sentence. We have a workable and teachable, if not a definitive, modern grammar; but we do not have, despite several titles, a modern rhetoric.

In composition courses we do not really teach our captive charges to write better—we merely *expect* them to. And we do not teach them how to write better because we do not know how to teach them to write better. And so we merely go through the motions. Our courses with their tear-out work books and four-pound anthologies are elaborate evasions of the real problem. They permit us to put in our time and do almost anything else we'd rather be doing instead of buckling down to the hard work of making a difference in the student's understanding and manipulation of language.

With hundreds of handbooks and rhetorics to draw from, I have never been able to work out a program for teaching the sentence as I find it in the work of contemporary writers. The chapters on the sentence all adduce the traditional rhetorical classification of sentences as loose, balanced, and periodic. But the term *loose* seems to be taken as a pejorative (it sounds immoral); our students, no Bacons or Johnsons, have little occasion for balanced sentences; and some of our worst perversions of style come from the attempt to teach them to write periodic sentences. The traditional grammatical classification of sentences is equally barren. Its use in teaching composition rests on a semantic confusion, equating complexity of structure with complexity of thought and vice versa. But very simple thoughts may call for very complex grammatical constructions. Any moron can say "I don't know who done it." And some of us might be puzzled to work out the grammar of "All I want is all there is," although any chit can think it and say it and act on it.

The chapters on the sentence all appear to assume that we think naturally in primer sentences, progress naturally to compound sentences, and must be taught to combine the primer sentences into complex sentences—and that complex sentences are the mark of maturity. We need a rhetoric of the sentence that will do more than combine the ideas of primer sentences. We need one that will *generate* ideas.

For the foundation of such a generative or productive rhetoric I take the statement from John Erskine, the originator of the Great Books courses, himself a novelist. In an essay "The Craft of Writing" (*Twentieth Century English,* Philosophical Library, 1946) he discusses a principle of the writer's craft which, though known he says to all practitioners, he has never seen discussed in print. The principle is this: "When you write, you make a point, not by subtracting as though you sharpened a pencil, but by adding." We have all been told that the formula for good writing is the concrete noun and the active verb. Yet Erskine says, "What you say is found not in the noun but in what you add to qualify the noun . . . The noun, the verb, and the main clause serve merely as the base on which meaning will rise . . . The modifier is the essential part of any sentence." The foundation, then, for a generative or productive rhetoric of the sentence is that composition is essentially a process of *addition*.

But speech is linear, moving in time, and writing moves in linear space, which is analogous to time. When you add a modifier, whether to the noun, the verb, or the main clause, you must add it either before the head or after it. If you add it before the head, the direction of modification can be indicated by an arrow pointing forward; if you add it after, by an arrow pointing backward. Thus we have the second principle of a generative rhetoric—the principle of *direction of modification* or *direction of movement*.

Within the clause there is not much scope for operating with this principle. The positions of the various sorts of close, or restrictive, modifiers are generally fixed and the modifiers are often obligatory—"The man who came to dinner remained till midnight." Often the only choice is whether to add modifiers. What I have seen of attempts to bring structural grammar to bear on composition usually boils down to the injunction to "load the patterns." Thus "pattern practice" sets students to accreting sentences like this: "This small boy on the red bicycle who lives with his happy parents on our shady street often coasts down the steep street until he comes to the city park." This will never do. It has no rhythm and hence no life; it is tone-deaf. It is the seed that will burgeon into gobbledegook. One of the hardest things in writing is to keep the noun clusters and verb clusters short.

It is with modifiers added to the clause—that is, with sentence modifiers— that the principle comes into full play. The typical sentence of modern English, the kind we can best spend our efforts trying to teach, is what we may call the *cumulative sentence*. The main clause, which may or may not have a sentence modifier before it, advances the discussion; but the additions move backward, as in this clause, to modify the statement of the main clause or more often to explicate or exemplify it, so that the sentence has a flowing and ebbing movement, advancing to a new position and then pausing to consolidate it, leaping and lingering as the popular ballad does. The first part of the preceding compound sentence has one addition, placed within it; the second part has 4 words in the main clause and 49 in the five additions placed after it.

The cumulative sentence is the opposite of the periodic sentence. It does not represent the idea as conceived, pondered over, reshaped, packaged, and delivered cold. It is dynamic rather than static, representing the mind thinking. The main clause ("the additions move backward" above) exhausts the mere fact of the idea; logically, there is nothing more to say. The additions stay with the same idea, probing its bearings and implications, exemplifying it or seeking an analogy or metaphor for it, or reducing it to details. Thus the mere form of the sentence generates ideas. It serves the needs of both the writer and the reader, the writer by compelling him to examine his thought, the reader by letting him into the writer's thought.

Addition and direction of movement are structural principles. They involve the grammatical character of the sentence. Before going on to other principles, I must say a word about the best grammar as the foundation for rhetoric. I cannot conceive any useful transactions between teacher and students unless they have in common a language for talking about sentences. The best grammar for the present purpose is the grammar that best displays the layers of structure of the English sentence. The best I have found in a textbook is the combination of immediate constituent and transformation grammar in Paul Roberts's *English Sentences*. Traditional grammar, whether over-simple as in the school tradition or over-complex as in the scholarly tradition, does not reveal the language as it operates; it leaves everything, to borrow a phrase from Wordsworth, "in disconnection dead and spiritless." *English Sentences* is oversimplified and it has gaps, but it displays admirably the structures that rhetoric must work with—primarily sentence modifiers, including nonrestrictive relative and subordinate clauses, but, far more important, the array of noun, verb, and adjective clusters. It is paradoxical that Professor Roberts, who has done so much to make the teaching of composition possible, should himself be one of those who think that it cannot be taught. Unlike Ulysses, he does not see any work for Telemachus to work.

Layers of structure, as I have said, is a grammatical concept. To bring in the dimension of meaning, we need a third principle—that of *levels of generality* or *levels of abstraction*. The main or base clause is likely to be stated in general or abstract or plural terms. With the main clause stated, the forward movement of the sentence stops, the writer shifts down to a lower level of generality or abstraction or to singular terms, and goes back over the same ground at this lower level.[1] There is no theoretical limit to the number of structural layers or levels, each [2] at a lower level of generality, any or all of them compounded, that a speaker or writer may use. For a speaker, listen to Lowell Thomas; for a writer, study William Faulkner. To a single independent clause he may append a page of additions, but usually all clear, all grammatical, once we have learned how to read him. Or, if you prefer, study Hemingway, the master of the simple sentence: "George was coming down in the telemark position, kneeling, one leg forward and bent, the other trailing, his sticks hanging like some insect's thin legs, kicking up puffs of snow, and finally the whole kneeling, trailing figure coming around in a beautiful right curve, crouching, the legs shot forward and back, the body leaning out against the swing, the sticks accenting the curve like points of light, all in a wild cloud of snow." Only from the standpoint of school grammar is this a simple sentence.

This brings me to the fourth, and last, principle, that of texture. *Texture* provides a descriptive or evaluative term. If a writer adds to few of his nouns or verbs or main clauses and adds little, the texture may be said to be thin. The style will be plain or bare. The writing of most of our students is thin—even threadbare. But if he adds frequently or much or both, then the texture may be said to be dense or rich. One of the marks of an effective style, especially in narrative, is variety in the texture, the texture varying with the change in pace, the variation in texture producing the change in pace. It is not true, as I have seen it asserted, that fast action calls for short sentences; the action is fast in the sentence by Hemingway above. In our classes, we have to work for greater density and variety in texture and greater concreteness and particularity in what is added.

I have been operating at a fairly high level of generality. Now I must downshift and go over the same points with examples. The most graphic way to exhibit the layers of structure is to indent the word groups of a sentence and to number the levels. The first three sentences illustrate the various positions

---

[1] Cf. Leo Rockas, "Abstract and Concrete Sentences," *CCC*, May 1963. Rockas describes sentences as abstract or concrete, the abstract implying the concrete and vice versa. Readers and writers, he says, must have the knack of apprehending the concrete in the abstract and the abstract in the concrete. This is true and valuable. I am saying that within a single sentence the writer may present more than one level of generality, translating the abstract into the more concrete in the added levels.

[2] This statement is not quite tenable. Each helps to make the idea of the base clause more concrete or specific, but each is not more concrete or specific than the one immediately above it.

of the added sentence modifiers—initial, medial, and final. The symbols mark the grammatical character of the additions: SC, subordinate clause; RC, relative clause; NC, noun cluster; VC, verb cluster; AC, adjective cluster; A + A, adjective series; Abs, absolute (i.e., a VC with a subject of its own); PP, prepositional phrase. The elements set off as on a lower level are marked as sentence modifiers by junctures or punctuation. The examples have been chosen to illustrate the range of constructions used in the lower levels; after the first few they are arranged by the number of levels. The examples could have been drawn from poetry as well as from prose. Those not attributed are by students.

1

1 He dipped his hands in the bichloride solution and shook them,
  2 a quick shake, (NC)
    3 fingers down, (Abs)
      4 like the fingers of a pianist above the keys. (PP)

                                    Sinclair Lewis

2

  2 Calico-coated, (AC)
  2 small-bodied, (AC)
    3 with delicate legs and pink faces in which their mismatched eyes rolled
      wild and subdued, (PP)
1 they huddled,
  2 gaudy motionless and alert, (A + A)
  2 wild as deer, (AC)
  2 deadly as rattlesnakes, (AC)
  2 quiet as doves. (AC)

                                William Faulkner

3

1 The bird's eye, / , remained fixed upon him;
  2 / bright and silly as a sequin (AC)
1 its little bones, / , seemed swooning in his hand.
  2 / wrapped . . . in a warm padding of feathers (VC)

                                  Stella Benson

4

1 The jockeys sat bowed and relaxed,
  2 moving a little at the waist with the movement of their horses. (VC)

                          Katherine Anne Porter

5

1 The flame sidled up the match,
  2 driving a film of moisture and a thin strip of darker grey before it. (VC)

6

1 She came among them behind the man,
  2 gaunt in the gray shapeless garment and the sunbonnet, (AC)
  2 wearing stained canvas gymnasium shoes. (VC)

Faulkner

7

1 The Texan turned to the nearest gatepost and climbed to the top of it,
  2 his alternate thighs thick and bulging in the tight trousers, (Abs)
  2 the butt of the pistol catching and losing the sun in pearly gleams. (Abs)

Faulkner

8

1 He could sail for hours,
  2 searching the blanched grasses below him with his telescopic eyes, (VC)
  2 gaining height against the wind, (VC)
  2 descending in mile-long, gently declining swoops when he curved and
    rode back, (VC)
  2 never beating a wing. (VC)

Walter Van Tilburg Clark

9

1 They regarded me silently,
  2 Brother Jack with a smile that went no deeper than his lips, (Abs)
    3 his head cocked to one side, (Abs)
    3 studying me with his penetrating eyes; (VC)
  2 the other blank-faced, (Abs)
    3 looking out of eyes that were meant to reveal nothing and to stir pro-
      found uncertainty. (VC)

Ralph Ellison

10

1 He stood at the top of the stairs and watched me,
  2 I waiting for him to call me up, (Abs)
  2 he hesitating to come down, (Abs)
    3 his lips nervous with the suggestion of a smile, (Abs)
    3 mine asking whether the smile meant come, or go away. (Abs)

11

1 Joad's lips stretched tight over his long teeth for a moment, and
1 he licked his lips,
  2 like a dog, (PP)
    3 two licks, (NC)
      4 one in each direction from the middle. (NC)

Steinbeck

12

1 We all live in two realities:
  2 one of seeming fixity, (NC)
    3 with institutions, dogmas, rules of punctuation, and routines, (PP)
      4 the calendared and clockwise world of all but futile round on round; (NC) and
  2 one of whirling and flying electrons, dreams, and possibilities, (NC)
    3 behind the clock. (PP)

Sidney Cox

13

1 It was as though someone, somewhere, had touched a lever and shifted gears, and
1 the hospital was set for night running,
  2 smooth and silent, (A + A)
  2 its normal clatter and hum muffled, (Abs)
  2 the only sounds heard in the whitewalled room distant and unreal: (Abs)
    3 a low hum of voices from the nurses' desk, (NC)
      4 quickly stifled, (VC)
    3 the soft squish of rubber-soled shoes on the tiled corridor, (NC)
    3 starched white cloth rustling against itself, (NC) and, outside,
    3 the lonesome whine of wind in the country night (NC) and
    3 the Kansas dust beating against the windows. (NC)

14

1 The beach sounds are jazzy,
  2 percussion fixing the mode—(Abs)
    3 the surf cracking and booming in the distance, (Abs)
    3 a little nearer dropped bar-bells clanking, (Abs)
    3 steel gym rings, / , ringing, (Abs)
      / 4 flung together, (VC)
    3 palm fronds rustling above me, (Abs)
      4 like steel brushes washing over a snare drum, (PP)
    3 troupes of sandals splatting and shuffling on the sandy cement, (Abs)
      4 their beat varying, (Abs)
        5 syncopation emerging and disappearing with changing paces. (Abs)

15

1 A small Negro girl develops from the sheet of glare-frosted walk,
  2 walking barefooted, (VC)
    3 her bare legs striking and coiling from the hot cement, (Abs)
      4 her feet curling in, (Abs)
        5 only the outer edges touching. (Abs)

16

1 The swells moved rhythmically toward us,
  2 irregularly faceted, (VC)
  2 sparkling, (VC)
  2 growing taller and more powerful until the shining crest bursts, (VC)
    3 a transparent sheet of pale green water spilling over the top, (Abs)
      4 breaking into blue-white foam as it cascades down the front of the wave, (VC)
      4 piling up in a frothy mound that the diminishing wave pushes up against the pilings, (VC)
        5 with a swishsmash, (PP)
      4 the foam drifting back, (Abs)
        5 like a lace fan opened over the shimmering water as the spent wave returns whispering to the sea. (PP)

The best starting point for a composition unit based on these four principles is with two-level narrative sentences, first with one second-level addition (sentences 4, 5), then with two or more parallel ones (6, 7, 8). Anyone sitting in his room with his eyes closed could write the main clause of most of the examples; the discipline comes with the additions, provided they are based at first on immediate observation, requiring the student to phrase an exact observation in exact language. This can hardly fail to be exciting to a class: it is life, with the variety and complexity of life; the workbook exercise is death. The situation is ideal also for teaching diction—abstract-concrete, general-specific, literal-metaphorical, denotative-connotative. When the sentences begin to come out right, it is time to examine the additions for their grammatical character. From then on the grammar comes to the aid of the writing and the writing reinforces the grammar. One can soon go on to multi-level narrative sentences (1, 9–11, 15, 16) and then to brief narratives of three to six or seven sentences on actions with a beginning, a middle, and an end that can be observed over and over again—beating eggs, making a cut with a power saw, or following a record changer's cycle or a wave's flow and ebb. (Bring the record changer to class.) Description, by contrast, is static, picturing appearance rather than behavior. The constructions to master are the noun and adjective clusters and the absolute (13, 14). Then the descriptive noun cluster must be taught to ride piggy-back on the narrative sentence, so that description and narration are interleaved: "In the morning we went out into a new world, a glistening crystal and white world, each skeleton tree, each leafless bush, even the heavy, drooping power lines sheathed in icy crystal." The next step is to develop the sense for variety in texture and change in pace that all good narrative demands.

In the next unit, the same four principles can be applied to the expository paragraph. But this is a subject for another paper.

I want to anticipate two possible objections. One is that the sentences are long. By freshman English standards they are long, but I could have produced far longer ones from works freshmen are expected to read. Of the sentences by students, most were written as finger exercises in the first few weeks of the course. I try in narrative sentences to push to level after level, not just two or three, but four, five, or six, even more, as far as the students' powers of observation will take them. I want them to become sentence acrobats, to dazzle by their syntactic dexterity. I'd rather have to deal with hyperemia than anemia. I want to add my voice to that of James Coleman (*CCC,* December 1962) deploring our concentration on the plain style.

The other objection is that my examples are mainly descriptive and narrative—and today in freshman English we teach only exposition. I deplore this limitation as much as I deplore our limitation to the plain style. Both are a sign that we have sold our proper heritage for a pot of message. In permitting them, the English department undercuts its own discipline. Even if our goal is only utilitarian prose, we can teach diction and sentence structure far more effectively through a few controlled exercises in description and narration than we can by starting right off with exposition (Theme One, 500 words, precipitates *all* the problems of writing). There is no problem of invention; the student has something to communicate—his immediate sense impressions, which can stand a bit of exercising. The material is not already verbalized—he has to match language to sense impressions. His acuteness in observation and in choice of words can be judged by fairly objective standards—is the sound of a bottle of milk being set down on a concrete step suggested better by *clink* or *clank* or *clunk?* In the examples, study the diction for its accuracy, rising at times to the truly imaginative. Study the use of metaphor, of comparison. This verbal virtuosity and syntactical ingenuity can be made to carry over into expository writing.

But this is still utilitarian. What I am proposing carries over of itself into the study of literature. It makes the student a better reader of literature. It helps him thread the syntactical mazes of much mature writing, and it gives him insight into that elusive thing we call style. Last year a student told of rereading a book by her favorite author, Willa Cather, and of realizing for the first time *why* she liked reading her: she could understand and appreciate the style. For some students, moreover, such writing makes life more interesting as well as giving them a way to share their interest with others. When they learn how to put concrete details into a sentence, they begin to look at life with more alertness. If it is liberal education we are concerned with, it is just possible that these things are more important than anything we can achieve when we set our sights on the plain style in expository prose.

I want to conclude with a historical note. My thesis in this paragraph is that modern prose like modern poetry has more in common with the seventeenth than with the eighteenth century and that we fail largely because we are operating from an eighteenth century base. The shift from the complex to the cumulative sentence is more profound than it seems. It goes deep in grammar, requiring a shift from the subordinate clause (the staple of our trade) to the cluster and the absolute (so little understood as to go almost unnoticed in our textbooks). And I have only lately come to see that this shift has historical implications. The cumulative sentence is the modern form of the loose sentence that characterized the anti-Ciceronian movement in the seventeenth century. This movement, according to Morris W. Croll,[3] began with Montaigne and Bacon and continued with such men as Donne, Browne, Taylor, Pascal. To Montaigne, its art was the art of being natural; to Pascal, its eloquence was the eloquence that mocks formal eloquence; to Bacon, it presented knowledge so that it could be examined, not so that it must be accepted.

But the Senecan amble was banished from England when "the direct sensuous apprehension of thought" (T. S. Eliot's words) gave way to Cartesian reason or intellect. The consequences of this shift in sensibility are well summarized by Croll:

> To this mode of thought we are to trace almost all the features of modern literary education and criticism, or at least of what we should have called modern a generation ago: the study of the precise meaning of words; the reference to dictionaries as literary authorities; the study of the sentence as a logical unit alone; the careful circumscription of its limits and the gradual reduction of its length; . . .[4] the attempt to reduce grammar to an exact science; the idea that forms of speech are always either correct or incorrect; the complete subjection of the laws of motion and expression in style to the laws of logic and standardization—in short, the triumph, during two centuries, of grammatical over rhetorical ideas.

Here is a seven-point scale any teacher of composition can use to take stock. He can find whether he is based in the eighteenth century or in the twentieth and whether he is consistent—completely either an ancient or a modern—or is just a crazy mixed-up kid.

Postscript

I have asserted that "syntactical ingenuity" can best be developed in narrative-descriptive writing and that it can be made to carry over into discursive writing. The count made for the article on sentence openers included all sentence modifiers—or free modifiers, as I prefer to call them. In the total number of free modifiers, the 2000 word samples were almost identical—1545 in the fiction and 1519 in the nonfiction, roughly one in three sentences out of four. But they differ in position:

---

[3] "The Baroque Style in Prose," *Studies in English Philology: A Miscellany in Honor of Frederick Klaeber* (1929), reprinted in *Style, Rhetoric, and Rhythm: Essays by Morris W. Croll* (1966) and A. M. Witherspoon and F. J. Warnke, *Seventeenth-Century Prose and Poetry*, 2nd ed. (1963). I have borrowed from Croll in my description of the cumulative sentence.

[4] The omitted item concerns punctuation and is not relevant here. In using this scale, note the phrase "what we should have called modern a generation ago" and remember that Croll was writing in 1929.

| Nonfiction | initial 575 | medial 492 | final 452 |
| Fiction | initial 404 | medial 329 | final 812 |

And they differ in some of the grammatical kinds used in the final position:

| Nonfiction | NC 123 | VC 63 | Abs   9 |
| Fiction | NC 131 | VC 218 | Abs 108 |

Thus the differences are not in the structures used, only in the position and in the frequency of the various kinds of structures. It will be well to look at a few more sentences of discursive prose.

17

1 His [Hemingway's] characters, / , wander through the ruins of Babel,
  2/ expatriates for the most part, (NC)
  2 smattering many tongues (VC) and
  2 speaking a demotic version of their own. (VC)

Harry Levin

18

1 From literal to figurative is one range that a word may take:
  2 from *foot* of a person to *foot* of a mountain, (PP)
    3 a substituted or metaphoric use. (NC)

1 From concrete to abstract is another range:
  2 from *foot* to *extremity,* (PP)
    3 stressing one of the abstract characteristics of foot, (VC)
      4 a contrast for which the terms *image* and *symbol* as distinguished
      from *concept* are also used. (NC)

Josephine Miles

19

  2 Going back to his [Hemingway's] work in 1944, (VC)
1 you perceive his kinship with a wholly different group of novelists,
  2 let us say with Poe and Hawthorne and Melville: (PP)
    3 the haunted and nocturnal writers, (NC)
    3 the men who dealt in images that were symbols of an inner world. (NC)

Malcolm Cowley

20

1 Even her style in it is transitional and momentous,
  2 a matter of echoing and reminiscing effects, and of little clarion notes
  of surprise and prophecy here and there; (NC)
    3 befitting that time of life which has been called the old age of youth
    and the youth of old age, (AC or VC)

4 a time fraught with heartache and youthful tension. (NC)

Glenway Wescott, of Colette's *Break of Day*

21

2 Aglow with splendor and consequence, (AC)
1 he [Sterne] rejoined his wife and daughter,
  2 whom he presently transferred to his new parsonage at Coxwold, (RC)
    3 an old and rambling house, (NC)
      4 full of irregular, comfortable rooms, (AC)
      4 situated on the edge of the moors, (VC)
        5 in a neighborhood much healthier than the marshy lands of Sutton. (PP)

Peter Quennell

22

1 It is with the coming of man that a vast hole seems to open in nature,
  2 a vast black whirlpool spinning faster and faster, (NC)
    3 consuming flesh, stones, soil, minerals, (VC)
    3 sucking down the lightning, (VC)
    3 wrenching power from the atom, (VC)
      4 until the ancient sounds of nature are drowned out in the cacophony of something which is no longer nature, (SC)
        5 something instead which is loose and knocking at the world's heart, (NC)
        5 something demonic and no longer planned—(NC)
          6 escaped, it may be—(VC)
          6 spewed out of nature, (VC)
          6 contending in a final giant's game against its master. (VC)

Loren Eiseley

The structures used in prose are necessarily the structures used in poetry, necessarily because prose and poetry use the same language. Poets may take more liberties with the grammar than prose writers are likely to do; but their departures from the norm must all be understood by reference to the norm. Since poets, like the writers of narrative, work more by association than by logical connection, their sentences are likely to have similar structures. They seem to know the values of the cumulative sentence.

The first example here consists of the first two stanzas of "The Meadow Mouse"; the slashes mark the line ends. The other example constitutes the last four of the five stanzas of "The Motive for Metaphor." It shows well how structural analysis of the sentence reveals the tactics of a difficult poem.

23

1 In a shoebox stuffed in an old nylon stocking / Sleeps the baby mouse I found in the meadow, /

2 Where he trembled and shook beneath a stick / Till I caught him up by the tail and brought him in, / (RC)
   3 Cradled in my hand, / (VC)
   3 a little quaker, (NC)
      4 the whole body of him trembling, / (Abs)
   3 His absurd whiskers sticking out like a cartoon mouse, / (Abs)
   3 His feet like small leaves, / (Abs)
      4 Little lizard-feet, / (NC)
      4 Whitish and spread wide when he tried to struggle away, / (AC)
         5 Wriggling like a minuscule puppy. (VC)

1 Now he's eaten his three kinds of cheese and drunk from his bottle-cap watering trough— /
  2 So much he just lies in one corner, / (AC)
   3 His tail curled under him, (Abs)
   3 his belly big / As his head, (Abs)
   3 His bat-like ears / Twitching, (Abs)
      4 tilting toward the least sound. (VC)

Theodore Roethke

24

2 In the same way, (PP)
1 you were happy in spring,
  2 with the half colors of quarter-things, (PP)
   3 The slightly brighter sky, (NC)
   3 the melting clouds, (NC)
   3 the single bird, (NC)
   3 the obscure moon—(NC)
      4 The obscure moon lighting an obscure world of things that would never be quite expressed, (NC)
         5 where you yourself were never quite yourself and did not want nor have to be, (RC)
            6 desiring the exhilarations of changes: (VC)
               7 the motive for metaphor, (NC)
            6 shrinking from the weight of primary noon, (VC)
               7 the ABC of being, (NC)
               7 the ruddy temper, (NC)
               7 the hammer of red and blue, (NC)
               7 the hard sound—(NC)
                  8 steel against intimation—(NC)
               7 the sharp flash, (NC)
               7 the vital, arrogant, fatal, dominant X. (NC)

Wallace Stevens

Some Tentative Strictures on Generative Rhetoric

Sabina Thorne Johnson

Johnson's essay is a healthy corrective to the implication in Christensen's article that the concept of free modifiers says all there is to say about sentences—an implication that, I think, Francis Christensen himself did not intend.

Johnson is not vandalistic in her comments; in fact, her essay might well be viewed as an extension of Christensen's work, not an attack upon it.

> Sussurare: to whisper, to mutter or murmure. Also to humme or buzze as Bees. Also to charme or forspeake with whispering words. Also to make a low, a soft or still noise as a gentle winde among trees, or a gentle gliding streame among pible-stones, or as birds chirping and chattring among woods.
>
> John Florio
> 17th c. Italian Dictionary

Such rich playfulness, such yokings of abstract meaning to images from life pervade Elizabethan and Jacobean writing; their absence, if I may be allowed an oxymoron, pervades ours. On the professional level, the lack is most noticeable in contemporary expository prose: the prose of magazines, both highbrow and middlebrow, of professional journals and the more dignified of our newspapers. (I am not concerned here with the journalistic equivalent of pulp fiction.) Such prose is utilitarian, whether the aim is an objective evaluation or a subjective response. And there is nothing wrong with purely functional writing, provided that it is clear and concise and that the content has enough interest to hold the attention of one's intended readers. Fortunately, many of the professionals who write articles do write clearly and concisely, and they would not be in the profession for long were they unable to choose topics of interest to their readers.

Such competent writers seldom vary from a purely utilitarian kind of prose. Ascertaining the reasons is not my concern, though I mention as a chief one our near obsession with seeming to be "scientific." With the increasing influence of scientific thought and methodology on us all, we tend less and less to write in words that are *dulce* as well as *utile*. We have forgotten that we write most usefully when we write most palatably. *Dulce,* of course, does not mean "sweet" in the sugary sense, but pleasant, lively, entertaining, appetizing —all those qualities that give "pile" to the fabric of words. In short, though there is nothing wrong with purely functional writing, there isn't a great deal right with it. It is generally pallid, thin and anemic, and saved from boring the reader only by the interest the reader brings to the topic being discussed. This, as I see it, is the chief problem of professional writers. What of the non-professionals, most particularly the young who learn how to write in school?

My own experience in reading essays and examinations on literature, written on the university level, is that the writing of college students is in even more need of a transfusion than is that of the professionals. All too often, ideas lie limply sprawled across the pages, like bloodless corpses. At other times, ideas are so contorted or garbled that there is no discerning their original shape. The number of articles in English journals about such problems indicates to me that other teachers are also concerned about colorless prose, vacuous prose, and tortuous prose.

There are, need I say, many recipes for writing. Some are harmful; most are ineffectual. Occasionally one appears that seems helpful, and if, like Francis Christensen's *Rhetoric Program* (Harper & Row, 1968), it challenges many of our basic assumptions about the teaching and learning of English sentence structure and the principles of composition, then one must give it a long, hard look.

What Christensen wants us to do first is cast away the belief that a mature style is one based on amplified main clause statements and frequent elaborate subordinations. His own examination of the styles of contemporary professional American writers has revealed to him that a mature style is of quite a different nature: it depends (unlike the preceding sentence) on short main clauses, especially short noun phrases, and on longer sentence modifiers, what he calls "free" modifiers, in contrast to "bound" or restrictive modifiers. Sentences of this sort he calls cumulative sentences because,

> The main clause . . . advances the discussion; the additions placed after it move backward, as in this sentence, to modify the statement of the base clause or more often to explain it or add examples or details to it, so that the sentence has a flowing and ebbing movement, advancing to a new posi-

tion and then pausing to consolidate it. (*Notes Toward a New Rhetoric* [Harper & Row, 1967], p. 5)

The cumulative sentence depends for much of its power on verb and noun clusters, notably participials and appositives used singly or in series, and on absolutes (participials containing their own subjects). By its very nature, it discourages the writer from producing what Christensen calls "pretzel prose," a term that needs no defining for those of us who have worked our labyrinthine way through perilous complex sentences. If, as Christensen contends, the fine writer is the master of the cumulative sentence, using it about fifty per cent of the time, then his advice is plausible: that we train our students to write short base clauses and to build their ideas by means of free modifiers.

Christensen makes this crucial point about the cumulative sentence:

> The main clause exhausts the mere fact of the idea; logically there is nothing more to say. The additions stay with the same idea, probing its bearings and implications, exemplifying it or seeking an analogy or metaphor for it, or reducing it to details. Thus the mere form of the sentence generates ideas. (*Notes,* p. 6)

The cumulative sentence form gives rise to what Christensen calls "the generative rhetoric of the sentence." In other words, "solving the problem of *how to say* helps solve the problem of *what to say,*" especially if students are asked to begin by doing "a few controlled exercises in description and narration [rather than] starting right off with exposition" (*Notes,* p. 15). And, as Christensen demonstrates in his *Program,* the generative rhetoric of the sentence as exemplified by the cumulative structure can, by analogy, be adapted to the paragraph and even larger units of thought.

What Christensen presents us with is a revolution in our assessment of style and in our approach to the teaching of composition.

II

Christensen's work is fresh, and appealingly simple, yet two aspects of it make me doubt the efficacy of his approach to composition. My first reservation pertains to his justification for teaching his method and to parts of the Rhetoric Program itself; the second concerns the way he arrives at his definition of a mature style. In going over these points I will move back and forth between Christensen's *Rhetoric Program;* his collection of essays, *Notes Toward a New Rhetoric;* and his article, "The Problem of Defining a Mature Style" (*English Journal,* 57, 1968, 572 ff.). Each contributes to his approach to the teaching of English composition.

First, here is a run-of-the-mill essay by a student currently enrolled in the remedial English course at Berkeley:

> The University has established breadth requirements to broaden the student's educational scope. Certain courses must be completed at the end of a four year period in order for the student to obtain a degree. The abolition

of the breadth requirements would promote a free educational atmosphere in which the student determines his own academic schedule. A student should not be compelled to enroll in Physics 10 if the subject does not appeal to his mental curiosity. An individual cannot force enthusiasm under this circumstance, and the University has no right to expect it. A great deal of valuable time is spent in satisfying these numerous requirements, time which should be devoted to studies supportive of a major.

Education is meant to be stimulating and involving; material should grasp the reader's interest to the point where one must force himself to cease. Breadth requirements in the latter sense are not representative of education; they are viewed as obstacles which must be conquered. It is imperative that a student select his own courses. These breadth requirements are not beneficial to the student and must be abolished.

If we evaluate this essay according to the criteria for writing established in Walter Loban's *The Language of Elementary School Children* (National Council of Teachers of English, 1963, p. 25), we find that the essay would barely qualify as "good" if the student were of elementary school age:

1. Uses limited sentence patterns
2. Uses few, if any, relational words
3. Begins to organize but strays from basis of organization
4. Displays monotonous vocabulary
5. Uses reasonably correct spelling and punctuation
6. Interprets only the obvious, barely achieving interpretation
7. Fails to be specific; tends to generalities

But this student is eighteen years old; he has had twelve years of instruction in English and has done well enough in other subjects in school to gain entrance to the University—none of which would matter except that the poor quality of this student's writing is typical of what we see in student essays written as remedial English assignments. Errors aside, the tendency to write a series of flat assertions, the lack of precise thinking and of any personal element, the monotony of language and sentence structure all make the essay boring, stale, clichéd, and, beyond that, pallid, thin and anemic. It is this sort of essay that I have at the back of my mind as I examine Christensen's theories and try to evaluate the efficacy of his Program.

Christensen gives a number of reasons for adopting his Program, several of which are based on what he considers the dangers of teaching sentence structure and composition in a traditional manner. They are the following:

1. We shouldn't teach subordination as it is hard to read. ("The Problem of Defining a New Style," *English Journal*, April, 1968, p. 576)
2. We shouldn't teach opening verb clusters, as they usually dangle. (*Notes,* p. 49)
3. We shouldn't teach the periodic sentence because a) "some of our worst perversions of style come from the attempt to teach [students] to write

periodic sentences" (*Notes,* p. 3), and b) "periodic sentences represent the idea as conceived pondered over, reshaped, packaged, and delivered cold." (*Notes,* p. 6)

4. We shouldn't teach balanced sentences because they have gone out of fashion. (*Notes,* p. 6)

Looking back at the student essay, we see that there are six examples of subordination, none of which is structurally faulty (there are obvious errors in word choice). And whatever the quality of the content, none is hard to read. In general, well-executed subordination is no harder to read than any other kind of modification, well-executed. In any event, if we should teach only what is easy to read, why don't we keep our students' writing at the primer level? I note what Christensen himself says in regard to Faulkner's cumulative style:

> To a single independent clause he may append a page of additions, but usually all clear, all grammatical, *once we have learned to read him.* (*Notes,* p. 8. Italics mine.)

If we must learn to read one kind of style, why shouldn't we learn to read another?

Second, there are no opening verb clusters in the student essay. In fact, there are no initial free modifiers at all. That is one of the main faults of the essay. Sentence after sentence runs subject, verb, complement, qualifier; that is, each sentence runs downhill. The student sample aside, I find that when students do dangle their initial verb clusters, it is easy for them to correct the fault.

Third, in our student essay there are no periodic sentences and no balanced sentences. There are only simple sentences and, using Christensen's definition, cumulative sentences. Unfortunately, the latter do not do what they are supposed to do: "advance the discussion." There is, in fact, no discussion going on in the essay, because it is merely a set of pronouncements. I wish the student had used a couple of balanced sentences. They are an extremely economical device for making the reader grasp the correlations between ideas,[1] as is evident from E. M. Forster's essays. For instance, here is an excerpt from "What I Believe":

> My law-givers are Erasmus and Montaigne, not Moses and St. Paul. My temple stands not upon Mount Moriah but in that Elysian Field where even the immoral are admitted. My motto is: Lord, I disbelieve—help thou my unbelief.

Periodic sentences are often horrendous, I agree, but if teachers have enough taste to distinguish between good and bad ones they can discourage

---

[1] Would we still remember John Kennedy's "Ask not what your country can do for you—ask what you can do for your country" had he presented the thought in less balanced form?

the writing of bad ones. But the second of Christensen's objections to the periodic sentence deserves some study. The periodic sentence is the antithesis in structure of the cumulative sentence. And, Christensen tells us, it is also the antithesis in spirit. The cumulative sentence

> does not represent the idea as conceived, pondered over, reshaped, packaged, and delivered cold. It is dynamic rather than static, representing the mind thinking. (*Notes*, p. 6)

Yet Churchill's World War II speeches are not static, nor Edmund Wilson's "Mr. More and the Mithraic Bull." What bothers me most about the distinction between seemingly spontaneous and pre-packaged thought is that it is a false distinction. Neither the cumulative nor the periodic sentence imitates thought, which by its nature is usually chaotic and inchoate. In any case, good cumulative sentences require as much forethought as good periodic sentences. If we pretend they do not, if we tell students to write short base clauses that will generate ideas, we will be telling them to do what they do now: postpone thinking. Looking back at our student essay, we see that each sentence is an assertion because each sentence is an aborted thought. The student, like so many I have taught, did not know where he was going when he started writing, did not know what he wanted to say. He had a vague idea, of course, but rather than thinking out the possibilities of the topic before he started to write, he trusted that ideas might come to him along the way. Thus, sentence after sentence begins with a short base clause and then runs downhill, as the momentum dies. Perhaps if he had preformed his ideas, his sentences would have had both vigor and variety. How can one know how one wants to say something unless one first knows what one wants to say?

This is perhaps the heart of my hesitancy about the Rhetoric Program. Christensen seems to believe that form can generate content (*Program*, p. vi). I don't believe it can, especially if the content is of an analytical or critical nature. Whatever he says of the generative power of the cumulative sentence, Christensen must be in tacit agreement with me, or he would not suggest that students first apply his method to description and narration, to topics that depend for content on immediate observation (*Notes*, p. 13). I can see that professional writers of narrative and description depend heavily on cumulative sentences, and also that students must learn how to write them. But I am aware of what happens to students who write only narrative and descriptive essays. On each remedial English examination at the University of California, a few students turn out such essays instead of the expository essay that we ask for. On retesting, these students usually fail to write passing expository essays. Why? Because their skills in the first two kinds of writing seldom carry over to the third kind.

The inspiration for Christensen's entire approach to sentences is to be found in certain remarks of John Erskine's:

> When you write, you make a point, not by subtracting as though you sharp-
> ened a pencil, but by adding. . . . What you say is found not in the noun
> but in what you add to qualify the noun. . . . The noun, the verb, and the
> main clause serve mainly as the base on which meaning will rise. . . . The
> modifier is the essential part of any sentence.
>
> (Quoted in *Notes,* p. 4)

For many writers—say, Hemingway or Eudora Welty—Erskine's statement
is applicable much of the time. My own word counts of other contemporary
authors indicate that the same holds true, though in lesser degree, for writers
of quite diverse styles. However, young students seldom write sound, precise
base clauses, and for them the writing of the cumulative sentence is not unlike
building a house on sand. Furthermore, I have found in conferring with students that they depend heavily on modifiers to make up for what they rightly
sense to be the inadequacy of their base clauses. This technique usually fails
—and they know it—so they try again with the next sentence, and the next,
adding words onto words, but never making their point securely.

Both Christensen and I feel that students have little to say and that they
say it badly. Christensen seeks to help them with a sentence form that he
believes will generate ideas, while restricting them at first to topics that demand direct observation. The result he hopes for is essays of substance written
in a lively style. I want that, too. He says he wants syntactic dexterity; so do I.
But he wants his students to "dazzle" him with their dexterity, to be "sentence
acrobats" (*Notes,* p. 14). I do not. I want students to dazzle me with their
ideas and to astonish me with their powers of persuasion. The weaknesses
I see in student writing—the paucity of thought, the monotony of style and
structure, the superficiality of analysis and explanation, the insensitivity to
words—all indicate to me that what students need first is training in how to
attack a topic.

Christensen's method has much to offer, especially in teaching students
how to use participials, appositives and absolutes as free modifiers. Writers
of grammar and composition texts give a disproportionate amount of attention to subordination at the cost of these forms of modification. For pre-
college students, his focus on narrative and descriptive topics cannot be
anything but fruitful. I find it less relevant for college students, whose academic well-being depends largely on their ability to handle abstractions and
to employ their powers of exposition. What I would like to see tried in freshman composition is use of Christensen for developing varied skills in modification. More experimentally, I would also like to see whether and to what
degree his method of building sentences can be made to carry over from the
narrative and descriptive to the expository essay. But concurrently, I want
to see students taught the necessity of sound base clauses (the shorter the
better), and the proper use of all kinds of secondary structures, both free
and bound. Finally, the student's motivation for using any of these sentence
elements must be that he has something he wants to say.

III

The basis for Christensen's *Program* is his analysis of professional writing. By studying excerpts of contemporary prose, Christensen discovered that "free modifiers, commonly called sentence modifiers, are the principal working units of the professional writer." He adds,

> It is these modifiers, not subordinate clauses, that make it possible for him to say much in little—to make his writing concrete and specific without making it prolix, to get the movement or rhythm that is the life of prose.
>
> (*Program*, p. vi)

Consequently, Christensen uses in his *Program* sentence models taken from professional writers. This is an excellent innovation, but the process by which Christensen arrives at his conclusions is in some ways puzzling. Leaving aside the difficulty of understanding some of his structural categories, and hence of duplicating his counts, I turn to the values that underlie his judgments.

Let us look again at Christensen's definition of the cumulative sentence. I underline the structure that concerns me:

> The main clause, which may or may not have a sentence modifier before it, advances the discussion; but the additions move backward . . . to modify . . . *so that the sentence has a flowing and ebbing movement,* advancing to a new position . . .(*Notes*, p. 5)

As Christensen's sentence indicates, expository sentences are hard to write without subordinate structures, because to keep order we must continually keep clear the relationships between ideas. Here is an example by Joseph Wood Krutch:

Those [who are appalled by the prospect of living in a universe	1st order: Rel. Cl.
[which, for the first time in several centuries, has ceased to seem	2nd order: Rel. Cl.
comprehensible]] may be somewhat reassured by the reminder	1st order: Noun Cl.
[that it is only the novelty of the modern instances [which is dis-	2nd order: Rel. Cl.
turbing]] and [that they have all along been living with other	1st order: Noun Cl.
irresolvable paradoxes [which did not trouble them [simply because	2nd order: Rel. Cl.
they had been for so long accepted]]].	3rd order: Sub. Cl.

Most of the sentence consists of subordinations, some set within others so that the whole is like a Chinese puzzle box. I don't suggest that anyone write an essay composed of sentences like the above; I do suggest that sometimes such constructions are necessary to express complex relationships and that students had best know how to write them correctly, which means that students had best devote far more time to mastering subordination than Christensen would have them do.

Looking at Krutch's sentence again, we see that "for the first time in several centuries" is sandwiched into a second order subordination. Sandwiching is characteristic of certain writers. It seems to go with subordination, and it is the two together that often supply the texture of a passage, as in this quote from James Baldwin's *Notes of a Native Son* (I italicize the elements that are sandwiched into the main content):

> When I was about nine or ten I wrote a play which was directed by a young, white schoolteacher, a woman, who then took an interest in me, and gave me books to read and, *in order to corroborate my theatrical bent,* decided to take me to see *what she somewhat tactlessly referred to as* "real" plays. Theatergoing was forbidden in our house, but, *with the really cruel intuitiveness of a child,* I suspected that the color of this woman's skin would carry the day for me. When, *at school,* she suggested taking me to the theater, I did not, *as I might have done if she had been a Negro,* find a way of discouraging her, but agreed that she should pick me up at my house one evening. I then, *very cleverly,* left all the rest to my mother, who suggested to my father, *as I knew she would,* that it would not be very nice to let such a kind woman make the trip for nothing. Also, *since it was a schoolteacher,* I imagine that my mother countered the idea of sin with the idea of "education," which word, *even with my father,* carried a kind of bitter weight.

Sandwiching creates a parenthetic style, one that gives the illusion of approximating well-turned speech. It does not flow as Christensen would like sentences to. One may object to it as just the sort of style that we want students to get away from, but if I had to have a steady diet of any one kind of sentence, I would prefer Baldwin's kind to the cumulative kind, with its absolutes and participles streaming away into the distance. Which brings me to my last and most fundamental objection to Christensen's theories and Program: their basically subjective nature.

Christensen based his ideas on a study of contemporary professional writing. When I decided to test his ideas, I chose the first writers that came to my mind. Some, like Cather and Fitzgerald, were among those Christensen used in his earlier studies; others were not. Like Christensen I chose narrative, descriptive, and expository prose passages. But in every instance, I came out with results significantly different from his.

Much of Christensen's essay, "Problems of Defining a Mature Style" (see 577 ff.), is devoted to analyzing passages from current *Harper's* articles written by both professionals and non-professionals. It is to the tabulations in this essay that I shall compare my own, because they have been made in a reproducible manner. Christensen broke down selected passages into T-units —main clauses, together with subordinate elements, each unit such that it might be worked by a capital letter at the beginning and a period at the end ("Problems," p. 573). Instead of using his own more complicated classifications, Christensen simply broke the T-units down into base clauses and free modifiers. Next he counted the total words in each passage and averaged them per T-unit; counted the words in the free modifications according to whether the modifications were in the initial, medial, or final position; counted their totals, averaged them per T-unit, and calculated what percentage they were of the total number of words in the passage.

His conclusion about the *Harper's* writers ("Problems," pp. 577–79) was that the writer he considered the best, David Halberstam, used the shortest base clauses and had the longest free modifiers and the greatest number of free modifiers in the final position:

Average number of words per base clause	13.3
Average number of words in free modifiers per T-unit	9.8
Total words in free modifiers in final position	313
Percentage of total words in free modification	42.6%

In contrast, the writer Christensen considered the worst, a non-professional named Barnes, had the longest base clauses and had the shortest free modifiers and the greatest number of free modifiers in the *initial* position:

Average number of words per base clause	15.1
Average number of words in free modifiers per T-unit	4.24
Total words in free modifiers in final position	55
Percentage of total words in free modification	21.91%

The authors from whom I chose samples were the following:

Fiction—Cather, Fitzgerald, Forster, Isherwood
Non-Fiction—Baldwin, Edmund Wilson, Auden, Forster, Orwell

Of all these authors, only one compared favorably in count to Halberstam, and that was Wilson:

Average number of words per base clause	12.84
Average number of words in free modifiers per T-unit	11.12
Total words in free modifiers in final position	545
Percentage of total words in free modification	46.42%

But Edmund Wilson's style, unlike Halberstam's, is not cumulative; it is periodic, and he depends for modifications, not on verbal clauses, appositives and absolutes so much as on relative and subordinate clauses, as in the following sentence:

> The moralist in Paul Elmer More, who had always been at war with the poet and who had scored over him so crushing a victory, could usually be counted upon to formulate clearly—though of course a clear formulation may misrepresent a poet—the case of any writer, however abhorrent, who had a serious moral basis, even though the provincial prig who inseparably accompanied the moralist might prevent him from appreciating the artist's achievement.
>
> "Mr. More and the Mithraic Bull"

Obviously, this style is not at all what Christensen has in mind. The sort of style Christensen advocates is exemplified by the passage I chose at random from Fitzgerald's *The Great Gatsby,* the opening of Chapter Three, in which we are told about Gatsby's parties. The sentences are largely cumulative, the content primarily descriptive. It is a beautiful piece of writing. But Fitzgerald's

Christensen's Count Drawn on Non-Fiction Samples from *Harper's*　　**TABLE A**

Relative Length of 1) T-units, 2) Free Modifiers and 3) Base Clauses (Based on 50 T-units)

	Non-professional		Semi-professional		Professional	
	Barnes	Szasz	Boroff	Good-man	Morris	Halber-stam
1) T-units—100% of total words						
Total words	967	832	944	911	1037	1155
Av. words per T-unit	19.3	14.6	18.9	18.2	20.7	23.1
2) Free Modifiers						
Initial	129	94	51	107	70	76
Medial	28	36	93	23	20	103
Final	55	106	154	169	242	313
Total words in Free Modification	212	236	298	299	382	492
Av. words per T-unit	4.24	4.72	5.84	6.0	6.6	9.8
% of total words	21.91%	28.37%	31.57%	32.82%	36.84%	42.6%
3) Base Clauses						
Words in T-units	967	832	944	911	1037	1155
Words in Free Mod.	212	236	298	299	382	492
Words in Base Clauses	755	596	646	612	705	663
Av. per Base Clause	15.1	11.9	12.9	12.2	14.1	13.3
% of total words	78.09%	71.63%	68.43%	67.18%	63.16%	56.4%

My Count Drawn on Fiction and Non-Fiction Samples   TABLE B

Relative Length of 1) T-units, 2) Free Modifiers and 3) Base Clauses
(Based on 50 T-units unless otherwise noted)

	Forster Fiction (51 T-units)	Isherwood Fiction	Cather Fiction (49 T-units)	Fitzgerald Fiction	Forster Non-fiction (51 T-units)	Orwell Non-fiction (52 T-units)	Auden Non-fiction	Baldwin Non-fiction	Wilson Non-fiction (49 T-units)
1) T-units = 100% of total words									
Total Words	489	602	880	1058	705	990	950	950	1174
Av. words per T-unit	9.59	12.04	18.12	21.16	13.84	19.02	19.0	19.0	23.96
2) Free Modifiers									
Initial	18	52	78	65	68	86	86	103	107
Medial	7	15	37	14	14	78	61	62	110
Final	55	89	191	246	171	88	127	88	328
Total words in Free Modification	80	156	306	325	253	252	274	253	545
Av. words per T-unit	1.57	3.12	6.24	6.5	4.96	4.85	5.48	5.06	11.12
% of total words	16.86%	25.91%	34.77%	30.72%	35.89%	25.45%	28.84%	26.63%	46.42%
3) Base Clauses									
Words in T-units	489	602	880	1058	605	990	950	950	1174
Words in Free Mod.	80	156	306	325	253	252	274	253	545
Words in Base Clauses	409	446	574	733	452	738	676	697	629
Av. per Base Clause	8.02	8.92	19.71	14.66	8.86	14.19	13.52	13.94	12.84
% of total words	83.64%	74.09%	75.23%	69.28%	64.11%	74.55%	71.16%	73.37%	53.58%

words in free modification amount to only 30.72% against Halberstam's 42.6%.

As one can see from the tabulations of Christensen's counts and my own (Tables A and B), all the other writers I selected have short base clauses, commensurate with Halberstam's, all have more free modifiers in the final position, except Baldwin, who has most in the initial position, but none comes near Halberstam in the percentage of words in free modification. If we are to measure the degree of skill in a writer by the percentage of words he has in free modification, then we should rate Cather, Fitzgerald, Forster, Isherwood, Baldwin, Auden and Orwell less skillful than Halberstam, or assume that my passages, chosen at random, are atypical.

My point is that Christensen's theories about sentence structure are based on his study of selected passages from certain professional writers. Generally, I chose to study passages from different authors, my taste in styles being different from Christensen's. Therefore, when I look at the evidence yielded by my counts, it occurs to me that were Christensen a man of different stylistic tastes his entire Program would be somewhat different. And who is to say objectively whether it would be better or worse?

IV

At the beginning of this essay I suggested that we need language that is both *dulce* and *utile* and that we should welcome any method of teaching sentence structure and composition that may counteract the flatness, emptiness, and monotony of student writing. Christensen's method seems to have this potential. Yet I have been critical of both the reasons Christensen gives for teaching his method and parts of the *Program* itself, and also of aspects of the technique by which he arrived at his method, including what I take as a basically subjective choice of professonal writers and styles.[2]

My rather negative response to his method is seldom relieved by the suggestion of positive alternatives. But this approach is intentional. I suspect that Christensen, in seeking to remedy the errors inherent in the more traditional approaches to composition teaching, has presented his theories and his method in far more absolute terms than they warrant. And I fear that English teachers, driven by despair to a rigid adoption of his theories and method, will find that an untempered and exclusive use of the *Rhetoric Program* will not be as fruitful as they had hoped—and, indeed, as it could be, used in a limited way—especially at the high school and college levels. I do not fundamentally challenge Christensen's attempt to teach a vigorous prose. With all my objections, I can see that what he has to offer is more promising than much of what we teach now.

---

[2] That on occasion his students chose the authors does not make the act of choosing less subjective.

Assumptions and Hypothesis
[of Transformational
Sentence-Combining]

John C. Mellon

Regardless of one's feelings about transformational generative grammar, that theory has awakened us to some undeniable facts about language. Like any grammatical theory—traditional, structural, tagmemic, stratificational—in essence it is nothing more than an attempt to give an account of what every speaker of a language knows intuitively. In constructing this account, grammarians have formulated the extremely useful concepts of deep and surface structure, which are easily illustrated.

It is obvious that the surface structure of Behave yourself! *does not have a word of any kind as its subject, but it is equally as obvious that the meaning of the sentence does contain the second person pronoun as subject. This is evidenced, first, by our interpretation of the sentence, second, by the reflexive "yourself" in the surface structure, and, third, by the allowable, ultraemphatic* You behave yourself! (or I'll take away your popcorn). *In other words, in giving an explicit account of the meaning of the sentence, we will say something like the following:* IMPERATIVE + YOU + BEHAVE + YOURSELF.

Even more crucial in the statement of deep structures is the reconstruction of sentences that are contained within sentences. For instance, the sentence You know the girl who chewed the bubble gum *obviously contains the sentence* You know the girl *and, just as obviously,* The girl chewed the bubble gum, *for the relative "who" would be meaningless and the sentence would be nonsense if we could not get at the exact meaning of "who," which it picks up from its antecedent "the girl."*

In Grinning broadly, the boy kicked the girl in the shins, *the sentences are* The boy was grinning broadly (or something very like that), *and, of course,* The boy kicked the girl in the shins, *for if we did not know who was doing the grinning, once again the sentence would be nonsensical.*

In other words, the language affords us the means to embed sentence within *sentence within sentence. . . . And it goes without saying that embedding devices (in the jargon, transformations) are the single most powerful instrument that the language affords us. Without embedding, a discourse would look like this (as, in fact, the prose of inept writers often does look):*

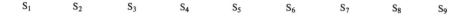

S_1 S_2 S_3 S_4 S_5 S_6 S_7 S_8 S_9

But embedding enables us, when necessary to convey meaning, and, where appropriate, to do this:

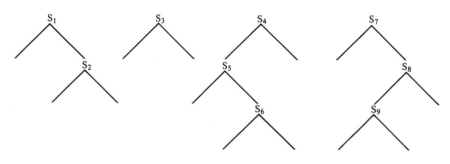

That is to say:

> [S_1] *The boy whistled happily.* [S_2] *The boy was mowing the lawn.* [S_3] *It was vacation time.* [S_4] *He had waited nine months.* [S_5] *He had waited to escape the tedium of classes.* [S_6] *The classes bored him.* [S_7] *Now he was planning his vacation.* [S_8] *His vacation was a trip to Mexico.* [S_9] *He would take the trip with his parents.*

> [S_1] *The boy (*[S_2] *mowing the lawn) whistled happily.* [S_3] *It was vacation time.* [S_4] *He had waited nine months (*[S_5] *to escape the tedium of classes (*[S_6] *which bored him)).* [S_7] *Now he was planning his vacation, (*[S_8] *a trip to Mexico (*[S_9] *which he would take with his parents)).*

This is just one example of what Mellon means by "syntactic fluency."

It is important to note that Mellon's study is arhetorical. That is, he does not claim that a syntactically fluent style is better than one that is not. And, of course, it makes no sense to claim that one way of writing is absolutely better than any other, for language is meaningful and effective only in relation to purpose and audience, that is, in relation to the rhetorical situation. A style that might be characterized as "choppy" in one situation could well be viewed as effectively staccato in another. Nonetheless, syntactic fluency as an ability is essential to the writer. The writer desperately needs the ability to embed when the situation calls for it.

It will be noted that six of Christensen's free modifiers are nothing more than embeddings, as can readily be illustrated:

Absolute
  The light becoming extremely dim, *we could no longer manage our fishing gear.*
  [S_1] *We could no longer manage our fishing gear.*
  [S_2] *The light was becoming extremely dim.*
Adjective Cluster
  The rose, delicate in its paleness, *drooped.*
  [S_1] *The rose drooped.*
  [S_2] *The rose was delicate in its paleness.*
Adverb Clause
  Students study because they want good grades.
  [S_1] *Students study.*
  [S_2] *Students want good grades.*
Noun Cluster
  My father, a roulette dealer, *was a mathematical genius.*
  [S_1] *My father was a mathematical genius.*
  [S_2] *My father was a roulette dealer.*
Relative Clause
  Norma, who is a masterful cook, *specializes in stews.*
  [S_1] *Norma specializes in stews.*
  [S_2] *Norma is a masterful cook.*
Verb Cluster
  Wanting the ultimate in pleasure, *the man smoked ten-cent cigars.*
  [S_1] *The man smoked ten-cent cigars.*
  [S_2] *The man wanted the ultimate in pleasure.*
The most serious limitation of Christensen's work is that he focuses on these six kinds of embeddings (and the prepositional phrase) to the exclusion of the various other kinds of sentence-combining that the language affords.

In Sentence-Combining: Improving Student Writing without Formal Grammar Instruction (*Urbana, Ill.: NCTE, 1973*), *Frank O'Hare extends Mellon's work. O'Hare's study is strongly recommended.*

Enhancing the Growth of Syntactic Fluency

The research discussed above [in Mellon's monograph] clearly shows that memorized principles of grammar, whether conventional or modern, play a negligible role in helping students achieve "correctness" in their written expression. It further suggests that pervasive emphasis upon the corrective aspects of grammar develops an error-oriented atmosphere which may inhibit growth of sentence structure and doubtless engenders a wide variety of negative and hostile feelings towards writing in general and linguistic studies in particular. For the moment, then, it would appear that additional experiments on existing notions of error therapy are unwarranted. On the other hand, the above research rather strongly implies the timeliness of experimentation related to the traditional claim that grammar practice results in the use of increasingly mature sentence structure. The present study reports one such experiment.

It has frequently been noted that the range of sentence types in free student writing increases in a continuous and sequential manner as the student matures. These increases have been studied in some detail, and the results of this developmental research are summarized below. In a general way, growth of sentence structure is reflected in a host of commonplace observations on developmental changes in student writing—that independent clauses grow longer, that sentences become more highly elaborated, that more subordination is used, that a wider range of sentence patterns is employed, or that sentences become on average more heavily and deeply embedded. Growth of sentence structure, however, is not a substantive phenomenon. It is merely evidence that the student, through gaining greater experience in the world around him, has learned to construe and take cognizance of this world and of his relation to it in an increasingly adult manner. It is this cognitive growth that results in his making fuller use of permitted grammatical operations and that produces the changes in his sentence structure noted above.

Growth of this sort, whether one speaks directly of cognition or more indirectly of the sentence structure which manifests cognition, occurs normally and without the aid of formally designed pedagogy. But normal growth need not be considered optimal growth. It refers merely to what has been observed; it should not be viewed as the maximum permitted by some presumably fixed schedule of "natural" growth. Indeed, the assumption that such growth is variable and thus amenable to treatment is supported by the widespread belief that differences in verbal ability between same-age children result in large part from widely discrepant prior language experiences in differing home and school environments. Thus the initial assumption of this study is that rates of growth towards more mature sentence structure may be enhanced by special treatment.

Maturity of sentence structure is here stipulatively defined, in a strictly statistical sense, in terms of the range of sentence types observed in representative samples of a student's writing. Since this is a rather lengthy and cumbersome phrase, the present study henceforth employs the term "syntactic fluency." The intention of this novel term is somewhat analogous to that of the more familiar "vocabulary fluency," in that both refer to ranges of linguistic types, the former being sentence types and the latter word types. The question to be considered, then, is whether grammar practice may enhance the growth of syntactic fluency.

Developmental Research on Normal Growth

Plans for stimulating the development of syntactic fluency obviously must be based on a knowledge of normal growth, since experimental treatments designed for use at certain grade levels would doubtless present students with sentence types which are known to appear subsequently in their writing but which are not generally characteristic of it at the time of presentation. Although syntactic fluency probably does not develop in exactly the same way for all children, it is possible to gain a fairly clear picture of mean growth parameters for representative groups of students at different ages.

Many studies of language development are reviewed by McCarthy (1954) and Carroll (1960), who summarize research on both spoken and written language. Early investigations of writing sought only to identify a single index for evaluating general maturity. Mean sentence length, percentage inventories of parts of speech and the major sentence types, and ratios of subordinate to total clauses were the measures most frequently used. Stormzand and O'Shea (1925), Frogner (1933), LaBrant (1933), Bear (1939), and Heider and Heider (1941) all find evidence of continuous growth from year to year on one or more of these measures, although certain methodological errors in these studies have recently been noted by Hunt (1964) and Mellon (1965). But the main difficulty is that any single index of maturity, while it may reflect syntactic fluency, does not characterize it fully enough to be useful in the sense suggested above.

Until recently, research on speech had produced more construction-count data than had writing research, but it is questionable whether findings based on spoken performance are applicable to writing. The work of Davis (1937), Templin (1957), and Loban (1963), for example, is based largely on "remarks" elicited from children during interviews. The high percentage of "functionally complete but structurally incomplete" responses indicates that considerable question-answering behavior was being measured. This presumably differs in structure from what the child might produce in written discourse. Indeed, Harrell (1957) has compared the use of subordinate clauses in oral and written compositions on identical topics. He finds that the number of subordinate clauses increases with age in both, but that these clauses are longer in oral compositions through grade eight, after which they become longer in the written ones. Variability of clause length at all grade levels is greater in writing than in speech. Few adjective clauses occur orally, while a great many are used in writing. One may thus conclude that developmental changes in written sentence structure are unique thereto and cannot be observed in studies of speech.

At the same time, however, one may ask whether research on aural/oral performance indicates that children have acquired full competence repertoires by the time they reach the writing age, probably grade four. The conclusion implied by Watts (1944), and in the studies reviewed by McNeill (1966), is that they have. Furthermore, Hunt (1964) finds that all the kernel-sentence types, including those with predicate complement embeddings, are used as fully and as frequently by fourth graders as by twelfth. The same is true of the simple transformations. Hunt also notes that all transformations which operate on embedded sentences have been acquired by even the youngest writers, although they are used more often by older ones. Treatments for promoting growth on the part of secondary school students may therefore be designed in the knowledge that these children have long since acquired, and that they normally use, the full roster of kernel-sentence types and transformation rules.

It follows, then, that growth of syntactic fluency can result only from increased use of sentence-embedding transformations. The recent work of Hunt (1964 and undated), as subsequently confirmed by O'Donnell, Griffin, and Norris (1967), depicts with reasonable clarity the norms of this growth. Hunt examined 1000 words of free writing per student as produced by groups of fourth, eighth, and twelfth graders, together with an equal number of 1000-word samples taken from nonfiction magazine articles published in *Harper's* and *The Atlantic*. The latter he terms "skilled adult." Although Hunt devotes considerable energy to showing that T-unit length is a more accurate index of maturity than are subordination ratios or length of orthographic sentence, it is his construction-count data based on complete grammatical analyses of all T-units examined that are of greatest importance to the present study. Curiously enough, however, Hunt reports this data on the basis of running words rather than number of T-units, apparently failing to recognize that his new unit is the base of analysis arithmetically as well as grammatically. In other words, the interesting question is not frequency of certain constructions per so many words; it is their frequencies per so many T-units. This has to be the case if frequency is to mean anything, since the sentence structure of skilled adults is so much more highly differentiated than that of fourth graders, for example, that adults write two and one third fewer T-units per given number of words than do these young children. Comparing absolute construction counts based on samples of equal numbers of words, as Hunt does, thus reduces the apparent magnitude of differences between age levels.

The following discussion, as well as the criteria subsequently employed in this experiment, is therefore based on a reworking of Hunt's data. Since the absolute totals of T-units and of the several construction types are given for each level, the construction totals may be converted by a simple ratio and proportion formula and shown as they would appear if produced in 100 T-units. The resulting figures are directly comparable across age levels and may be regarded as parameters of normal growth. Hunt's findings show that intra-T-unit coordinate conjunction, comparative conjunction, and adverbial clauses do not fluctuate with age. In the case of adverbials, however, radical decreases in temporal clauses obscure the fact that the concessives, causals, and conditionals do increase somewhat. But in general, it is the nominal and relative transforms whose consistently greater frequencies per T-unit characterize growth of syntactic fluency. Table 1 presents Hunt's findings on these transforms, converted by the method given above and summarized under the six construction categories listed.

Table 1

Frequencies of Constructions per 100 T-units (Hunt)

Construction Type	Grade 4	Grade 8	Grade 12	Adult
Nominal clauses (fact and question)	9	12	27	21
Nominal phrases (gerund and infinitive)	6	10	23	not available
Relative clauses (less time and place)	5	9	16	25
Relative phrases (post-noun modifiers)	13	28	46	92
Relative words (pre-noun modifiers)	33	68	81	152
Unique dominant nominals	9	20	34	not available

The "dominant nominals" mentioned in Table 1 refer to the full nominal constructions in the primary grammatical functions of T-units—subject, object, and so forth. Notice also that in dominant nominals containing one or more embeddings, the four age levels average the following numbers of these embeddings per nominal:

Grade 4	Grade 8	Grade 12	Adult
1.19	1.39	1.43	2.42

Another way to view the tabled figures is to divide them by 100, in which case they represent the percentage of likelihood that the associated construction will occur in an individual T-unit.

Clearly, Hunt has shown that the hallmark of mature syntactic fluency is the ability to "say more," on average, with every statement. Increased use of relative transforms means in effect that the student more often makes secondary statements, either fully formed or elliptical, about the nouns in his main sentences. Greater use of nominalized sentences means that he more often predicates upon statements, as it were, rather than upon simple nouns. Furthermore, transformed sentences will be recursively embedded at increasingly deeper levels, and relative transforms will be more frequently used in parallel "clusters" surrounding single nouns. Notice that by grade twelve, one out of every three dominant nominals produced by the student will be a unique type, whereas in grade four only one in ten would be. And most striking of all, it would seem, is how far even the oldest students have to go in order to match the performance of skilled adults. Generally speaking, then, the above embedding transforms, together with measures of depth of embedding, cluster size, and unique nominal patterns, constitute the appropriate criteria for describing growth of syntactic fluency. In like manner, example sentences used in the secondary grades as practice exercises designed to enhance this growth would feature many of these transforms in concert and would exemplify the widest possible diversity of grammatical patterns.

Existing Proposals for Grammar Practice

Several grammar-related activities have already been mentioned which would cause students to experience given sentences in certain specially planned ways and would thus presumably lead to enhancement of syntactic fluency. Four proposals have been cited—modeled writing, applied transformation rules, pattern practice, and traditional sentence parsing. Each may be rejected in turn. First, modeled writing differs from the other procedures listed in that it requires only the straightforward imitation of style and thus is not really contingent in any way on prior grammar study. Furthermore, it results in the production of discourse and presumably therefore entails a response to some rhetorical occasion. In short, modeled writing is actually a disguised form of composition. But as noted, this activity misrepresents to the student the nature of the composing process, and it contains no provision for specifying the purpose of the writing it invites. In general, a condition required of schemes for grammar-related language practice is that they be a-rhetorical in nature and not give the appearance of pertaining to the student's work in composition. Certain advantages of this approach are discussed below.

A second proposal for research was that investigated in the Bateman and Zidonis study, namely, that the student learn the transformation rules of a generative grammar so that he can later apply these rules in writing. As pointed out, however, students who have reached the writing age have already acquired complete sets of these rules in their internalized competence. And even if they had not, it would be absurd to believe that memorizing formulations of rules might occasion their acquisition, just as it is idle to pretend that transformations can be consciously applied in the production of sentences. People simply do not behave in these ways. Then too, it has just been shown that maturity of sentence structure does not stem so much from the use of particular rules in isolation as from their more frequent use together in single statements. Thus a second condition on grammar-related practice activities is that they must in some way confront the student with actual sentences of mature structure. It is not enough to present transformation rules alone, nor to exemplify them by means of sentences embodying the given rule but no others.

Pattern practice and traditional sentence parsing, although they are a-rhetorical and may indeed feature mature sentences, are unacceptable for still other reasons. Pattern practice requires the student to write sentences whose structures conform to given strings of grammatical terms. While the final behavior elicited from the student is the production of a pre-described sentence, the weakness of this activity is that it forces him to provide his own content, apropos of no purpose whatever, to be grafted onto the stipulated grammatical framework. But searching for pointless content surely distracts him from the very thing to which he is supposed to be attending, namely, the given pattern. Traditional parsing, on the other hand, begins with actual sentences and requires that their constituents be segmented and labeled. Here the student experiences no part of the production process. And while he does attend initially to the interrelationships between content and structure in fully formed statements, his attention subsequently becomes focused within isolated constructions and in the end is directed to the wholly irrelevant problem of selecting correct terminological labels.

To be acceptable, then, routines for grammar-related language practice must satisfy two further conditions. One of these is that the final behavior elicited from the student must be the writing of a fully formed statement whose structure is predetermined and characteristic of mature expression. The other is that the content of such pseudo-production activities must be provided at the outset and must be given in a grammatical format which optimally and unobtrusively facilitates the student's realization of this content in the form of the desired statement. Since the above proposals for enhancing syntactic fluency fail to meet the foregoing conditions, they almost certainly do not merit experimental study. Consequently, it was decided that some alternative procedure should be considered in their stead.

Transformational Sentence-Combining

The grammar-related practice activity examined in this study was designed to satisfy the four conditions outlined above. It was presented to the student in the form of sentence-combining problems to be solved in connection with his study of a transformational grammar. In solving these problems, the student experienced the pseudo-production of a range of sentences more mature in structure than those typical of his writing at the time. In general, the aim of these problems was to direct a maximum of the student's attention to the way that content initially expressed in collections of separately represented kernel sentences may be collapsed into single statements. The overt tasks required of the student were first that he transform the separate sentences according to directions keyed to rule formulations he had earlier studied, then that he embed these transforms as constituents in other sentences according to a simple embedding format employed in all problems, and finally that he write out the result in the form of a single fully developed complex sentence. In short, the student was given a set of kernel sentences plus directions for combining these sentences into a single complex statement, which he was then required to write out.

The following is an example illustrating the form of these transformational sentence-combining problems. A problem such as this would appear in about the seventh month of the grammar course:

Problem:

The children clearly must have wondered SOMETHING.
  The bombings had orphaned the children.
  SOMETHING was humanly possible somehow. (T:wh)
    Their conquerors pretended SOMETHING. (T:infin—T:exp)
      Chewing gum and smiles might compensate for the losses. (T:fact)
        The losses were heartbreaking.
        They had so recently sustained the losses.

Write-out:

  (Here the student writes the fully formed sentence.)

_____

_____

The student would have studied the transformations involved, and he would also have become thoroughly familiar with the details of format, which are purely mechanical and readily learned. Briefly, the right-hand indentations show how the embedding is to proceed. The first sentence is always the main clause. The sentence or sentences immediately beneath it and spaced one place to the right are to be embedded therein, and so on down the list of successively right-spaced sentences. The capitalized word "SOMETHING" indicates an open nominal position, repeated nouns signal relativization, and parenthetical items are abbreviated transformational directions where necessary.

In solving problems such as the above, the student begins with the main-clause sentence incremented by the first embedded transform. Since he is not to write the sentence until it is fully formed, his first step above is simply to relativize the second sentence and to say the following:

The children whom the bombings had orphaned clearly must have wondered something.

He then nominalizes the third sentence as a question clause, inserts it in place of "SOMETHING," and says the following as a second approximation of the final sentence:

The children whom the bombings had orphaned clearly must have wondered how something was humanly possible.

This process is continued until all sentences are transformed and embedded. Finally, while holding the fully formed sentence in memory, the student writes it out as follows:

The children whom the bombings had orphaned clearly must have wondered how it was humanly possible for their conquerors to pretend that chewing gum and smiles might compensate for the heartbreaking losses which they had so recently sustained.

Additional illustrations of these sentence-combining problems are given in Appendix B. Several further comments may be made at this time. Pre-experiment trials indicated that junior high school students of virtually all ability levels are capable of solving these problems. Bright students, in fact, soon become adept at reading out the final complex sentence after a single run-through of the listed kernels, whereas average and slower students follow the strategy outlined above, rehearsing the sentence after incrementation by each successive embedding until the finished product is achieved. Motivation for these problems arises in part from the student's desire to grapple with increasingly challenging sentences, and in part from his curiosity to know what each completed sentence has to say. Notice that while the kernel sentences taken together embody the total content of the final statement, reading them separately provides only an intriguing suggestion as to how they may be ultimately interrelated. Finally, the student learns to rely, obviously, on his inherent sense of grammaticality to test the correctness of the sentences produced. The automatic perception of grammaticality acts much like a special kind of positive reinforcement noted each time the student rehearses all or any preliminary part of a given sentence. Everything considered, solving these problems seems to constitute a reasonably pleasurable experience for the student.

As required in the conditions for grammar practice set forth above, these sentence-combining activities elicit from the student the writing of a fully formed sentence whose content has been provided in advance. Its structure is also predetermined and may be made to represent an unending variety of sentence types. Grammatical knowledge *per se* is invoked only at the outset, when the student must decide from the transformation-rule tags how each kernel sentence should be transformed. In the case of relative embeddings, in fact, such tags are unnecessary. In rehearsing the full statement while forming it and appraising its grammaticality, the student experiences it repeatedly and thus in a particularly intensive manner. Lastly, he must retain the fully formed sentence in memory while he writes it, and practice in this mnemonic skill may indeed be crucial. The findings reported by Harrell (1957), for example, may be interpreted as evidence that older students learn to keep sentences of increasing length in mind while their hands trace them on paper, whereas younger students cannot do this with facility—a conclusion which would explain why the latter children write shorter sentences than they normally speak.

Furthermore, in being a-rhetorical, these problems are unaccompanied by whatever interferences attend the need to select sentences according to their appropriateness in larger contexts—paragraphs, discourses, and finally the total rhetorical setting. The student is free to experience, intensively and without distraction, networks of intrasentence relationships among increasing numbers of kernel statements appropriately formed and arrayed in context of the full sentences they comprise. The record of this experience, added to that representing the many occasions of naturalistic language use which the student encounters daily and which this practice merely supplements in a specially structured way, constitutes the basis out of which his maturing cognition presumably develops and on which the subsequent production of mature language is thus contingent.

It should be emphasized that these sentence-combining problems were an integral part of the student's work in grammar. They were not represented as lessons in composition, nor should they be viewed as any kind of a "linguistic approach" to writing. As the rhetorician correctly notes, the writing act occurs only in response to some rhetorical occasion and can neither be routinized nor artificially duplicated. As discussed below, it was assumed that schoolchildren would obviously continue to study full programs of composition along with their grammar courses. Furthermore, the sentence-combining practice was not advertised to the student as a simulation of the composition process. He was not expected to "imitate" patterns of practice sentences when he wrote, nor was he admonished to try to "use" sentence-combining strategies in any conscious manner. The assumption was simply that when he came to writing, the student would, as a natural result of prior sentence-combining practice, produce sentences whose structures would be more mature than those of the sentences he would otherwise have written.

Lastly, this sentence-combining practice did not represent an attempt to condition students to favor complexity of expression. Indeed, the term "complexity" is quite misleading and probably should be avoided. In general, of course, mature writing is on average more complex grammatically than is immature writing. But even here the notion of complexity may be construed in various ways. Complexity of deep structure, for example, differs from that of surface structure. Grammatical complexity is not the same as psychological complexity. Deviations from grammaticality, as in the case of metaphor, often produced complexity of a tantalizing sort, whereas deviations from acceptability, in the sense used by Chomsky (1965), produce a less desirable kind. What the rhetorician intends by "complexity" as a deprecatory term is not at all easy to define. Doubtless it covers a variety of ineptitudes, none of which one would wish to encourage. Enhanced growth of syntactic fluency, however, merely means that children of a certain age, after a given period of sentence-combining practice, would produce writing whose structural parameters had theretofore been associated with the normal productions of children some years older. It is unlikely that this writing would be considered undesirably complex.

Principal Curricular Assumptions

Clearly, a general curricular assumption underlying this experiment was that what one ordinarily thinks of as secondary school English consists in fact of three autonomous component subjects—literature, composition, and linguistics. How this curriculum might be structured in the future—by how many teachers it might be taught, in how many different classrooms, for how many hours weekly, and under what subject names—is an open question quite beyond the scope of this discussion. The point is only that in order to create appropriately a-rhetorical conditions for the sentence-combining practice, linguistic study had to be viewed as an independent academic subject. No longer was it to be considered an expendable activity defined solely in terms of its overt intracurricular utility relative to the goals of composition. It can and perhaps should be argued, of course, that these studies are independent and self-justifying without benefit of assumption. When presented as rational inquiry into the many aspects of human language behavior, linguistics leads to the acquisition of knowledge and the formation of attitudes which are humanistic in outlook, liberalizing, and in the long run of unquestionable worth.

In any event, one result of the above assumption was that composition instruction became an independent variable in this study. Insofar as possible, it was held constant for both the experimental and the control groups. Such an arrangement distinguishes the present experiment from the majority of its predecessors, which held in effect that the way to measure the results of grammar instruction in student writing is to have some of the students learn less grammar and practice more writing. In reality, these were experiments on various approaches to composition, and grammar was by implication viewed as no more than one such approach.

The position in this study, however, is that linguistics and composition are separate subjects in pursuit of separate goals and that both can be accommodated in school curriculums. It was assumed that the composition course would be an ideal one, featuring an optimal sequence of writing assignments and maximally helpful criticism of the student's written performance. But it was assumed further that the nature of this performance is also a function of the student's experience with language encountered outside and prior to the composition class. Thus the general goal of this experiment was to determine whether the sentence-combining practice, an activity presented solely as an exercise in linguistics and not at all as a task in composition, might be counted as an instance of such prior language experience known to enhance the growth of syntactic fluency, although to do so in ways totally indiscernible to the student and thus quite "naturalistically."

A second outgrowth of the above assumption may be seen in the chracter of the grammar course in whose setting the sentence-combining problems were presented. The chief purpose of this course was neither to rectify the student's language behavior nor to facilitate the sentence-combining practice. Rather, it was to present to junior high school students, in an obviously introductory manner, an elementary transformational grammar describing the language competence they and all other speakers already possess. As with contemporary studies in other curriculums, the main justification for this course was given in terms of the experiences and learnings generated by the inquiry it occasioned. Furthermore, as an activity designed to reinforce and further illustrate transformations earlier learned by the student, the problem-solving practice was considered an integral part of the grammar course and may be viewed in this light quite without regard for its possible effects upon syntactic fluency. Its role was very much like that of the straightforward exercises in formula application which are employed, for example, in modern secondary school algebra.

Procedural Assumptions

The seventh grade was selected as the level on which to conduct this experiment. It represents a time just in advance of the high school years, when the most noteworthy growth of syntactic fluency normally occurs among the students. Also, as the first year of junior high school, the seventh grade is in the writer's opinion the earliest point at which grammar or linguistics should be introduced into the curriculum. Otherwise, however, the choice of grade level was actually quite arbitrary, as was the decision to confine the study to a single academic year. These topics are discussed further in the final chapter of this report.

Two assumptions pertaining to the measurement of syntactic fluency are also of importance. First, it is obvious that enough writing must be secured from each student to constitute a representative sample of his performance. Frogner (1933) and Hunt (1964) have shown that mode of discourse influences sentence structure counts. Consequently, the writing selections obtained from each student should range over a variety of modes, including at least narrative, expository, and descriptive. In any case, parameters of syntactic fluency cannot be extrapolated from observations based on single compositions. Anderson (1937) has demonstrated the complete unreliability of the 150-word samples used by LaBrant (1933) and recommends securing several times this much writing. Chotlos (1944) finds, however, that 1000-word samples are as reliable as ones of 3000 words in the case of junior high school students. Although no consistency studies are recorded for adult writers employing highly differentiated sentence structure, samples of 1000 words were assumed herein to be minimally adequate for schoolchildren. Since Hunt's eighth graders have a mean T-unit length of about 11 words, it was decided to collect per-student samples of 90 T-units. Such samples would represent at least six or seven compositions in as many discourse modes as possible.

Second, it was imperative that all writing represent the student's own free and uncoached responses to presented topics. The student was to be allowed to write naturally, and above all he was not to be made to feel that his sentence structure or any other single aspect of his writing was particularly on trial, or that he ought to affect any kind of artificial style. Obviously, he was to be denied access to parental assistance or material which he might be tempted to plagiarize.

Thus all writing examined in this experiment would be secured on an in-class basis under conditions similar to those of the one-hour Writing Sample used by the College Entrance Examination Board. The students were not to be told that their writing would be analyzed, or even that a particular experiment was in progress. They were to be free to write partial or complete rough drafts and to revise their initial sentences in any way they desired. The only requirement was that they produce finished essays on the given topic by the end of the class hour. Additional information on procedures used in securing the writing sample is given below.

Hypothesis and General Plan

The overall hypothesis of this study was that practice in transformational sentence-combining would enhance the normal growth of syntactic fluency. The rationale for this hypothesis, as alluded to throughout the foregoing discussion, was that such practice occasions intensive and undistracted experiences with sentences of mature grammatical form. These experiences, in turn, were assumed to count not only as specially structured instances of language input promoting the cognitive development on which subsequent mature output depends, but also as cases of the pseudo-production of such mature sentences in a way that provides their content in advance, thus bypassing the conception process and featuring only their construction and inscription. The sentence-combining practice was obviously intended as a supplement to, not a replacement of, the student's normal activities in reading and writing.

The plan of this study was to test the above hypothesis at the seventh grade level in an experiment of one year's duration. Samples of before and after writing were to be used as a basis for determining syntactic fluency. Comparisons of growth observed in the experimental group would be made with the normative data advanced by Hunt (1964) and with the growth observed in equivalent before and after writing of students in two control groups. One of these groups would study traditional grammar and perform associated practice activities, and the other would study no grammar but would read extra literature selections and receive direct-method instruction in techniques for varying sentence structure when writing. Equal numbers of inter-test composition assignments were to be given to all three groups. Except as noted, the inter-test literature requirements would be identical throughout. The amount of sentence-combining practice experienced by the experimental group was the maximum possible, subject to two important conditions. It was not to exceed the time block allotted to the grammar course, nor could it compromise the chief purpose of this course as given above. Detailed descriptions of the experimental treatments, and of the other design features, are given in the following chapter of this report.

Finally, it was obviously necessary to stipulate the amount of enhanced growth required in order for a confirmation of the hypothesis to be regarded as having educational significance. As shown by Hunt (1964), Harris (1962), and others, normal growth of syntactic fluency during the school years proceeds with glacial slowness. Indeed, differences in certain transform frequencies from one year to the next may not be great enough to attain statistical significance. Between grades four and eight, for example, Hunt's data show that children's per-year gains are one noun clause and one relative clause in each 100 T-units, although they become three clauses per year during high school. At the same time, however, schoolchildren have tremendous growth in store for themselves as they come to approximate adult norms. Surely the syntax of *Harper's* and *The Atlantic,* Hunt's adult sample, is not beyond the potentiality of senior high school students. In any event, it was decided that an extra year's growth per year, or twice the normal rate, would be the minimum criterion specified in the hypothesis. This would mean in the long run that students completing grade nine, if they had begun programs of sentence-combining in grade seven, and if an enhanced growth rate had been sustained throughout the three-year period, would demonstrate an average syntactic fluency heretofore associated with twelfth graders. Clearly, such development would be most desirable within the present goal structure of the English curriculum.

C
D
E
F   0
G   1
H   2
I   3
J   4